T0330420

Competition in the Provision of Local Public Goods

STUDIES IN FISCAL FEDERALISM AND STATE–LOCAL FINANCE

Series Editor: Wallace E. Oates, *Professor of Economics, University of Maryland and University Fellow, Resources for the Future, USA*

This important series is designed to make a significant contribution to the development of the principles and practices of state–local finance. It includes both theoretical and empirical work. International in scope, it addresses issues of current and future concern in both East and West and in developed and developing countries.

The main purpose of the series is to create a forum for the publication of high quality work and to show how economic analysis can make a contribution to understanding the role of local finance in fiscal federalism in the twenty-first century.

Competition in the Provision of Local Public Goods

Single Function Jurisdictions and Individual Choice

Alexandra Petermann Reifschneider

Freiburg University, Germany and Chilean Construction Chamber, Santiago, Chile

STUDIES IN FISCAL FEDERALISM AND STATE–LOCAL FINANCE

Edward Elgar
Cheltenham, UK • Northampton, MA, USA

Published by
Edward Elgar Publishing Limited
Glensanda House
Montpellier Parade
Cheltenham
Glos GL50 1UA
UK

Edward Elgar Publishing, Inc.
136 West Street
Suite 202
Northampton
Massachusetts 01060
USA

A catalogue record for this book
is available from the British Library

Library of Congress Cataloguing in Publication Data

Petermann Reifschneider, Alexandra, 1972–
    Competition in the provision of local public goods: single function
jurisdictions and individual choice/Alexandra Petermann Reifschneider.
        p.   cm. — (Studies in fiscal federalism and state–local finance series)
    Includes bibliographical references and index.
    1. Public goods. 2. Local finance. 3. Intergovernmental fiscal relations.
I. Title. II. Studies in fiscal federalism and state–local finance.
HJ193.R45   2005
363'.09173'2—dc22

2005050624

ISBN-13: 978 1 84542 369 8
ISBN-10: 1 84542 369 0

Printed and bound in Great Britain by MPG Books Ltd, Bodmin, Cornwall

Contents

Acknowledgements

This book is based on my doctoral thesis from the University of Freiburg. In connection with this work, I should like to acknowledge the following.

First, I am greatly indebted to Professor Thomas Gehrig, my doctoral thesis adviser, for his continuous encouragement, help and suggestions, which were invaluable in developing the book.

I am also grateful to Professor Günther Schulze, the second adviser for my thesis, who offered valuable suggestions and comments.

I would also like to thank the staff at the University of Freiburg. In particular, I acknowledge the contributions of all the members of the Institute for the Research of Economic Development.

I owe a special debt of gratitude to the DAAD (Deutscher Akademischer Austauschdienst), who financed my doctoral studies.

Finally, I am grateful to my family and friends for their continuous encouragement. In particular, I would like to express my deepest appreciation to my parents, Ivonne and Victor, to my sister Andrea, to Cristina, to my two children, Víctor and Sebastián, and to my husband Andrés, whose unfailing encouragement and patience enabled me to complete this book.

General introduction

NATURE OF THE BOOK

In many modern megacities, especially those located in developing countries, the supply of an adequate urban infrastructure, in the sense of local public goods and services such as refuse collection, police departments, fire brigades, medical support and educational systems, among many others, is a pressing problem. It is precisely in these cities, where the problems emerging from the interactions among people are more acute, and local public goods and services are more urgently required. However, many of these cities suffer from a lack of an adequate urban infrastructure. This problem may result from a lack of competition among jurisdictions for the provision of local public goods in those large urban regions.

Therefore, the central purpose of this book is to analyse the optimal allocation of local public goods or services in large urban agglomerations and the allocation consequences of increasing competition in their provision. We take two innovative aspects of the concept of 'functional overlapping competing jurisdictions' (FOCJ)[1] – 'de-localized membership' and 'uni-functionality of jurisdictions' – which seek to increase competition among jurisdictions for the provision of local public goods.

De-localized membership means that individuals have the opportunity to choose, independent of their place of residence, the local government (or local service provider) they wish to patronize for the provision of local public goods. This should increase competition among jurisdictions, compared to traditional jurisdictions where individuals are obliged to consume the local public goods offered by the jurisdiction where they live. On the other hand, *uni-functionality* means that different local service providers provide each facility with the various types of local public goods. This should also help to increase competition, compared to traditional jurisdictions which offer a bundle of such goods to individuals located in their territory. This book specifically analyses the effect of these two aspects on competition among jurisdictions in large urban agglomerations, and the impact this probable increase in competition may have on the achievement of the optimal allocation of local public goods.

1

URBAN REVOLUTION, CITY SIZE AND THE IMPORTANCE OF URBAN INFRASTRUCTURE (LOCAL PUBLIC GOODS AND SERVICES)

In the twentieth century, the entire world experienced an urban revolution. From 1300 to 1800, the proportion of the global population living in cities remained relatively stable, at just below 9 per cent (Bairoch, 1985). This figure rose to approximately 16 per cent by 1900, 30 per cent by 1950, and 47 per cent by 2000, and it is projected to reach 60 per cent by 2030 (ibid.; United Nations, 2002). Virtually all of the population growth expected at the world level between 2000 and 2030 will be concentrated in urban areas, with most of it (approximately 95 per cent) in urban zones of less-developed regions (ibid.).

Furthermore, the size of these urban agglomerations has increased dramatically. During the millennia between the origins of urbanization and the onset of the Industrial Revolution, hardly a city in the world had a population exceeding one million. By 1900, however, the world already had a dozen such cities, and around 1980 there were more than 230, with a collective population close to or slightly higher than that of the entire world population in 1700 (Bairoch, 1985). In 1975, 4.7 per cent of the world's population lived in cities with more than 5 million inhabitants. This figure was 6.5 per cent in 2000, and it is projected to be 8.4 per cent in 2015. Most of these large cities are located in developing countries. In 2001, just nine of the 40 cities with 5 million inhabitants or more were located in developed countries. By 2015, the world is expected to have 58 cities with more than 5 million inhabitants, and only 10 of these will be in the developed world (United Nations, 2002).

There are many reasons for humanity's ongoing shift from an autarkic agricultural form of living to an urban one, and a considerable number of the reasons given in the literature for this concentration of population are economic in nature. According to Alfred Marshall ([1890] 1920), externalities are crucial to the formation of economic agglomerations such as cities. In his well-known *Principles of Economics*, Marshall describes what he considers to be the most relevant externalities: mass production, the formation of a highly specialized labour force, the emergence of new ideas, the availability of specialized input services and the existence of a *modern infrastructure*.[2]

Throughout history, the availability of urban infrastructure has been one of the most notable characteristics of cities. The congregation of a large number of people facilitates the mutual provision of *collective services* or *local public goods*, which could not have been obtained in isolation (Fujita and Thisse, 2002). Examples include the Roman aqueduct for providing water to the population, the construction of city walls in medieval Europe to protect urban dwellers, the *agora* in Greek civilization and many of today's local public facilities or city services such as refuse collections and police departments, among others. This is in line with Mills's (1967) view that cities develop in the economy because of *scale economies in production*.

Nevertheless, despite the presence of increasing returns in production (particularly in the production of local public goods), urban areas are bounded. They have a limited size, based on the number of urban dwellers. Therefore, scale economies in production are damped by *scale diseconomies arising in transportation*. As also acknowledged by Mills (ibid.), an important factor in determining a city's size is the trade-off between increasing returns and transportation costs. As stated by Fujita and Thisse (2002), in the absence of scale economies in production, there would be no cities (backyard capitalism), whereas with no transportation costs, there would be a single city in the economy (the world megalopolis). In addition to scale diseconomies in transportation, there are many other problems and negative externalities involved in large agglomerations, such as pollution and crime, which discourage a high concentration of population and suggest the possible existence of an optimal city size.[3]

The criteria for evaluating the optimal size of a city have varied with time and place. The dominant feeling across the various disciplines related to urbanization is that most cities are just too big. Most current urban policies are implicitly based on this assumption. Megacities are viewed as gigantic and dangerous autonomous organisms, whose growth should be curbed. In these huge cities, local governments are unable to solve urban problems, which increase in number and complexity as the population increases. One of the crucial urban problems faced by local governments is how to ensure adequate provision of local public goods or, in Marshall's words, 'infrastructure', such as refuse collection, police departments, fire brigades, medical support, educational systems, transportation services, water and sewer services, and in general collective goods aimed at solving problems linked to the agglomeration of people. This problem is extremely severe in large urban regions, where the provision of local public goods must be continuously and rapidly expanded in order to satisfy the growing demand.

As suggested by Marshall, the existence of modern infrastructure is one of the crucial externalities that explain the formation of economic agglomerations in the first place. Nevertheless, in many modern megacities, especially those located in developing countries,[4] the supply of adequate infrastructure is currently more of a problem needing to be addressed rather than a motivation for the agglomeration of people. It is possible that when these cities first arose, the level of urban infrastructure served as an incentive for people to concentrate there. But today, although many of the cities suffer from a lack of adequate infrastructure, their populations continue to increase. For the local governments of these large urban regions, such cities have become excessively big and unmanageable. Why have local governments failed to achieve the adequate provision of local public goods in these large urban regions?

THE PROBLEM OF THE PROVISION OF LOCAL PUBLIC GOODS FROM THE ECONOMIC PERSPECTIVE

Before answering the previous question, let us first discuss some important contributions to the economic literature relating to the problem of the provision of local public goods, which has been viewed as problematic by many authors. Paul Samuelson defined public goods as 'collective consumption goods . . . which all enjoy in common in the sense that each individual's consumption of such a good leads to no subtraction from any other individual's consumption of that good' (Samuelson, 1954, p. 387). In his well-known paper 'The pure theory of public expenditures', he argues that in some sense, no 'market-type', solution exists to achieve the optimal provision of public goods.

Charles M. Tiebout was the first to point out that most public goods are locally supplied. In his classic paper, Tiebout (1956) suggests that in an economy of local public goods, the optimal allocation can be decentralized through competition among local governments. Tiebout imagines a system of jurisdictions in which each government offers its own package of public goods/tax structures, and these compete with one another for consumers. By migrating to the jurisdiction that respects their tastes in public goods/tax schemes, consumers reveal their preferences. Competition among jurisdictions and 'voting with the feet' may lead to the efficient provision of local public goods. Tiebout did not specify a complete model; it was left to later authors to suggest different models in which his 'competing jurisdictions' result in the optimal provision of local public goods.

Following these later studies, we can identify the conditions under which Tiebout's hypothesis holds. The first crucial condition is the *costless mobility of people among jurisdictions*. Tiebout's intuition proved correct with respect to the relevance of individuals' mobility among jurisdictions to the achievement of the optimal provision of local public goods. The opportunity to change one's place of residence and move to another jurisdiction if a particular local government does not fulfil one's expectations frees individuals from becoming 'captured demand' for their local governments. This may motivate local governments to provide the local public goods preferred by individuals at the lowest possible cost in order to keep these citizens under their jurisdiction, and thus to provide the public goods efficiently. Nevertheless, costless mobility of individuals guarantees only that the achievable utility for identical individuals is equalized across jurisdictions. It cannot eliminate inefficiencies, which are common to all local governments.[5]

A second crucial assumption required for the Tiebout hypothesis to hold is the *existence of a large number of jurisdictions*. This assumption, explicitly made by Tiebout in his original paper, is crucial in order to ensure competition among jurisdictions and to avoid situations such as the one described in the example in note 5. If there are a large number of local governments (or local service providers), the impact of the actions chosen by any single local government on the common utility level is negligible, and thus local governments can be seen as 'utility takers' (this would be equivalent to competitive firms that are price takers). It can be shown that if local governments take the common utility level in the economy as given, the first best optimum can be sustained as a free-entry equilibrium among local governments. In the literature, utility-taking local governments are referred to as 'perfectly competitive jurisdictions'.

Nevertheless, perfect competition among jurisdictions is extremely unlikely, since perfect competition requires an infinity of jurisdictions, just as perfect competition between firms requires an infinity of firms. In an economy with a finite number of jurisdictions, jurisdictions will not be 'utility takers', as noted by Scotchmer (1986). In this case, local governments may seek to manipulate the utility level of individuals. However, despite the existence of a limited number of local governments, the equilibrium allocation will be similar to the optimal one as long as there is *free entry and exit* in jurisdiction formation. In this case, the local monopoly power of the incumbent local governments will be constrained by the threat of an entrant who can steal their customers. The equilibrium allocation converges to the optimal one as the optimal jurisdiction size decreases with respect to the economy.[6]

Another relevant assumption is the *existence of an appropriate number of people in the economy*. In the literature, this assumption is usually referred to as 'the integer problem'.[7] This assumption may appear very technical; however, its implications are important for what follows. If N/n^* is not an integer (where N is the total population and n^* the optimal number of individuals in a jurisdiction), this implies that the population cannot be divided into optimal consumption groups. If N/n^* is not an integer and there are a large number of local governments (implying that they are utility takers), the utility-taking equilibrium will not exist.[8] On the other hand, if the optimal jurisdiction size is large with respect to the population, implying that there are only a few jurisdictions which will behave strategically with respect to one another, and there is free entry and exit in jurisdiction formation, the fact that N/n^* is not an integer matters because the jurisdiction sizes will be much bigger than the optimal size. However, it will still not pay to form a new jurisdiction, and thus the utility of the individuals will be much lower than at the optimal allocation. The equilibrium allocation converges to the optimal level as the optimal jurisdiction size decreases with respect to the economy.

Up to this point, all of the crucial assumptions that we have analysed in order for the Tiebout hypothesis to hold are similar to those necessary for a market of private goods provided by firms with U-shaped average cost curves which are 'perfectly contestable', in the sense used by Baumol (1982). They are also similar to the necessary conditions for the optimal allocation of club goods within a system of profit-maximizing clubs.[9]

Nevertheless, in pointing out the analogy between private goods and local public goods, Tiebout did not specify the objective function of the jurisdictions. Much of the debate arising from his work has focused on this question. The answer to the question of whether the provision of local public goods by local jurisdictions *à la* Tiebout will be efficient depends on the objective pursued by these local governments. Different authors assume different objectives to be pursued by local governments; for instance, some presume that jurisdictions will coalesce whenever it is in the interest of all members of a coalition to do so, that jurisdictions will seek to maximize the welfare of current residents, or that fiscal policies are decided by vote. Other authors view local governments as less benevolent to residents, and thus seeking, for example, to maximize their budgets subject to zero loss constraint, in a situation where the salaries of the local administrators depend on the level of expenditures.[10]

When the provision of local public goods is cast into the framework of club theory without regard to geography, each local public good can be fully financed by the appropriate user charge. The user charges are not only sufficient to cover the costs involved, but they also yield the appropriate incentive for optimal decision making regarding the supply of local public goods, as in the standard private-good case. Hence, in this 'lack of geography' setting, the optimal allocation of local public goods can be decentralized through a Tiebout system of local jurisdictions whose *objective is to maximize profits*. However, local public goods are not supplied by flying clubs to flying individuals. The services are provided at specific locations, and the beneficiaries of the services reside at other specific locations. This follows from the fact that residence requires space, and therefore, individual customers are spread out geographically. Thus, the provision of local public goods is associated with specific costs, such as transportation to the facility supplying the local public good, or a decreasing level of service with increasing distance between the public facility and the beneficiaries' residential location. When the club theory setting is modified by assigning locations to local public goods and their patrons, the optimal allocation can no longer be sustained through user charges alone. At the optimal allocation, the revenue derived from the user charge falls short of the provision cost, and the deficit is just equal to the aggregate land rent generated by the differences in accessibility to the local public goods experienced by users. In this case, the optimal allocation can be decentralized if local jurisdictions *maximize profits plus land rent* (Hochman et al., 1995).

According to several authors, there is a missing agent in Tiebout's local public-good setting; namely, a land developer who capitalizes the benefits of the public good in the land rent. In such an institutional context, competition among land developers may lead to the efficient provision of local public goods. Indeed, jurisdictions which are identified with land developers can profit by respecting their residents' tastes when the provision of public goods is capitalized into land prices. Thus, if capitalized land values are included in profits, jurisdictions have an incentive to organize their affairs efficiently (Fujita and Thisse, 2002).

In summary, if (i) there is costless mobility of people between jurisdictions, (ii) there are a large number of jurisdictions or free entry and exit in jurisdiction formation, (iii) there are an appropriate number of people in the economy or the optimal jurisdiction size is small with respect to the economy and (iv) local governments maximize profits plus land rent, this decentralized mechanism of competing jurisdictions *à la* Tiebout will result in the optimal provision of local public goods.

However, these crucial assumptions of Tiebout's hypothesis are unlikely to materialize in reality, especially in countries with large metropolitan regions. This makes it problematical to achieve the optimal provision of local public goods by means of Tiebout's competing jurisdictions.

Let us now return to the initial question of why local governments have failed to achieve the adequate provision of local public goods in large urban regions. The reasons for local governments' failure to achieve this goal vary from region to region. To gain an idea of the possible problems involved, let us consider the case of one of these large cities, Santiago de Chile.

SANTIAGO DE CHILE: A CASE OF LACK OF COMPETITION AMONG JURISDICTIONS FOR THE PROVISION OF LOCAL PUBLIC GOODS

According to the last census (2002), the metropolitan region of Santiago had a population of approximately six million, with a growth rate of some

1.5 per cent per year (INE, 2001).[11] The units of government responsible for the provision of an important part of the local public goods at the local level are the so-called 'municipalities'. The municipalities provide various types of local public goods[12] (such as refuse collection services, basic health-care centres, security systems, schools and so on) and enjoy a territorial monopoly within their particular area, which means in general terms that all the people living there are obliged to pay taxes to their municipality and to use the services it provides.[13] These jurisdictions are relatively independent from the central government, despite the fact that there is a body of the central government above them, the Ministry of Housing and Urban Planning (MINVU), which in some sense plays the role of a metropolitan local government in the provision of local public goods or solutions to urban problems involving many municipalities (such as metropolitan parks, link roads and so on).[14] As the population of the city of Santiago has increased, so has that of some municipalities to the point where the central government has decided to form a new municipality. The creation of a new municipality to provide the full range of services for a new population group is a very complex and time-consuming process in contrast to the rapid increase in urban population, and during this process, the existing municipalities are unable to satisfy the increasing demand for local public goods.

In the case of Santiago, this local government structure results in a very low level of competition among local governments for the provision of local public goods. As explained above, there are two levels of local government, the local jurisdictions (municipalities) and the central government body acting as a metropolitan government (MINVU), each of them faced with varying degrees of intensity with regard to competition among governmental units for the provision of local public goods.

In the case of the local jurisdictions, a small and finite number of municipalities comprise the metropolitan region. It is very difficult for new municipalities to emerge. On the one hand, the decision to create a new municipality is made centrally. At the same time, many of the local public goods provided by municipalities involve sunk costs, in the sense that many of them are tied to a location and their use is not easily altered. Furthermore, the fact that a municipality must provide the full range of services to the new population means that a very high investment is involved in the formation of a new municipality, including many types of sunk costs, as previously explained. All these factors suggest that there are high barriers to entry and exit in municipality formation, and thus that the number of jurisdictions is relatively fixed in the metropolitan region of Santiago.

On the other hand, competition among existing municipalities is not very intense, because there is low mobility of individuals among different locations. High costs are incurred in a move from one place of residence to another, such as those involved in the search for new housing. In addition, individuals incur a variety of sunk costs at their current residences, and there are many other reasons why individuals are relatively fixed to their locations. In the case of the MINVU, there is no competition at all, because it is a central government body.[15]

All these factors suggest that there is a lack of competition among local governments in the metropolitan region. On the one hand, competition among municipalities is restricted by individuals' mobility costs, the limited number of jurisdictions and the barriers to entry and exit in municipality formation. On the other, the MINVU is in effect monopolistic with respect to the provision of local public goods or the solution of urban problems involving many municipalities. This lack of competition may serve to impede the adequate provision of local public goods in the case of large urban agglomerations such as Santiago.

Several questions emerge from the previous discussion. How can competition among local governments in large urban agglomerations be increased? And, if it is possible to increase local government competition, would this gain in competition result in the efficient provision of local public goods in such agglomerations, or at least in an improvement over the original situation? At what point will an increase in competition represent an improvement in public welfare? Who will be the winners and/or losers of such an increase in competition?

INCREASING COMPETITION AMONG JURISDICTIONS BY UNI-FUNCTIONALITY AND DE-LOCALIZATION OF MEMBERSHIP

A new approach has emerged in the literature which seeks to increase competition among jurisdictions by *unbundling* the activities of a jurisdiction and opening up each individual activity to competition. In order to generate competition among these new 'uni-functional jurisdictions' effectively, the proponents of this approach argue in favour of *de-localization of membership*. These two factors, the unbundling of activities (uni-functionality) and de-localized membership, seem to be crucial for increasing competition among local jurisdictions in large metropolitan areas.

De-localized membership means that individuals have the opportunity to choose, independent of their place of residence, the local government (or local service provider) they wish to patronize for the provision of local public goods. This would lead to additional local competition among neighbouring jurisdictions, which is absent from Tiebout's classical jurisdiction concept, as well as from Santiago's municipalities.[16] This is because while people may remain relatively fixed to their locations, and thus moving to another jurisdiction may be very costly, the opportunity to choose the jurisdiction they want to patronize, independently of where they live, reduces the jurisdictions' monopoly power. Nevertheless, because local public goods are provided at specific locations in space, while the users of these services reside at other locations, the use of these local public goods will involve specific costs (such as transportation costs to the facility supplying the local public good, or decreasing levels of service as the distance between the public facility and the users' residence increases), and thus we should expect that jurisdictions will still enjoy some kind of local monopoly power over the people living nearby.

At the same time, the unbundling of activities is also important for increasing competition, because if each facility of the various types of local public goods is provided by different local service providers, free entry and exit in at least some types will be more likely than in the case of a complex multi-purpose jurisdiction supplying many types of local public goods, as seen in Tiebout's classical jurisdiction concept as well as Santiago's municipalities. Furthermore, uni-functionality would also reduce the severity of the integer problem, at least for the provision of some local public goods, namely those whose optimal consumption group is small in comparison with the region's total population.

The idea of introducing these two elements in order to increase competition among local governments and thus achieve the optimal provision of local public goods was first presented by Frey and Eichenberger (1995, 1996a, 1997, 1999), who introduced the FOCJ concept.[17]

This concept proposes a new kind of political unit aimed at solving specific local problems, such as the provision of local public goods or services. Briefly, FOCJ are democratic governmental units which provide only one local public good to a group of people (uni-functionality), who freely choose to join this FOCJ, independently of the place of residence (de-localized membership), in order to obtain the benefits of the local public good, and who pay a fee (or tax) directly to the FOCJ for their use of it.

FOCJ are 'functional', because they specialize in one function and their size (in number of users) is determined endogenously, in the sense that the size is not established previously, but has to match its tasks in order to exploit economies of scale, reduce the possible spillovers and adapt the supply to citizen demand. Accordingly, they differ from the traditional jurisdictions, which provide all local public goods in a predefined territory, where the extension of the jurisdiction is a given and people who live at a specific location have to patronize the local public goods provided by the specific jurisdiction responsible for that territory.

Because each FOCJ provides a different kind of local public good, with different cost functions and preference levels, the optimal FOCJ size in terms of members will vary among different local public goods, and thus the FOCJ will *overlap*. Accordingly, FOCJ that perform different tasks overlap and a citizen is, therefore, a member of several jurisdictions.

FOCJ are subject to two competition mechanisms, forcing them to cater for the preferences of their members: the option for citizens to exit FOCJ (without changing their place of residence)[18] establishes competition similar to markets, and in addition their voting rights establish political competition.

FOCJ are formal political units with power to regulate and to tax, and are thus called 'jurisdictions'. These governmental units are financially independent from the central government. Consequently, the prices they charge to users must at least equal the costs of providing the local public good.

It is argued that the increase in competition for the provision of local public goods implied by the creation of FOCJ, should lead to the optimal provision of these kinds of local public goods, or at least should represent an improvement over the classical concept of jurisdiction[19] in the achievement of this goal.

This concept has been discussed extensively to date, relying on verbal economic reasoning. While it appears to offer several advantages, many open questions remain regarding this new concept of jurisdiction:

- How many different types of FOCJ should exist? What is their optimal size, and what are the determinants of this?
- Does competition between FOCJ lead to an optimum? In particular, will the equilibrium location of their local public goods be efficient? How should exit and entry be regulated? (What about the possibilities of excessive or insufficient entry?) How would price policies be determined? How can they be optimized?
- Do FOCJ really overlap, and is this overlapping efficient? Are there areas of interdependence among different types of FOCJ, such as complementarities? What implications does this have? (Possible monopolization?) Are FOCJ 'better' in comparison with the classical all-purpose jurisdictions (Tiebout's jurisdictions)?[20]
- Is some degree of coordination between FOCJ necessary? Can cooperation between FOCJ solve the allocation problems that emerge in competition? Under what circumstances? What degree of cooperation between FOCJ is adequate? (Partial or full cooperation?) How should cooperation between FOCJ be regulated? Would cooperation between FOCJ lead to the formation of a cartel of local service providers? (Possible collusion?)

SCOPE AND PLAN OF THE BOOK

This book analyses the optimal allocation of local public goods in a spatial context[21] and the allocation consequences of increasing competition in a decentralized provision of them. We take two innovative aspects from the FOCJ concept – de-localized membership and uni-functionality of jurisdictions – and examine the effects of these two specific aspects on competition among jurisdictions in large urban agglomerations, and the impact that this probable increase in competition is likely to have on the achievement of the optimal allocation of local public goods.

We concentrate on local public goods with high fixed costs, where it pays for groups to consume collectively (since the average cost decreases with the group size), and it is also possible to exclude others from consumption of the group's own units of the good (for example, refuse collection, medical services, public transport, school systems, water and sewer services and so on).[22]

Although the FOCJ concept has many interesting dimensions as explained above, it is not the intention of this book to analyse fully all the aspects involved in it. However, the analysis presented here serves as a benchmark in order to study these two features. Thus we shall address the earlier questions with regard to this new concept of jurisdiction, with the proviso that when we refer to FOCJ we are referring only to our interpretation of the concept relative to the aspects of it that are under consideration.

This work differs from that of Frey and Eichenberger (whose comprehensive treatment can be found in Frey and Eichenberger, 1999) and provides additional insight, in that they analyse the multi-dimensional concept of FOCJ, relying on verbal economic reasoning, while the present book focuses fundamentally on only two aspects, namely de-localized membership and uni-functionality of jurisdictions, and conducts a formal analysis of them. This analysis helps to clarify the forces that are involved and to understand the benefits and problems that the concept may generate regarding the provision of local public goods.

The term 'local service providers' rather than 'local governments' is used in the analysis for the decentralized provision of the local public goods. This is to underline that there is no political process involved in the analysis and that the only objective of the local service providers in this setting is to maximize profits. This is the main difference with the concept of FOCJ, where voting is involved and several objectives may be pursued. However, the analysis in this book is valid even for political competition to the extent that running public services is a source of tax income for any politician.[23]

The intention of the analysis is not to discourage or to support such a decentralized provision of local public goods as a FOCJ system, but to discover the advantages and possible problems that such a system may have in order to encourage its positive aspects and to solve any problems that may arise.

The book is structured in three chapters. In what follows, the central point of each chapter will be explained and the developed framework will be used to provide some answers to the open questions posed above regarding this new concept of jurisdiction, namely FOCJ.

CHAPTER 1: MAXIMUM LOT-SIZE REGULATION

In Chapter 1, we discuss the sample case of policies currently being implemented in the metropolitan region of Santiago, which are aimed at solving problems caused by the inefficient provision of local public goods in the region. This example provided the motivation for analysing the problem of the provision of local public goods in large urban agglomerations such as Santiago.

In the case of Santiago, it is argued that the costs for some urban infrastructure (local public goods such as police and fire departments, schools, medical services, transportation systems and so on), which increase with the extension of the city and are borne by the government, are not taken into account by people when they choose their location in the city and the amount of land to occupy, since these individuals assume that a minimum provision of infrastructure already exists at any location. Thus, the outcome is that people use more land, and the city area extends further than would be the case if such costs were taken into account. This situation accordingly results in diminished welfare.

In an effort to correct this inefficiency, a number of policies are currently being implemented in Santiago which aim to reduce the city's expansion by penalizing the use of large amounts of urban land (through, for instance, a tax on vacant land) or by providing incentives for the occupation of less space (as with a reduction of property taxes on smaller houses). In general, these policies seek to restrict the space occupied by individuals in the city in order to limit the city's expansion and therefore the government's infrastructure costs. Nevertheless, the real problem in this case seems to be the lack of adequate incentives for individuals and local governments to achieve the optimal provision of local public goods.

CHAPTER 2: COMPETING JURISDICTIONS FOR THE PROVISION OF LOCAL PUBLIC GOODS

Chapter 2 corresponds to the central part of the book. A framework is developed to analyse the question about the optimal provision of local public goods in large metropolitan regions. We examine the effects of de-localized membership and uni-functionality of jurisdictions on competition among jurisdictions in large urban agglomerations and the impact that this probable increase in competition may have on the achievement of the optimal provision of local public goods.

Using this framework, some answers can be given to the open questions regarding this new concept of jurisdiction, namely FOCJ.[24]

How many different types of FOCJ should exist? What is their optimal size, and what are the determinants of this?

An important factor in determining the optimal number of FOCJ in a region and their optimal sizes in terms of users is the existing trade-off between fixed and transportation costs, a classical aspect of location models.

For example, taking the case of educational systems within this framework, we should have fewer universities than schools at the optimum allocation in a region, if we assume that the levels of investment for the former are higher than those required for schools. On the other hand, local public goods characterized by high infrastructure costs (such as universities) will have a higher user population at the optimal allocation than local public goods requiring lower infrastructure costs. Furthermore, higher transportation costs mean that at the optimum there will be more facilities providing each local public good, because the price of infrastructure relative to transportation will be lower in this case.

Does competition between FOCJ lead to an optimum? In particular, will the equilibrium location of their local public goods be efficient? How should exit and entry be regulated? (What about the possibilities of excessive or insufficient entry?) How would price policies be determined? How can they be optimized?

With regard to these questions, we find that the effect of competition between FOCJ on efficiency will crucially depend on the technology type of the local public good provided, the price policy implemented and the level of competition among regions.

In the case of local public goods characterized by 'no location sunk cost technology',[25] their equilibrium locations will be unique and efficient, in the sense that they minimize total transport costs for individuals, if the FOCJ that provide them can charge discriminatory prices. However, if they had to charge mill prices (that is, at the point where the service is produced, the price is the same for everybody), the equilibrium locations could be inefficient. In the case of 'location sunk cost technology',[26] the efficient locations are also an equilibrium when price discrimination is possible, but in addition to this, we have other possible location equilibria. So in this case, we have a multiplicity of equilibria, and we can also have location equilibria that are inefficient.

If there is intense competition from other regions,[27] competition between FOCJ inside the region will lead to an optimum in the case of local public goods characterized by no location sunk costs in their provision, in terms of the optimal number and location of local public goods, if price discrimination is possible. Nevertheless, in the case of local public goods that imply location sunk costs in their provision, intense competition from other regions may lead to insufficient entry of FOCJ for the provision of these local public goods, and thus to inefficient allocation of these types of local public goods by FOCJ. This implies that intense competition from other regions will not always bring about efficient allocation under FOCJ. The effect of this competition on efficiency will depend on the type of technology of the local public good provided.

However, if competition from other regions is very weak,[28] competition will lead to excessive entry of FOCJ and correspondingly to excess capacity in the region, in the case of local public goods characterized by no location sunk costs in their provision.[29] In the case of local public goods with location sunk costs in their provision, very weak competition from other regions may cause either excessive or insufficient entry. The precise nature of the equilibrium pattern of FOCJ in this case, and the possible resulting inefficiency, will depend on the history of the particular region.

We also find that FOCJ offering local public goods will choose, at equilibrium, to charge discriminatory prices based on location, in favour of the more distant locations. As argued above, the achievement of an efficient allocation of local public goods by FOCJ necessarily requires spatial price discrimination.[30] Mill pricing will typically increase the inefficiencies identified under discriminatory pricing (at least for the case of no location sunk cost technologies) and in general, the opportunity to charge discriminatory prices with respect to location increases competition and improves welfare in a spatial context.

Do FOCJ really overlap, and is this overlapping efficient? Are there areas of interdependence between different types of FOCJ, such as complementarities? What implications does this have? (Possible monopolization?) Are FOCJ 'better' in comparison with the classical all-purpose jurisdictions (Tiebout's jurisdictions)?

In the case of Tiebout's jurisdictions, which provide all types of local public goods (as with the case of Santiago's municipalities), overlapping of jurisdictions[31] is not possible, because each one has a territorial monopoly over a particular region, meaning that all the people living there must pay taxes to that jurisdiction and use the services it provides. An important element of the idea of FOCJ is the possibility that these jurisdictions may overlap, in the sense that many different local service providers may extend over the same geographical area, thus potentially increasing competition and utility for the individuals living there. It is reasonable to expect that the incorporation of de-localized membership in addition to uni-functionality of jurisdictions in the case of FOCJ may imply the overlapping of jurisdictions. However, in the case of FOCJ offering homogeneous local public goods,[32] optimality requires no overlapping, and at equilibrium they will never overlap.

The possibility of *overlapping* and the idea of *unbundling* the services provided by local service providers is related to the existence of different types of local public goods which are not perfect substitutes for one another. For example, in the case of schools, if these are identical in all aspects, at equilibrium individuals will simply choose the nearest school. This implies that FOCJ providing identical schools will never overlap. This will also represent the optimal distribution of individuals, since if everyone patronizes the nearest school, total transport costs will be minimized. However, if schools can be differentiated, for example in the second language that they teach, with some offering English and others French, they will no longer be perfect substitutes for each other. Some people may prefer English and others French, and in this case, these particular FOCJ may overlap. If local public goods are not substitutes at all, but rather perfect complements – as, for example, schools and universities – their particular FOCJ will always overlap.

Thus, in order to analyse the question of overlapping service areas and the idea of unbundling the services provided by local service providers, we consider a setting containing different types of local public goods. In such a setting, if competition among regions is very weak, the opportunity to unbundle activities may increase competition and the aggregate utility for individuals in a region. Nevertheless, this will only be possible if there is competition for all types of local public goods. If there is a monopoly local government for at least one type, and we assume that local public goods are perfect complements between types, all the gains from increased competition in the other types of local public goods will be redistributed to the monopoly local service provider.

It is important to make clear that this result should not be interpreted as a rejection of the concept of FOCJ in the sense that it can be understood as a statement about FOCJ being never beneficial to the individuals or that the assumptions for them to increase the utility of individuals are too unrealistic or too tough to be satisfied. Actually, we could expect that, within our model, FOCJ increase the utility of the individuals with respect to all-purpose jurisdictions. This is because the assumption of competition in all local public-good types is not necessarily so unrealistic. We could expect to have some degree of competition always, if the market areas are not too big (de-localized membership allows that) and because local public goods are likely to have some degree of substitution between types. In addition, in the case of all-purpose jurisdictions, low mobility among individuals leads to less intense competition among jurisdictions. In such a situation, the addition of de-localized membership under FOCJ introduces a new source of local competition into the system, which is absent in all-purpose jurisdictions, and guarantees a minimum utility level for individuals, which is higher than in all-purpose jurisdictions.

Furthermore, the fact that the competitive pressures may be increased with FOCJ, *could* imply that the utility of the individuals increases. However, this is not always so. Actually and as explained above, in the case of homogeneous local public goods, we could get insufficient entry (by fixed technology) under a decentralized provision like the one under FOCJ, which will imply a lower utility for the individuals than that at the optimal allocation. In this case we should be ready to take measures to increase entry and so enhance the utility of individuals. On the other hand, an increase in the competitive pressures does not necessarily mean that this will increase welfare,[33] and this is an important variable to look at when we evaluate the benefits of alternatives for the provision of local public goods.

The point of the result discussed here, and of the main results of the analysis, is to shed some light on which aspects we should be aware of in order to achieve gains with a decentralized provision of local public goods such as a FOCJ system, in terms of utility for the individuals in this particular case, or more generally in terms of welfare in the case of other important results of the book (such as that of the necessity of price discrimination for efficiency).

CHAPTER 3: COOPERATION BETWEEN COMPETING JURISDICTIONS

In Chapter 3, we address the question about the possible benefits and problems resulting from cooperation between FOCJ. One alleged problem of this system of uni-functional competing jurisdictions concerns coordination among the large number of FOCJ. Many critics of FOCJ argue that some coordination should exist among them. However, as argued by the proponents of this system, although such coordination often makes sense, and it is possible if required, it is not good in itself, but it can be used to maintain a cartel in which to evade, or even exploit, the desires of the population (Frey and Eichenberger, 1995; Frey, 1997).

Accordingly, we use the framework of Chapter 2 to analyse the equilibrium allocation of a system of FOCJ characterized by cooperation, in order to compare this equilibrium allocation with that achieved through competition and with the optimal allocation. Using this framework, we can provide some answers to the open questions mentioned above regarding the possibility of cooperation with respect to our interpretation of this new concept of jurisdiction.

Is some degree of coordination between FOCJ necessary? Can cooperation between FOCJ solve the allocation problems that emerge in competition? Under what circumstances? What degree of cooperation between FOCJ is adequate? (Partial or full cooperation?) How should cooperation between FOCJ be regulated? Would cooperation between FOCJ lead to the formation of a cartel of local service providers? (Possible collusion?)

As we explain in Chapter 2, the absence of coordination between FOCJ may fail to achieve an optimal allocation of local public goods under some circumstances.[34] Accordingly, some level of coordination could be necessary. However, we find that the possibility that cooperation between FOCJ may solve the allocation problems that emerge in competition will crucially depend on the degree of cooperation and the relevant geographical structure for the analysis.[35]

Under partial cooperation (that is, the non-cooperative choice of locations followed by cooperative pricing), the equilibrium locations of the local public goods provided by two FOCJ would be inefficient if we consider an asymmetrical geographical structure as in the Hotelling (1929) setting.[36] This holds for both price regimes: mill and discriminatory prices. Under such a geographical structure, discriminatory prices with respect to locations can help solve this problem and achieve the optimal location choices at equilibrium, but only if competition is guaranteed and partial cooperation is ruled out.[37] Accordingly, partial cooperation leads to additional efficiency problems with respect to competition in this context.

However, as Chapter 3 explains, the inefficient location choices crucially depend on the asymmetrical geographical structure of the Hotelling setting. If we consider instead a symmetrical geographical structure, as in

the Salop (1979) setting, we would find that competition and partial cooperation lead to the same location choices at equilibrium under both mill and
discriminatory pricing, which are the optimal locations.

In general, under the assumption of a symmetrical geographical structure, efficient equilibrium location choices will always be obtained for local
public goods provided by FOCJ. The problem of inefficient equilibrium
location choices arises when there is some 'hinterland' to be captured and
FOCJ have to charge mill prices. In this case, competition and partial cooperation both lead to inefficient location choices, as explained above.
Accordingly, we should analyse whether a higher degree of cooperation
may lead to the optimal allocation of local public goods in this case.
Consequently, in the last part of Chapter 3, we analyse whether *full cooperation* (that is, the cooperative choice of locations and prices) can achieve
this goal.

Normally, we would expect that full cooperation would be equivalent to
a monopoly situation, and under both symmetrical and asymmetrical geographical structures, and under both price regimes, a monopoly local government would choose the optimal locations for its local public goods in
order to maximize its profits, and thus it would be efficient in this sense.[38]

Accordingly, in our setting, this would imply that full cooperation by
FOCJ under an asymmetrical geography and mill pricing should lead to
efficient location choices for their local public goods at equilibrium, and in
this sense it would imply increased efficiency when compared with competition or with partial cooperation. Nevertheless, and as we show in
Chapter 3, full cooperation is not completely equivalent to a monopoly
local government, as explained above. Under mill pricing, full cooperation
can lead to inefficient location choices in an asymmetrical space, as would
competition and partial cooperation under mill pricing in such a setting.

Under full cooperation, local service providers remain independent units,
and thus, once the locations of their local public goods are chosen in a cooperative manner (assuming that these are difficult to change once chosen),[39]
they may still deviate in prices, because these can easily be changed.

If the penalty for deviating from the cooperation price agreement is very
low, as reflected in a relatively low value of the discount parameter, full
cooperation with optimal pricing will not be sustainable at all locations,
and it may not be sustainable at the efficient locations. Thus, in order to
choose the location pair that maximizes their cooperative profits, FOCJ will
have to look for a location pair that will result in the highest possible *sustainable cooperative profits*, given such a low discount parameter. In the case
of relatively low discount parameters, sustainable cooperative profits will
be maximized at locations that are farther away than the efficient ones, and
for low enough values of the discount parameter, maximum differentiation

from full cooperation will be obtained at equlibrium, as with competition. So, for a low discount parameter, competition, partial cooperation and full cooperation between FOCJ will lead to inefficient location choices for local public goods under mill pricing within an asymmetrical space, which will be equivalent in terms of welfare (total transport costs will be identical in all three cases).

NOTES

1. FOCJ is a concept that proposes a new kind of political unit aimed at solving specific local problems, such as the provision of local public goods or services and was developed by Frey and Eichenberger (1995, 1996a, 1997, 1999).
2. Most of the factors currently used in the field of economics to explain economic agglomerations can be found in the work of von Thünen ([1826] 1966) and Fujita and Thisse (2002). See Fujita (2000) for more details.
3. The problem of city size is not new. In fact, both Plato and Aristotle addressed it with regard to Greek civilization. Aristotle insisted upon the existence of a minimum and particularly a maximum size – a limit that should never be surpassed. Plato was more explicit, stating that the ideal republic would have 5040 citizens. If one interprets 'citizens' as being equivalent to heads of household, this implies a population on the order of twenty thousand people. Aristotle stressed the problems of security in overly large cities. But for both, by far the most important criterion for determining the proper size of cities was political in nature, and intimately linked with the problem of communication. The city must remain sufficiently small to permit the holding of public meetings with all citizens present (Bairoch, 1985).
4. As stated above, most of these large cities are located in developing countries.
5. For example, suppose that for some reason there were only two local governments (or local service providers), each providing only one local public good, such as a school, which is limited in capacity. Let us also assume that there is a large population, which would like to attend one of these schools; that is, a population that by far exceeds the capacity of both schools. In this case, despite the mobility of the individuals involved, both local service providers would be able to charge extremely high taxes to the population and provide them with low-quality services, because competition between individuals for the service provided by the local service providers is very high. Thus, the two local service providers would not really compete with each other. In this case, they would act as two monopolists. The fact that people can move freely between schools, or decide not to attend any school, only means that at equilibrium individuals will obtain the same utility. But this utility will be much lower than that which could be achieved at the optimal allocation, if local service providers were providing an appropriate number of schools for the population.
6. See Scotchmer (1985) for a derivation of this result in the case of club goods.
7. See ibid. for a discussion about this assumption in the case of club goods.
8. This is shown in ibid.
9. See Berglas (1976b) and Scotchmer and Wooders (1987).
10. See Wagner and Weber (1975).
11. INE: Instituto Nacional de Estadísticas (National Statistics Institute), Santiago de Chile.
12. 'Provide' does not necessarily mean that the service is directly supplied to the individuals by public enterprises. In many cases, these services are financed by the municipality but supplied to the individuals by private firms.
13. This is a very simplified way of describing how this system works, which we have given in order to concentrate on the aspects of it that are relevant for our study.

14. There are other bodies of the central government that act at a city level, but the MINVU is one the most important ones.
15. Note that the possible creation of a truly metropolitan government, which is being widely discussed in Santiago, does not guarantee that competition at this level will increase. As we shall explain below, a metropolitan government for Santiago would face almost no competition from other metropolitan regions. On the one hand, the country has few if any other large cities, which offer similar living conditions to the population, and thus individuals are relatively 'locked' into their metropolitan region. On the other, individuals' decisions to live in one city or another seem to be determined mainly by the location of their employment. The supply of local public goods is a less important variable in their location choice. This implies that in metropolitan regions, the location of people is not very sensitive to changes in the provision of local public goods, above some minimum level, and thus we can consider people to be relatively fixed to their locations. Furthermore, the barriers to entry and exit in municipality formation, as discussed above, would be substantially increased in the case of metropolitan regions. The complexity involved in the formation of a new metropolitan region is well known, and it is also well known that once such a region is formed, there is a kind of 'snowball effect' in which a growing number of agents seek to congregate in order to benefit from a greater diversity of activities and a higher level of specialization (Fujita and Thisse, 2002). All these arguments suggest that competition among metropolitan regions for the provision of local public goods or solutions to urban problems that involve many municipalities would be virtually non-existent.
16. In Tiebout's local public goods model, individuals are mobile in the sense that they can choose a jurisdiction or location to occupy, but once they have settled there, their level of access to public goods is irrelevant. Individuals cannot use the public goods of a neighbouring locality even if those public goods are physically closer to them. In the case of Santiago, the municipalities exercise a territorial monopoly over their particular areas, meaning that all their inhabitants must pay taxes to them and use the services that they provide. In this sense they are similar to Tiebout's jurisdictions. Providing individuals with the opportunity to choose the local service provider they wish to patronize for the provision of local public goods, independent of the location of their residence, brings a new, competing force into the system.
17. Although the singular of FOCJ is FOCUS, in the text FOCJ will be used for both the singular and plural forms.
18. Note that this source of competition is possible, because of de-localized membership. Furthermore, uni-functionality is also relevant for increasing competition, as explained above.
19. The 'traditional' or 'classical' jurisdictions, comprise the Tiebout concept of jurisdiction, which was explained above. The Santiago municipalities are similar to this concept of jurisdiction, as stated earlier.
20. The Tiebout concept of jurisdiction encompasses 'traditional', 'classical' or 'classical all-purpose' jurisdictions. The Santiago municipalities are similar to this concept, as explained above.
21. By 'spatial context' we mean basically considering transport costs.
22. These are also the types of local public goods on which Frey and Eichenberger (1995, 1996a, 1997, 1999) mainly concentrate in their analysis.
23. It would be interesting to analyse political inefficiencies and self-interested behaviour of politicians and whether the incentives of politicians are different in FOCJ (in the broad sense of the concept) compared with the all-purpose jurisdictions for reasons other than competition. However, this is beyond the remit of the present analysis.
24. Note, 'FOCJ' refers to the interpretation of the concept relative to the aspects considered in this book.
25. 'No location sunk cost technology' refers to the local service provider's ability to reallocate its local public good without incurring any additional costs; that is, there are no sunk costs in its chosen location and corresponding market segment. This is the case, for example, with the technology used in collective transportation services such as buses and

taxis, where there may be high fixed costs represented by the buses and taxis serving a particular area, but these can easily be reallocated to another area if necessary, at almost no cost. Thus, if competition in a region is too intense, the local service provider offering the transportation service can easily (in terms of cost) reallocate its vehicles to another region where it can achieve higher profits. Another example of local public goods with no location sunk cost technology is refuse collection services.

26.   'Location sunk cost technology' refers to the local service provider's inability to change its chosen location and corresponding market segment once it has been selected. Local public goods that are located in space are typical examples of sunk cost technologies, for example, schools and health-care centres. Once they are located at a point in space, it would be very costly to change their location. Their fixed costs are location specific.

27.   'Very intense competition from other regions' means that there is costless mobility of people among regions, and a large number of regions exist, or there is free entry and exit in the formation of regions, and this will be reflected in that the achievable utility in alternative regions will be the highest possible within the economy in question (that is, the utility obtained when the local public goods are provided efficiently, at the optimal allocation).

28.   'Very weak competition from other regions' means that there are high costs involved in changing one's place of residence, or the number of competing regions is low and there are entry and exit barriers to the formation of new jurisdictions, and this will be reflected in a very low utility level achievable in alternative regions.

29.   One example of excessive entry when the technology of the local public good is characterized by no location sunk costs is the case of the collective transportation services in the metropolitan region of Santiago, particularly the *micros* (buses). The *micros* are provided by independent small firms (each having a very small number of *micros*, many with only one) which compete with one another for customers. The result of their competition is an excess capacity of *micros* in the region, as evident in the extremely low average passenger rate for each bus.

30.   This is also true in Tiebout's setting. Actually, charging taxes (or prices) according to land rent values to achieve optimality in Tiebout's setting is a form of spatial price discrimination.

31.   'Overlapping of jurisdictions' means that more than one is active in the same geographical area.

32.   'Homogeneous local public goods' are local public goods that are identical in all aspects, except for their location in space. In a spaceless framework, these local public goods would be perfect substitutes.

33.   The increase in competition may imply excessive entry and be inefficient in this sense, as explained above.

34.   Competition among FOCJ may lead to inefficiencies such as inefficient location choices for local public goods when charging mill prices or excessive or insufficient entry of local service providers, with a correspondingly reduced level of welfare.

35.   We analysed only the case of cooperation among FOCJ that provide homogeneous local public goods.

36.   In this case, minimum differentiation (that is, both facilities located at the centre of the region at $L/2$, where space in the region is described by the interval $X = ([0, L])$) is the only equilibrium. Given that the efficient locations are those that minimize total transport costs (in this case at $L/4$ and $3L/4$), this equilibrium is inefficient.

37.   As we explain in Chapter 2, under competition, the use of discriminatory pricing leads to the optimal location choices of two competing local service providers in an asymmetrical geographical structure.

38.   Actually, Friedman and Thisse (1993) argue that, in a Hotelling model with quadratic transportation costs, the equilibrium locations under mill pricing and full cooperation with equal profits are the same as the efficient locations.

39.   Here we are assuming fixed technology for the local public goods.

1. Maximum lot-size regulation

1.1 INTRODUCTION

Most current urban policies implicitly assume that cities are simply too big. Megacities are viewed as enormous and unsafe autonomous organisms whose growth should be limited. The alleged problems of these large urban areas vary from region to region, as do the policies implemented in order to correct them. In the case of Chile, several problems have been identified with respect to the large size of the metropolitan region of its capital, Santiago, many of which are related to the location of economic activity in space.

One alleged problem stemming from the size of Santiago's metropolitan region is related to the distribution of economic agents within the region.[1] In this case, it is not clear whether the market alone will lead to an optimal distribution, or whether there are inefficiencies justifying intervention in the market process in order to improve welfare. In the case of Santiago, a range of regulations are currently in place which seek to influence the location of economic agents within this region, but it is not yet apparent whether they truly serve to improve welfare.

In this chapter we focus on this problem. We consider one specific inefficiency that is said to exist in the case of Santiago, which implies an inefficient distribution of economic agents within this region and for which several regulations have been implemented in order to correct it. The inefficiency is that there may be some urbanization or infrastructure costs,[2] increasing with the city's extension, which are borne by the city government and are not taken into account by individuals when they choose their location in the city, because they assume that a minimum level of infrastructure exists at any location.[3] The outcome of this is a city that extends further than it would if people considered these costs, and thus welfare is lower.

Under the assumption that this inefficiency exists and that the city is correspondingly 'overly extended' (with each agent occupying too much territory), the Santiago authorities have implemented a number of policies in an attempt to correct this problem. These policies seek to limit the city's extension by penalizing the use of large amounts of urban space (for example, through taxes on vacant land) or by providing incentives for the occupation of less space (as with the reduction of property taxes on smaller houses). In general, these policies attempt to restrict the space occupied by people in the city in order to limit the city's expansion and thus reduce the urbanization costs faced by the city government.[4]

In order to exemplify these policies, we consider a policy that penalizes the establishment of large sites in the city simply by prohibiting the existence of sites bigger than some fixed level s_M. We call this regulation the 'maximum lot size regulation' (henceforth the 's_M regulation').[5] This is not an actual policy; it is used only as an example of policies tending in this direction. In this chapter we examine, within the context described above, whether it is reasonable to think that this kind of regulation can improve welfare. We then analyse the possible existence of an optimal s_M regulation and the exogenous variables of the economy on which it would depend, in order to evaluate the circumstances under which such regulations would or would not improve welfare.

The framework we use is the 'basic model of residential choice', based on von Thünen's ([1826] 1966) central concept of bid-rent curves, which was extended to an urban context by Alonso (1964), Mills (1967) and Muth (1969) and was rigorously treated in Fujita (1989) and Fujita and Thisse (2002). This model focuses on the fundamental trade-off between accessibility and space in the area of residential choice.

Structure of the Chapter

The chapter is structured as follows. Section 1.2, describes the equilibrium land-use patterns within the framework of the basic model of residential choice. Section 1.3 analyses the consequences of our fictitious s_M regulation within the context of this model, in terms of its allocative consequences and distributional issues, setting aside the problem of urbanization costs. It is clear that in this setting, such a regulation can only imply a decrease in welfare, because it can be shown that the competitive equilibrium in this model is efficient, and thus any distortion of it will reduce welfare. Section 1.4 introduces the problem of urbanization costs, which are the responsibility of the city government, so people do not take them into account when choosing a place to live. Thus, the competitive equilibria of residential land markets will no longer be socially efficient. In this setting, policy makers may have reason to believe that policies inducing people to choose smaller sites than they would otherwise have chosen, as with our maximum lot-size regulation, may be welfare improving. Using such a setting, we seek to determine both whether such a policy can help improve welfare, and the variables upon which the answer depends. Section 1.5 offers some concluding remarks.

1.2   THE BASIC MODEL OF RESIDENTIAL CHOICE

First, we examine the equilibrium land rent and land-use patterns under the basic model of residential choice in the absence of regulation, which will allow us to compare this situation with the case in which regulations are present, so that we can assess their impact.

Assumptions

Consider a monocentric city with a prespecified centre, called the central business district (CBD), where all jobs are located. For simplicity, the CBD is treated as a point, and space is assumed to be homogeneous in all aspects except for distance to the CBD. Thus, the only spatial characteristic of a location in this setting is its distance from the CBD.

In this model, there are three types of economic agents that interact with one another. The first are the so-called 'landlords', who have no active role in the model and are assumed to live outside the city. They own the land, and their only rational choice is to rent it at the highest possible rate. Second, there are N identical 'households' in the city, whose members must commute to the city centre in order to work there, incurring transportation costs of $T(r)$, which depend on the location where they choose to live, r.[6] They have a fixed income Y, and their preferences are described by a 'well-behaved' utility function $U(z, s)$,[7] where z represents the amount of composite consumer good with a price equal to 1 and s is their consumption of land, or lot size. The third type of economic agents present in the model are the 'farmers'. The activity of farming is independent of the city (farmers do not need to travel to the city centre); there is free entry in this activity, and the surplus a farmer can obtain from one unit of land dedicated to farming is constant and equal to R_A.

The land market is assumed to be perfectly competitive at every location in space. This means that all participants have perfect information about land rents throughout the city and take the land rents in the city as given. Here, as in the von Thünen model, land-rent formation is a process through which land at any point is allocated to an activity according to a bidding process. In this process, the economic agent (household or farmer) offering the highest bid secures the lot in question. This notion rests on the idea that land at a particular location represents a single commodity whose price cannot be determined by the textbook interplay among a large number of sellers and buyers, since 'land as space is a homogeneous good and land at a location is a continuously differentiated good' (Alonso, 1964). The price-taking assumption in the land market can be justified in this context on the ground that land in the close vicinity of any location belonging to a continuous space is highly substitutable, thus making the competition for land highly intense.

Description of the Competitive Equilibrium

The competitive equilibrium in this model is defined by a land-rent function $R(r)$ as well as by the areas in which each activity or economic agent is located, so that no one finds it optimal to change his/her location at the prevailing land rents.

As we explain in detail in Appendix 1A1, the land-rent function $R(r)$, the household distribution $n(r)$,[8] the lot size $s(r)$,[9] the utility level of the individuals u^* and the city border r_f,[10] together represent an equilibrium land use in this model, if and only if the following conditions are satisfied:

$$R(r) = \Psi(r, u^*) \qquad \text{for } r \leq r_f$$
$$= R_A \qquad \qquad \text{for } r > r_f \qquad (1.1)$$

$$s(r) = s(r, u^*) \qquad \text{for } r \leq r_f$$
$$= 0 \qquad \qquad \text{for } r > r_f \qquad (1.2)$$

$$n(r) = L(r)/s(r, u^*) \quad \text{for } r \leq r_f$$
$$= 0 \qquad \qquad \text{for } r > r_f \qquad (1.3)$$

$$\int_0^{rf} [L(r)/s(r, u^*)] \, dr = N \qquad (1.4)$$

$$\Psi(r_f, u^*) = R_A, \qquad (1.5)$$

Where, $\Psi(r, u^*)$ is the bid-rent curve, which represents the maximum each household is willing to pay for a unit of land at every location in order to achieve a utility level of u^*; $s(r, u^*)$ is the bid-max lot size, which represents the amount of land each individual will demand at each location for a land-rent price given by $\Psi(r, u^*)$ and $L(r)$ is the amount of land available at each location r (land supply at each r).

Let us now analyse this competitive equilibrium. As explained above, the land at each location will be assigned to the economic agent offering the highest bid. Appendix 1A1 explains that the maximum that the farmers will be able to offer for a unit of land is the value of what they can produce with a unit of land, which is R_A. On the other hand, the bid-rent function $\Psi(r, u)$ gives the maximum each household is willing to pay for a unit of land at every location in order to achieve a utility level u. Thus, for a given utility level, because the bid-rent function $\Psi(r, u)$ is continuous and decreasing in r,[11] while the agricultural activity bid-rent function, R_A, is independent of r, the equilibrium land rent at each location (equation (1.1))

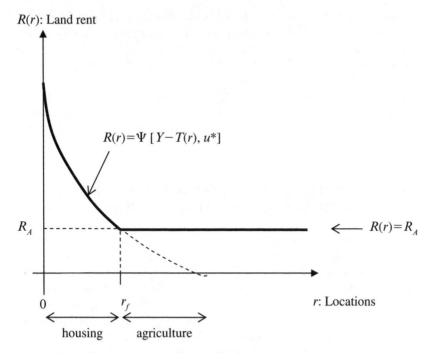

Figure 1.1 Competitive equilibrium land-use pattern

will coincide with the maximum of the equilibrium bid rent and the agricultural rent, as we can see in Figure 1.1. At each distance $r \leq r_f$, housing development takes place, because households are able to offer more for land than are farmers. Here the equilibrium lot size $s(r)$ for each household will coincide with the bid-max lot size $s(r, u^*)$ (equation (1.2)). After r_f, agricultural activity is undertaken.

The equilibrium households' distribution (equation (1.3)) will be determined by the fact that at equilibrium, the demand of land must be equal to its supply.

Up to this point we have described the equilibrium situation for a given utility level. We now need to examine how the equilibrium utility level u^* and fringe distance r_f, are determined. The element that is relevant for determining this is the population (N) that will be accommodated in the city (population constraint, equation (1.4)) as we explain in Appendix 1A1.[12] A larger population will imply lower levels of utility at equilibrium in this model and will influence the urban boundary, r_f. This is because more people must be accommodated in space, implying a reduction in the amount of land used by each household, with the corresponding utility reduction, or alternatively, implying a greater expansion of the city (extension of the city boundary, r_f). In this case, because of the existence of transport costs which will be borne by the CBD, a greater expansion also implies a lower level of utility for individuals.[13]

Finally, under the assumptions made about preferences, income and commuting costs, the existence of a unique residential equilibrium can be shown to hold. It can also be shown that this residential equilibrium is always efficient.[14]

1.3 COMPETITIVE EQUILIBRIUM UNDER THE MAXIMUM LOT-SIZE REGULATION

In order to simplify our analysis and understand the possible implications of such a policy, we worked with an example of an explicit form of 'well-behaved' utility function. In Appendix 1A2 we describe the competitive equilibrium for this specific utility function. In the following section we use the example of Appendix 1A2 in order to analyse the consequences of this fictitious 'maximum lot-size regulation' (s_M regulation) in the context of this model, relative to its allocative implications and distributional issues, setting aside for the moment the issue of urbanization costs.

As stated in the introduction, we analyse the consequences of a policy that penalizes the use of large amounts of land in the city, by simply prohibiting the existence of sites larger than a constant lot size s_M. In order to examine the impact of such a regulation, we introduce the new bid-rent function associated with the regulation.[15] Given that the specific utility function that we used is given by equation (1A2.1), the maximization problem of the households is now as follows:

$$\text{Max}_{r,z,s}\,\alpha\log z + \beta\log s,$$
$$\text{subject to } z + R(r)s = Y - T(r) \text{ and } s \leq s_M. \tag{1.6}$$

Hence, the associated bid-rent function can be defined as:

$$\Psi(r,u;s_M) = \text{max}_{s \leq s_M}[Y - T(r) - Z(s,u)]/s. \tag{1.7}$$

We know from Appendix A2 that, for the specific utility function we are using in this example, $Z(s,u) = s^{-\beta/\alpha}e^{u/\alpha}$. Hence, the bid-rent function can be written as:

$$\Psi(r,u;s_M) = \text{max}_{s \leq s_M}(Y - ar - s^{-\beta/\alpha}e^{u/\alpha})/s, \tag{1.8}$$

and the associated bid-max lot function linked with (1.8) is $s(r, u; s_M)$. Our next step is to obtain the competitive equilibrium under this regulation.

As explained above, land at each location will be assigned to the activity offering the highest bid, and the equilibrium price at that location will be equal to this highest bid. Therefore, in order to describe the competitive equilibrium under this regulation, we need to determine the bid-rent curves for both activities which compete here for land. We know that all individuals are equal, so they will have the same urban bid-rent curves, $\Psi(r, u; s_M)$, for each given utility level u. We also know that the opportunity cost for land is $R_A = 0$, which is the agricultural activity bid-rent curve.

Since the number of households is equal to N, this will determine the maximum utility level u' attainable for the households in the city under this regulation. This implies that there is a unique urban bid-rent function for this utility level (for all individuals), which is $\Psi(r, u'; s_M)$.

This means that land will be assigned to an urban household if the bid-rent function at that location is positive (and so it can outbid the agricultural activity), and the equilibrium price of land at that location will be given by the urban bid-rent function $\Psi(r, u'; s_M)$. Therefore, we can specify the equilibrium land rent $R(r)$, with its corresponding land-use pattern, as

$$R(r) = \Psi(r, u'; s_M) \quad \text{for } r \leq r_f'$$
$$= 0 \quad \text{for } r > r_f', \tag{1.9}$$

where r_f' is the maximum distance at which urban activity is undertaken under this regulation. The equilibrium lot size $s(r)$, from which we can derive the equilibrium density at r, given $L(r)$, will be provided by the bid-max lot function $s(r, u'; s_M)$ associated with $\Psi(r, u'; s_M)$

$$s(r) = s(r, u'; s_M) \quad \text{for } r \leq r_f'$$
$$= 0 \quad \text{for } r > r_f'. \tag{1.10}$$

Thus, in order to describe the equilibrium situation, we need to specify the form of $\Psi(r, u; s_M)$ for any utility level, and then determine the equilibrium utility level that will be reached, given that the population is fixed at N.

Consider Figure 1.2. We define $r_M \equiv r_M(Y, u, s_M)$ as the distance determined by the intersection between the $s(r, u')$ curve (which is the bid-max lot size without regulation for a given utility u') and the horizontal s_M line, which defines the maximum permitted lot size. Since the $s(r, u)$ curve is increasing in r, for all $r < r_M$, $s(r, u') < s_M$, the restriction is inactive and thus the equilibrium lot size $s(r) = s(r, u'; s_M) = s(r, u')$, for those values of r. This also implies that for those values of r, $\Psi(r, u'; s_M) = \Psi(r, u')$

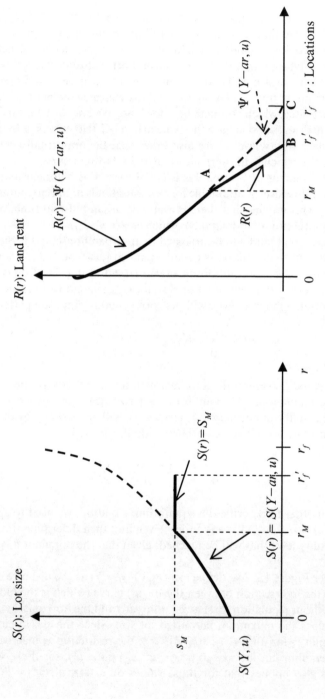

Figure 1.2 Equilibrium lot size (S(r) curve) and land rent (R(r) curve) under s_M regulation

(which is the bid-rent curve without regulation), and therefore, for those values, $R(r) = \Psi(r, u')$.

For values of r that are greater than r_M, $s(r, u')$ (the equilibrium lot-size value without regulation, given utility u') will be greater than s_M, so the restriction will oblige individuals residing at distances greater than r_M to live on lots of size s_M, which are smaller than the lots they would have chosen without this regulation. Thus, in order to maintain the same utility level (u'), the maximum price that they will be able to offer for land at those locations (which defines the bid-rent function for the locations) will be lower than it would have been without the restriction, because they must substitute composite good for land (they alter their optimal consumption pattern). The bid-rent function will be a straight line, decreasing with distance, because the value of the lot size is given, s_M, and thus the only factor which determines the difference in land price between two locations is the transport cost, which is linear and decreases with distance.

As a result, the lot-size curve $s(r)$ and land-rent curve $R(r)$ at the residential land market equilibrium under this regulation will be as follows:

$$
\begin{aligned}
s(r) &= s(r, u') \quad \text{for } r \le r_M (Y, u', s_M) \\
&= s_M \qquad \text{for } r_M (Y, u', s_M) < r \le r_f'.
\end{aligned}
\tag{1.11}
$$

$$
\begin{aligned}
R(r) &= \Psi(r, u') && \text{for } r < r_M (Y, u', s_M) \\
&= (Y - ar - s_M^{-\beta/\alpha} e^{u'/\alpha})/s_M && \text{for } r_M (Y, u', s_M) \le r \le r_f'.
\end{aligned}
\tag{1.12}
$$

From the second line of equation (1.12), it is clear that the bid-rent functions for these locations (that is, the maximum that individuals are willing to pay for a unit of land at these locations, while maintaining a utility level of u') is a straight line, decreasing in r. Here, Y, s_M, and u' are given, so, as stated above, the only difference between locations is the transport cost, $T(r) = ar$, which is linear and decreasing with distance.

In our example in Appendix 1A2, the bid-max lot-size and bid-rent functions without the regulation are given by equations (1A2.4) and (1A2.5), respectively. Using equation (1A2.4), we can obtain r_M by solving the following equation:

$$
s_M = \alpha^{-\alpha/\beta} (Y - ar_M)^{-\alpha/\beta} e^{u'/\beta}.
\tag{1.13}
$$

Therefore, we can define the effective distance as follows:

$$
r_M (Y, u', s_M) = 1/a (Y - \alpha^{-1} s_M^{-\beta/\alpha} e^{u'/\alpha}).
\tag{1.14}
$$

We assume for the moment that $s_M \ge s(r = 0, u')$.

Up to now, we have determined the equilibrium land rent $R(r)$ and lot size $s(r)$ for a given utility level u' and a corresponding r_f' under this regulation. In order to determine the equilibrium values of u' and r_f', let us consider the following additional equilibrium conditions:

$$\int_0^{rf'} (\theta/s(r))dr = N \tag{1.15}$$

$$R(r_f') = 0. \tag{1.16}$$

From (1.16) and (1.12), we have that:

$$r_f' = 1/a\,(Y - s_M^{-\beta/\alpha}e^{u/\alpha}). \tag{1.17}$$

Therefore, $r_M < r_f' < r_f$.

As the regulation becomes less restrictive (s_M increases), r_f' approaches the value of r_f, but never reaches it. Thus, as long as there is a restriction, the urban boundary will shrink.

Now we want to determine the equilibrium utility level. As mentioned above, the equilibrium utility level will be determined by the exogenously given population, N. As the population increases, the maximum utility level that can be reached for all individuals decreases, because the transport costs for people living far away from the centre will be higher. Using (1.15), (1.17) and (1.11), we can obtain the following equation:

$$\int_0^{rM} (\theta/s(r,u))\,dr + \int_{rM}^{rf'} (\theta/s_M)\,dr = N. \tag{1.18}$$

Solving this equation and using (1.14), we get:

$$((\theta/a)\beta\alpha^{\alpha/\beta}\,e^{-u/\beta}\,Y^{1/\beta}) - ((\theta/a)\beta\alpha^{-1}e^{u/\alpha}s_M^{-1/\alpha})$$
$$+ ((\theta/a)\beta\alpha^{-1}e^{u/\alpha}s_M^{-1/\alpha}) = N \tag{1.19}$$

The equilibrium utility level thus obtained is:

$$e^{u'} = \alpha^\alpha(\beta\theta/aN)^\beta Y = e^{u*}. \tag{1.20}$$

By substituting (1.20) into (1.11), (1.12) and (1.17), we obtain the equilibrium functions of $s(r)$, $R(r)$ and the urban boundary r_f' (which depends on s_M).

The utility level of the households remains the same (as in equation (1A2.13)), despite the restriction. This can be explained as follows. We know that nothing has changed for the households between 0 and r_M, so they enjoy the same utility as they did without the regulation, u^*. The possible utility change is for the households between r_M and r_f', because they are obliged to live on sites smaller than those they would have freely chosen. However, they still have the freedom to choose the distance from the city at which they wish to live.

In order to understand this, look at Figures 1.3 and 1.4. We defined the bid-rent function as the maximum rent per unit of land that the household can pay to reside at distance r, while enjoying the fixed utility u, and this will be the prevailing land rent at equilibrium. The maximum rent that each individual is willing to pay at r_M will be $\Psi(r_M, u^*)$, which is determined by the optimal choice of land consumption s_M and composite good z_M in order to achieve utility u^*. This is at point M in Figure 1.3. For the case in which no regulation is present, for distances greater than r_M, such as r_2, the optimal consumption choice would be s_2 and z_2, at point 2, and the bid rent would thus be $\Psi(r_2, u^*)$.

However, with the lot-size restriction, at distance r_2 the individual must consume s_M, so in order to obtain utility u^*, he/she must consume z_M. This implies point M in Figure 1.3 for any distance. However, at distance r_2, transportation costs are higher than at distance r_M, so the maximum he/she is now willing to pay for a unit of land at r_2, in order to obtain u^*, will be $\Psi(r_2, u^*)'$, which is smaller than $\Psi(r_2, u^*)$ (the bid rent without regulation), because the individual cannot optimally choose his/her level of land consumption.

Hence, it is clear that the utility remains the same, because we define the bid rent as the maximum rent an individual is willing to pay to enjoy a fixed utility u^*, and as long as there is a positive price for land that satisfies this condition (because the opportunity cost for land is 0), this will be the land rent at that location, and the utility will still be u^*. All of the losses caused by the suboptimal consumption choices will be reflected in lower land prices and will thus be borne by the landlords.

The key element, then, which allows the households to maintain a constant utility level is that the *urban boundary is left free to adjust*. Despite the fact that people are obliged to live in sites smaller than they would have chosen, they still have the freedom to choose the distance from the centre at which to live. This freedom allows them to adjust this distance (now the maximum distance is $r_f' < r_f$), permitting them to consume s_M and z_M and to pay their transportation costs to the centre as well as the opportunity cost for land (the minimum they can offer for land). If they were also obliged to live at the same distances as before, those at distances greater than r_f' would not be able to consume z_M in order to maintain utility u^*, because at these distances $Y - T(r) < z_M$, so they would have to consume a smaller amount of z, and thus would obtain a lower utility.[16]

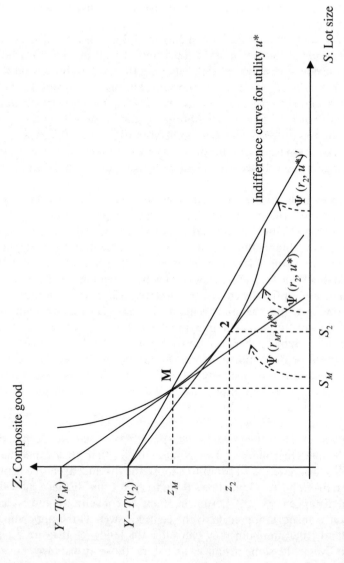

Figure 1.3 *Changes in the bid rent* $\Psi(r, u)$ *under the maximum lot-size regulation* s_M *with an increase in the distance to the centre,* r

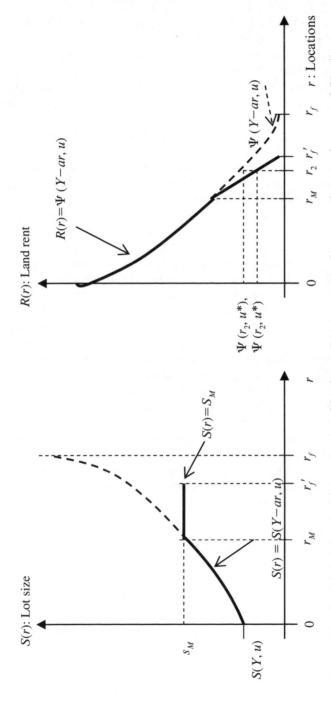

Figure 1.4   Equilibrium lot size (S(r) curve) and land rent (R(r) curve) under s_M regulation, when s_M ≥ S(Y, u)*

As mentioned above, landowners play a passive role in this theory of land use, and their only rational choice is to rent their land at market prices, which are determined by the bid-rent functions of the individual tenants. Thus, if individuals are willing to pay less for some locations (the bid-rent function has moved downwards), in order to achieve the same utility at each place and thus to achieve equilibrium, landowners will receive the market price for their land, which will then be lower.

It is clear that in this context, under the assumption of competitive land markets, any restriction will cause a loss in utility for some economic agents. In this case, the interesting issue is that all the losses are assumed by only one of the groups present in the model, the landlords, and the utility of the other groups remains the same.

In the previous analysis, we assumed that $s_M \geq s(r=0, u^*)$, and thus the utility level was independent of the regulation s_M. As we can see in Figure 1.5, the smallest city that we can obtain without changing the households' utility level is r_{f1}, when $s_M = s_{M1} = s(r=0, u^*)$. We know that $s(r = 0, u^*) = (\beta\theta/aN)Y$. Then, using (1.17) and (1.20), we can see that $r_{f1} = \beta(Y/a)$. Thus, when there is a high preference for land (a high value of β), the smallest city we can obtain without lowering households' utility is larger than that which we would obtain if the preference for land were lower.

However, we can see that if $s_M < s(r=0, u^*)$, the households' utility will also be reduced. The urban boundary will be smaller, and the land-rent curve will be lower, as can be seen in Figure 1.5.

Thus, if $s_M \geq s(r=0, u^*)$, a regulation such as the one in this example can result in a smaller city without lowering the utility for households. This result is attractive, since it suggests that if there are reasons to believe that cities have extended more into territory than they should have, such a regulation could reduce the expansion of a city without reducing the welfare of the households in it, because all the losses are reflected in decreasing land rents. The losses for society as a whole (households and landowners) can be specified exactly in this model, since they are represented by the decrease in land rents, corresponding to the area ABC in the right-hand diagram in Figure 1.2.

The effects of the maximum lot-size regulation in this framework can be summarized in the following result.

Result 1.1 In this setting, the presence of a maximum lot-size regulation will imply that:

1. the territorial extension of the city will be reduced, because the urban boundary is now smaller ($r_f' < r_f$);
2. generally, density and land rent will remain the same at distances near to the CBD (between the CBD and r_M), because the restriction is

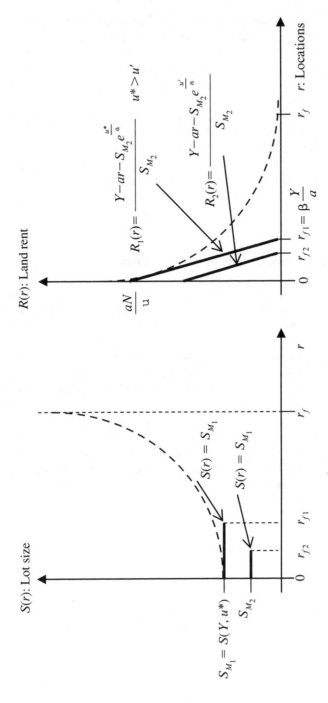

Figure 1.5 Equilibrium lot size (S(r) curve) and land rent (R(r) curve) under s_M regulation, when s_M ≥ S(Y,u*)

inactive there, while for farther away locations (from r_M to r_f') the density will increase and the land rent will decrease;
3.   the utility level for households will be unchanged, despite the restriction, if the regulation is not strongly restrictive, $s_M \geq s(r=0, u^*)$. If the regulation is so restrictive that $s_M < s(r=0, u^*)$, the equilibrium utility level of the households will decrease; and
4.   all the losses due to the households' suboptimal consumption choices will be reflected in lower land prices and thus will be borne by the landlords, if the regulation is not strongly restrictive, $s_M \geq s(r=0, u^*)$. If the regulation is so restrictive that $s_M < s(r=0, u^*)$, the losses will be borne by both landlords and households in this model.

1.4   OPTIMAL MAXIMUM LOT-SIZE REGULATION

Determining the Optimal Maximum Lot-size Regulation

It is clear that in the foregoing setting, the regulation under discussion could only bring about a decrease in welfare, because we know that the competitive equilibrium without it was efficient, and thus any distortion of it will reduce welfare.

However, many arguments can be made to support the view that the competitive equilibrium described in the model (without the presence of regulations) may not be truly efficient and would justify this kind of regulation. The argument we discuss here, which is the one presented in favour of this kind of policy in the case of Santiago de Chile, maintains that there are some urbanization costs which increase with the city's expansion, are borne by the city government, and are not taken into consideration by individuals when they choose the location of their residences (because they assume that a minimum provision of infrastructure exists at any location), and therefore the outcome is a city that extends further than it would have if these costs were considered by individuals, and thus a lower level of welfare.

Examples of such costs are those of providing local public goods such as green spaces, police and fire departments, medical support systems and so forth. In order to simplify the analysis we assume that there is only the cost of one kind of these local public goods that is not taken into account by individuals when they choose their locations in the city. We can then define the total non-considered cost of urbanization relative to this specific local public good (C_T) as follows:

$$C_T = \sum_{i=1}^{n} K_i, \tag{1.21}$$

where n is the number of facilities of this particular kind of local public-good (for example, the number of police departments) in the city and K_i the cost of providing the specific facility i of this type of local public good. We could also define this type of local public good as a 'composite local public good', comprising all of the local public goods needed in the region whose costs are not taken into account by individuals when they choose their locations in the city. We assume that some *standards* are defined by the city government in relation to the provision of these local public goods, as follows:

1. *Coverage requirement*: This states that there should be at least 1 unit of the local public good for every q units of urban land, in order to guarantee that all locations are covered by some unit of the local public good.
2. *Level of service requirement*: This states that there should be c amount of service per person in the city. (A police department, for instance, may require one police officer for every 100 people, so that $c = 0.01$.)

We shall not discuss here the methods for determining these kinds of standards, but merely assume that they seek to guarantee some minimum level of provision for the local public goods, which the individuals take as given.[17] We denoted the amount of land at each location by $L(r) = \theta$, and thus the area that will be taken up by the city will be θr_f. Then we can define the required number of local public goods as:

$$n = (\theta r_f)/q. \tag{1.22}$$

We define the average cost of providing the local public goods as:

$$K = b_0 + b_1 (cN/n), \tag{1.23}$$

where b_0 is the fixed cost of providing each local public good, b_1 is the cost of providing one unit of service of the public good, and (cN/n) is the average amount of service required per local public good, given the fixed population N living in the city.[18] In the case of a police department, for example, b_0 would be the cost of the station, while b_1 could be interpreted as the wage rate for each policeman.

Thus, total urbanization costs can be expressed as:

$$C_T = (\theta r_f/q)b_0 + b_1 cN. \tag{1.24}$$

It can be seen that in this context, the provision costs for these local public goods will depend on the urban boundary, and an extension to the city limits will imply higher costs for the local government. It is clear that this is due to the existence of fixed costs in providing these local public goods. If fixed costs were zero, the total urbanization cost would then be independent of the city's expansion, because the only relevant cost issue would be the service requirement for the fixed population N, and this could be divided into the number of units of public goods necessary to satisfy the coverage requirement, without increasing the total cost.

As discussed above, the s_M regulation leads to a smaller urban boundary (r_f') and thus it will lead to savings in urban infrastructure costs for the government. The cost savings due to this policy can be expressed as follows:

$$C_S(s_M) = [(\theta r_f/q)b_0 + b_1 cN] - [(\theta r_{f'}/q)b_0 + b_1 cN] \qquad (1.25)$$

$$C_S(s_M) = (\theta/q)b_0(r_f - r_{f'}). \qquad (1.26)$$

In order to determine whether the implementation of this policy improves welfare, we must compare these savings with the losses brought about by the decrease in land rents, which we define as R_L. These losses are given by the following expression:

$$R_L(s_M) = \int_{rM}^{rf} \Psi(r, u^*)dr - \int_{rM}^{rf} [(Y - ar - s_M^{-\beta/\alpha}e^{u^*/\alpha})/s_M] \, dr. \qquad (1.27)$$

It is clear that in this setting there is a trade-off between savings in urbanization costs and losses in land rents. If the regulation is highly restrictive, s_M is lower, the urban boundary is smaller, and therefore urbanization costs are lower, but on the other hand, greater losses are incurred due to lower land rents. Therefore, if $C_S(s_M) \geq R_L(s_M)$, then the s_M regulation is welfare improving in this context. We could then identify a value for s_M at which this difference is maximized. This would be the optimal s_M regulation, and would be given by the following expression:

$$s_M^* = \text{argmax} \, [C_S(s_M) - R_L(s_M)]. \qquad (1.28)$$

where the $C_S(s_M)$ and $R_L(s_M)$ functions are given by the following expressions:

$$C_S(s_M) = (\theta/q)b_0 e^{u^*/\alpha}(1/a)s_M^{-(\beta/\alpha)} \qquad (1.29)$$

$$R_L(s_M) = (1/2a)[\beta^2/(1+\beta)](1/\alpha)e^{2(u^*/\alpha)}s_M^{-[(1+\beta)/\alpha]}. \qquad (1.30)$$

Solving equation (1.28), we can obtain the optimal s_M regulation, which is as follows:

$$s_M^* = (1/2)^\alpha (\beta/\alpha)^\alpha \theta^\alpha (q/b_0)^\alpha e^{u*}. \qquad (1.31)$$

where

$$e^{u*} = \alpha^\alpha (\beta\theta/aN)^\beta Y. \qquad (1.32)$$

Hence, the optimal s_M regulation, in terms of the exogenous variables of the model, is given by:

$$s_M^* = (1/2)^\alpha \beta \theta^{\beta-\alpha} (q/b_0)^\alpha (1/aN)^\beta Y. \qquad (1.33)$$

We can summarize these results as follows:

Result 1.2 If there are fixed costs involved in the provision of local public goods, then:

1. the total amount of the provision costs for local public goods will depend on the expansion of the city, and a more extended city will imply higher costs for the local government, given a fixed population; and
2. there is a trade-off between savings in urbanization costs for the local government and losses for the landlords, as reflected in the decrease in land rents when the city expansion is reduced. If the cost savings are greater than the losses for landlords, $C_S(s_M) \geq R_L(s_M)$, then the s_M regulation is welfare improving in this context. There is a value for s_M at which this difference is maximized, and this constitutes the optimal s_M regulation.

Analysing the Optimal Maximum Lot-size Regulation

In this section, we analyse how the optimal s_M regulation varies with the parameters of the model.

An increase in fixed costs b_0 or a decrease in the coverage requirement q
It is intuitively clear that if the fixed cost, b_0, of providing each local public-good increases, or the coverage requirement q decreases (which means that more units of the local public goods are required in space), the optimal s_M regulation will be a more restrictive one, because the gains derived from a smaller city (which implies a more restrictive regulation) will increase. This is because this change affects only the $C_S(s_M)$ function, thus increasing the savings at each level of the s_M regulation, since the $R_L(s_M)$ function remains the same, and thus the losses due to this regulation also remain the same, because the bid-rent and bid-max lot-size functions, which determine the $R_L(s_M)$ function, have not changed.

This can be seen in Figure 1.6. Let us suppose that for a given value of $(b_0/q)^*$, the optimal s_M regulation is s_M^*, which determines the land-rent and lot-size functions as well as the urban boundary (r_f'). In this case, the gains deriving from the s_M^* regulation are reflected in the area BCDE, while the losses are represented by the area ABC. Because s_M^* is the optimal regulation for the given parameters of the economy, we know that a very minor deviation from it, such as a more restrictive regulation, s_M^{**}, which determines a smaller urban boundary $r_f'(s_M^{**})$, will lead to extra gains represented by the area $B'BEE'$, which will be smaller than the extra losses of area $B'BAA'$. However, if (b_0/q) has increased to $(b_0/q)^{**}$, the extra gains from a more restrictive regulation such as s_M^{**} have increased in the area EGHE', while the extra losses remain the same, so that a reduction in s_M will increase the gains from the policy, and thus the optimal regulation will be a more restrictive one.

If there is a high preference for land (high β or low α), an increase of b_0 or a reduction of q will imply a smaller reduction of s_M^* than in the case of a low preference for land, because the losses due to the restriction in the first case will be higher than in the second instance. This can be seen in Figure 1.7. Here we can see that a higher preference for land (or higher β) implies a flatter bid-rent curve, because the substitution between land and good z in order to maintain a constant utility is more difficult to achieve, since z is valued very little. In the extreme case, where the consumption of land is the only possibility (because z is not valued at all), the price decline in land as we move away from the centre will form a straight line, reflecting only the increase in transportation costs, which is linear. This flatter bid-rent curve implies that at every distance, people will be willing to pay a higher price for land than before. Thus, the losses due to a more restrictive s_M regulation will be higher, and in consequence it is reasonable to assume that the reduction in s_M^* as b_0 increases or q decreases will be smaller as the preference for land increases.

An increase in the income level of households, Y

An increase in income implies that the equilibrium utility level of the households will increase (equation (1.32)). The only possibility for increasing utility is consuming more goods, z or s. Because we know that land is a normal good (the income effect on the Marshallian demand for land is positive), the increase in income will result in an increase in land consumption at each location ($s^*(r)$ increases, as we can see in equation (1A2.15)). This implies that any s_M regulation will now be more restrictive than before, because the overall level of lot sizes is now higher. Thus, the optimal s_M regulation should be relaxed (increased) as income rises. This is clear in equation (1.33).

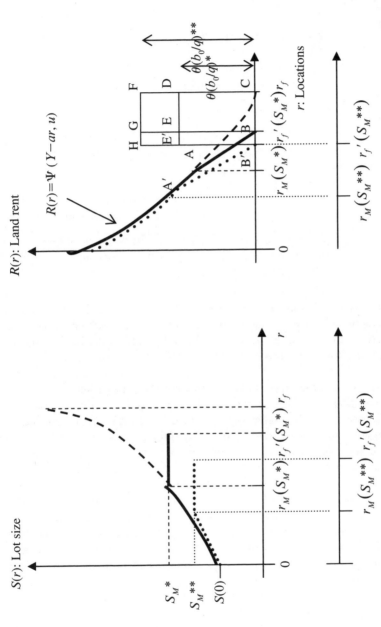

Figure 1.6   Equilibrium lot size (S(r) curve) and land rent (R(r) curve) under the optimal s_M regulation, for different values of (b_0/q)

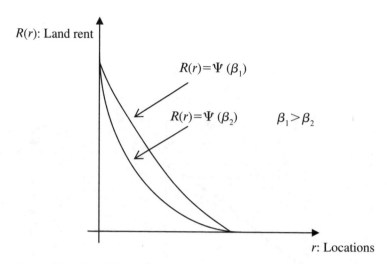

Figure 1.7   Equilibrium land rent (R(r) curve) for different values of preference for land, where a higher β implies a higher preference for land

Thus, we can see that any change in the exogenous variables of the model resulting in an increase in the equilibrium utility for households will lead to an increase in lot sizes at each location, and therefore the level of the s_M regulation should be adjusted to this new level by relaxing it.

An increase in θ, the supply of land (or space) at each location
We now discuss an increase in θ, which is the supply of land (or space) at each location. If θ is higher (which can be interpreted, for example, as the presence of a larger number of tall buildings in the city, so that while at each location there is still θ amount of land, the space available is now larger than θ, so the supply of space at each location increases), we would expect s_M^* to be more restrictive than in the case of a smaller supply of space, because a higher θ means that it is necessary to provide more units of public goods in the city (because of the coverage requirement), so a more restrictive regulation would provide greater cost savings than before.

However, this is only the direct effect of the increase in θ, which can be seen in equation (1.31). There is also an indirect effect of the increase in θ, which is that the equilibrium utility increases (equation (1.32)), because people will now be able to consume more land (or space) at each distance as the supply of land (or space) increases for each distance (equation (1A2.15)). This increase in the utility level increases the optimal s_M regulation, as explained above.

Hence, the net effect of the regulation will depend on the magnitude of each phenomenon, and this will in turn depend on the importance of consuming land (or space) for individuals (β), in comparison with the importance of the consumption of the composite good (α), as we can see in equation (1.33).

This first effect dominates the second one, and thus the s_M^* regulation gets stricter (decreases), when individuals' preference for consuming the composite good, α, is larger than that for consuming land, β, that is $(\beta - \alpha) < 0$. However, if there is a high preference for consuming space, so that $(\beta - \alpha) > 0$, a larger supply of it will imply a relatively large increase in the utility level. Therefore, this effect will dominate the other one, and the optimal s_M^* will increase, which means that the optimal regulation should be less restrictive in these cases.

Accordingly, if there is a high preference for space in a city as well as an ample supply of space θ at each location, the optimal maximum lot-size regulation should be less strict than in the case of a city with a smaller supply of space at each location. In consequence, if for some reason the city government expects the supply of space in the city to increase (for example, because higher densities or taller buildings are permitted, or because previously unavailable land is being developed), and the population shows a strong preference for land (or space) relative to other goods, then regulations aimed at restricting lot sizes (or living space) in order to reduce the size of the city and save on urbanization costs should be relaxed in order to improve welfare.[19]

1.5 CONCLUDING REMARKS

In this chapter, we discussed an example of a policy similar to those currently being implemented in the metropolitan region of Santiago, in an attempt to solve problems arising from the inefficient provision of local public goods in the region. This example provided the original motivation for analysing the problem of the provision of local public goods in large urban agglomerations such as Santiago, as presented in the following chapters. In the Santiago case, it is argued that some infrastructural costs (for local public goods such as police and fire departments, schools, medical facilities, transportation services and so on), which increase with the city's extension and are borne by the city government, are not taken into account by individuals when they choose their locations in the city and the amount of land to consume (because they assume that a minimum infrastructure exists at any location). Therefore, the outcome is that people consume excess land and the city is more extensive than it would be if these costs were considered by individuals, thus lowering welfare.

In an attempt to correct this inefficiency, a number of policies have been implemented in Santiago which seek to reduce the city's extension by penalizing the use of large amounts of land in the city (through, for instance, a tax on vacant land) or by providing incentives for the occupation of less space (as with the reduction of property taxes on smaller houses), and in general by restricting the space occupied by individuals in the city in order to limit the city's extension and thus reduce the infrastructure costs for the city government. Nevertheless, in this case the real problem seems to be the lack of adequate incentives for individuals and local governments to promote the optimal provision of local public goods.

The results of this chapter can be summarized as follows. In the framework of the basic model of residential choice, we can see that regulations aimed at penalizing the use of larger lots in cities, such as the regulation we have analysed here, do not affect households' utility as long as the regulation is not overly restrictive, as we discussed in this chapter. All the losses involved are borne by the landlords, because land rents decrease. It is clear that in this context, because the competitive equilibrium of the basic model of residential choice was efficient, any restriction such as this regulation will cause a utility loss for some economic agents. Note that all the losses are assumed by only one group among those present in the model, the landowners, and the utility of the other groups remains the same. Thus, the losses from such a policy are clearly identified.

Hence, if we believe that some urbanization costs, which increase with the city's extension and are the responsibility of the city government, are not taken into account by individuals when choosing their locations, the competitive equilibrium of residential land markets will not be socially efficient, and thus policy makers may have reason to believe that policies aimed at reducing the city's size, such as the maximum lot-size policy under discussion here, may be welfare improving. This will be the case if the cost savings deriving from a smaller city size are greater than the land-rent losses arising from the households' suboptimal choice of their consumption bundle.

The optimality of regulations aimed at restricting the space occupied by individuals in the city in order to limit the city's extension will depend on the exogenous variables of the model, s_M^* (β, θ, q, b_0, a, N, Y). As we can then see, in spite of the existence of some urbanization costs which increase with the city's extension and are not taken into account by individuals when choosing their locations, if the specific parameters of the economy call for a very relaxed s_M^* regulation (that is, a very high s_M^*) – for example, if households have very high incomes – a very restrictive regulation could also decrease welfare.

It is also important to note that since this regulation's optimal level depends on the parameters of the economy, which change over time, such a regulation should also change in order to be efficient. Yet normally, this kind of regulation is not adjusted once it has taken effect. This is the case in Santiago, where, if we examine the exogenous parameters determining the optimal s_M^* regulation, those which have clearly changed are N and Y, while the others have remained relatively unaltered. We can see from the available data that the average growth rate of per capita income $Y(GDP/N)$ was approximately 5 per cent during the past decade, while the average growth rate for the population N was 1.5 per cent. (INE, 2001). Therefore, Y/N^β has increased over time (and with it the optimal s_M^* regulation), implying that such regulations should have been relaxed in order to improve welfare. Yet we know in the case of Santiago that these regulations are very rigid. Thus, even if the optimal s_M^* regulation had been chosen at the beginning, as time passed and Y/N^β increased, this regulation would have become more restrictive than the optimum, and might even have led to a decrease in welfare.

Accordingly, in a case such as that analysed here (in which the city is overly large in relation to its optimal extension, because of the inefficiencies mentioned above), policy makers should be aware that regulations aimed at restricting the city's extension by limiting the size of the space people can occupy can potentially improve welfare, but they can also decrease welfare, and the final result of these policies is difficult to determine. Policy makers should concentrate their efforts on trying to find mechanisms that aim to solve the real problem, which in this case appears to be the lack of adequate incentives for individuals and local governments to achieve the optimal provision of local public goods. Accordingly, in the following chapters we shall shed some light on the discussion about the optimal provision of local public goods.

APPENDIX 1A1 DETERMINATION OF THE COMPETITIVE EQUILIBRIUM UNDER THE BASIC MODEL OF RESIDENTIAL CHOICE

The competitive equilibrium in this model is defined by a land-rent function $R(r)$ as well as by the areas in which each activity or economic agent is located, so that no one finds it optimal to change his/her location at the prevailing land rents.

As explained in the chapter, in this model the land-rent formation is a process in which land at any point is allocated to an activity according to a bidding process in which the economic agent (household or farmer) offering the highest bid secures the corresponding lot. Accordingly, in order to determine this equilibrium land-rent function and the corresponding equilibrium locations of the economic agents, we need to identify the maximum that each agent is able to offer for each unit of land at each location.

We know that the maximum that the farmers will be able to offer for a unit of land is the value of what they can produce with a unit of land, which is R_A. This will also be the minimum price that the landlords will accept for land at each location, because there is free entry into the activity of farming.

Let us now analyse the price that the households will offer at each location. We know that all the households are equal, so at equilibrium (with equilibrium land prices), they must achieve the same utility, independent of where they choose to locate. If this were not the case, the agents at a location where they obtain a lower utility would seek to move to a location with higher utility, and thus the prevailing situation would not be an equilibrium.[20] Therefore, equilibrium prices should be those at which the utility for households at all locations is equal.[21]

We assume for the moment that households' utility is exogenously given, but we know that at equilibrium, all the households should have the same utility.

What, then, is the maximum rent per unit of land that a household can pay to reside at distance r while enjoying a fixed utility level u? This maximum price is the best offer it can make for this piece of land. If it were to make a lower offer than the best it can do for the land at that location, then it would obtain a higher utility, and another household would be able to make a better offer (because they are all equal) in order to obtain that location. If the household in question makes a better offer than that, it will obtain a lower utility and thus will seek to change its location. Hence, it will not offer more than that.

To respond to the previous question, let us consider the situation of a household that is looking for a residence in the city. As is typical in the economic analysis of consumer behaviour, the assumption is that the household will maximize its utility subject to a budget constraint.

The household earns a fixed income Y per unit of time, which is spent on the composite good, on land and on transportation. If the household is located at a distance r from the CBD, the budget constraint is given by $z + R(r)s = Y - T(r)$, where $R(r)$ is the rent per unit of land at r, $T(r)$ is the transport cost at r and $Y - T(r)$ is the net income at r. It is assumed that $T(r)$ is continuous and increasing for all $r \geq 0$, where $0 \leq T(0) < Y < T(\infty)$. Thus, we can express the residential choice of the household as:

$$\max_{r,\, z,\, s} U(z,s), \text{ subject to } z + R(r)s = Y - T(r). \qquad (1A1.1)$$

The only variation from the standard consumer problem is that here the consumer must also choose a residential location, $r \geq 0$, which affects both the land rent he/she pays and his/her commuting cost. This problem involves a trade-off between accessibility, measured by $T(r)$, and land consumption, measured by s.

In this context, then, what would be the maximum rent per unit of land that a household could pay to reside at distance r, while enjoying a fixed utility level u? This is given by the following expression, which is called the 'bid-rent function', $\Psi(r, u)$:

$$\Psi(r,u) = \max_{z,\,s}(\{[Y - T(r) - z]/s\}/U(z, s) = u) \qquad (1A1.2)$$

This can be seen in Figure 1A1.1. In fact, for a household residing at distance r and selecting the consumption bundle (z, s), $Y - T(r) - z$ is the money available for land payment, so that $[Y - T(r) - z]/s$ represents the rent per unit of land at r. The bid rent $\Psi(r, u)$ is then obtained when this rent is maximized by choosing the appropriate consumption bundle (z, s) subject to the utility constraint $U(z, s) = u$. In the maximization problem of equation (1A1.2), the utility constraint $U(z, s) = u$ can be solved for z to obtain the equation for an indifference curve $z = Z(s, u)$. Then the bid-rent function can be redefined as:

$$\Psi(r,u) = \max_{s}[Y - T(r) - Z(s, u)]/s, \qquad (1A1.3)$$

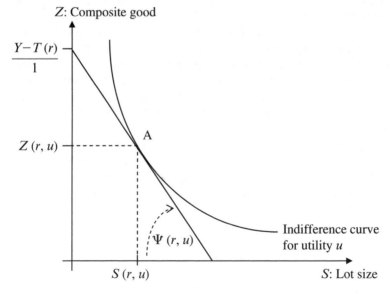

Figure 1A1.1   Bid rent $\Psi(r, u)$ and bid-max lot size $S(r, u)$.

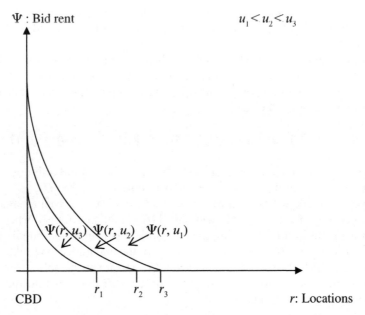

Figure 1A1.2   General shapes of bid-rent curves

which is an unconstrained maximization problem. When we solve it, we obtain the optimal lot size $S(r, u)$, which is the 'bid-max lot size'.

In Figures 1A1.2 and 1A1.3 we can see that for each utility level, we can obtain a bid-rent curve and corresponding lot-size curves. Thus, for an exogenously given utility, there is one bid-rent curve which represents the maximum each household is willing to pay at every location in order to achieve this utility, as well as one lot-size function, which represents the amount of land each person will demand for this land-rent price at each location.

As mentioned above, the land at each location will be assigned to the economic agent offering the highest bid. For a given utility u^*, because the bid-rent function $\Psi(r, u)$ is continuous and decreasing in r, while the agricultural activity bid-rent function is independent of r, the equilibrium land rent will thus be:

$$R(r) = \Psi(r, u^*) \quad \text{for } r \le r_f$$
$$= R_A \qquad\quad \text{for } r > r_f. \tag{1A1.4}$$

We define r_f as the maximum distance at which urban activity is undertaken. $R(r)$ is the equilibrium land rent with its corresponding land-use

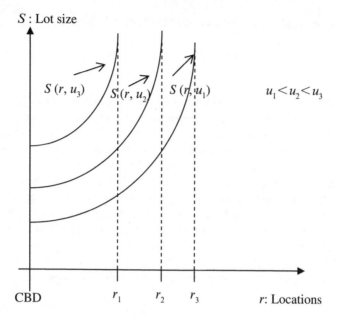

Figure 1A1.3   General shapes of lot-size curves

pattern, because for this land rent: (i) no agent is interested in changing his/her current location, because the land rent at a location different from the chosen one is higher than he/she is able to offer at that location, and (ii) given the utility u^* for urban activity and the free-entry condition in agricultural activity, land rent must be equal to the bid-rent curves for each activity ($\Psi(r, u^*)$ and R_A, respectively).

Figure 1.1 shows the competitive equilibrium land-use pattern. At each location, the market land rent coincides with the maximum of the equilibrium bid rent and the agricultural rent.

At each distance $r \le r_f$, the equilibrium lot size $s(r)$ for each household coincides with the bid-max lot size $s(r, u^*)$, which is the demand for land at that location:

$$s(r) = s(r, u^*) \quad \text{for } r \le r_f \tag{1A1.5}$$

Let us define $L(r)$ as the amount of land available at each distance r (for example, in a circular city, $L(r) = 2\pi r$); that is, the supply of land at each location. At equilibrium, demand must be equal to supply, so:

$$n(r) \, s(r, u^*) = L(r), \tag{1A1.6}$$

where $n(r)$ is the population density at each distance r.

Thus, the equilibrium household distribution is given by:

$$n(r) = L(r)/s(r, u^*) \quad \text{for } r \le r_f, \qquad (1A1.7)$$
$$= 0 \qquad\qquad \text{for } r > r_f.$$

Up to this point we have described the equilibrium situation for a given utility level. We now need to examine how u^* and r_f are determined.

In the literature, it is traditional to classify market models as 'closed-city models', in which the population of the city is exogenous, and 'open-city models', in which households are assumed to be able to move from city to city in a costless manner; hence, the residents' utility equals that of the rest of the economy, which is exogenously fixed, while the population of the city is determined endogenously. For our later analysis of policy implications, we shall use a closed-city model approach, where the utility level is endogenously determined within the model, because we want to examine the potential effects of such a policy on utility levels for households residing in a city.

Since N households reside in the city, the population constraint is:

$$\int_0^{rf} [L(r)/s(r, u^*)]dr = N. \qquad (1A1.8)$$

We also know that the bid rent of both activities must be equal at r_f. This implies that:

$$\Psi(r_f, u^*) = R_A.$$

Summarizing, $R(r)$, $n(r)$, $s(r)$, u^* and r_f together represent an equilibrium land use for the closed-city model approach, if and only if conditions (1A1.4)–(1A1.9) are satisfied. Two real unknowns are the equilibrium utility u^* and fringe distance r_f.

APPENDIX 1A2   AN EXAMPLE OF COMPETITIVE EQUILIBRIUM WITHOUT THE REGULATION

Suppose that the utility function in (1A1.1) is given by the following log-linear utility function:

$$U(z, s) = \alpha \log z + \beta \log s, \qquad (1A2.1)$$

where $\alpha > 0$, $\beta > 0$ and $\alpha + \beta = 1$. We can confirm that this utility function is a well-behaved utility function, in the sense that it satisfies the conditions mentioned above. Thus, the residential choice behaviour of each household can be described as:

$$\max_{r,\,z,\,s} \alpha\log z + \beta\log s, \text{ subject to } z + R(r)s = Y - T(r). \quad (1A2.2)$$

As explained in Appendix 1A1, this is equivalent to:

$$\Psi(r, u) = \max_s([Y - T(r) - Z(s, u)]/s). \quad (1A2.3)$$

Given this, we can obtain the following bid-max lot-size and bid-rent functions:[22]

$$s^*(r, u) = \alpha^{-\alpha/\beta}[Y - T(r)]^{-\alpha/\beta} e^{u/\beta} \quad (1A2.4)$$

$$\Psi^*(r, u) = \alpha^{\alpha/\beta}\beta[Y - T(r)]^{1/\beta} e^{-u/\beta} \quad (1A2.5)$$

Suppose that:

$$T(r) = ar \quad (1A2.6)$$

$$R_A = 0 \quad (1A2.7)$$

$$L(r) = \theta \text{ (Linear city)} \quad (1A2.8)$$

$$Y = Y^0. \quad (1A2.9)$$

We want to determine $R^*(r)$, $n^*(r)$, $s^*(r)$, u^* and r_f, which together represent the equilibrium land use for the closed-city model approach in this example,[23] if and only if conditions (1.1)–(1.5) are satisfied. From these equilibrium conditions, we can see that:

$$\int_0^{rf} [L(r)/s^*(r, u)]\, dr = N \quad (1A2.10)$$

$$\Psi^*(r_f, u) = R_A \quad (1A2.11)$$

From (1A2.5), (1A2.6), (1A2.7), (1A2.9) and (1A2.11), we obtain:

$$r_f = Y^0/a \quad (1A2.12)$$

Then, using (1A2.4), (1A2.6), (1A2.8) and (1A2.10), we obtain the equilibrium utility u^*:

$$e^{u^*} = \alpha^\alpha(\beta\theta/aN)^\beta Y \quad (1A2.13)$$

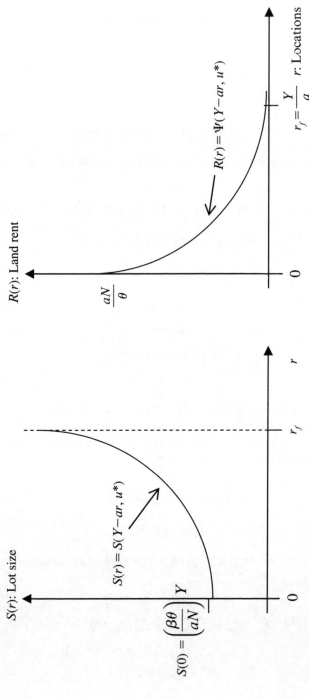

Figure 1A2.1   Competitive equilibrium land-use pattern in the example

$$u^* = \alpha \log \alpha + \beta \log(\beta\theta/aN) + \log Y. \qquad (1A2.14)$$

Finally, replacing (1A2.13) in (1A2.4) and (1A2.5), we obtain the equilibrium lot-size curve $s^*(r)$ and equilibrium land-rent curve $R^*(r)$:

$$s^*(r) = (\beta\theta/aN)\ Y^{1/\beta}(Y - ar)^{-\alpha/\beta} \qquad (1A2.15)$$

$$R^*(r) = \beta(\beta\theta/aN)^{-1}\ Y^{-1/\beta}(Y - ar)^{1/\beta} \qquad (1A2.16)$$

$$n^*(r) = (aN/\beta)\ Y^{-1/\beta}(Y - ar)^{\alpha/\beta} \qquad (1A2.17)$$

$$s^*(0) = (\beta\theta/aN)Y \qquad (1A2.18)$$

$$R^*(0) = aN/\theta > \qquad (1A2.19)$$

Figure 1A2.1 shows the equilibrium land use for the closed-city model approach in this example.

NOTES

1. Another important alleged problem is related to the unequal distribution of economic activity in the country, which is generally seen as a socially inefficient outcome. Within the framework of the neoclassical model, and assuming homogeneous space, we would expect economic activity to be equally distributed in space. Of course, if space is not homogeneous, some places will enjoy advantages for the production of certain goods compared to others, and we can expect firms to agglomerate in places where production is facilitated. However, if space is homogeneous, transport is costly and we are in a competitive setting (that is, prices are given and there are constant returns to scale), the rational choice for a firm will be to (that is, to produce at each location where its goods are in demand) in order to minimize transport costs. Yet this is not what we observe; economic activity is highly concentrated in space. Policy makers are concerned with this unequal distribution of economic activity. However, they do not agree as to whether this unequal distribution is a socially efficient outcome or a result of inefficiencies, and thus whether it would be justified to intervene to some extent in the market process in order to produce a more equal distribution and thus to improve welfare.

    In the case of Chile, this issue is a very important one, because the country exhibits a highly unequal distribution of population and production activities, with more than 40 per cent of its population (6 million people) living in the capital city or metropolitan region of Santiago, where more than 47 per cent of the entire country's GDP is produced (INE, 2001). Numerous policies are being implemented in an attempt to reverse this unequal distribution, such as tax reductions in outlying regions (those very far from the metropolitan region). However, it is not clear whether a more equal distribution of economic activity would improve welfare at the national level.

    Fujita and Thisse (2002, Chapter 11) have recently derived results that shed some light on this discussion. The main message seems to be that agglomeration may well be the territorial counterpart of economic growth, in much the same way as growth seems to foster inequality among individuals. However, a higher level of welfare may accompany inequalities even for those living on the periphery (outside the agglomeration). If such results were to be confirmed, they would have far-reaching implications for the modern space-economy as well as for the design of more effective economic policies.

2. These include local public goods such as green spaces, police and fire departments, medical support systems and so forth.

3. People assume this, because the government has always provided this infrastructure (or at least part of it) to those settled in new territories, at almost no cost to them. This infrastructure is mostly financed by general taxes, which are borne by the whole population and therefore have a negligible impact on the taxes paid by individuals settled in new territories. Thus, people assume that the government will continue with this strategy.

4. There is also a regulation that directly limits the extension of Santiago's metropolitan region simply by prohibiting urban development outside a certain 'urban boundary'. The justifications for this regulation have varied over time. One recurrent argument has been the reduction of urbanization costs for the city government. An analysis of the consequences of this policy in the case of the metropolitan region can be found in Petermann (1998, 2005).

5. Fujita (1989, Chapter 7) analyses the opposite policy: minimum lot-size regulation. This regulation requires the lot size per household to be no less than a given constant s_M. Although the focus of the analysis is very different, the framework used there is very useful for our analysis, so we utilize it here.

6. r measures the distance of a location to the CBD.

7. By a 'well-behaved' utility function, we mean that it is continuous and increasing for all $z > 0$ and $s > 0$, all indifference curves are strictly convex and smooth, and they do not cut across axes. Both z and s are essential and normal goods.

8. $n(r)$ is the population density at each location r.

9. $s(r)$ is the amount of land that each individual demands at each location r.

10. r_f is the maximum distance at which urban activity is undertaken. Beyond this distance, agricultural activity is undertaken.

11. In Figure 1A1.2 we show that the bid-rent function $\Psi(r, u)$ decreases with distance, otherwise people who are located farther away from the centre and thus have higher transportation costs would obtain a lower utility.

12. Equation (1.5) reflects the fact that the bid rent of both activities must be equal at the urban fringe r_f.

13. As we explain in Appendix 1A1, for our later analysis of policy implications, we used a closed-city model approach, in which the population of the city is exogenous and the utility level is endogenously determined within the model, because we want to examine the potential effects of such a policy on utility levels for households residing in a city.

14. The proof of this can be found in Fujita (1989).

15. The detailed analysis of the concept of bid-rent function is in Appendix 1A1.

16. The fact that the utility does not change can also be seen by looking at equation (1.18). The first term on the left-hand side (which is equivalent to the first and second terms on the side of equation (1.19)) is the same as it would be without the regulation. The term which changes is the second on the left-hand side (equivalent to the third on the left-hand side of equation (1.19)). Thus, this regulation implies a smaller constant $s(r)$ between r_M and r_f', which makes this term increase, but on the other hand r_f' is reduced in a manner which exactly compensates for this increase, so the term is exactly the same as without the regulation, and a change in utility is not needed in order to satisfy the population constraint. Without the regulation, condition (1.18) would be:

$$\int_0^{rM} [\theta/s^*(Y - ar, u)]\,dr + \int_{rM}^{rf} [\theta/s^*(Y - ar, u)]\,dr = N.$$

From this, we obtain exactly the same expression as in equation (1.19).

17. Note that we are not determining here the optimal provision of these local public goods.

18. In areas with a higher population density, the amount of required service will be higher than in places with lower density, but on average the requirement will be cN/n.

19. In the case of Santiago, some current policies are aimed at increasing the space available at each location by increasing the permitted density. At the same time, other policies seek to reduce the lot sizes occupied by each household, in order to reduce the city's size and

save on urbanization costs. However, we know from the previous model that if the households' preference for land (or space) is high relative to their preference for consuming other goods, an increase in the space available at each location would imply that the s_M^* regulation, or policies aiming in this direction, should be relaxed, as explained above.

20. We are assuming perfect mobility of individuals.
21. Intuitively we know that equilibrium prices must decrease with distance; otherwise people who are located farther away from the centre and thus have higher transportation costs would obtain a lower utility.
22. Equations (1A2.4) and (1A2.5) were obtained as follows:

(1) $(\partial\,[(Y - T(r) - Z(s, u)]/s)/\partial s = [-1/s\,\partial Z(s, u)/\partial s] - \{1/s^2[Y - T(r) - Z(s, u,)]\} = 0 \Rightarrow$
(2) $-\partial Z(s, u)/\,\partial s = [Y - T(r) - Z(s, u)]/s$
(3) $Z(s, u) = e^{u/\alpha} s^{-\beta/\alpha}$.

Using (2) and (3), we obtain (1A2.4) and (1A2.5).

23. As we explained in Appendix 1A1, for our later analysis of policy implications, we used a closed-city model approach, in which the population of the city is exogenous and the utility level is endogenously determined within the model.

2. Competing jurisdictions for the provision of local public goods

2.1 INTRODUCTION

Tiebout (1956) envisaged an original decentralized mechanism to achieve the optimal provision of local public goods. He suggested that in an economy with local public goods, the optimal allocation could be decentralized through a system of competing jurisdictions. His concept of jurisdiction was one in which local service providers offer a bundle of services (all-purpose jurisdiction or multi-functionality of jurisdictions) to individuals living in a predefined region, where all of the individuals living there must pay taxes and consume the services provided by their local jurisdiction (localized membership). His idea was that by migrating to the jurisdiction that reflects their tastes in public goods and tax schemes, consumers would reveal their preferences. Tiebout argued that competition among jurisdictions and 'voting with the feet' may lead to the efficient provision of local public goods.

Nevertheless, this decentralized mechanism of competing jurisdictions *à la* Tiebout will result in the optimal provision of local public goods only if some critical assumptions are satisfied. Among them, the most important are: (i) there is costless mobility of people between jurisdictions and (ii) there are a large number of jurisdictions or free entry and exit in jurisdiction formation. However, and as discussed in the general introduction, these crucial assumptions of Tiebout's hypothesis are unlikely to materialize in reality, especially in countries with large metropolitan regions. The lack of competition among their jurisdictions makes it problematical to achieve the optimal provision of local public goods by means of Tiebout's competing jurisdictions.

In general, the literature examining the possibility of decentralizing the optimal provision of local public goods assumes, whether directly or indirectly, some version of Tiebout's setting, as in Berglas (1984), Scotchmer (1986), Berglas and Pines (1981) and Hochman (1981), among many others. The original idea of the concept of functional overlapping competing jurisdictions (FOCJ) (Frey and Eichenberger, 1995, 1996a, 1997, 1999), that of unbundling the various functions (uni-functionality of jurisdictions[1]) and incorporating de-localized membership[2] in order to increase competition in the provision of local public goods has not, until now, been integrated into a unified framework which would allow discussion of the advantages and problems that this new type of jurisdiction may imply for the optimal provision of local public goods.

In this chapter, we develop a framework to be used to analyse the optimal allocation of local public goods in a spatial context (that is, considering transport costs) and the allocation consequences of increasing competition in a decentralized provision. For this we take these two innovative aspects present in the concept of FOCJ: *de-localized membership* and *uni-functionality of jurisdictions.* We analyse the effects of these two specific aspects on competition among jurisdictions in large urban agglomerations, and the impact this probable increase in competition may have on the achievement of the optimal allocation of local public goods.

For the development of this framework, we incorporated aspects from different areas of the literature, including that on local public goods (Tiebout, 1956; Arnott and Stiglitz, 1979; Berglas, 1984; Scotchmer, 1986), but also from club theory (Buchanan, 1965; Berglas, 1976b; Sandler and Tschirhart, 1980; Scotchmer, 1985), location theory (Hotelling, 1929; D'Aspremont et al., 1979; Salop, 1979), market and industry structure theory (Baumol, 1982) and urban economics (Alonso, 1964; Muth, 1969; Fujita 1989), among others.

Note that the analysis presented here serves as a benchmark in order to study these two aspects present in the concept of FOCJ, but it is not an analysis of the entire concept. As explained in the general introduction, FOCJ is a multi-dimensional concept, and although many of these dimensions may be of interest, in this chapter we concentrate only on the two aspects mentioned above. Thus, we shall discuss several aspects related to this concept, with the proviso that 'FOCJ' refers only to our interpretation of the concept.

Structure of the Chapter

The chapter is structured as follows. First, we develop the framework to be used in the analysis of these issues. We make the assumption that there is a group of individuals living in the same region, each endowed with units of some composite good. Each individual derives utility from the composite good, the amount of land he or she occupies and the use of the various types of local public goods.[3] The amount of the local public good and the corresponding provision cost for each type are fixed and equal for all goods of the same type. Each specific facility for each type of local public good is provided by an independent local service provider (uni-functionality of jurisdictions, unbundling of activities), and these different local service providers compete with one another for customers in order to maximize profits.[4]

In our setting, independent of their place of residence, individuals are free to choose the local service provider they wish to patronize for the provision of each local public good (de-localized membership in jurisdictions). However, in order to enjoy the local public goods, an individual located at some point in space must travel to the chosen facilities, incurring transportation costs.[5]

Each local service provider must make three decisions: whether to enter the local public-good market, the location at which it will offer its local public good, and the price (or tax) it will charge its customers in order to maximize its profits.[6]

We also assume that individuals are fixed to their locations within the region under analysis, but that they have the opportunity to move to another region where they can achieve an alternative level of utility. The level of this exit option utility is related to the level of competition among regions.[7]

In Section 2.2, the basic model is presented, and in Section 2.3, the case of homogeneous local public goods[8] is analysed. We identify the equilibrium pattern of a system of independent and competing local service providers supplying homogeneous local public goods, comparing this with the welfare-maximizing pattern.[9]

In Section 2.3, first we discuss the optimal allocation for this economy. We find that an important factor in determining the optimal allocation of local public goods in such a setting is the existing trade-off between transportation costs and fixed costs, a classical aspect of location models.

Second, we analyse the equilibrium patterns of a system of uni-functional competing jurisdictions, and we solve backwards for the subgame perfect Nash equilibria. We start with the third-stage subgames, in which the prices are set by the local service providers and find that in general, local service providers will choose to charge discriminatory prices with respect to location, in favour of the more distant locations. Then we analyse the location choices of the second stage. Here, the assumption about the flexibility of the local service providers' chosen locations and corresponding market areas is crucial. In the case of no location sunk cost technology (in which no location-specific fixed costs are present), the equilibrium locations for competing local service providers will be unique and efficient, in the sense that they will minimize total transport costs for individuals, if local service providers can charge discriminatory prices. However, in the case of location sunk cost technology we have a multiplicity of equilibria, and we can also have location equilibria that are not efficient. Finally we discuss the entry decisions involved in the first stage. Here the assumption about the technology of local public goods is also crucial. In the case of no location sunk cost technology, the equilibrium allocation under free entry of local service providers in the region is unique and is characterized by excessive entry, when the competition represented by other regions is very weak. Only when we have perfect competition from other regions is this allocation optimal. However, in the case of location sunk cost technology, the optimal allocation is a free-entry equilibrium, but we can also have free-entry equilibria with excessive and insufficient entry. In this case we have a multiplicity of equilibria.

Third, we compare the different free-entry price-location equilibria characterized in the previous sections, in terms of the winners and losers between the local service providers and the individuals living in their service areas, and in terms of welfare. We shall see that equilibria with higher entry levels are better in terms of utility for individuals and worse for local service providers in terms of profits than equilibria with lower levels of entry. Note that deviations from the optimal allocation are more costly in terms of welfare when they represent a reduction in the number of local public goods than when they represent an increase. Furthermore, the presence of distant competition is not always welfare increasing. We show that the result will depend on the type of technology of the local public good provided.

Fourth, we check the robustness of our results by considering demand that responds to price. We find that, if the local public goods technology is characterized by no location sunk costs and there is free entry in the region, the free-entry price-location equilibrium will be characterized by excessive entry, as in the inelastic demand case. Thus, this result does not depend on demand elasticity and is in this sense robust. Nevertheless, if the local public-good technology is characterized by location sunk costs and there is free entry in the region, the free-entry price-location equilibrium may be characterized by insufficient or excessive entry, as in the inelastic demand case, but it can also be characterized only by excessive entry.

We also check the robustness of our results relative to price-setting restrictions, and then finally in Section 2.3, we discuss what happens to the equilibrium patterns identified earlier if local service providers are no longer free to set prices and are forced to charge fixed rates (mill pricing), independent of location. We find that the inefficiencies identified under discriminatory pricing are increased under mill pricing, and that in general the opportunity to charge discriminatory prices based on location increases competition and improves welfare in a spatial context.

In Section 2.4, we analyse the case of heterogeneous local public goods,[10] in order to incorporate the uni-functionality of jurisdictions into the analysis and to evaluate the consequences of unbundling local governments' activities. We find that, if competition from other regions is very weak, the possibility of unbundling activities may increase competition and aggregate utility for the individuals in a region. Nevertheless, this will only be possible if there is competition in all types of local public goods. If there is a monopoly local service provider in the region, even for only one type of service, all the gains from the increased competition in all other types of local public goods will be redistributed to the monopoly local service provider, and individuals will obtain the same utility as if there were no competition in any type at all. The result in terms of utility for individuals will be equivalent to the case of the classical all-purpose jurisdictions.

Finally, Section 2.5 provides a summary and gives some explanations of the main results of the chapter.

2.2   THE MODEL

Consider a group of N identical individuals living in the same region, each endowed with Y units of some composite good. Each individual derives utility from the composite good, z, from the amount of land he/she occupies, s, and from the use of K types of local public goods according to a utility function, $u(z, s, G_1, G_2, \ldots, G_k)$. For the sake of simplicity, we assume that the amount of land occupied by each individual is fixed at one unit ($s = 1$), so that $u(z, G_1, G_2, \ldots, G_k)$.

We assume that individuals have quasilinear preferences, represented by the following *quasilinear utility function*:[11]

$$u(z, G_1, G_2, \ldots, G_k) = z + g(G_1, G_2, \ldots, G_k). \qquad (2.1)$$

Each of the K types of local public goods is supplied in the region by m_i facilities, identified by ij, where $i \in \{1, 2, \ldots, K\}$ denotes the type of local public good provided, and $j \in \{1, 2, \ldots, m_i\}$ denotes the index of the specific facility. The amount of the local public good of each type, G_i, is fixed and equal for all of the same type. The provision cost for each type of local public good is $c(G_i) = G_i$. For example, local public goods for which it pays for groups to consume collectively, but it is possible to exclude others from the consumption of the group's own units of the goods, as with educational systems, fire and police protection and domestic refuse collection, among many others.

Space in the region is described by the interval $X = [0, L]$, where at each point $r \in X$ the amount of land is $L(r) = 1$, and space is homogeneous except for the presence of the service facilities, each located at one specific

Competing jurisdictions for the provision of local public goods

location, r_{ij}. We assume that $L = N$, so that no vacant land exists within the region, and each point in space is identified with one individual. In order to consume the local public goods, an individual located at r must travel to one chosen facility of each type located at $r_{1, j1(r)}, r_{2, j2(r)}, \ldots, r_{K, jK(r)}$, where $j_i(r)$ corresponds to the specific facility j of the local public-good type i chosen by the individual located at r.[12] The transportation cost for an individual located at r and patronizing facility ij is given by $t_{ij}(r) = a(|r - r_{ij}|)$. We also assume that the local public goods do not occupy space.

In this setting, an *allocation* is a system of $\Sigma_{i=1}^k m_i$ facilities, in which each facility ij is described by its location r_{ij}, its number of customers N_{ij}, the residential location of its customers relative to it $X_{ij} \in X$ (its market area), where $X_{ij} = [r_{ij}^{bl}, r_{ij}^{br}]$ and r_{ij}^{bl} and r_{ij}^{br} represent the borders of the market area to the left and right of the facility ij, respectively, and their consumption of z. We denote by $\underline{r} = \underline{r}(m_1, m_2, \ldots, m_K) = (r_{1,1}, r_{1,2}, \ldots, r_{1,m1}, r_{2,1}, r_{2,2}, \ldots, r_{2,m2}, \ldots, r_{K,1}, r_{K,2}, \ldots, r_{K,mK})$ the vector describing the number of facilities of each type and their corresponding locations.

Let us consider now the *optimal allocation* for this economy. Imagine a region-wide planner whose objective is to maximize the aggregate utility achieved by the N individuals of the region, subject to the resources constraint. The planner's role is to determine the number of facilities of each type, their locations and their tax or pricing structure, designated as $\phi(r)$, which is used to finance them. We denote by $\underline{r}^*(m_1^*, m_2^*, \ldots, m_K^*) = (r_{1,1}^*, r_{1,2}^*, \ldots, r_{1,m1}^*, r_{2,1}^*, r_{2,2}^*, \ldots, r_{2,m2}^*, \ldots, r_{K,1}^*, r_{K,2}^*, \ldots, r_{K,mK}^*)$ the vector describing the optimal number of facilities of each type and their corresponding optimal locations, and $\phi^*(r)$ will represent the optimal taxation scheme (the amount, in units of composite good, charged by the central planner to the individuals located at each r) used to finance the local public goods.

Since we assume that individuals are identical in all aspects, except for their locations in space, and that travelling to the facilities involves a cost, different $\underline{r}$ and $\phi(r)$ chosen by the planner will lead to different indirect utility levels for individuals, which will depend on their locations relative to the locations of the facilities as well as the amount they must pay at their location to finance the facilities. Let us denote the constraint indirect utility function[13] for an individual located at r, for a given $\underline{r}$ and $\phi(r)$, as:

$$V[r, \underline{r}, \phi(r), G_1, G_2, \ldots, G_K] = u\{z[r, \underline{r}, \phi(r)], G_1, G_2, \ldots, G_K\}, \quad (2.2)$$

where $z[r, \underline{r}, \phi(r)]$ is given by:

$$z[r, \underline{r}, \phi(r)] = Y - \sum_{i=1}^{K} a(|r - r_{ij_i(r)}|) - \phi(r). \quad (2.3)$$

Equation (2.3) describes the amount of income that is left free for an individual located at r for consumption of the composite good, after travelling to the chosen facilities providing each type of local public good and paying the tax or fee charged by the planner at r in order to finance them. Given that all the facilities providing the same type of local public good are identical in every way except their locations, each individual will choose the nearest one in order to maximize his or her utility.

The planner's problem is then:

$$\text{Max}_{\underline{r}(m_1, m_2, \ldots, m_K), \phi(r)} \int_{r=0}^{N} V(\cdot) dr \qquad (2.4)$$

$$\text{s.t.} \int_{r=0}^{N} \phi(r) dr \geq \sum_{i=1}^{K} m_i G_i, \qquad (2.5)$$

where $\int_{r=0}^{N} V(\cdot) dr$ corresponds to the aggregate constraint indirect utility function.

In this setting, an optimal allocation is therefore a system of $\Sigma_{i=1}^{K} m_i^*$ facilities, located as described by the vector $\underline{r}^*(m_1^*, m_2^*, \ldots, m_K^*)$ and financed by $\phi^*(r)$, which solves (2.4) s.t. (2.5). We denote the optimal allocation as the vector $[\underline{r}^*, \phi^*(r)]$.

In the following sections, we discuss the potential benefits and problems of a decentralized provision of local public goods in this economy. In support of this aim, we analyse the equilibrium patterns of such a system and compare it with the welfare-maximizing pattern.

We identify in our setting with a decentralized system for the provision of local public goods a system of independent local service providers where each of them supplies only one local public good (or facility) to individuals (uni-functionality) and independently of their place of residence, individuals are free to choose the local service provider they wish to patronize for the provision of each local public good (de-localized membership). These local service providers compete with one another for customers. This is a 'system of uni-functional competing local service providers'.

The local service providers can be viewed as units of local government or as private firms that supply the service in question, whose only objective is to maximize profits, since they are completely independent of the central government and behave as private firms in our model.[14]

Each local service provider decides whether to enter the local public-good market, the location at which it will offer its local public good, and the price it will charge to its customers. These choices are made in a game consisting of three stages. In the first stage, local service providers simultaneously decide whether to enter the market. In the second stage, each local service provider decides on the location for its local public good. In the third stage, given the location choices of all of the other local service providers, each local service provider determines its prices. This structure of the game is natural, since local service providers may decide on a pricing scheme over the short term, the location of their local public goods over the long term, and entry into the market over the very long term.

We assume that the local service providers are allowed to choose the price structure they prefer and that they can verify the location of origin of each individual. We also assume that each local service provider possesses complete information about the price structures chosen by the other local service providers and that each individual is aware of the prices charged by the local service providers at his or her location.

Each individual chooses his/her consumption of z, as well as the local service provider he/she will patronize in order to maximize his/her utility, given that individual's location, income, the location of the facilities and the prices charged by each local service provider.

We assume that individuals are fixed to their locations within the region under analysis, but that they have the opportunity to move to another region where they can achieve an alternative level of utility, u^{DC}. The level of this exit option utility is related to the level of competition among regions and is given by:

$$u^{DC} = \gamma V^*, \tag{2.6}$$

where V^* is the maximum utility achievable in the economy if the local public goods are provided in the optimal manner and the parameter $\gamma \in [0, 1]$ reflects the level of competition presented by the other regions for the analysed region. A higher value of γ reflects more intense competition from other regions. Hence, $\gamma = 0$ reflects no competition from other regions, while $\gamma = 1$ reflects perfect competition among regions.

Two important factors help determine the level of competition experienced from one region to another. On the one hand, if individuals face high costs in changing their place of residence, competition from other regions will be relatively low, and this will be reflected in a low value of γ. There are numerous reasons why individuals may be restricted in their residential mobility. For instance, many costs are involved in a move from one place of residence to another, such as the costs of searching for a new place to live, sunk costs at the current residence, and many others which discourage individuals from changing their place of residence. In addition, individuals' residential location decisions seem to be more strongly influenced by job alternatives than by the provision of local public goods, as long as an acceptable level of the latter is present.

On the other hand, the other region or regions may be a poor substitute for the analysed region. For example, in the case of Latin American countries, there are generally only a few metropolitan regions (and perhaps only one) within a country offering similar characteristics to individuals. This would imply that competition from other regions would be relatively low, resulting in a low value of γ.

We define u^A as the utility that can be obtained by an individual in autarky (refraining from using any local public goods and consuming only z with all his/her income). In the case of our specific form of utility function, given by equation (2.1), u^A is given by:

$$u^A = Y. \tag{2.7}$$

Finally we define $V^E(r)$ as the constraint indirect utility achieved at equilibrium (that is, given the equilibrium prices of the local service providers) by an individual located at r in the region. Under these assumptions, the only decision that an individual can really make is that of moving to another region, living in a state of autarky or participating in the consumption of the local public goods in his/her current region. His/her decision will depend on the utility implied by each of those alternatives.

2.3   HOMOGENEOUS LOCAL PUBLIC GOODS, $K = 1$

The Optimal Allocation

From the previous analysis we can see that for the case of homogeneous local public goods the optimal allocation in this economy will be characterized by a system of m^* facilities, located as described by the vector $\underline{r}^*(m^*)$ and financed by $\phi^*(r)$, which solves (2.8) s.t. (2.9).

$$\text{Max}_{\underline{r}(m), \phi(r)} \int_{r=0}^{N} V(\cdot) \, dr \tag{2.8}$$

$$\text{s.t.} \int_{r=0}^{N} \phi(r) dr \geq mG. \tag{2.9}$$

As we explain in Appendix 2A1, the optimal number of facilities and their corresponding optimal locations are given in this case by:

$$m^* = \frac{1}{2} \left(\frac{a}{G} \right)^{\frac{1}{2}} N \tag{2.10}$$

$$\underline{r}^* = (r_1^*, r_2^*, \ldots, r_m^*) \tag{2.11}$$

$$r_j^* = \left[\frac{(2j-1)}{2m^*} \right] L, \tag{2.12}$$

where $j \in \{1, 2, \ldots, m^*\}$.

This result is not surprising and is classical in location models. It shows the trade-off between transportation costs and the costs of supplying the local public goods involved in determining the optimal number of facilities (that is, the number that maximizes the aggregate utility achieved by individuals in the region, subject to the resources constraint). On the one hand, a large number of facilities will allow total transportation costs to fall, and thus the aggregate indirect utility will increase. On the other hand, a higher number of facilities will involve higher fixed costs and thus a lower aggregate indirect utility.

This implies that for local public goods with high fixed costs, the optimal number of facilities will be smaller than that for local public goods involving lower fixed costs. For example, in the case of educational systems within this framework, we should see fewer universities than schools at the optimal allocation in a region, if we assume that the investment for a university is higher than that required by a school. We can also see that for a given level of fixed cost of a local public good, higher transportation costs will imply that there should be a larger number of facilities providing this good at the optimum than there would be if transportation costs were lower.[15]

The result also shows that the optimal locations for the facilities providing homogeneous local public goods in a region will be those that minimize total transport costs, which correspond to the symmetrical locations (that is, the locations that divide space into equal market areas for each facility). This is because by reducing as much as possible the transport costs, the utility of the individuals increases since they have to incur in smaller costs for acquiring the services of the local public goods and can spend the savings in the composite good. For example and as we explain in Appendix 2A1, in the case of one facility, the optimal location will be at the centre of the region at $r^* = 1/2L$ and in the case of two facilities, the optimal locations will be $r_1^* = 1/4L$ and $r_2^* = 3/4L$, respectively.

Thus, for this economy we have identified the optimal number of facilities and their corresponding locations, $\underline{r}^*(m^*)$. We can see that, given $\underline{r}^*(m^*)$, there is a wide range of possible tax or pricing schemes to sustain it. The only condition that must be satisfied by the optimal taxation scheme is that the collection covers the fixed costs of the local public goods, which means:

$$\int_{r=0}^{N} \phi(r) dr = m^* G. \tag{2.13}$$

For all $\phi(r)$ that satisfies this condition, the aggregate constraint indirect utility will be the maximum one. We can now determine, for this economy, the maximum possible aggregate constraint indirect utility that can be achieved by the region's individuals, for a given population (N), income (Y), local public-good cost (G) and transportation costs (a). This will be given by:[16]

$$\int_{r=0}^{N} V[r, \underline{r}^*(m^*), G]\,dr = N[Y - G^{\frac{1}{2}}a^{\frac{1}{2}} + g(G)]. \qquad (2.14)$$

We can see that the maximum aggregate constraint indirect utility is independent of the specific pricing scheme. However, different pricing schemes will imply a different level of constraint indirect utility at each location, and thus some people will be better off under some pricing schemes than with others. There is only one pricing scheme for which the utility will be the same for all individuals at each location. We denote this specific pricing scheme as $\phi^*(r)$. This is given by:

$$\phi_j^*(r) = G^{\frac{1}{2}}a^{\frac{1}{2}} - t(r) \quad \text{for } r_j^* - \frac{N}{2m^*} \le r \le r_j^* + \frac{N}{2m^*}, \qquad (2.15)$$

for each facility $j \in \{1, 2, \ldots, m^*\}$.

This pricing scheme implies that individuals located at more distant locations with respect to the facilities are subject to lower charges than those located nearer to them in order to compensate for the higher transport costs of distant locations and so to guarantee that the utility for all individuals at each location is the same. Note that all taxation schemes that satisfy condition (2.13) are equivalent in terms of optimality (or efficiency) and in this sense the definition of $\phi^*(r)$ is only a matter of redistribution between individuals.

We can see then that at the optimal allocation given by $\underline{r}^*(m^*)$, and for the pricing scheme $\phi^*(r)$, all individuals will obtain the same and maximum possible constraint indirect utility, which will be:

$$V^*[r, \underline{r}^*(m^*), G] = Y - G^{\frac{1}{2}}a^{\frac{1}{2}} + g(G). \qquad (2.16)$$

Finally, we assume that the local public goods are of a nature such that their collective provision will always be preferable, in terms of aggregate constraint indirect utility, to auto-provision (that is, where each individual provides his or her own facility), and it will always be better that they are provided by the central planner than if they were not provided at all.

The first assumption means that the aggregate constraint indirect utility of providing the local public good in a collective manner must be higher than that obtained through auto-provision, which implies the following condition:[17]

$$a < G. \tag{2.17}$$

Under the second assumption, if a central planner provides the local public goods in the optimal manner, the aggregate constraint indirect utility will be higher than the aggregate indirect utility would be if they were not provided at all, while each individual consumes his/her entire income in z.[18] This implies the condition:

$$g(G) > G^{\frac{1}{2}}a^{\frac{1}{2}}. \tag{2.18}$$

Equation (2.18) expresses the fact that if the provision of a local public-good is socially optimal, the benefit resulting from its provision for each individual, $g(G)$, must be higher than the cost in terms of consumption of good z that it implies for him/her, $G^{\frac{1}{2}}a^{\frac{1}{2}}$ (this includes transportation costs and fixed costs). From equation (2.18), we can see that when transportation costs are low (high) it is more probable that the local public good should (not) be provided, for a given level of fixed costs and preferences in relation to it.

We can summarize this result as follows:

Result 2.1   The optimal allocation in this economy can be described fundamentally by a number of facilities providing homogeneous local public goods and their corresponding locations in a region, for which welfare is maximized. The optimal number of facilities crucially depends on the trade-off between transportation costs and the costs of supplying the local public goods; their optimal locations in the region will be those that minimize total transport costs, which correspond to the symmetrical locations (that is, the locations that divide space into equal market areas for each facility).

Equilibrium Patterns in a System of Uni-functional Competing Local Service Providers

In this section, we analyse the equilibrium patterns of a system of uni-functional competing local service providers, as described above, offering local public goods in a region, in order to compare it with the welfare-maximizing pattern identified above.

Price equilibrium

We start by analysing the last stage of the game. At this stage, we have an established number of independent local service providers in the region, m, who have already chosen the location of their local public goods, $\underline{r}(m) =$ $(r_1, r_2, \ldots, r_m)$. They choose their taxation scheme or 'price structure', as it will be called from now on, non-cooperatively. We then seek to determine the nature of the equilibrium price structure for each local service provider, as well as the factors it will depend upon.

At this stage, a local service provider has only one strategic variable to choose: the prices it will charge the individuals who want to patronize its facility, in order to maximize its profits,[19] which are described by:

$$\Pi_i = \int_{X_i(\underline{P})} [P_i(r)n(r)]dr - G, \tag{2.19}$$

where $P_i(r)$ is the price structure or function chosen by the local service provider i, $i \in \{1, 2, \ldots, m\}$; $n(r)$ is the population density at each location (in this version of the model, $n(r) = 1$); $\underline{P} = [P_1(r), P_2(r), \ldots, P_i(r), \ldots, P_m(r)]$ is the vector describing the price structure chosen by each local service provider; and $X_i \in X$ represents the location of the individuals choosing to patronize facility i (the market area) given $\underline{P}$.

This price structure $(P_i(r))$ defines the prices charged by service provider i, at the point where it locates its facility (r_i). The specific price charged there by it to each individual who comes to its facility to consume the local public good provided there, can be different, depending on the location of origin of each individual (r). This is why the price structure of each local service provider depends on r.[20]

Monopoly price equilibrium, m = 1   What price structure would be chosen by a monopoly local service provider?

As mentioned above, we have assumed that the objective function of local service providers is to maximize their profits, as represented by equation (2.19). Thus, given the location of its local public good, r_1, a local service provider, in order to maximize its profits, will choose the highest possible prices it can at each location. The presence of only one local service provider implies in this case that it enjoys some kind of monopoly status in the region. However, its monopoly power to set prices is restricted in two ways. The first restriction is given by the competition from other regions, which we call the 'distant competition restriction', as represented by the minimum utility, u^{DC}, that must be guaranteed at each r in order to persuade the customers to remain in the region. The other restriction results from the fact that the local service provider must also guarantee a utility level of u^A at each location, in order to motivate individuals residing at those locations to participate in the consumption of the local public goods. Otherwise, they will prefer to remain in a state of autarky. We call this the 'autarky restriction'.

Thus, $P^E(r)$ is a price equilibrium for the monopoly local service provider if and only if:

$$P^E(r) = \arg \max \Pi[P(r), X\{V[r, P(r)]\}] \tag{2.20}$$

$$\text{s.t. } V^E[r, P^E(r)] \geq \max [u^{DC}; u^A] \quad \text{for all } r \in X\{V[r, P^E(r)]\} \tag{2.21}$$

$$\text{s.t. } \Pi[P^E(r)] \geq 0. \tag{2.22}$$

We can see that the local service provider will seek to have as many customers paying positive prices as possible. This is because the local public-good is not subject to congestion, and thus the number of customers does not affect the price that people are willing to pay at each location.

We denote by $P^{DC}(r, u^{DC})$ the price function that describes the maximum prices that the local service provider can charge at each location in order to guarantee u^{DC} to its customers and so persuade them to remain in the region, and we denote by $P^A(r, u^A)$ the price function that describes the maximum prices that it can charge at each location in order to guarantee u^A to its customers and thus make them participate in consuming the local public good. We normalize the location of the monopoly local service provider to $r_1 = 0$.

We can see that $P^{DC}(r, u^{DC})$ and $P^A(r, u^A)$ are given by the following expressions:[21]

$$P^{DC}(r, u^{DC}) = g(G) - t(r) - (u^{DC} - Y) \tag{2.23}$$

$$P^A(r, u^A) = g(G) - t(r). \tag{2.24}$$

In Figure 2.1, we have drawn price functions that describe the maximum prices that the local service provider can charge at each location in order to guarantee a corresponding utility level to its customers. In a *continuous* line we have drawn the price function $P^*(r, V^*)$ that results in equal utility levels of V^*[22] for the individuals at all locations within the monopoly local service provider's market area. This price function implies zero profits for the local service provider, because the prices just cover the local public goods' cost.

In this setting, because u^A is given and equal to Y, we have only one $P^A(r, u^A)$,[23] and for every value of u^{DC}, we have one different $P^{DC}(r, u^{DC})$, as we can see in Figure 2.1, in a *dashed* line and in *dotted* lines respectively. The differences between each price function, $P(r, u)$, and $P^*(r, V^*)$ in Figure 2.1 correspond to the profits (when $u < V^*$) or losses (when $u > V^*$) for the local service provider.

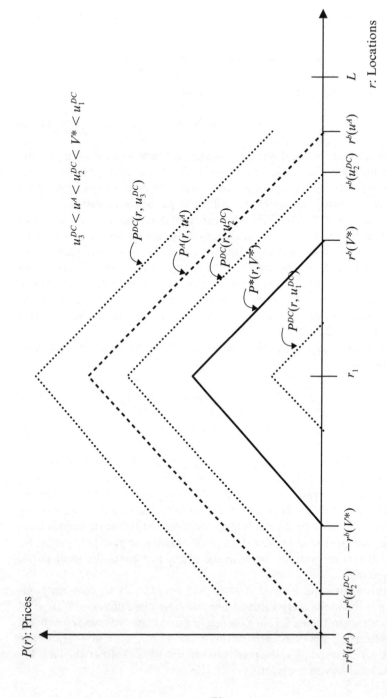

Figure 2.1 *Price functions set by the monopoly local service provider that imply different utility levels for the individuals at each location*

Thus, $P^E(r)$ will be given by:

$$P^E(r) = \min[P^{DC}(r, u^{DC}); P^A(r, u^A)] \qquad (2.25)$$

$$\text{s.t. } \Pi[P^E(r)] \geq 0. \qquad (2.26)$$

Assuming that there is an adequate potential market on both sides of the facility, the borders of its market area (r^{bl} and r^{br}) are determined by the locations where the prices that the monopolist can charge, in order to encourage people to participate in the consumption of the local public good, are just zero. For farther away locations, the monopolist would be obliged to charge negative prices or in other words to pay people to partici-pate. This would obviously reduce profits and for that reason these loca-tions are excluded from the monopolist's market.

In Appendix 2A2 we show the nature of the price equilibrium by defin-ing it for different levels of distant competition. We can see there that when competition from other regions is so weak that only the autarky restriction is binding ($u^{DC} \leq u^A$), the monopoly local service provider will be able to take advantage of its monopoly power in the region and so charge the maximum possible equilibrium prices ($P^E(r) = P^A(r, u^A)$), obtaining the corresponding highest possible profits, independent of the exact value of u^{DC}. Nevertheless, the prices it can charge are still limited by the possibility that individuals remain in a state of autarky.

As competition from other regions increases, the monopoly power of the local service provider is undermined, which implies that the equilibrium prices and profits are reduced. Finally, when competition from other regions is at its maximum intensity, $u^{DC} = V^*(\gamma = 1)$, the monopoly power of the local service provider is completely eliminated and the equilibrium prices it can charge just cover its costs, resulting in zero profits.

Thus, we have a unique price equilibrium for each value of u^{DC}, between $P^E(r, u^{DC} \leq u^A) = P^A(r, u^A)$ and $P^E(r, u^{DC} = V^*)$, and this price equilibrium will be characterized by discriminatory pricing with respect to locations, in favour of individuals coming from more distant locations,[24] as we can see in Figure 2.1. This shows that the monopoly power of the local service provider is also limited by space and the corresponding transportation costs that have to be incurred in order to use the local public good. Thus, its local monopoly power is more intense at locations nearer to the facility, where it can charge higher prices, but is reduced for farther away locations where it must charge lower prices in order to encourage people living there to consume the local public good, because of the higher transportation costs that those locations imply.

We can summarize this result as follows:

Result 2.2 Given a monopoly local service provider in a region, whose local monopoly power is restricted by the competition of a distant region (represented by u^{DC}), by the possibility that individuals remain in a state of autarky (represented by u^A) and by the fact that individuals have to incur transport costs to use the local public good,

1. the equilibrium price function set by the monopoly local service provider is unique for a given level of the distant competition. It reaches its upper limit when competition from the distant region is very weak and only the autarky restriction is binding ($P^A(r, u^A)$) and reaches its lower limit when there is perfect competition from the other region ($P^*(r, V^*)$);
2. the equilibrium price function set by the monopoly local service provider will involve discriminatory pricing with respect to locations, in favour of the more distant locations;
3. the equilibrium indirect utility achieved by each individual in the region, given the equilibrium prices set by the provider, will be equal for all and will always be equivalent to the maximum utility between the one achievable at the other region and in autarky ($V^E(r) = \max [u^A, u^{DC}]$);
4. the equilibrium indirect utility achieved by each individual in the region, given the equilibrium prices set by the provider, will be the highest possible that can be achieved (V^*) only if there is perfect competition from the other region ($\gamma = 1$).[25] If the competition from the other region is less fierce ($\gamma < 1$), the indirect utility achieved by each individual in the region will be lower than that ($V^E(r) < V^*$); and
5. the equilibrium profits of the monopoly local service provider increase with income and the valuation that the individuals give to the local public good (Y and $g(G)$) and decrease with transport costs (a), the cost of providing the local public good (G) and the intensity of the distant competition (γ).

We can see here that when there is a monopoly local service provider in the region, the only case in which the equilibrium aggregate constraint indirect utility reaches its potential maximum, represented by equation (2.14), is when competition from other regions is so intense that it guarantees a utility of V^* for individuals who move to another region. However, this is only the case when two conditions are satisfied: first, that the utility at the other region is V^*, and second, that there are no costs involved in moving to the other region.

Regarding the first condition, in order to achieve a utility of V^* in the other region (or regions), the local public goods in that other region must be provided efficiently (meaning that the allocation must be the optimal one, $(\underline{r}^*(m_1{}^*),\ P^*(r))$, in order to guarantee V^*. For this to be true, we can imagine two scenarios. In the first, there are so many regions in the country that the actions taken by any single local service provider in one region have no impact on individuals' common utility levels, and thus all local service providers in each region take V^* as given. This would imply that each local service provider in each region, when choosing its strategy in order to maximize profits, will choose $(\underline{r}^*(m_1{}^*),\ P^*(r))$, given V^*. But normally, individuals face the choice of only a few metropolitan regions (or only one) within a country that offers them similar living conditions.

In the other imaginable scenario, although there are only a few metropolitan regions within a country, which compete with one another through their respective local service providers, the possibility of the emergence of a new region that can attract their inhabitants forces them to offer the highest possible utility, V^*. However, the creation of a new region is a very complicated and time-consuming process involving numerous irreversible costs, which implies that the 'market of metropolitan regions' (if we can call it that) is very far from being a contestable one, in the sense used by Baumol (1982).

Thus, we can see that if there are only a few regions in competition with one another, as is usually the case in a country, it is probable that the local service providers of each region are not utility takers, and thus their competition is strategic in the sense that they choose $[\underline{r}(m_1),\ P(r)]$, given the strategies chosen by the other regions, and therefore the utility achieved in the other regions will be smaller than V^*.

Regarding the second condition, what we normally observe is that moving to another region involves a number of costs, in addition to transportation costs, such as those involved in leaving one's current job and finding alternative employment in the new region. In this case, the fact that costs are incurred in moving to another region makes the utility achieved in the other regions smaller than V^*.

Accordingly, we would expect the competition represented by other regions to be relatively weak for a monopoly local service provider, $u^{DC} < V^*(\gamma < 1)$. This gives the local service provider a high degree of monopoly power, which will imply high profits for it and a low utility level for individuals, $V^E(r) = u^{DC} < V^*$.

Price equilibrium by competing local service providers, m > 1

THE CASE OF TWO COMPETING LOCAL SERVICE PROVIDERS   In this case, we have at the present stage two independent local service providers in the region, who have already chosen the location of their local public goods, $\underline{r} = (r_1, r_2)$. We want, then, to find out what the equilibrium price structure and the corresponding aggregate constraint indirect utility achieved by individuals will look like, as well as what factors they will depend upon.

Thus, given that the locations of the local service providers are fixed at this stage,[26] each local service provider, in order to maximize its profits, will choose the highest possible prices at each location. Since there are transportation costs involved in gaining access to the local public good, each of the two local service providers in this case will enjoy some degree of local monopoly power over the individuals living near it. However, its local monopoly power to set prices will be restricted in three ways.

As in the monopoly case, each service provider faces a restriction given by the minimum utility, u^{DC}, that must be guaranteed at each r in order to maintain the customers in the region (the 'distant competition restriction'), as well as the one that it must guarantee a utility level of u^A at each location (the 'autarky restriction'), in order to persuade the individuals living in its area to participate in the consumption of the local public good. But now, in addition to these two restrictions, each of the two local service providers face competition from the other provider located in the region, which we call 'local competition'. This is represented by the minimum utility, $u_j^{LC}[r, P_j(r)]$ (which is the utility achieved at location r from patronizing facility j, where $j \neq i$ and $i, j \in \{1, 2\}$) that must be guaranteed at each location within the market area X_i of facility i in order to prevent the customers from patronizing the facility offered by the other local service provider j. This local competitive force is generated by the opportunity for individuals to patronize the facility they choose, independently of where they live (de-localized membership).

Thus, $\underline{P}^E = [P_1^E(r), P_2^E(r)]$ is a *price equilibrium* if and only if:

$$P_i^E(r) = \arg \max \Pi_i[P_i(r), X_i(\underline{P}^E)] \qquad (2.27)$$

$$\text{s.t. } V^E(r, \underline{P}^E) \geq \max\{u^{DC}; u^A; u_j[r, P_j^E(r)]\} \quad \text{for all } r \in X_i(\underline{P}^E) \quad (2.28)$$

$$\text{s.t. } \Pi_i[P_i^E(r), X_i(\underline{P}^E)] \geq 0. \qquad (2.29)$$

In game-theory terms, this means that the price equilibrium is a Nash equilibrium of a non-cooperative game, whose players are local service providers, payoffs are profits and strategies are prices, which are functions of location.

As before, we denote with $P_i^{DC}(r, u^{DC})$ and $P_i^A(r, u^A)$ the price functions that describe the maximum prices that local service provider i can charge at each location in order to guarantee u^{DC} and u^A, respectively, to its customers. We denote by $P_i^{LC}\{r, u_j^{LC}[r, P_j(r)]\}$ the price function that describes the maximum prices that provider i can charge at each location, in order to prevent its customers from switching to the other provider j.

We can see that $P_i^{DC}(r, u^{DC})$, $P_i^A(r, u^A)$ and $P_i^{LC}\{r, u_j^{LC}[r, P_j(r)]\}$[27] are given by the following expressions:

$$P_i^{DC}(r, u^{DC}) = g(G) - t_i(r) - (u^{DC} - Y) \tag{2.30}$$

$$P_i^A(r, u^A) = g(G) - t_i(r) \tag{2.31}$$

$$P_i^{LC}\{r, u_j[r, P_j(r)]\} = t_j(r) - t_i(r), \tag{2.32}$$

where $i \neq j$ and $i, j \in \{1, 2\}$. Equations (2.30) and (2.31) are the same as equations (2.23) and (2.24), which represent the maximum price that can be set, given the distant competition and autarky restrictions. However, in this case, an additional restriction is imposed by local competition, which is represented by equation (2.32).

Thus, $\underline{P^E} = P_1^E(r), P_2^E(r)$ will be given by:

$$P_i^E(r) = \min[P_i^{DC}(r, u^{DC}); P_i^A(r, u^A); P_i^{LC}(r)] \tag{2.33}$$

$$\text{s.t. } \Pi_i[P_i^E(r)] \geq 0, \quad \text{where } i \in \{1, 2\}. \tag{2.34}$$

If we suppose that the exit option dominates the autarky option ($u^{DC} > u^A = Y$) and that $P_i^{LC}(r) < P_i^{DC}(r, u^{DC})$ throughout the relevant range, which implies that the distant competition is very weak, $\underline{P^E} = P_1^E(r), P_2^E(r)$ will be given by:

$$P_i^E(r) = P_i^{LC}(r) = t_j(r) - t_i(r) \tag{2.35}$$

$$\text{s.t. } \Pi_i[P_i^E(r)] \geq 0. \tag{2.36}$$

This price equilibrium implies that when for a given location, neither competing local service provider has a location advantage relative to the other, $t_j(r) - t_i(r) = 0$, they will compete in price until prices fall to zero. This is a classical Bertrand competition result. Beyond this location, one of them will have an advantage in terms of lower transport costs over the other, so it will be able to charge positive prices. Nevertheless, the maximum price that it will be able to charge at each location is the differential cost for the individual living there of patronizing the alternative facility. This differential cost corresponds to the difference in transportation costs incurred by the individual when patronizing this alternative facility. On the other hand, the maximum that the alternative facility will be able to charge at equilibrium in this region is zero.

In order to show the nature of the price equilibrium in our setting and to understand the influence of the distant competition on it, in Appendix 2A3 we define this price equilibrium for different levels of distant competition. There we can see that the new source of competition introduced through the presence of additional local service providers offering the local public-good in the region, along with the opportunity for individuals to choose their local service providers independently of where they live (de-localized membership), will guarantee to the individuals living in the region a minimum level of utility, $V[r, P^{LC}(r)]$, regardless of how weak the distant competition is.[28] However, local competition alone is not enough to guarantee that the individuals obtain the highest possible utility (V^*). Only when we have perfect competition from the other region ($\gamma = 1$) is the local monopoly power of the local service providers completely restricted, $\underline{P}^E = \underline{P}^*$, profits are zero and all the individuals obtain V^* at all locations.

It is important to note that in the present case, both local public goods are identical in all aspects except for their location in space. They are substitutes for each other, because individuals may choose only one of the possible facilities offering the local public good in order to enjoy its benefits. Nevertheless, their degree of substitution varies among individuals' locations, depending on the relative proximity of each facility to each residence. A smaller (larger) difference in the distance from an individual's specific location to the various facilities implies a higher (lower) degree of substitution. Only in the case where the distances to the facilities providing the local public good are identical at a particular location, as at the centre location in the example of Appendix 2A3, are these facilities perfect substitutes for each other at that location.

THE CASE OF M COMPETING LOCAL SERVICE PROVIDERS   We can generalize the equilibrium price structure of each local service provider, as determined above, for any given number of local service providers, m. For this, we use the same model presented in the previous section, but now we assume that space in the region is described by a circle of perimeter L rather than an interval $[0, L]$, and we use X to denote the set of locations in this circle. This change in the model is made to avoid the special cases that appear at the extremes of the interval, and thus to make every point in the region equivalent. This allows us to concentrate on the general results.

In this case, given the locations $\underline{r} = (r_1, r_2, \ldots, r_m)$, the *price equilibrium* $\underline{P}^E = [P_1^E(r), P_2^E(r), \ldots, P_m^E(r)]$ will be given by:

$$P_i^E(r) = \min[P_i^{DC}(r, u^{DC}); P_i^A(r, u^A); P_i^{LC}(r)] \qquad (2.37)$$

$$\text{s.t. } \Pi_i[P_i^E(r)] \geq 0, \tag{2.38}$$

where $P_i^{DC}(r, u^{DC}), P_i^A(r, u^A)$ and $P_i^{LC}(r)$ are given by the following expressions:

$$P_i^{DC}(r, u^{DC}) = g(G) - t_i(r) - (u^{DC} - Y) \tag{2.39}$$

$$P_i^A(r, u^A) = g(G) - t_i(r) \tag{2.40}$$

$$P_i^{LC}(r) = \min[t_{-i}(r)] - t_i(r), \tag{2.41}$$

where $t_{-i}(r) = [t_1(r), \ldots, t_{i-1}(r), t_{i+1}(r), \ldots, t_m(r)]$.

If we suppose that the exit option dominates the autarky option ($u^{DC} > u^A = Y$), and that $P_i^{LC}(r) < P_i^{DC}(r, u^{DC})$ over all of the relevant range, $\underline{P}^E = [P_1^E(r), P_2^E(r), \ldots, P_m^E(r)]$ will be given by:

$$P_i^E(r) = P_i^{LC}(r) = \min[t_{-i}(r)] - t_i(r) \tag{2.42}$$

$$\text{s.t. } \Pi_i[P_i^E(r)] \geq 0. \tag{2.43}$$

This price equilibrium is, in fact, the familiar discriminating-price equilibrium of spatial competition, originally identified by Hoover (1937) and considered later by many authors, for example, Lederer and Hurter (1986), Hobbs (1986), Thisse and Vives (1988), MacLeod et al. (1988), and Eaton and Schmitt (1994), among others. These authors show that the equilibrium price at each point is equal to the marginal cost experienced by the firm in the market with the second-lowest marginal cost. This is because this price is the highest that the firm with the lowest marginal cost can charge in order to prevent people from switching to the firm with the second-lowest marginal cost and on the other hand is the minimum price that the firm with the second-lowest marginal costs can charge without incurring losses.

We can see that our equilibrium price functions have a similar property. The maximum price that a local service provider can charge at each location is the differential cost for the individual living there of patronizing the alternative nearest facility (the one that implies the second-lowest marginal cost). This differential cost corresponds to the difference in transportation costs incurred by the individual when patronizing the alternative nearest facility.[29]

We can summarize the results as follows:

Result 2.3   Given a system of competing local service providers in a region whose local monopoly power is restricted by the competition of a distant region (represented by u^{DC}), by the possibility that individuals remain in a state of autarky (represented by u^A), by the fact that individuals have to incur transport costs to use the local public good and by the local competition represented by the other local service providers:

1. the equilibrium price function set by each local service provider is unique and reaches its upper limit ($P^{LC}(r)$), when distant competition is relatively weak ($u^{DC} \leq \bar{u}$),[30] and it is determined by the differential transportation costs of patronizing the other provider with the second-lowest transportation cost. For a relatively more intense distant competition ($\bar{u} < u^{DC} \leq V^*$), the equilibrium price function set by each local service provider is unique for each level of distant competition. This equilibrium price function reaches its lower limit ($P^*(r, V^*)$) when we have perfect distant competition;

2. the equilibrium price function set by each of the competing local service providers will involve discriminatory pricing in favour of the more distant locations for all locations in their market area. These equilibrium price functions will involve more price discrimination than in the monopoly case;

3. the indirect utility achieved by each of the individuals in the region, given the equilibrium prices set by the local service providers, can differ between individuals and will always be equivalent to the maximum utility between the one achievable in autarky, at the other region and by patronizing the alternative facilities in the region ($V^E(r) = \max [u^A, u^{DC}, u^{LC}]$ for each $r \in X$);

4. a minimum level of utility will be guaranteed to the individuals living in the region ($V[r, P^{LC}(r)]$), regardless of the level of the distant competition and the autarky option; and

5. the indirect utility achieved by each of the individuals in the region, given the equilibrium prices set by the local service providers, will be equal to the highest possible utility achievable (V^*) only if we have perfect distant competition ($u^{DC} = V^*$).[31] If this is not the case (and $u^{DC} < V^*$), the utility achieved by each individual at equilibrium will be lower than that ($V^E(r) < V^*$), except for the individual located where the transportation cost of patronizing at least two facilities is identical (that is, where no local service provider has an advantage over the other).[32] This individual will always obtain V^*.

Location equilibrium
We now analyse the second stage of the game, in which the number of competing local service providers is given, and the strategic variables are the locations of the local public goods.

A crucial assumption for the analysis of this stage of the game is that of the local service providers' flexibility in choosing their locations and corresponding market areas. This flexibility will depend on the type of fixed costs involved in the provision of each local public good. Thus, we distinguish two extreme cases with regard to the types of fixed costs: (a) flexible technology, where no location-specific fixed costs are present (no location sunk costs), and (b) fixed technology, where only location-specific fixed costs are present (location sunk costs).

Flexible technology, absence of location-specific fixed costs (absence of location sunk costs)   Flexible technology refers here to the local service provider's opportunity to relocate its local public good without incurring any additional costs; that is, there are no sunk costs in its chosen location and corresponding market segment. In order to understand this, let us discuss some examples. This kind of flexible technology can be found, for example, in the case of refuse collection services. There may be high fixed costs associated with the acquisition of the refuse trucks that serve a specified area, but these trucks can easily be transferred to another area if necessary, at almost no cost. This implies that if competition in a region is too intense, the local service provider offering refuse collection services can easily (in terms of costs) relocate its trucks to another region where it can achieve higher profits. Another example of a local public good with this type of technology is collective transportation (buses and taxis). In this case, there may also be high fixed costs represented by the buses required to provide services to an area, but here it is also easy for the collective transportation service provider to change its service area, if desired.

With flexible technology, therefore, we have at this stage a given number of independent local service providers in the region, m, who have to choose the location of their local public good, $\underline{r}(m) = (r_1, r_2, \ldots, r_m)$, non-cooperatively. Local service providers evaluate the location choices for their local public good at the equilibrium of the price subgame that these locations imply. Thus, when a local service provider contemplates a change of location for its local public good, it takes into account not only the resulting change in its own price, but also the resulting changes in the prices of all other local service providers. The use of flexible technology implies here that the local service provider will always move its local public good to its most preferred location, given the locations of the others, because there are no costs involved in a change of location.

We then want to find out whether a price-location equilibrium exists, what it will look like and what it will depend upon.

Note that at any price-location equilibrium, we never have two local public goods located in the same place, because if this were the case, neither local service provider would have a location advantage over the other, so $t_j(r) - t_i(r) = 0$ for all r, and thus they will compete until prices fall to 0 at all r (this is a standard Bertrand result applied to this game). Therefore, both local service providers will incur losses equal to their fixed costs. By offering their local public goods at a slightly different location, either of these two local service providers will be able to charge positive prices for a range of r, and thus do better than at this common location. Accordingly, at equilibrium no local public goods will share the same location.

MONOPOLY LOCATION EQUILIBRIUM, $M = 1$ We now discuss the location that will be chosen by a monopoly local service provider.

First, we consider the case in the *absence of distant competition*. The monopoly local service provider must choose a location r_1 that maximizes its profits, knowing that, given r_1, the prices it can charge are the equilibrium prices identified in Appendix 2A2 and are given by the first line of equation (2A2.7). These equilibrium prices are drawn in Figure 2.2.

In the figure, we can see that the choice of location r_1 will crucially depend on the relationship between the size of the region the monopolist seeks to cover $X_1 = [r^{bl}(u^A), r^{br}(u^A)]$ (where $r^{bl}(u^A)$ and $r^{br}(u^A)$ represent the borders of the market area to the left and right of the facility, respectively) and the total size of the region, $X = [0, L]$.

From our earlier analysis, we know that:[33]

$$r^{bl}(u^A) = r^{br}(u^A) = \frac{g(G)}{a}. \tag{2.44}$$

So if:

$$\frac{2g(G)}{a} \geq L \Rightarrow r_1^E = \frac{L}{2}. \tag{2.45}$$

This means that if the total size of the region is relatively small with respect to the size of the region the monopolist seeks to cover, the location that will maximize profits for the monopolist will be the centre of the region and this will be the location it will choose at equilibrium in this case.

We can see that the optimal location for the monopoly local service provider in this case is the location at which total transportation costs are minimized, which is the midpoint of the region, as shown in Figure 2.2. This is because if individuals' transportation costs are minimized, they will be able to pay more for the local public good, and thus the monopolist's profits will be higher. The area $0LABC$ minus fixed costs gives these profits in this case. If the monopolist chooses another location, for example r_1' in

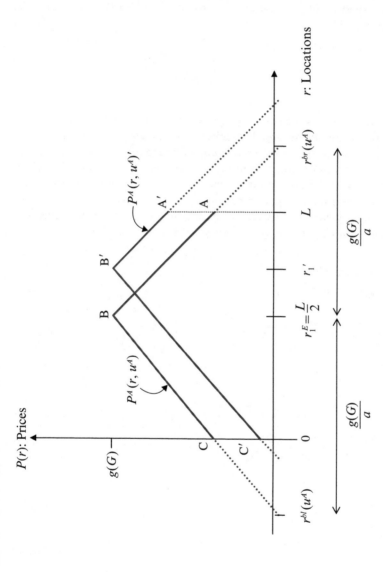

Figure 2.2   Monopoly price-location equilibrium when the total size of the region is relatively small with respect to the size of the region the monopolist seeks to cover and distant competition is absent

the figure, its profits would be given in that case by the area $0LA'B'C'$ minus fixed costs, which is clearly smaller than the area $0LABC$ minus fixed costs. Therefore, in this case, the location chosen by the monopoly local service provider will be equal to the optimal one, $r^* = L/2$, as we can see in Appendix 2A1.

But if:

$$\frac{2g(G)}{a} < L \Rightarrow \frac{g(G)}{a} \le r_1^E \le L - \frac{g(G)}{a}. \tag{2.46}$$

Therefore, if the total size of the region is relatively large with respect to the size of the region the monopolist seeks to cover, there will be a whole range of location equilibria, as shown in a *dotted* line in the x-axis in Figure 2.3.

Let us now discuss the case in the *presence of distant competition*, and what happens if the exit option is binding. In this case, given r_1, the prices that a monopoly local service provider can charge will be given by the second line of equation (2A2.7). These equilibrium prices are drawn in *dashed* lines in Figure 2.4, for a given $u^{DC} < u^A$.

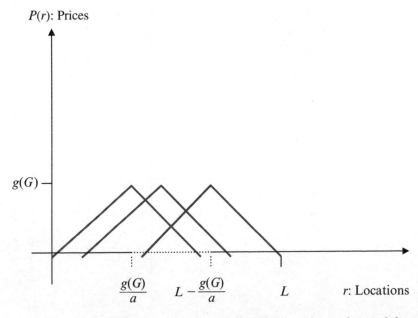

Figure 2.3   Monopoly price-location equilibrium when the total size of the region is relatively large with respect to the size of the region the monopolist seeks to cover and distant competition is absent

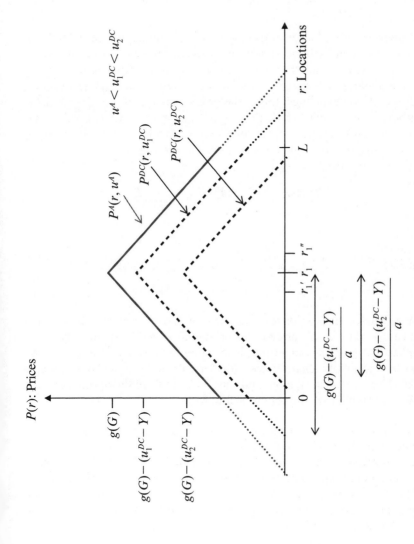

Figure 2.4   Monopoly price-location equilibrium when distant competition is binding

85

We can see that the size of the region that the monopolist seeks to cover, $X_1 = [r^{bl}(u^{DC}), r^{br}(u^{DC})]$, is reduced in this case as a result of the existence of distant competition:[34]

$$r^{bl}(u^{DC}) = r^{br}(u^{DC}) = \frac{g(G) - (u^{DC} - Y)}{a}. \tag{2.47}$$

This is because when distant competition is binding, the utility that must be guaranteed at each location in order to encourage people to remain in the region is now higher than the one obtained in autarky. This implies that the maximum prices that the monopolist can charge at each location are reduced. As we explained above, the prices charged by the monopolist at the borders of its market area are zero. Consequently, these border locations will now be closer to the facility, because farther away locations imply higher transport costs and consequently a lower utility.

Thus, in this case if:

$$\frac{2[g(G) - (u^{DC} - Y)]}{a} \geq L \Rightarrow r_1^E = \frac{L}{2} \tag{2.48}$$

and if:

$$\frac{2[g(G) - (u^{DC} - Y)]}{a} < L \Rightarrow \frac{g(G) - (u^{DC} - Y)}{a} \leq r_1^E \leq L - \frac{[g(G) - (u^{DC} - Y)]}{a}. \tag{2.49}$$

We can see that as distant competition becomes more intense (u^{DC} increases), the set of price-location equilibria will also increase. This implies that intense competition from other regions makes it more likely that the monopoly local service provider will choose a location different from the centre of the region, and thus different from the optimal one.

We can summarize the results as follows:

Result 2.4 Assume that technology is flexible. Given a monopoly local service provider in a region, whose local monopoly power is restricted by the competition of a distant region (represented by u^{DC}), by the possibility that individuals remain in a state of autarky (represented by u^A) and by the fact that individuals have to incur transport costs to use the local public good, and whose equilibrium prices are the ones in the price subgame, described in Result 2.2, then:

1. if the total size of the region is relatively small with respect to the size of the region the monopolist seeks to cover ($L \leq 2[g(G) - (u^{DC} - Y)]/a$), then the equilibrium location chosen by the monopoly local service

provider will be unique and optimal (that is, at the centre of the region); and

2. if the total size of the region is relatively large with respect to the size of the region the monopolist seeks to cover $(L > 2[g(G) - (u^{DC} - Y)]/a)$, then there will be multiple location equilibria described by $r_1^E \in \{g(G) - (u^{DC} - Y)]/a, L - [g(G) - (u^{DC} - Y)]/a\}$. As distant competition becomes more intense (u^{DC} increases), the range of location equilibria increases.

LOCATION EQUILIBRIUM AMONG COMPETING LOCAL SERVICE PROVIDERS, $M > 1$ First, we shall consider the case of two competing local service providers. In order to show the existence of a price-location Nash equilibrium, we must demonstrate the existence of location choices on the part of these two local service providers, r_1^E, r_2^E, such that:

$$\Pi_1(r_1^E, r_2^E, \underline{P}^E) \geq \Pi_1(r_1, r_2^E, \underline{P}^E) \quad \forall r_1 \in X$$
$$\Pi_2(r_2^E, r_1^E, \underline{P}^E) \geq \Pi_1(r_2, r_1^E, \underline{P}^E) \quad \forall r_2 \in X \tag{2.50}$$

where $\underline{P}^E$ is the vector of equilibrium prices in the price subgame. We call the values of $(r_1^E, r_2^E, \underline{P}^E)$ that satisfy (2.50) a price-location equilibrium.

Consider first that the distant competition restriction is very weak and is therefore not binding. It can be shown that a price-location equilibrium exists for two competing local service providers and that $(r_1^E, r_2^E, \underline{P}^E)$ is a price-location equilibrium with locations (r_1^E, r_2^E) and where $\underline{P}^E$ is the vector of equilibrium prices in the price subgame,[35] if and only if:[36]

$$TTC(r_1^E, r_2^E, \underline{P}^E) \leq TTC(r_1, r_2^E, \underline{P}^E) \quad \forall r_1 \in X$$
$$TTC(r_2^E, r_1^E, \underline{P}^E) \leq TTC(r_2, r_1^E, \underline{P}^E) \quad \forall r_2 \in X \tag{2.51}$$

where $TTC(r_1, r_2)$ represents the total transportation costs incurred in aggregate terms by individuals when the local public goods are located at (r_1, r_2). We explain this result in more detail in Appendix 2A4.

This implies that the existence of a price-location equilibrium depends on the existence of locations for which each location minimizes total transportation costs relative to the other locations of the local public goods. Such locations do exist, and in our two-dimensional setting, there is only one equilibrium pair: that which minimizes total transportation costs, which is the optimal location pair (r_1^*, r_2^*), as described in Appendix 2A1. As a result, the equilibrium locations of these two competing local service providers are efficient.

This result is remarkable because it shows that a decentralized provision of local public goods can guarantee optimality in this case, even though each local service provider is only looking after its own interest.

Note that, as we explain in Appendix 2A4, the equilibrium locations of these two competing local service providers are independent of the specific form of the transport-cost function. Accordingly, the unique price-location equilibrium of two competing local service providers offering local public goods with flexible technology is efficient, independent of the form of the transport-cost function.

This implies that if a local service provider anticipates that equilibrium prices will be used by the other local service providers, and the locations of the other local public goods will be fixed, the local service provider in question will minimize total transportation costs, not only the cost of going to its own facility, in order to maximize profits. However, note that, in a three-dimensional space, equilibrium locations need not necessarily minimize total transport costs globally.[37] Accordingly, in that case there are multiple price-location equilibria in this game, and one equilibrium pair is that which minimizes total transport costs globally, (r_1^*, r_2^*). Nevertheless, in our two-dimensional space, there is only one equilibrium pair, that which minimizes total transport costs globally, which corresponds to the optimal locations (r_1^*, r_2^*).

Let us now consider the restriction imposed by distant competition on the equilibrium prices, in order to see whether this affects the equilibrium locations of the price-location equilibria identified before. As we explain in Appendix 2A4, such a restriction has no effect on the equilibrium location pairs identified above. Consequently, the equilibrium locations of these two competing local service providers are efficient, independently of the presence of distant competition.

The second case to consider is that of m competing local service providers. We have shown above that at this stage a unique price-location equilibrium exists in the case of two competing local service providers, which is the optimal location pair, $\underline{r}^* = (r_1^*, r_2^*)$. We can generalize this result for any given number of local service providers, m, as we show in Appendix 2A4.

As before, the existence of a price-location equilibrium will depend on the existence of locations such that each minimizes total transport costs with regard to the locations of the other local public goods. In this case, there is only one equilibrium vector: that which minimizes total transport costs, which represents the optimal locations $\underline{r}^* = (r_1^*, r_2^*, \ldots, r_m^*)$ (the symmetrical locations), as described in Appendix 2A1.

We can summarize the results as follows:

Result 2.5 Assume that technology is flexible. Given a system of m competing local service providers in a region whose local monopoly power is restricted by the competition of a distant region (represented by u^{DC}), by the possibility that individuals remain in a state of autarky (represented by u^A), by the fact that individuals have to incur transport costs to use the local public good and by the local competition represented by the other local service providers, and whose equilibrium prices are those in the price subgame, described in Result 2.3, then:

1. the equilibrium locations will be those which each minimize total transport costs with regard to the other local public-good locations;
2. there is a unique price-location equilibrium in this game, and it is the vector that minimizes total transport costs, $(r_1^*, r_2^*, \ldots, r_m^*)$ which is in this sense efficient;
3. the equilibrium locations are independent of the specific form of the transport-cost function. As a result, the unique price-location equilibrium of this game is efficient, independent of the form of the transport-cost function; and
4. the restriction imposed by distant competition on equilibrium prices has no effect on the equilibrium location vectors identified above.

Fixed technology, location-specific fixed costs (location sunk costs) 'Fixed technology' refers here to the situation in which it is very costly for a local service provider to change its local public goods' location and corresponding market segment once it has been chosen. Local public goods that are located in space are typical examples of fixed technologies. This is the case, for example, with public schools. Once they are located at a point in space, it would be very costly to change their locations. Their fixed costs are location specific.[38]

Here, the price-location equilibrium identified in the case of flexible technology will also represent a price-location equilibrium. In this sense the optimal locations will also be an equilibrium in this case. However, and as we show in Appendix 2A5, we also have additional price-location equilibria, which will not be efficient. This is because the existence of location sunk costs ensures that once a location is chosen, it is costly for a local service provider to change it and accordingly this location will have costs advantages with respect to the others. This implies that, although the optimal locations are those that maximize revenues for the local service providers, there will also be other location pairs that will represent an equilibrium, because the cost of changing that location to the optimal one is higher than the gains of the increased revenues.

This can be summarized in the following result:

Result 2.6 Assume that technology is fixed. Then the range of possible price-location equilibria is enlarged compared with the flexible technology case and we would also have additional price-location equilibria, which are inefficient.

Entry

We now analyse the first stage of the game, during which local service providers simultaneously decide whether to enter the market. At this stage we identify the equilibrium number of competing local service providers in the region. As for the second stage of the game (location decisions), the assumption about local service providers' flexibility in choosing their locations and corresponding market areas is crucial for the analysis of this stage.

As before and in order to simplify the analysis, we assume that the exit option dominates the autarky option ($u^{DC} > u^A = Y$) and that a circle of perimeter L describes space in the region.[39]

Flexible technology, no location-specific fixed costs (no location sunk costs)
We show that in cases where technology is completely flexible as to location, the free-entry price-location equilibrium will be unique, given a level of distant competition (represented by u^{DC}). This free-entry price-location equilibrium will be characterized by a number of competing local service providers in the region, which we denote by m_{flex}^E, located symmetrically at locations $\underline{r}^E$,[40] whose profits will be zero and so:

$$\Pi_i(\underline{r}^E, \underline{P}^E) = 0 \quad \forall i \in \{1, 2, \ldots, m_{flex}\}. \tag{2.52}$$

This is the only possible equilibrium in this case, because if the number of local service providers were smaller than m_{flex}^E, each of them would make positive profits, which would provide an incentive for new providers to enter the region. Given that technology is completely flexible, as new providers enter the region, they would relocate in order to maintain the symmetrical locations and so maximize profits. This entry and following relocation would continue until profits are zero, which is when m_{flex}^E local service providers are in the region. On the other hand, if more than m_{flex}^E providers were to enter the region and profits would therefore be negative, some of them would leave the region until the profits of the prevailing ones are zero.

We now determine m_{flex}^E within our model. First, we analyse the price-location equilibrium for a given number of competing local service providers, identified above. In order to do this, we examine the case of local service provider i and normalize its location as $r_i = 0$, as we can see in Figure 2A6.1. We disregard for the moment the existence of distant competition, the implications of which we shall analyse later.

PRICE-LOCATION EQUILIBRIUM FOR A GIVEN NUMBER OF COMPETING LOCAL
SERVICE PROVIDERS, M In the *absence of distant competition*, the price-
location equilibrium for a given number of competing local service
providers, m, can be described as follows. $\underline{P}^E$ will be given by:[41]

$$P_i^E = P_i^{LC}(r,m) = t_j(r) - t_i(r) = \frac{Na}{m} - 2a|r| \quad \forall r \in X_i \tag{2.53}$$

$$\text{s.t. } \Pi_i[P_i^E(r)] \geq 0, \tag{2.54}$$

Because of the symmetrical equilibrium locations and the equilibrium
prices $\underline{P}^E$, X_i is given by:

$$X_i = [-r^b; r^b], \tag{2.55}$$

where

$$r^b = \frac{N}{2m}. \tag{2.56}$$

We define $\Pi_i(m)$ as the equilibrium profits of local service provider i in
the absence of distant competition, depending only on m. They will be
given by:[42]

$$\Pi_i(m) = 2\left[\int_0^{r^b} P_i^{LC}(r, m)dr \right] - G = \frac{N^2a}{2m^2} - G. \tag{2.57}$$

Let us now consider the *presence of distant competition*. In this case, the
price-location equilibrium for a given number of competing local service
providers, m, can be described as follows. $\underline{P}^E$ will be given by:

$$P_i^E(r) = \min[P_i^{DC}(r, u^{DC}); P_i^{LC}(r)] \tag{2.58}$$

$$\text{s.t. } \Pi_i[P_i^E(r)] \geq 0, \tag{2.59}$$

where $P_i^{LC}(r,m)$ is given by equation (2.53) and $P_i^{DC}(r,u^{DC})$ is given by the
following expression:[43]

$$P_i^{DC}(r, u^{DC}) = g(G) - t_i(r) - (u^{DC} - Y) = g(G) - a|r|$$
$$- (u^{DC} - Y) \quad \forall r \in X_i. \tag{2.60}$$

In this case, X_i is given again by equations (2.55) and (2.56).

In Appendix 2A6 we show the nature of the price-location equilibrium here and how it depends upon the disciplinary influence imposed on the local service providers by the two forces of competition (distant and local competition, reflected by u^{DC} and m, respectively). We can see that in general, an increase in competition implies a decrease in the local monopoly power enjoyed by each of the local service providers within its region with the consequent reduction in the equilibrium prices charged by them and the resulting increase in the equilibrium utility levels for the individuals.

Nevertheless, these price reductions are different, depending on which competition (distant or local) is augmented. If the distant competition is the one that increases (represented by an increase in the level of utility offered at the alternative region), then the price reductions will mostly affect the individuals located at the central region of the market areas of the local service providers. These were the regions where the providers could most effectively exploit its local monopoly power (recall that it could offer the lowest utility to individuals located at the centre of its market area, because this was the location most distant from the other local service providers in the region). On the other hand, if the local competition is the one that is augmented (represented by a higher number of providers in the region), the price reductions will mostly affect those located at the borders of the market areas of the providers. This is because a higher number of providers will reduce the distance between them, thus making them better substitutes.

Having determined $\underline{P^E}$ for a given u^{DC} and m, we can see that the equilibrium profit function for local service provider i will be given in this case by the following expression:

$$\Pi_i(m, u^{DC}) = 2\left[\int_0^{r^0} P_i^{DC}(r, u^{DC})dr + \int_{r^0}^{r^b} P_i^{LC}(r, m)dr\right] - G, \quad (2.61)$$

where r^0 is given by:[44]

$$r^0 = \frac{N}{m} - \frac{1}{a}[g(G) - (u^{DC} - Y)]. \quad (2.62)$$

Equation (2.61) can be written as follows:[45]

$$\Pi_i(m, u^{DC}) = \frac{N^2 a}{2m^2} - G - \left(\left\{\frac{N}{m} - \frac{1}{a}[g(G) - u^{DC} + Y]\right\}\right.$$

$$\left.\left\{\frac{Na}{m} - [g(G) - u^{DC} + Y]\right\}\right). \quad (2.63)$$

In equation (2.63), we determined the equilibrium profits obtained by each local service provider for a given u^{DC} and m.

FREE-ENTRY PRICE-LOCATION EQUILIBRIUM   Now we determine the equilibrium number of local service providers with flexible technology $m^E_{flex}(u^{DC})$, for a given level of distant competition u^{DC}, if there is free entry in the establishment of providers. In Appendix 2A7 we show that this is given by:[46]

$$m^E_{flex}(u^{DC}) = \left[\frac{x + \left(\dfrac{x^2 - aG}{2} \right)^{\frac{1}{2}}}{G + \dfrac{x^2}{a}} \right] N. \qquad (2.64)$$

This means that in those cases where technology is completely flexible as to location, the free-entry price-location equilibrium will be unique for a given level of distant competition.

As we can see in Appendix 2A7, when distant competition is relatively weak, this unique free-entry price-location equilibrium will be characterized by excessive entry (or excessive capacity in the region) in the sense that the equilibrium number of competing local service providers is larger than the optimal one. The equilibrium number of providers decreases steadily as the intensity of the distant competition increases. This is because the presence of distant competition reduces equilibrium profits and thus incentives for entry, leading to a reduction of the mentioned inefficiency (that of excessive entry).

As we explain in Appendix 2A7, only if we have a very intense distant competition will we obtain the optimal number of competing local service providers under flexible technology. This is the implicit assumption made by Tiebout in order to obtain optimality in a system of competing providers. Otherwise we get excessive entry. This means that without the disciplinary force of distant competition, local competition alone is not enough to ensure optimality.

One example of excessive entry when the technology of the local public-good is flexible is the case of the collective transportation services in the metropolitan region of Santiago, particularly the *micros* (buses). Santiago's *micros* are provided by independent small firms (each with a very small number of them, many with only one), which compete with one another for customers. The result of their competition is an excess capacity of *micros* in the region, as is evident in the extremely low average occupancy rate of each vehicle.

We can summarize the results as follows:

Result 2.7   Assume that technology is flexible. Then there will be a unique free-entry price-location equilibrium for competing local service providers in a region for a given level of distant competition, u^{DC}. This free-entry location price equilibrium will be characterized by symmetrically located competing local service providers, whose equilibrium prices are those in the price subgame, described in Result 2.3 and for which profits are zero. The equilibrium number of these competing local service providers and the consequent efficiency of this equilibrium allocation, in the sense of being equivalent to the optimal one, will depend upon the intensity of the distant competition as follows:

1. if distant competition is not perfect ($u^{DC} < V^*$), this equilibrium allocation will be characterized by excessive entry and will thus be inefficient;
2. as competition from the other regions increases (higher u^{DC}), the equilibrium number of competing local service providers decreases and thus the inefficiency is reduced; and
3. only if distant competition is perfect ($u^{DC} = V^*$), will this equilibrium allocation be efficient, because the equilibrium number of competing local service providers in the region will in this case be equivalent to the optimal one.

Fixed technology, location-specific fixed costs (location sunk costs)   We show that in those cases where technology is completely fixed to its location, after a location is chosen, there will be multiple free-entry price-location equilibria for a given level of distant competition (represented by u^{DC}). These free-entry price-location equilibria can be symmetrical or asymmetrical. We now characterize the symmetrical free-entry price-location equilibria. From these equilibria, the asymmetrical ones that can exist can easily be identified.[47]

SYMMETRICAL FREE-ENTRY PRICE-LOCATION EQUILIBRIA   These involve a number of competing local service providers, which we denote by m_{fix}^E, located symmetrically at locations $\underline{r}^E(m_{fix}^E)$, for which:

$$\Pi_e[r_e, \underline{r}^E(m_{fix}^E), \underline{P}^E] \leq 0, \qquad (2.65)$$

$$\Pi_i[\underline{r}^E(m_{fix}^E), \underline{P}^E] \geq 0, \qquad (2.66)$$

where $\Pi_e[r_e, \underline{r}^E(m_{fix}^E), \underline{P}^E]$ are the profits that an entrant can make by entering at the most profitable location, r_e, given the equilibrium locations of the existing providers, $\underline{r}^E$, and their equilibrium prices, $\underline{P}^E$, while $\Pi_i[\underline{r}^E(m_{fix}^E), \underline{P}^E]$ are the equilibrium profits of each provider in the region. If $\Pi_e[r_e, r^E (m^E_{fix}), P^E]$ > 0, there will be incentives for new providers to emerge and to enter at r_e, so that m^E_{fix} would not constitute an equilibrium. On the other hand, if $\Pi_i[r^E(m^E_{fix}), P^E] < 0$, some providers were to leave the region and so in this case m^E_{fix} would also not constitute an equilibrium. However, in the case of fixed technology we may have equilibria with positive profits for the local service providers in the region. This is because, once a location distribution of providers is established, it is very costly to change it (sunk costs are involved). Thus, the entry of new providers into the region will not necessarily imply a relocation of the existing ones to their most profitable location, which are the symmetrical locations, as explained above. As a result, location distributions with positive profits can be sustained as free-entry location price equilibria in the case of fixed technology.

We now determine m^E_{fix} in our model in the *absence of distant competition*. For this purpose, we disregard for the moment the existence of distant competition, the implications of which we analyse below.

In the case of fixed technology, the symmetrical price-location equilibrium for a given number of competing local service providers (m) will be equivalent to the unique price-location equilibrium under flexible technology, described above. Thus, in the absence of distant competition, the symmetrical price-location equilibrium for a given number of competing providers under fixed technology can be described by equations (2.53), (2.54), (2.55), (2.56) and (2.57).

Let us now analyse the incentives for the entry of a new local service provider into the market. If locations are fixed and symmetrical, as explained above, the most profitable location for an entrant, r_e, given the equilibrium prices of the existing local service providers, is given by:

$$r_e = \frac{N}{4m}, \qquad (2.67)$$

that is, at the midpoint between two existing facilities in the region. By entering at this point, the entrant can minimize transportation costs for those living in the segment between these two established facilities. This implies that these individuals will be willing to pay the highest possible amount to patronize the entrant's facility, and thus it will maximize its profits. These profits are given by:[48]

$$\Pi_e[r_e, \underline{r}^E(m), \underline{P}^E] = \frac{N^2 a}{8m^2} - G. \qquad (2.68)$$

For m^E_{fix} to be a free-entry price-location equilibrium, equations (2.65) and (2.66) must be satisfied, and thus, given equations (2.68) and (2.57), we can obtain $m_{fix}^{\min}$, which denotes the minimum number of symmetrically located facilities at which an entrant would make no positive profits by entering at the best possible location and $m_{fix}^{\max}$ which is the maximum number of facilities at which all existing local service providers in the region make non-negative profits:[49]

$$m_{fix}^{\min} = \frac{1}{2\sqrt{2}} a^{\frac{1}{2}} G^{-\frac{1}{2}} N \le m_{fix}^E \le \frac{1}{\sqrt{2}} a^{\frac{1}{2}} G^{-\frac{1}{2}} N = m_{fix}^{\max}. \qquad (2.69)$$

Any m_{fix} that satisfies equation (2.69) will be a symmetrical free-entry price-location equilibrium for the fixed technology case, m_{fix}^E. We then have a whole range of possible symmetrical free-entry price-location equilibria.

The distance between local public goods at a symmetrical free-entry price-location equilibrium for the fixed technology case will fall within the following ranges:[50]

$$d_{fix}^{\max}(m_{fix}^{\min}) = 2\sqrt{2} a^{-\frac{1}{2}} G^{\frac{1}{2}} \ge d_{fix}^E \ge \sqrt{2} a^{-\frac{1}{2}} G^{\frac{1}{2}} = d_{fix}^{\min}(m_{fix}^{\max}), \qquad (2.70)$$

where $d_{fix}^{\max}(m_{fix}^{\min})$ and $d_{fix}^{\min}(m_{fix}^{\max})$ are the maximum and minimum possible equilibrium distance between local public goods, respectively.

In the case of fixed technology, the optimal allocation (where the optimal number of competing local service providers is given by equation (2.10)) can be sustained as a free-entry price-location equilibrium, but allocations with insufficient and excessive entry can also be sustained as free-entry price-location equilibrium among independent local service providers.

This implies that in the case of fixed technology, a monopoly local service provider (for example, some kind of metropolitan local service provider), who provides all the facilities in the region, could solve the inefficiency derived from the coordination problem of independent providers (possible excessive or insufficient entry) and maximize welfare by providing all the local public goods through an optimal number of facilities at the optimal locations in the region, because this is the allocation that will maximize its profits.[51] This is possible because in this case, no independent local service provider would have any incentive to enter the region. On the contrary, in the case where technology is flexible, the threat of an entrant makes it impossible for a monopoly local service provider to sustain such an optimal equilibrium. So, in the case of flexible technology it would be impossible for a monopoly provider to solve the inefficiency derived from this coordination problem, which generates excessive entry.

So far, we have disregarded the potential effect of distant competition on the free-entry price-location equilibria with fixed technology identified above. We may expect, perhaps, as in the case of flexible technology, that the presence of distant competition might tend to correct the deviation from the optimal number of competing local service providers.

Let us now analyse what happens in the *presence of distant competition*. In this case, we have, for each level of distant competition, a whole range of possible symmetrical free-entry price-location equilibria, where $m_{fix}^E(u^{DC})$ is an equilibrium number of local service providers if it satisfies the following condition:

$$m_{fix}^{\min}(u^{DC}) \leq m_{fix}^E(u^{DC}) \leq m_{fix}^{\max}(u^{DC}). \tag{2.71}$$

As before, the distance between local public goods at each symmetrical free-entry price-location equilibrium for the fixed technology case will fall within the following ranges:

$$d_{fix}^{\max}[m_{fix}^{\min}(u^{DC})] \geq d_{fix}^E(u^{DC}) \geq d_{fix}^{\min}[(m_{fix}^{\max}(u^{DC})], \tag{2.72}$$

where $d_{fix}^{\max}[m_{fix}^{\min}(u^{DC})]$ and $d_{fix}^{\min}[m_{fix}^{\max}(u^{DC})]$ are the maximum and minimum possible equilibrium distance between local public goods, for each level of distant competition, respectively. Accordingly, we analyse the effect of distant competition on $m_{fix}^{\max}(u^{DC})$ and $m_{fix}^{\min}(u^{DC})$, respectively.

The maximum number of local service providers (the zero profits equilibrium), $m_{fix}^{\max}(u^{DC})$, is equivalent to the free-entry equilibrium number of providers under flexible technology, under the presence of distant competition, $m_{flex}^E(u^{DC})$, which is given by equation (2.64). Thus, as in the flexible technology case, the existence of distant competition will decrease the profits of a given number of providers. It is clear, then, that $m_{fix}^{\max}(u^{DC})$ will decrease with the intensity of distant competition (represented by u^{DC}), and only when we have perfect distant competition ($u^{DC} = V^*$) will the maximum number of providers be the optimal one (m^*). As in the case with flexible technology, intense distant competition reduces the tendency towards excessive entry and can even completely correct this inefficiency if distant competition is perfect.[52]

However, on the other hand, the existence of distant competition will serve even more strongly to prevent the entry of new local service providers in the insufficient entry equilibria, because of the decrease in profits an entrant can make, given a particular number of providers. As we can see in Appendix 2A8, the minimum equilibrium number of providers $[m_{fix}^{\min}(u^{DC})]$ will decrease with the intensity of distant competition and in this sense distant competition will increase this inefficiency.

Thus, for example, when we have perfect distant competition ($u^{DC} = V^*$), for $m_{fix}^E(u^{DC} = V^*)$ to be a free-entry price-location equilibrium, equations (2.65) and (2.66) must be satisfied, and therefore:[53]

$$m_{fix}^{\min}(u^{DC} = V^*) = \frac{1}{4}a^{\frac{1}{2}}G^{-\frac{1}{2}}N \le m_{fix}^E(u^{DC} = V^*) \le \frac{1}{2}a^{\frac{1}{2}}G^{-\frac{1}{2}}N$$

$$= m_{fix}^{\max}(u^{DC} = V^*) = m^*. \qquad (2.73)$$

We can see that very intense distant competition eliminates the potential excessive entry equilibria, as in the flexible technology case, but it also increases the range of possible insufficient entry equilibria.

It can be shown that, as u^{DC} increases, $m_{fix}^{\min}(u^{DC})$ and $m_{fix}^{\max}(u^{DC})$ decrease in absolute value, but $m_{fix}^{\max}(u^{DC})$ decreases more than $m_{fix}^{\min}(u^{DC})$, so that the interval $[m_{fix}^{\min}(u^{DC}), m_{fix}^{\max}(u^{DC})]$ shrinks as u^{DC} increases, and thus the number of possible free-entry price-location equilibria is reduced. When $u^{DC} = V^*$, there is still a whole range of free-entry price-location equilibria, now characterized by $m_{fix}^E(u^{DC}) \in [m_{fix}^{\min}(u^{DC} = V^*), m_{fix}^{\max}(u^{DC} = V^*) = m^*]$ (equation (2.73)), but the number of possible free-entry price-location equilibria is at its minimum. In this case, the optimal allocation is still an equilibrium, but the number of possible equilibria with insufficient entry is enlarged.

ASYMMETRICAL FREE-ENTRY PRICE-LOCATION EQUILIBRIA In addition to the symmetrical equilibria identified above, we can see that there will be a whole range of asymmetrical free-entry price-location equilibria for the fixed technology case, determined by the fact that the maximum and minimum possible equilibrium distance between local public goods is given by equation (2.72).

Therefore, in the case of fixed technology there are a *multiplicity* of free-entry location price equilibria. This implies that the precise nature of the free-entry location price equilibrium among competing local service providers providing local public goods with location sunk cost technology in a particular region will depend upon the history of that region.

We can summarize the results as follows:

Result 2.8 Assume that technology is fixed. Then there will be multiple free-entry price-location equilibria for a given level of distant competition (u^{DC}), which can be symmetrical or asymmetrical. The equilibrium number of these competing local service providers and the consequent efficiency of this equilibrium allocation, in the sense of being equivalent to the optimal one, will depend upon the intensity of the distant competition as follows:

1. in the absence of active distant competition, the optimal allocation will be a free-entry price-location equilibrium, but we can also have equilibria with excessive and insufficient entry;
2. as competition from the other regions increases (higher u^{DC}), the equilibrium number of competing local service providers decreases and thus the number of possible free-entry price-location equilibria with excessive entry are reduced, but those with insufficient entry are increased; and
3. only if distant competition is perfect ($u^{DC} = V^*$), will we have no equilibrium allocation with excessive entry, but the number of possible free-entry price-location equilibria with insufficient entry is maximal. The optimal allocation will still be a free-entry price-location equilibrium in this case.

SEQUENTIAL FREE-ENTRY PRICE-LOCATION EQUILIBRIUM   Up to this point, we have demonstrated the existence of multiple free-entry price-location equilibria when the local public-good technology is fixed. Nevertheless, as is usually the case with a multiplicity of equilibria, we cannot identify which equilibrium will actually result. As suggested by Prescott and Visscher (1977, p. 379), when relocation costs are high, 'it may be more reasonable to model firms as making location decisions once and for all, one firm at a time, with firms being aware of the relative permanence of their decisions and thus taking some care to anticipate the decision rules firms entering later in the sequence will follow'.

We follow this suggestion in order to analyse which of the equilibria identified above will be a sequential free-entry price-location equilibrium. For this purpose, we assume that local service providers enter the market and choose their locations one at a time in our model.[54] Each local service provider is assumed to choose the profit-maximizing location, based on the observed choices of the providers that have already chosen their locations, as well as the location rules that subsequent, equally rational potential entrants will use. Thus, each provider will take into consideration the effect of its location decision upon the ultimate configuration of the industry.

In our setting, this implies that a unique sequential free-entry price-location equilibrium will exist for a given level of distant competition, represented by u^{DC}. This sequential free-entry price-location equilibrium will be characterized by a number of competing local service providers, which we denote by m_{fix}^{SE}, located at locations $\underline{r}^{SE}(m_{fix}^{SE})$.

We now determine m_{fix}^{SE} and $r^{SE}(m_{fix}^{SE})$ within our model. As before, we disregard for the moment the existence of distant competition, the implications of which we shall analyse later.

Let us start with the location decision of the first entrant in the *absence of distant competition*. Because space is completely homogeneous on the circle, the first local service provider entering the region will be indifferent with respect to where to place its local public good. Thus, it will locate with equal probability at any location on the circle, which we define as r_1.

The second local service provider to enter knows that after its entry, there will be free entry of other providers until there is no available location where non-negative profits can be achieved. Thus, given the location of the first local service provider, r_1, the second one will choose a location r_2 which is as far as possible away from r_1 without inviting entry in between. This guarantees that after all have entered, it will at least obtain its maximum profits in the area $|r_2 - r_1|$ on a sustainable basis with no entry. We already know that the maximum distance between two local service providers without inviting entry is given by $d_{fix}^{max}(m_{fix}^{min})$, in equation (2.70).

Given the locations of the first and second local service providers, the third provider will choose a location r_3 as far away from r_1 or r_2 as possible without inviting entry in between (it will locate with equal probability at any of these two locations). The entry process will continue in this manner until there is no available location where non-negative profits can be achieved.

If we assume that N/d_{fix}^{max} is an integer,[55] we can see that the sequential free-entry price-location equilibrium can be described by m_{fix}^{SE} evenly spaced local service providers, whose facilities are separated by a distance $d_{fix}^{SE}(m_{fix}^{SE})$, where:

$$m_{fix}^{SE} = m_{fix}^{min}, \tag{2.74}$$

$$d_{fix}^{SE}(m_{fix}^{SE}) = d_{fix}^{max}(m_{fix}^{min}). \tag{2.75}$$

Thus, m_{fix}^{SE} corresponds to the lowest number of evenly spaced local service providers consistent with no entry (m_{fix}^{min} in equation (2.69)), as identified in the case without sequential entry.

Note that:

$$m_{fix}^{SE} < m^*, \tag{2.76}$$

which implies that in this case there will be *insufficient entry* of competing local service providers in the region.

Accordingly, in the case where technology is completely fixed to its location, and under the assumption of sequential entry, there will be a unique free-entry price-location equilibrium characterized by m_{fix}^{SE} symmetrically located competing local service providers in the region, charging the equilibrium prices described in the previous sections. This equilibrium will be inefficient, because there will not be enough entry of local public goods into the region.

Thus, the presence of location sunk cost technology together with the assumption that local service providers anticipate the decision rule of local service providers entering later in the region, act as some kind of entry barrier that allows the local providers in the region to obtain positive profits without inviting entry and so in this case competition of local providers is not enough to guarantee optimality.

Let us now analyse what happens in the *presence of distant competition*. Equivalent to the previous case and assuming that N/d_{fix}^{max} is an integer,[56] we can see that the sequential free-entry price-location equilibrium can be described by $m_{fix}^{SE}(u^{DC})$ evenly spaced local service providers, whose facilities are separated by a distance $d_{fix}^{SE}(u^{DC})$, where:

$$m_{fix}^{SE}(u^{DC}) = m_{fix}^{min}(u^{DC}) \tag{2.77}$$

$$d_{fix}^{SE}(u^{DC}) = d_{fix}^{max}(u^{DC}). \tag{2.78}$$

As before, $m_{fix}^{SE}(u^{DC})$ corresponds to the lowest number of evenly spaced local service providers consistent with no entry ($m_{fix}^{min}(u^{DC})$ in equation (2A8.3)), as identified in the case without sequential entry.

Accordingly, in the case in which technology is completely fixed to its location and we assume sequential entry, there will be a unique free-entry price-location equilibrium for every given level of distant competition (u^{DC}), characterized by $m_{fix}^{SE}(u^{DC})$ evenly spaced competing local service providers in the region, charging the equilibrium prices described in the previous sections. As we explain in Appendix 2A8, in the case of fixed technology, the equilibrium number of competing local service providers will decrease as distant competition increases. This is because the existence of distant competition will decrease the profits of a given number of local service providers, and it will more strongly discourage the entry of new providers, because of the decrease in potential profits for an entrant, given a particular number of local providers. Thus the presence of distant competition causes the equilibrium number of competing local service providers to deviate even further from its optimal level.

Therefore, under sequential entry in our setting, we always have insufficient entry and this problem will become more severe as distant competition increases.

We can summarize the results as follows:

Result 2.9   Assume that technology is fixed and local service providers choose their locations sequentially. Then there will be a unique sequential free-entry price-location equilibrium for a given level of distant competition (represented by u^{DC}), which will be characterized as follows:

1. the equilibrium number of competing local service providers will correspond to the lowest number consistent with no entry;
2. this equilibrium will always be inefficient in the sense that it will be characterized by insufficient entry, independently of the level of distant competition; and
3. the equilibrium number of competing local service providers decreases steadily as the level of distant competition increases. Therefore, in this case, the presence of distant competition will lead to a greater deviation from the optimal number of competing local service providers.

Redistribution and Welfare Analysis at the Symmetrical Free-entry Price-location Equilibria[57]

We now compare the various symmetrical free-entry price-location equilibria identified above in terms of the winners and losers among the local service providers and the individuals living in their service areas at these equilibria (*redistribution among equilibria*) and in terms of efficiency (*welfare among equilibria*). We disregard for the moment the presence of distant competition, the implication of which we shall discuss later.

As before and in order to simplify the analysis, we assume that a circle of perimeter L describes space in the region.[58]

Redistribution among the equilibria
Let us first analyse the situation of the *competing local service providers* at the various symmetrical free-entry price-location equilibria. Given a number of m symmetrically located competing local service providers in a region, we know from the previous analysis that the profits made by each of them will be given by equation (2.57) and in aggregate terms will be given by:

$$\Pi^T(m) = \sum_{i=1}^{m} \Pi_i^E(m) = \frac{1}{2}\frac{N^2 a}{m} - mG. \qquad (2.79)$$

Equilibria featuring a higher number of local service providers will result in smaller profits for each provider, and thus in aggregate terms smaller profits for all of them. Therefore, local service providers will logically prefer equilibria with the lowest possible number of providers, because this will give them more local monopoly power, and thus they can charge higher prices.

$$\frac{\partial \Pi^T(m)}{\partial m} = -\frac{1}{2}\frac{aN^2}{m^2} - G < 0. \tag{2.80}$$

As we can see in equation (2.80), if the number of local service providers in the region increases by one, the losses for the providers in aggregate terms are caused, on the one hand, by the *reduction in aggregate prices* (reflected by the first term on the right-hand side of the equation), and on the other hand, by the *additional fixed cost* due to the additional local service provider (reflected by the second term on the right-hand side of the equation).

Let us now analyse the situation of *individual customers* at the various free-entry price-location equilibria. We can see that given m symmetrically located local service providers, the indirect utility achieved by the individuals in aggregate terms is given by:[59]

$$V^T[\underline{r^E(m)}, \underline{P^E}] = N[Y + g(G)] - \left(\frac{1}{2}\frac{aN^2}{m} + \frac{1}{4}\frac{aN^2}{m}\right). \tag{2.81}$$

The aggregate utility of the individuals increases with m. Thus, in aggregate terms, the individuals will be better off in equilibria with higher numbers of competing local service providers.

$$\frac{\partial V^T[\underline{r^E(m)}, \underline{P^E}]}{\partial m} = \frac{1}{2}\frac{aN^2}{m^2} + \frac{1}{4}\frac{aN^2}{m^2} > 0. \tag{2.82}$$

As we can see in equation (2.82), if the number of providers in the region increases by one, the benefits for the individuals in aggregate terms are derived, on the one hand, from the *reduction in aggregate prices* (reflected by the first term on the right-hand side of the equation) and on the other hand, from the *reduction in transport costs* thanks to the additional provider (reflected by the second term on the right-hand side of the equation).

Welfare among the equilibria

Now we compare the free-entry price-location equilibria in terms of welfare. We consider as a measure of welfare in our case the sum of the profits made in aggregate by the competing local service providers and the utility obtained by all the individuals in the region. Thus, welfare will be given by:

$$W(m) = \Pi^T(m) + V^T[r^E(m), P^E]$$

$$= N[Y + g(G)] - \left(\frac{1}{4}\frac{aN^2}{m}\right) - mG$$

$$= Ng(G) + NY - TTC(m) - mG. \tag{2.83}$$

Once again, we can see here the well-known trade-off between transportation costs and fixed costs present in location models. In the last line of equation (2.83), on the one hand, a higher number of facilities will result in lower total transport costs, and thus higher welfare, while on the other hand, a higher number of facilities will imply higher fixed costs, and thus lower welfare. The losses caused by lower prices for the local service providers when m increases represent gains in the same amount for the individuals (this is only a redistribution effect), and thus they do not affect welfare.

By maximizing equation (2.83) with respect to m, we can once again obtain the optimal number of competing local service providers identified above, m^*. Therefore, in terms of welfare, the best free-entry price-location equilibrium is the one with m^* symmetrically located providers. All other equilibria where $m^E < m^* < m^E$ produce lower levels of welfare, and welfare decreases as we move away from m^*.

The lowest welfare levels will be achieved at the equilibria with the extreme values of m, m_{fix}^{min} and $m_{fix}^{max} = m_{flex}^E$, in equation (2.69). Note that at both of these equilibria, welfare will be the same, despite the fact that m_{fix}^{min} and m_{fix}^{max} are not symmetrically located with respect to m^*; $(m_{fix}^{max} - m^*) > (m^* - m_{fix}^{min})$, as we can see in Figure 2.5. This implies that deviations from m^* are more costly in terms of welfare when they represent a reduction in the number of local service providers than when they represent an increase.

Let us now discuss what happens when we include distant competition in the setting. It is clear that the existence of distant competition, for a given m, reduces the profits obtained by local service providers (because of the price reduction), while increasing by the same amount the benefits for individuals, as we can see in the area $ABCD$ in Figure 2A6.1. Thus, welfare relative to a given number of providers remains the same (the welfare function in Figure 2.5 remains the same). Where change can be seen, however, is in m_{fix}^{min} and $m_{fix}^{max} = m_{flex}^E$ (given by equations (2A8.3) and (2A7.3), respectively), as explained earlier. As u^{DC} increases, $m_{fix}^{min}(u^{DC})$ and $m_{fix}^{max}(u^{DC}) = m_{flex}^E(u^{DC})$ decrease in absolute value, and the interval

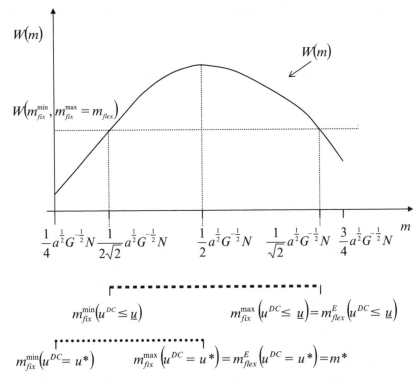

Note: The *dashed* and *dotted* lines represent the possible equilibrium number of symmetrically located local service providers under the absence and presence of perfect distant competition ($u^{DC} = u^*$), respectively.

Figure 2.5   *Relationship between the level of welfare (W(m) in the y-axis) and the number of competing local service providers (m in the x-axis).*

$[m_{fix}^{min}(u^{DC}), m_{fix}^{max}(u^{DC})]$ also decreases. In Figure 2.5 we have drawn $[m_{fix}^{min}, m_{fix}^{max}]$ for $u^{DC} \leq \underline{u}$ (insignificant distant competition) in a *dashed* line and $[m_{fix}^{min}, m_{fix}^{max}]$ for $u^{DC} = u^*$ in a *dotted* line.

We can summarize the results as follows:

Result 2.10

In the case of flexible technology,

1. and in the absence of active distant competition, the free-entry price-location equilibrium, characterized by the largest equilibrium number of competing local service providers, $m_{flex}^E(u^{DC} \leq \underline{u})$, will be the least

favourable in terms of welfare and in terms of profits for the local service providers, but the most favourable for individuals; and

2. as the intensity of distant competition increases, the equilibrium number of local service providers decreases. Accordingly, welfare at this equilibrium increases, and profits for the local service providers increase, while the aggregate indirect utility for individuals decreases. When we have perfect distant competition ($u^{DC} = u^*$), the free-entry price-location equilibrium, characterized by the minimal equilibrium number of competing local service providers, $m^E_{flex}(u^{DC} = u^*) = m^*$, is the most favourable in terms of welfare and in terms of profits for the local service providers, but the least favourable for individuals.

In the case of fixed technology,

3. and in the absence of active distant competition, there is a whole range of symmetrical free-entry price-location equilibria, characterized by an equilibrium number of competing local service providers, $m^E \in [m^{min}_{fix}(u^{DC} \leq \underline{u}), m^{max}_{fix}(u^{DC} \leq \underline{u})]$, where m^{min}_{fix} and m^{max}_{fix} correspond to the minimum and maximum possible equilibrium number of competing local service providers in this case. Among these, the equilibria with m^{max}_{fix} and m^{min}_{fix} competing local service providers are the least favourable in terms of welfare, but the equilibrium with m^{max}_{fix} local service providers is the best for individuals and the least favourable for the local service providers, while the opposite is true for the equilibrium with m^{min}_{fix} local service providers; and

4. if the intensity of the distant competition increases, m^{min}_{fix} and m^{max}_{fix} decrease in absolute value, but m^{max}_{fix} decreases more than m^{min}_{fix}, so the interval $[m^{min}_{fixED}, m^{max}_{fixED}]$ shrinks as the intensity of distant competition increases. When we have perfect distant competition ($u^{DC} = u^*$), there is still a whole range of free-entry price-location equilibria, now characterized by $m^E \in [m^{min}_{fix}(u^{DC} = u^*), m^*]$. The lowest welfare is obtained at $m^{min}_{fix}(u^{DC} = u^*)$, and it is much lower than at the equilibria where distant competition is absent ($u^{DC} \leq \underline{u}$).

Elastic Demand

In the previous sections, we have seen that the free-entry price-location equilibrium with flexible technology will be inefficient and characterized by excessive entry. However, in the case of fixed technology, the optimal allocation may be sustained as a free-entry price-location equilibrium, but allocations with insufficient and excessive entry may also be sustained as free-entry price-location equilibria among independent local service providers. As we argued above, this implies that in the case of fixed technology, a monopoly local service provider (for example, some kind of metropolitan local service provider) could solve the inefficiency derived from the coordination problem of the independent local service providers (potential excessive or insufficient entry) and maximize welfare by providing all the local public goods through an optimal number of facilities at the optimal locations in the region, because this is the allocation that will maximize its profits.[60] As explained above, this is possible because in this case, no independent local service provider would have any incentive to enter the region.

The previous results hold when the individual demand for the local public goods is not responsive to price. In our setting, this implies that individuals travel only once to a facility in order to enjoy the service of the local public good (or the service of the local public-good is delivered to their residential locations only once). However, we can imagine situations in which individuals may choose to patronize the facility more frequently (or to request the service more frequently at their residential locations), depending on the price charged for the service. For example, in the case of refuse collection services, individuals may choose to have their rubbish collected once a month, once a week or daily, depending on the price of the service. Another example of a local public good with price-responsive demand may be seen in the case of a public swimming pool, which individuals may decide to visit more or less frequently, depending on the admission fee.

As we shall see in the following example, if demand is price responsive, the optimal allocation under fixed technology will no longer be sustained as a free-entry price-location equilibrium if the frictions (transport costs and fixed costs), are relatively low. In this case, a metropolitan local service provider could only partially solve the inefficiency generated by independent local service providers,[61] because when the optimal allocation is no longer sustainable and there are incentives for independent local service providers to enter the region, the metropolitan local government will have to choose the smallest number of facilities consistent with no entry, and this will imply some excessive capacity in the region.

In our example, we assume that individuals exhibit the following demand function, at each r, for the local public good of local service provider i located at r_i:

$$q_i(r) = \begin{cases} \dfrac{1}{P_i^T(r)} & \text{if} \quad P_i^T(r) \le g(G) \\ 0 & \text{if} \quad P_i^T(r) > g(G) \end{cases} \tag{2.84}$$

$$P_i^T(r) = P_i(r) + t_i(r). \tag{2.85}$$

Here, as in the previous sections, $P_i(r)$ is the price structure or function[62] chosen by the local service provider i, $i \in \{1, 2, \ldots, m\}$. We define $P_i^T(r)$ as the full price that an individual must pay at his/her location r in order to consume one unit of the local public good offered by local service provider i at location r_i (this price includes the transport costs that the individual must incur).[63] In the following analysis we disregard the existence of distant competition and concentrate only on local competition.

As before and in order to simplify the analysis, we assume that a circle of perimeter L describes space in the region.[64]

The optimal allocation

In order to determine the nature of the optimal allocation in this case, we imagine a region-wide planner (a monopolist) whose objective is to maximize profits. The planner's role is to determine the number of facilities m^{ED} and their corresponding locations, as well as the taxation scheme (which we henceforth refer to as the pricing scheme) denoted by $P_i(r)$, for $i \in \{1, 2, \ldots, m^{ED}\}$, which is used to finance these facilities. We denote by $r^{ED*}(m^{ED*}) = (r_1^{ED*}, r_2^{ED*}, \ldots, r_m^{ED*})$ the vector describing the optimal number of facilities (m^{ED*}) and their corresponding optimal locations, and by $P_i^*(r)$ the optimal price scheme in order to finance these local public goods.[65]

From the previous sections we know that given a particular number of facilities, the configuration that minimizes total transport costs is an evenly spaced distribution of the facilities (symmetrically located facilities). Therefore, this will be the distribution chosen by the monopoly local service provider and will then be the optimal distribution of facilities, $r^{ED*}(m^{ED*})$.[66]

In Appendix 2A9 we determined the number of evenly spaced facilities that a monopolist will choose in order to maximize its profits in the case of an elastic demand, which is equivalent to the optimal number of facilities, m^{ED*}, and is given by:

$$m^{ED*} = \frac{1}{2} \left[\frac{a}{Gg(G)} \right]^{\frac{1}{2}} N. \tag{2.86}$$

Here we can see that the expression that determines the optimal number of facilities in the case of an elastic demand (equation 2.86) is similar to that obtained for the case of an inelastic demand (equation 2.10).[67] Equivalent to the inelastic demand case, equation (2.86) shows the trade-off between transportation costs and the cost of supplying the local public goods involved in choosing the number of facilities to install.

However, contrary to what happens in the case of an inelastic demand, the value that the individual gives to the local public good, represented in some way by $g(G)$, influences the optimal number of facilities ($m^{ED}*$) in this case. In order to understand this relationship, let us analyse what happens with $m^{ED}*$ if $g(G)$ increases. In the case of an increase in the valuation that people give to the local public good ($g(G)$), they will be willing to pay a higher price for the use of the local public good. Nevertheless and because demand is sensitive to price changes, this higher price will imply a reduction in the quantity demanded, which will cause them to travel less frequently. As a result, the impact of transportation cost on revenues of the monopolist will be reduced. Accordingly, as $g(G)$ increases, the total revenues of the monopolist will be less sensitive to transportation cost, and so the optimal number of facilities will be smaller, in order to reduce the fixed costs that additional facilities imply.

Free-entry price-location equilibrium in a system of one-purpose competing local service providers

As in the previous sections, we start by analysing the final stage of the game. At this stage, we have an established number of independent local service providers in the region, m, who have already chosen the locations of their local public goods, $\underline{r}(m) = (r_1, r_2, \ldots, r_m)$. In the present stage, they choose their pricing structure in a non-cooperative manner. We then want to find out what each local service provider's equilibrium pricing structure will look like and what it will depend upon, if demand is responsive to price, as in our example.

Given the demand function discussed earlier, local service provider i offering a local public good at location r_i will charge the highest price it can at each location in order to maximize its profits.[68] However, as in the case with inelastic demand, its local monopoly power to set prices will here be constrained by the autarky restriction as well as by local competition.

Thus, in this case, given the locations $\underline{r} = (r_1, r_2, \ldots, r_m)$, the price equilibrium $P^E = P_1^E(r), P_2^E(r), \ldots, P_m^E(r)$ is:

$$P_i^E(r) = \min[P_i^A(r); P_i^{LC}(r)] \qquad (2.87)$$

$$\text{s.t. } \Pi_i[P_i^E(r)] \geq 0, \qquad (2.88)$$

where $P_i^A(r)$ is given by equation (2A9.2), and $P_i^{LC}(r)$ is given by equation (2.41), as explained in the previous sections.

If we assume that $P_i^{LC}(r) < P_i^A(r)$ over all the relevant range, $\underline{P}^E = [P_1^E(r), P_2^E(r), \ldots, P_m^E(r)]$ will be given by equations (2.42) and (2.43). Thus, given this price-responsive demand function, the price equilibrium is identical to the one in the inelastic demand case.

Let us now discuss what happens at the second stage of the game, where the industry structure, m, is given, and the strategic variables are the locations of the local public goods. Then we shall discuss what happens at the first, or entry, stage. As explained earlier, the assumption about the flexibility of the local service providers' chosen locations and corresponding market areas is crucial for the analysis of these stages of the game.

Flexible technology, no location-specific fixed costs (no location sunk costs)
In this case, the fact that demand is now responsive to price does not affect the price-location equilibrium identified in the inelastic demand case, because the equilibrium prices have not changed. This implies that, as before, the existence of a price-location equilibrium depends on the existence of locations such that each one minimizes total transport costs with respect to the other locations for the local public goods. As explained above, there is a unique price-location equilibrium in this case. The equilibrium locations of a given a number of competing local service providers are those that minimize total transport costs, which are the symmetrical locations. Accordingly, the symmetrical locations of the m local service providers represent the unique price-location equilibrium under flexible technology, including the case in which demand is responsive to price.

Let us now discuss what happens at the entry stage when we have free entry. We can see that, as in the inelastic demand case, the free-entry price-location equilibrium will be unique. This equilibrium will be characterized by a number of competing local service providers, which we denote by m_{flexED}, located symmetrically at locations r^E, for which:

$$\Pi_i(\underline{r^E}, \underline{P^E}) = 0 \quad \forall i \in \{1,2, \ldots, m_{flexED}\}. \tag{2.89}$$

The equilibrium number of evenly spaced local service providers in this case will be:[69]

$$m_{flexED} = \frac{2N[1 - \ln(2)]}{G}. \tag{2.90}$$

Thus, in this case, there will always be a free-entry price-location equilibrium with excessive entry, as in the inelastic demand case.[70]

Fixed technology, location-specific fixed costs (location sunk costs)   As in the case of inelastic demand, we see that in the case of price-responsive demand when technology is completely fixed to its location, there will be multiple symmetrical free-entry price-location equilibria, characterized by a number of local public goods and the corresponding distance between them, given by:

$$m_{fixED}^{min} \leq m_{fixED}^E \leq m_{fixED}^{max} \tag{2.91}$$

$$d(m_{fixED}^{min}) \geq d_{fixED}^E \geq d(m_{fixED}^{max}), \tag{2.92}$$

where m_{fixED}^{min} and m_{fixED}^{max} are the minimum and maximum symmetrical equilibrium number of local public goods, and $d(m_{fixED}^{min})$ and $d(m_{fixED}^{max})$ are the corresponding maximum and minimum distances between local public goods that can exist in a symmetrical equilibrium, respectively.

As before, we can see that in addition to the symmetrical equilibria, there will be a whole range of asymmetrical free-entry price-location equilibria for the case of fixed technology, with the maximum distance between local public goods being $d(m_{fixED}^{min})$ and the minimum distance $d(m_{fixED}^{max})$.

We now want to see what m_{fixED}^{min} and m_{fixED}^{max} will look like, in order to compare the possible equilibria with the optimal number of local public goods, m^{ED*}, and to see whether the optimal allocation is again a possible equilibrium.

As in the inelastic demand case, m_{fixED}^{max} will be identical to the equilibrium number under flexible technology:

$$m_{fixED}^{max} = m_{flexED}. \tag{2.93}$$

where m_{flexED} is given by equation (2.90).

On the other hand, the minimum equilibrium number of evenly spaced local service providers consistent with no entry, m_{fixED}^{min}, in this case are:[71]

$$m_{fixED}^{min} = \frac{N[1 - \ln(2)]}{G}. \tag{2.94}$$

This implies that the symmetrical equilibrium number of local public goods in the case of price-responsive demand will be characterized by:

$$m_{fixED}^{min} = \frac{N[1 - \ln(2)]}{G} \leq m_{fixED}^E \leq \frac{2N[1 - \ln(2)]}{G} = m_{fixED}^{max}. \tag{2.95}$$

We would thus have a whole range of possible symmetrical free-entry price-location equilibria. However, in this case, m^{ED*} may be or may be not a free-entry price-location equilibrium.

We can see that if:[72]

$$\frac{aG}{g(G)} \geq \{2[1 - \ln(2)]\}^2, \tag{2.96}$$

$m^{ED}*$ will be a free-entry price-location equilibrium, as in the inelastic demand case. However, if:[73]

$$\{2[1 - \ln(2)]\}^2 > \frac{aG}{g(G)},\tag{2.97}$$

$m^{ED}*$ will not be a free-entry price-location equilibrium, and we would have only equilibria with excessive entry.

In order to understand why we would have only equilibria with excessive entry in the case of price-responsive demand if condition (2.97) holds, and $m^{ED}*$ is no longer a free-entry price-location equilibrium, we analyse a situation in which condition (2.97) holds, which is when transport costs are relatively low (represented by a lower-case a), and how this setting differs from the case of inelastic demand.[74]

If transport costs are relatively low, in both the inelastic and elastic demand cases, we would have at the optimum a relatively small number of local public goods (in comparison with higher values of a), because we would observe more travel by individuals relative to fixed costs, since the former becomes less expensive in relation to the latter.

In the case where demand is inelastic, lower transport costs will result in smaller equilibrium profits for an entrant as well as for the local service providers already in the region (because their monopoly power decreases, local public goods are better substitutes for one another and thus prices are lower), and so the minimum and maximum number of evenly spaced local public goods consistent with no entry and with positive profits will also be smaller when transport costs are relatively low. The whole range of equilibria will shift towards equilibria with smaller numbers of local public goods. As a result we would still have equilibria with insufficient and excessive entry, and $m*$ will always be a possible equilibrium in the case of inelastic demand, independent of the level of transport costs. This implies, as explained above, that in the case of fixed technology and inelastic demand, a monopoly local service provider (for example, some kind of metropolitan local service provider), who provides all the facilities in the region, could solve the inefficiency derived from the coordination problem of independent local service providers (possible excessive or insufficient entry) and maximize welfare by providing all the local public goods through an optimal number of facilities at the optimal locations in the region, because this is the allocation that will maximize its profits. This is possible because in this case, no independent local service provider would have any incentive to enter the region.

Nevertheless, when demand is responsive to price, transport costs do not influence the profits of new entrants or of the local service providers already in the region.[75] Lower transport costs will lead to a reduction in the price that can be charged because local public goods are better substitutes for one another, as in the inelastic demand case, but now, reduced prices and lower transport costs will result in an expansion of demand which will not alter the level of profits. This implies that the minimum and maximum number of evenly spaced local public goods consistent with no entry and positive profits will be the same (they are not sensitive to changes in transport costs). However, because m^{ED*} is sensitive to changes in transport costs and is now smaller, it can be the case that m^{ED*} now lies outside the possible equilibria, and thus we would get only equilibria with excessive entry. This implies that, in this case, a monopoly local service provider could only partially solve the inefficiency derived from the coordination problem between independent local service providers (which will be only excessive entry in this case), because when the optimal allocation is no longer sustainable and there are incentives for independent local service providers to enter the region, the monopoly local service provider will have to choose the smallest number of evenly spaced facilities consistent with no entry, and this will imply some excessive capacity in the region.

Note that when the technology of the local public good is fixed and demand is responsive to price, as in the case of a public swimming pool, smaller frictions (transport costs and G), may imply that the optimal allocation is impossible to sustain as a free-entry price-location equilibrium, and we would always get excessive entry.

We can summarize the results as follows:

Result 2.11 If individual demand for the local public good is responsive to price and is given by equations (2.84) and (2.85):

1. given a specific number of local service providers and their locations, the price equilibrium will be identical to that of the inelastic demand case;
2. if technology is flexible and there is free entry, the free-entry price-location equilibrium will be characterized by excessive entry, as in the inelastic demand case; and
3. if technology is fixed, there is free entry and the frictions (transport costs, a, and fix costs, G) are relatively high, the optimal allocation can be sustained as a free-entry price-location equilibrium, but if the frictions are relatively low (a and G are low), the optimal allocation cannot be sustained as a free-entry price-location equilibrium, and there will always be equilibria with excessive entry.

Restrictions on Price Setting: Constant Fees (Mill Pricing)

In the previous sections, we allowed the local service providers to charge their preferred prices, and we saw that the prices they charged at equilibrium were *discriminatory prices* with respect to location.[76] However, discriminatory price policies are usually difficult to implement in practice. On the one hand, there can be technical problems in implementing them. For example, if transportation is under the customers' control, it can be difficult to verify every customer's address, and people will have incentives to claim that they live at more distant locations in order to obtain lower prices. These technical problems would be solved if transportation were under the control of the providers of the local public goods, as in the case of refuse collection services. But with other types of local public goods, such as educational systems, transportation costs are under the customers' control, and thus discriminatory pricing is technically difficult to implement. On the other hand, there may also be institutional constraints that prevent price discrimination. Hence, in many cases local service providers will have to charge *mill prices* (that is, the price charged to all individuals at the point where the service is provided is the same). Therefore we shall analyse what happens to the equilibrium patterns identified above if local service providers are no longer free to set prices and are forced to charge constant fees, independent of location.

The following section characterizes the equilibrium pattern under mill pricing, comparing it with the optimal allocation and with that achieved under the possibility of price discrimination. It will be seen that mill pricing increases the inefficiencies identified under price discrimination.

As is well known in location economic theory, no free-entry price-location equilibrium would exist in our setting if local service providers charged mill prices. Nevertheless, as shown by D'Aspremont et al. (1979), under quadratic transportation costs this lack of equilibrium can be solved. We shall then consider a slightly modified version of the model presented in the previous sections, in which transportation costs are quadratic rather than linear and are given by $t_j(r) = a(|r_j - r|)^2$.

In order to be able to evaluate the efficiency of the equilibrium allocation under mill prices using quadratic transport costs and to compare the inefficiencies under both price regimes, discriminatory and mill prices, in Appendix 2A10 we characterize the optimal allocation and the equilibrium allocation of competing local service providers under the possibility of discriminatory pricing, as in previous sections, but now using quadratic instead of linear transport costs.

We assume that the technology of the local public goods is flexible and that the exit option (distant competition) is not present, in order to simplify the analysis and concentrate on the general results.

Price-location equilibrium with two competing local service providers[77]

As we explain in Appendix 2A4, in order to show the existence of a price-location equilibrium, we must demonstrate the existence of location choices on the part of these two local service providers, $(r_1{}^E, r_2{}^E)$, such that equation (2A4.1) is satisfied. In the present case, the restriction set on local service providers, which are obliged to charge mill prices, will affect the price-location equilibrium identified for the case where price discrimination was possible (Appendix 2A10).

In Figure 2.6, we have drawn the location of local public good 1 provided by local service provider 1 at r_1; the location of local public good 2 provided by local service provider 2 at r_2; and the location of a consumer indifferent to the choice of patronizing local public good 1 or local public good 2 at w.

The equilibrium prices, market areas, demands and profits as a function of locations in the case of mill prices are given by:[78]

$$P_1^{LC} = \frac{a}{3}(r_2 - r_1)(2L + r_1 + r_2)$$

$$X_1 = \left[0, \frac{2L + r_1 + r_2}{6}\right] \Rightarrow D_1^{LC} = \frac{2L + r_1 + r_2}{6}$$

$$\Pi_1^{LC} = a(r_2 - r_1)\frac{(2L + r_1 + r_2)^2}{18} \tag{2.98}$$

$$P_2^{LC} = \frac{a}{3}(r_2 - r_1)(4L - r_1 - r_2)$$

$$X_2 = \left[\frac{2L + r_1 + r_2}{6}, L\right] \Rightarrow D_2^{LC} = \frac{4L - r_1 - r_2}{6}$$

$$\Pi_2^{LC} = a(r_2 - r_1)\frac{(4L - r_1 - r_2)^2}{18} \tag{2.99}$$

Note that both Π_1^{LC} and Π_2^{LC} fall as r_1 rises, and both fall as r_2 falls. At equilibrium, the local service providers increase their profits as they move farther apart, and thus the equilibrium locations in this case are those of maximum differentiation, 0 and L, respectively.

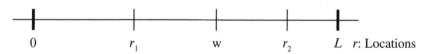

$$0 \qquad\qquad r_1 \qquad\qquad w \qquad\qquad r_2 \qquad\quad L \quad r\text{: Locations}$$

Figure 2.6 Location of a consumer indifferent to the choice of patronizing local public good 1 at r_1 *or local public good 2 at* r_2, *which is represented by* w.

As we explain in Appendix 2A10, the optimal locations for two facilities in this setting would be at $\frac{1}{4}L$ and $\frac{3}{4}L$, respectively. Accordingly, the equilibrium locations under mill pricing identified above are inefficient. Nevertheless, as we also explain in the appendix, under the possibility of discriminatory pricing, the equilibrium locations of the two local service providers in this setting are at $\frac{1}{4}L$ and $\frac{3}{4}L$, respectively. Thus, under the possibility of discriminatory pricing the equilibrium locations are efficient. This implies that the possibility of discriminatory pricing solves the inefficient equilibrium locations of two local service providers under mill pricing.

Result 2.12 The unique price-location equilibrium of two local service providers offering local public goods with flexible technology under mill pricing and quadratic transport costs is characterized by maximum differentiation.[79] Accordingly, if two competing local service providers offering local public goods with flexible technology are obliged to charge mill prices, the locations at equilibrium will be inefficient and in this sense welfare will be reduced in comparison with the case where local service providers are allowed to charge discriminatory prices with respect to location, because in this latter case equilibrium locations are efficient.

The fact that under mill prices the equilibrium locations of two competing local service providers are inefficient is because in this case, local service providers have to charge the same price for all locations, and thus, in order to reduce price competition, they will seek to locate as far away as possible from their competitors, that is, at inefficient locations. However, in the case of discriminatory pricing, price competition is present at every point in space, and thus local service providers have no opportunity to reduce price competition by changing their locations. Therefore, as explained earlier, local service providers will maximize their profits by choosing the locations that minimize total transportation costs, which are the efficient locations.

Free-entry price-location equilibrium
We now characterize the free-entry price-location equilibrium under mill pricing and quadratic transport costs. As in the case of linear transport costs, we assume that space in the region is described by a circle of perimeter L rather than an interval $[0, L]$, and the set of locations in this circle is called X. This change in the model is made to avoid the special cases that appear at the extremes of the interval and thus make every point in the region equivalent, which allows us to concentrate on the general results.

Given prices and locations, in competition, the market areas and corresponding demand levels and profits of local service provider i, for $i \in \{1, 2, \ldots, m\}$, will be given by:[80]

$$X_i^{LC} = [w_{i-1}, w_{i+1}] \Rightarrow D_i^{LC} = \frac{1}{2}\left[\frac{P_{i+1} - P_i}{a(r_{i+1} - r_i)} + \frac{P_{i-1} - P_i}{a(r_i - r_{i-1})} + r_{i+1} - r_{i-1}\right]$$

(2.100)

$$\Pi_i^{LC} = P_i^{LC}D_i^{LC} - G = \frac{P_i}{2}\left[\frac{P_{i+1} - P_i}{a(r_{i+1} - r_i)} + \frac{P_{i-1} - P_i}{a(r_i - r_{i-1})} + r_{i+1} - r_{i-1}\right] - G,$$

(2.101)

where r_i is the location of the facility operated by local service provider i; r_{i-1} and r_{i+1} are the locations of the facilities provided by local service provider$_{i-1}$ and local service provider$_{i+1}$, located to the left and right of local service provider$_i$, respectively; while w_{i-1} is the individual indifferent between the facilities provided by local service provider$_{i-1}$ and local service provider i, and w_{i+1} is the individual indifferent between the facilities provided by local service provider i and local service provider$_{i+1}$, as we can see in Figure 2.7.

At the third stage of the game (where m local service providers have entered the region and have already chosen their locations), it can be shown that the price equilibrium is unique and is characterized by:

$$P_i = \frac{1}{2}\left[\frac{P_{i+1}(r_i - r_{i-1})}{(r_{i+1} - r_{i-1})} + \frac{P_{i-1}(r_{i+1} - r_i)}{(r_{i+1} - r_{i-1})} + a(r_{i+1} - r_i)(r_i - r_{i-1})\right]$$ (2.102)

for $i \in \{1, 2, \ldots, m\}$.[81]

At the second stage of the game (where m local service providers have entered the region), it can be shown that a symmetrical price-location equilibrium exists.[82] We now characterize this symmetrical price-location equilibrium. The equilibrium prices, market areas, demands and profits for each

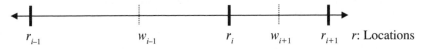

r_{i-1} w_{i-1} r_i w_{i+1} r_{i+1} r: Locations

Figure 2.7   Location of the individual indifferent between the facilities provided by local service provider$_{i-1}$ (local service provider i) and local service provider i (local service provider$_{i+1}$), represented by w$_{i-1}$ (w$_{i+1}$)

local service provider at the symmetrical price-location equilibrium as a function of the distance between local service providers (d) will be given by:

$$P_i^{LC}(d) = ad^2 \tag{2.103}$$

$$X_i^{LC}(d) \Rightarrow D_i^{LC}(d) = d \tag{2.104}$$

$$\Pi_i^{LC}(d) = ad^3 - G. \tag{2.105}$$

We now analyse the first stage of the game, in which local service providers decide whether to enter the region. It can be shown that a free-entry price-location equilibrium exists and that it is characterized by:

$$m^{EMQ} = \left(\frac{a}{G}\right)^{\frac{1}{3}} L \tag{2.106}$$

$$d^{EMQ} = \left(\frac{G}{a}\right)^{\frac{1}{3}}, \tag{2.107}$$

where m^{EMQ} is the equilibrium number of local service providers sustainable under free entry, and d^{EMQ} is the distance between providers at the free-entry price-location equilibrium under mill pricing and quadratic transport costs.

We can see here that:

$$m^{EMQ} > m^{EDQ} > m^{*Q}, \tag{2.108}$$

where m^{EDQ} is the free-entry equilibrium number of local service providers under discriminatory pricing and quadratic transport costs (given by equation (2A10.5) and m^{*Q} is the optimal number of local service providers under quadratic transport costs (given by equation (2A10.1).

Therefore, under mill pricing we obtain the excessive entry of local service providers offering local public goods with flexible technology in the region, as in the case of discriminatory prices. Nevertheless, in the case of mill pricing, the inefficiency is increased in comparison with discriminatory pricing: more excessive entry is observed under mill pricing. This is because in the case of mill pricing, competition is less intense than in the case of discriminatory pricing, where local service providers compete in price for each location in space, and at the borders of the service areas, competition is so intense that equilibrium prices fall to zero. This implies that the profits for a given number of providers are higher under mill pricing than under discriminatory pricing, serving as an incentive for additional entry in the former case.

Accordingly, the following result can be derived.

Result 2.13   The symmetrical free-entry price-location equilibrium under mill pricing and quadratic transport costs is characterized by the excessive entry of local service providers offering local public goods with flexible technology in the region. Nevertheless, this free-entry price-location equilibrium is more inefficient in terms of entry than that under discriminatory pricing. Accordingly, the inefficiencies identified under discriminatory pricing are increased under mill pricing, and in general, the opportunity to charge discriminatory prices based on location increases competition and improves welfare in this context.

2.4   HETEROGENEOUS LOCAL PUBLIC GOODS, $K \geq 2$

In the case of traditional all-purpose jurisdictions that provide local public goods, such as Tiebout's jurisdictions and the municipalities of Santiago, the overlapping of local service providers is not possible. This is because each local authority enjoys a territorial monopoly in its region, meaning that all people living there must pay taxes to the authority and use the services it provides. An important aspect of the idea of FOCJ is the possibility that these jurisdictions may overlap, in the sense that there may be many different service providers extending over the same geographical area. The proponents of FOCJ argue that this should increase competition as well as utility for individuals. However, we have seen that in the case of FOCJ offering homogeneous local public goods, optimality requires no overlapping, and at equilibrium they will never overlap.

The possibility of overlapping is related to the existence of different types of local public goods, which are not perfect substitutes for one another. For example, in the case of educational systems, if schools are identical in all aspects, at equilibrium individuals will simply choose the nearest school, which implies that the FOCJ offering schools will never overlap. This will also be the optimal distribution of individuals, because by patronizing the nearest school, their total transport costs are minimized. However, if schools can be differentiated, for example in the second language that they teach, with some offering English and others French, they will no longer be perfect substitutes. Some people may prefer English and others French, and in this case these FOCJ may overlap. If local public goods are not substitutes at all, and are instead perfect complements, such as schools and universities, for example, these FOCJ will always overlap.

Therefore we should analyse a setting in which the overlapping of FOCJ[83] occurs, in order to examine the possible advantages and problems that may arise from this overlapping. In the following section, we discuss an example in which overlapping takes place. In this example, there are two different types of essential local public goods, type 1 and type 2. By essential local public goods we mean that an individual must consume all the types of existing goods in order to obtain utility from them. As in the case of homogeneous local public goods, these local public goods are identical if they are of the same type. Thus, in our example, the *local public goods are perfect complements between types* and *perfect substitutes within a type*.[84] However, the two different types differ in the fixed cost of their facilities, implying different sizes of consumption groups in order to break even. For example, a primary school requires a lower investment than a university, and thus the size of the population needed to finance the former is smaller than that of the latter.

We assume that the number and locations of the local public goods are given and optimal for both types, and we concentrate only on price competition. We analyse the price equilibrium patterns of such a system and compare it with the price equilibrium patterns of a system of traditional all-purpose jurisdictions, in order to examine the potential effects on utility that this additional force of competition introduced by FOCJ, by *unbundling functions within jurisdictions*, may have for the individuals living in the region.[85]

In order to see how competition and overlapping among local service providers may affect the utility achieved by individuals, we consider in our example a situation in which there is *competition in local public-good type 1*, but *a monopoly in local public-good type 2*, and then we generalize the results for different degrees of competition in the different types.

The Optimal Allocation

First, we characterize in greater detail the optimal allocation for the case of two types of local public goods, $K = 2$. The planner's problem in this case is:

$$\text{Max}_{r(m_1, m_2)}, \, \phi(r) \int_{r=0}^{N} V(\cdot) \, dr \tag{2.109}$$

$$\text{s.t.} \int_{r=0}^{N} \phi(r) dr \geq m_1 G_1 + m_2 G_2, \tag{2.110}$$

where $V(\cdot)$ is described by equations (2.2) and (2.3).

As in the case of homogeneous local public goods, we work with an explicit form of utility function, $u(z, G_1, G_2) = z + g(G_1, G_2)$, where for $G_1 = 0$, $g(G_1, G_2) = 0$ and for $G_2 = 0$, $g(G_1, G_2) = 0$ and only if $G_1 > 0$ and $G_2 > 0$, $g(G_1, G_2) \geq 0$. This specific utility function, along with the fact that the amount of local public good of each type is given (G_i is fixed), reflects that there is no substitution between the local public goods of different types: they are *perfect complements*. This means that individuals, in order to derive utility from the consumption of the local public goods, must consume all the existing types. Thus, if consuming the local public goods is preferable to remaining in autarky, individuals will patronize one chosen facility for each type. They will travel to the nearest facility of each type.

Equivalent to the case of one type of local public good, the optimal number of facilities of each type will be given by the following expressions:[86]

$$m_1^* = \frac{1}{2}\left(\frac{a}{G_1}\right)^{\frac{1}{2}} N \qquad (2.111)$$

$$m_2^* = \frac{1}{2}\left(\frac{a}{G_2}\right)^{\frac{1}{2}} N. \qquad (2.112)$$

Thus, given the optimal number of facilities of each type, their corresponding optimal locations will be given by $\underline{r}^*(m_i^*)$, for $i \in \{1, 2\}$, as explained in Appendix 2A1. As before, given $\underline{r}^*(m_i^*)$, there is a whole range of possible pricing schemes that can support these facilities. The only condition that the optimal pricing scheme must satisfy is that:

$$\int_{r=0}^{N} \phi(r)dr = m_1 G_1 + m_2 G_2. \qquad (2.113)$$

For all $\phi(r)$ satisfying this condition, the aggregate constraint indirect utility will be the maximum one, and it will be given by the following expression:[87]

$$\int_{r=0}^{N} V[r, \underline{r}^*(m^*), G]dr = N[Y - G_1^{\frac{1}{2}} a^{\frac{1}{2}} - G_2^{\frac{1}{2}} a^{\frac{1}{2}} + g(G_1, G_2)]. \qquad (2.114)$$

As in the case of homogeneous local public goods, we also see in this case that the aggregate constraint indirect utility is independent of the specific pricing scheme. However, as before, different pricing schemes will imply different levels of constraint indirect utility at each location. There is only one pricing scheme for which the utility is the same for all individuals at each location. This is given by:

$$\phi^*(r) = G_1^{\frac{1}{2}}a^{\frac{1}{2}} + G_2^{\frac{1}{2}}a^{\frac{1}{2}} - t_{1j}(r) - t_{2j}(r) \quad \text{for } 0 \le r \le L, \quad (2.115)$$

where j is the specific facility of each type patronized by the individual located at r.

We can see that at the optimal allocation, given by $\underline{r}^*(m_i^*)$, for $i \in \{1, 2\}$, and with the pricing scheme $\phi^*(r)$, all of the individuals will obtain the same constraint indirect utility, which is:

$$V^*(\cdot) = Y - G_1^{\frac{1}{2}}a^{\frac{1}{2}} + G_2^{\frac{1}{2}}a^{\frac{1}{2}} + g(G_1, G_2). \quad (2.116)$$

As explained above, we consider in our example a situation in which there is competition in local public-good type 1, but a monopoly in local public-good type 2, and then we generalize the results for different degrees of competition in the different types. We then assume that the relationship among the fixed costs for each type of local public good, the transportation costs and the total population in the region is such that the optimal number of facilities for the case of local public-good type 1 is $m_1^* = 2$ and for type 2 is $m_2^* = 1$. This implies that, given equations (2.111) and (2.112), the relationship between G_1 and G_2 must satisfy the following condition:

$$G_2 = 4G_1. \quad (2.117)$$

Thus, equations (2.114), (2.115) and (2.116) become, respectively:

$$\int_{r=0}^{N} V[r, \underline{r}^*(m^*), G] dr = N[Y - 3G_1^{\frac{1}{2}}a^{\frac{1}{2}} + g(G_1, G_2)] \quad (2.118)$$

$$\phi^*(r) = 3G_1^{\frac{1}{2}}a^{\frac{1}{2}} - t_{1j}(r) - t_{21}(r) \quad \text{for } 0 \le r \le L \quad (2.119)$$

$$V^*(\cdot) = Y - 3G_1^{\frac{1}{2}}a^{\frac{1}{2}} + g(G_1, G_2). \quad (2.120)$$

Figure 2.8 shows the optimal allocation for this example, which is described by $\underline{r}^* (r_{11}^*, r_{12}^*, r_{21}^*)$, as well as the pricing scheme, $\phi^*(r)$, for which the utility achieved at each location is the same and the maximum possible and equal to V^* in equation (2.120).

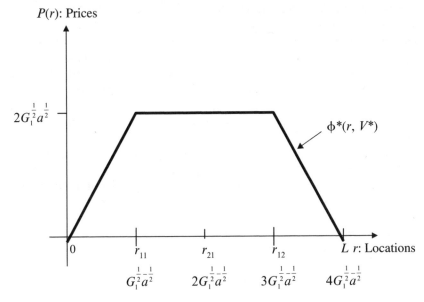

Figure 2.8 *Optimal allocation, described by r* (r_{11}*, r_{12}*, r_{21}*) in the x-axis, and pricing scheme ϕ*(r) in the y-axis, for the example where m_1* = 2 and m_2* = 1*

Price Equilibria in a System of One-purpose Competing Jurisdictions

This section discusses the nature of the equilibrium aggregate utility achieved by the individuals in this economy, relative to the maximum described by equation (2.114), if the local public goods are provided by a system of independent uni-functional local service providers, each providing one local public good and competing with one another for customers under de-localized membership.

We assume that the number of local service providers and the locations chosen by each of them for their facilities are both optimal and fixed, as explained above. Thus, the local service providers compete with one another for customers only in the pricing scheme that they choose in order to finance their own facilities. We shall then examine the nature of the equilibrium taxation scheme or price structure of each local service provider, and the factors upon which it will depend, in order to analyse the equilibrium aggregate utility.

Consider the same setting described above for the case of exclusively homogeneous local public goods (Section 2.3), but now for the example in this section. Let us then ask, given these optimal and fixed facility locations, each corresponding to one local service provider: what would be the equilibrium prices charged by each local service provider? As before, we assume that each local service provider sets its prices so as to maximize its profits (given by equation (2.19)). Accordingly, each local service provider, in order to maximize its profits, will choose the highest possible prices at each location. We denote the local service provider operating facility ij as local service provider$_{ij}$, where $i \in \{1, 2\}$ denotes the type of the local public good provided and $j \in \{1, 2, \ldots, m_i\}$ represents the index of the specific facility. We also denote as $P_{11}(r)$, $P_{12}(r)$ and $P_{21}(r)$ the price functions (or taxation schemes) set by local service provider$_{11}$, local service provider$_{12}$ and local service provider$_{21}$, respectively, and as $P_{11}^E(r)$, $P_{12}^E(r)$ and $P_{21}^E(r)$ the equilibrium price functions set by local service provider$_{11}$, local service provider$_{12}$ and local service provider$_{21}$, respectively.

We can then state that in this case, $\underline{P^E} = [P_{11}^E(r), P_{12}^E(r), P_{21}^E(r)]$ is a *price equilibrium* if and only if:

$$P_{ij}^E(r) = \arg \max \Pi_{ij}[P_{ij}(r), X_{ij}(\underline{P^E})] \tag{2.121}$$

$$\text{s.t. } V^E(r, \underline{P^E}) \geq \max\{u^{DC}; u^A; u_{il}[r, P_{il}^E(r)]\} \quad \text{for all } r \in X_{ij}(\underline{P^E}) \tag{2.122}$$

$$\text{s.t. } \Pi_{ij}[P_{ij}^E(r), X_{ij}(\underline{P^E})] \geq 0, \tag{2.123}$$

where $u_{il}[r, P_{il}^E(r)]$ is the utility obtained by an individual located at r when patronizing the facility of local service provider$_{il}$ for $l \neq j$ and $l \in \{1, 2, \ldots, (j-1), (j+1), \ldots, m_i\}$. This level of utility must be guaranteed by local service provider$_{ij}$ at location r in order to prevent its customers from patronizing another provider of local public-good type i.

Before continuing, some points that differ here from the case of exclusively homogeneous local public goods will be clarified. In our example, local public goods of different types are perfect complements. There is no substitution between the local public goods of different types. This means that in order to obtain utility from the consumption of the local public goods, individuals must consume all of the existing types. Thus, if the indirect utility achieved by individuals when patronizing their chosen facilities for each type of local public good is higher than the utility they could obtain in another region, u^{DC}, or by remaining in autarky, u^A, then they will consume all of the types of local public goods. But if the indirect utility when consuming the local public goods is smaller than that of the other two alternatives, they will not consume any type of the local public goods. This means that, for all local service providers, the prices set by the local service providers offering other types of local public goods will influence the prices they can charge, because the prices set for all types of local public goods will determine the indirect utility each individual will obtain at each location when consuming local public goods. This implies that there is a new sort of local competition, 'indirect local competition', which imposes some kind of restriction on each local service provider when they are setting their prices.

Let us define $P_T(r)$ as the total amount spent by each individual for local public goods at each location. It is then given by the following expression:

$$P_T(r) = P_{1j}(r) + P_{21}(r), \tag{2.124}$$

where j is the specific type 1 facility chosen by the individual located at r.

Analogous to the case of exclusively homogeneous local public goods, we denote by $P_T^{DC}(r, u^{DC})$ and $P_T^A(r, u^A)$ the price functions that describe the maximum prices that can be charged *in total* at each location in order to guarantee a utility of u^{DC} and u^A to the individual located at r, respectively. We can see that $P_T^{DC}(r, u^{DC})$ and $P_T^A(r, u^A)$ are given by the following expressions:[88]

$$P_T^{DC}(r, u^{DC}) = Y - t_{1j}(r) - t_{21}(r) + g(G_1, G_2) - u^{DC} \tag{2.125}$$

$$P_T^A(r, u^A) = g(G_1, G_2) - t_{1j}(r) - t_{21}(r), \tag{2.126}$$

where j is the specific type 1 facility chosen by the individual located at r.

We now analyse separately the case of the local service providers offering each type of local public good, in order to determine the prices they will set at each location.

The monopoly local service provider: type 2
In the case of local public-good type 2, the presence of only one service provider implies that in this case it enjoys some kind of monopoly situation in the region. However, its monopoly power to set prices is now restricted in three ways. As in the case of exclusively homogeneous local public goods, it is restricted by distant competition, represented by the minimum utility u^{DC} that must be guaranteed at each r in order to maintain its customers in the region, as well as by the fact that it must also guarantee a utility level of u^A at each location, in order to persuade the individuals residing at those locations to participate in the consumption of the local public goods. In this case, however, in addition to these two restrictions, the provider also faces a kind of indirect local competition presented by the providers of local public-good type 1, because the prices they charge and the locations they choose will influence the maximum prices it can charge at each location,

given u^{DC} and u^A.[89] As before, we denote by $P_{ij}^{DC}(r, u^{DC})$ and $P_{ij}^A(r, u^A)$ the price functions that describe the maximum prices that local service provider$_{ij}$ can charge at each location in order to guarantee a utility of u^{DC} and u^A to the individual located at r, respectively. We can see that $P_{21}^{DC}(r, u^{DC})$ and $P_{21}^A(r, u^A)$, given the prices set by local service provider$_{1j}$ (which is the local service provider the individual living at r chooses to patronize for local public-good type 1) are given by the following expressions:[90]

$$P_{21}^{DC}(r, u^{DC}) = P_T^{DC}(r, u^{DC}) - P_{1j}(r) \qquad (2.127)$$

$$P_{21}^A(r, u^A) = P_T^A(r, u^A) - P_{1j}(r), \qquad (2.128)$$

where $j \in \{1, 2\}$.

Thus, given $P_{1j}(r)$, the price set by local service provider$_{21}$, $P_{21}(r)$, will be:

$$P_{21}(r) = \min[P_{21}^{DC}(r, u^{DC}); P_{21}^A(r, u^A)] \qquad (2.129)$$

$$\text{s.t } \Pi_{21}[P_{21}(r)] \geq 0. \qquad (2.130)$$

The competing local service providers: type 1

For the case of the providers of local public-good type 1, the maximum prices they can charge will depend, as before (in the case of only one type of local public good) on distant competition, on the autarky option and also on the direct local competition presented by the other provider of local public-good type 1. However, in this case, in addition to these three restrictions, these providers also face some kind of indirect local competition presented by the provider of local public-good type 2, because the prices it charges and the location it chooses will influence the maximum price they can charge at each location, given u^{DC}, u^A and $u_{1j}[r, P_{1j}(r)]$ (as defined above). We denote by $P_{11}^{LC}\{r, u_{12}[r, P_{12}(r)]\}$ the price function that describes the maximum prices that local service provider$_{11}$ can charge at each location in order to prevent its customers from switching to local service provider$_{12}$ (and equivalently for local service provider$_{12}$).

We can see that $P_{11}^{DC}(r, u^{DC})$, $P_{11}^A(r, u^A)$ and $P_{11}^{LC}\{r, u_{12}^{LC}[r, P_{12}^A(r)]\}$, given the prices set by local service provider$_{21}$ and local service provider$_{12}$, are given by the following expressions (and equivalently for local service provider$_{12}$):

$$P_{11}^{DC}(r, u^{DC}) = P_T^{DC}(r, u^{DC}) - P_{21}(r) \qquad (2.131)$$

$$P_{11}^A(r, u^A) = P_T^A(r, u^A) - P_{21}(r) \qquad (2.132)$$

$$P_{11}^{LC}\{r, u_{12}[r, P_{12}(r)]\} = t_{12}(r) - t_{11}(r) + P_{12}(r). \qquad (2.133)$$

We can see from equations (2.131) and (2.132) that the local public goods offered by local service provider$_{11}$ (or local service provider$_{12}$), type 1, and local service provider$_{21,}$ type 2, are complementary goods,[91] and from equation (2.133) we can see that the local public goods provided by local service provider$_{11}$ and local service provider$_{12}$ are substitutes.[92]

Thus, given $P_{21}(r)$ and $P_{12}(r)$, the price set by local service provider$_{11}$ (equivalently by local service provider$_{12}$), $P_{11}(r)$, will be:

$$P_{11}(r) = \min(P_{11}^{DC}(r, u^{DC}); P_{11}^A(r, u^A); P_{11}^{LC}\{r, u_{12}[r, P_{12}(r)]\}) \qquad (2.134)$$

$$\text{s.t } \Pi_{11}[P_{11}(r)] \geq 0. \qquad (2.135)$$

Price equilibria when there is a monopoly in one type of local public good
In order to show the nature of the price equilibrium $\underline{P^E}$ in a system of one-purpose competing jurisdictions under heterogeneous local public goods, Appendix 2A11 analyses it for different ranges of the value of distant competition, represented by u^{DC}.

We show that the presence of a monopoly service provider, at least in one type of local public good, causes all possible gains for individuals derived from the existence of competition in the other local public-good types (because this competition imposes maximum prices that they can charge) to be completely captured by the monopoly service provider. This is due to the impossibility of substitution between different types of local public goods. Hence, if there is only one provider for one type of service, while all other types are offered by several providers in competition, in all of the equilibria the utility achieved by the individuals at each location will be the maximum between u^{DC} and u^A, but never higher than that, regardless of how many competitors are present in the other local public-good types. This means that the only restrictions to the monopolistic power of a single local public-good provider are imposed by the existence of alternative regions and by the autarky option, regardless of how intense the local competition may be in all other types of local public goods.

The principal results of the analysis presented in Appendix 2A11 can be summarized as follows:

Result 2.14 Given a system of competing local service providers offering different types of local public goods in a region, where the different types are perfect complements, and goods of the same type are perfect substitutes, with a distant competition restriction represented by u^{DC} and an autarky restriction represented by u^A, and with a monopoly local service provider for one type of local public good:

1. there are multiple equilibria in price functions for every value of distant competition;
2. the indirect utility achieved by each individual in the region at each equilibrium will be the maximum among the utility obtained in autarky (u^A) and the one obtained in the alternative region (u^{DC});
3. the indirect utility achieved by each individual in the region, given the equilibrium prices, will be equal to the maximum possible to be obtained (V^*) only if we have perfect distant competition (that is, $u^{DC} = V^*$). If distant competition is not so intense and $u^{DC} < V^*$, then the indirect utility achieved by each individual in the region will be smaller than V^*;
4. for relatively low levels of distant competition (that is, $u^{DC} \leq \underline{u}$)[93] the monopoly local service provider will enjoy positive profits at all equilibria; and
5. the gains for individuals represented by the competition among local service providers will be completely captured by the existence of a monopoly local service provider in one local public-good type.

It can be seen that if all local public goods were provided by a single all-purpose jurisdiction, as in Tiebout's jurisdictions and the municipalities of Santiago, the equilibrium price, depending on u^{DC}, would be given by $P_T^{DC}(r, u^{DC})$, as shown in *thin dotted* lines in all of the figures of Appendix 2A11. For all values of u^{DC}, individuals will achieve u^{DC} throughout the entire region. In this example, then, the utility obtained from a single all-purpose jurisdiction or from one-purpose competing service providers will be the same, and it will depend only on the exit option for individuals. The structure of local service providers in the region would then be irrelevant in this context, in terms of aggregate utility for individuals.

However, the fact that the equilibrium utility obtained by each individual in the case of competing local service providers is always equal to u^{DC} (regardless of how low u^{DC} falls), which is the same as the utility they would obtain from a single all-purpose jurisdiction, is given because there is only one provider of at least one type of local public good, and thus the monopoly local service provider absorbs all the gains for the individuals derived from the competition among local service providers. If there were more than one provider for each type of local public good, a minimum aggregate constraint indirect utility level would exist, determined by the existence of local competition in all types of local public goods. In that case, the aggregate constraint indirect utility achieved by the individuals in the region within a system of uni-functional competing local service providers would be higher than that which they could achieve in a single all-purpose jurisdiction, as we show in the next example.

Price equilibria when there is competition in all types of local public goods
Consider now that the relationship between the fixed costs for each type of local public good, the transportation costs and the total population in the region is such that $m_1^* = 3$ and $m_2^* = 2$. This implies that there is some degree of competition in both types of local public goods in the region, as we can see in Figure 2.9.

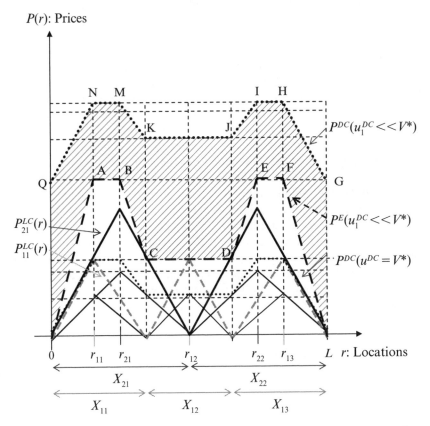

Figure 2.9   *Price equilibrium when there is competition in both types of local public goods, in the case of an all-purpose jurisdiction (dotted line for u_1^{DC}) and in the case of uni-functional competing jurisdictions (black dashed line)*

In the figure, we have assumed that space in the region is described by a circle of perimeter L rather than an interval $[0, L]$, in order to avoid the special cases that appear at the extremes of the interval, and thus to make every point in the region equivalent. This allows us to concentrate on the general results. The figure shows, in a *grey dashed* line and in a *thick black continuous* line, the maximum equilibrium prices that the local service providers offering local public goods types 1 and 2, respectively, can charge at each location, given the local competition among the local service providers offering local public goods of the same type. The *black dashed* line shows the sum of these two maximum prices for each location. This reflects the maximum prices individuals will have to pay at equilibrium at each location and the corresponding minimum utility that they will obtain under such a system. We can see that even with a very unfavourable exit option, such as u_1^{DC} in the figure, competition in both types of local public goods will guarantee a minimum utility level for each individual at each location in the region, and individuals will achieve $V(r) \gg u_1^{DC}$ throughout the region.

If all local public goods were provided by a classical single all-purpose jurisdiction in this case (as Tiebout's jurisdictions or Santiago municipalities), the equilibrium price, depending on u^{DC}, would be given by $P_T^{DC}(r, u_1^{DC})$, as shown in the *dotted* line in the figure, and all individuals would obtain u_1^{DC}. In this example, then, where there is competition in both types of local public goods, a system of uni-functional competing jurisdictions (like FOCJ) will increase the aggregate equilibrium utility level for the individuals in the region, compared to an all-purpose jurisdiction. The minimum aggregate utility gain for individuals under a system of FOCJ in this case is shown by the shaded area in the figure.

As the number of service providers offering the local public goods in the region increases for all types of local public goods, FOCJ will lead to a more favourable result, in terms of aggregate utility for individuals, than an all-purpose jurisdiction, and this aggregate utility will approach the maximum that can be achieved. This is the advantage of the additional competitive force introduced into the system by FOCJ. Nevertheless, because of the perfect complementarity of the local public goods, and the corresponding overlapping of jurisdictions, if there is only one local service provider present in the market for one type of local public good, this monopoly local service provider will absorb all the gains for individuals given by the competition among local service providers for all other types.

Result 2.15   Given a system of competing local service providers offering different types of local public goods in a region, where the different types are perfect complements and goods of the same type are perfect substitutes, with a distant competition restriction represented by u^{DC} and an autarky restriction represented by u^A, and with competition in all local public-good types in the region,

1. there will be a maximum equilibrium price that individuals will have to pay at equilibrium at each location, independent of the level of distant competition, u^{DC}, which will be less than or equal to the equilibrium price that an all-purpose jurisdiction would charge for each location, $P_T^{DC}(r, u^{DC})$;

2. there will be a minimum indirect utility level for the individuals at equilibrium at each location, independent of the level of distant competition, u^{DC}, which will be greater than or equal to this level of distant competition for each location;

3. the indirect utility achieved by the individuals in the region, given the equilibrium prices, will be equal to the maximum possible to be obtained, V^*, only if we have perfect distant competition ($u^{DC} = V^*$). If this is not the case ($u^{DC} < V^*$), the equilibrium utility will be lower than that but always higher than the one achievable under an all-purpose jurisdiction ($u^{DC} < V^E(r) < V^*$); and

4. the gains for individuals deriving from the competition among local service providers will increase as the competition in all types increases and as substitution between types increases.

FOCJ versus classical all-purpose jurisdictions[94]
In order to clarify the new forces of competition introduced into the system by FOCJ in comparison with classical all-purpose jurisdictions, we examine one final example. Assume that we have a region with two classical all-purpose jurisdictions, APJ_1 and APJ_2. In each all-purpose jurisdiction, the number and locations of the local public goods are optimal, and the utility obtained by moving to another jurisdiction is given by u^{DC}. In each jurisdiction, the relationship between the fixed costs of each type of local public good, the transportation costs and the total population in the jurisdiction is such that $m_1^* = 3$ and $m_2^* = 2$. Each jurisdiction's territory and the locations of the local public goods will appear in this case as shown in Figure 2.9. As explained above, the equilibrium price charged by each APJ will be given by $P_T^{DC}(r, u^{DC})$, as shown in a *dotted* line in Figure 2.10, and it will depend only on u^{DC}. The equilibrium utility for individuals will be given by u^{DC}. What will happen to the aggregate utility for the individuals in the region in this context if FOCJ provide the various local public goods instead of APJ?

As discussed in previous sections, there are two aspects of FOCJ that introduce new competitive forces into the system. On the one hand, individuals have the opportunity to choose the local service provider they wish

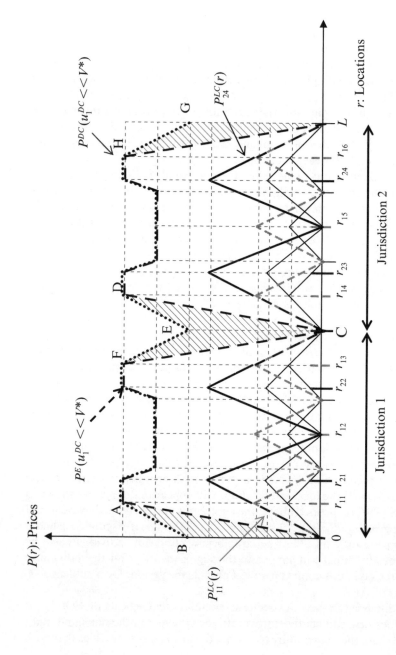

Figure 2.10   Price equilibrium in the case of two classical all-purpose jurisdictions (dotted line) and in the case of the introduction of de-localized membership (black dashed line).

to patronize for each type of local public good, independent of their place of residence; in other words, there is de-localized membership. At the same time, the jurisdictions are uni-functional.

We analyse separately the effects of each of these two factors on equilibrium prices and the corresponding aggregate utility for the individuals in the region. First, then, assume that the jurisdictions are still all-purpose, with each jurisdiction having three facilities offering local public-good type 1 and two offering local public-good type 2, located at the optimal locations. However, individuals now have the opportunity to decide which jurisdiction to patronize for the provision of all types of local public goods. In this case, the equilibrium prices and corresponding aggregate utility for the individuals will be as shown in a *black dashed* line in Figure 2.10. The aggregate utility gains in this case are represented by the shaded area in the figure.

This is because, although people may be relatively fixed to their locations and thus moving to another jurisdiction may be difficult (as reflected in a low u^{DC}), the opportunity to choose the jurisdiction that they want, independently of where they live, will reduce the monopoly power of the jurisdictions. Nevertheless, because the local public goods are provided at specific locations, while the beneficiaries of these services reside at other specific locations, and thus using the local public goods involves transport costs, the jurisdictions will still enjoy some degree of local monopoly power, which will be reduced only at the extremes of the jurisdictional territories.

This increase in competition and the corresponding increase in aggregate utility are possible only because the two jurisdictions are relatively close to each other (that is, transport costs to the other jurisdiction are not excessively high). If they were located far apart, patronizing the other jurisdiction's facilities would then be too expensive, and therefore, although individuals would have the choice of patronizing the other jurisdiction's facilities, at equilibrium they would not do so, and both jurisdictions would be equivalent to classical APJ.

Assume now, in addition to the specification that individuals may choose their jurisdictions, that these jurisdictions are uni-functional. In this case, the equilibrium prices and corresponding aggregate utility for the individuals will be as shown in a *black dashed* line in Figure 2.11, and the gains in utility will be given by the shaded area in the figure. In this case, uni-functionality increases local competition in the region, with a corresponding increase in aggregate utility for individuals. Nevertheless, if there remained only one facility for some local public-good in each previous APJ, the equilibrium prices and aggregate utility would be as in Figure 2.10, and uni-functionality would imply no additional gain in comparison with all-purpose jurisdictions.

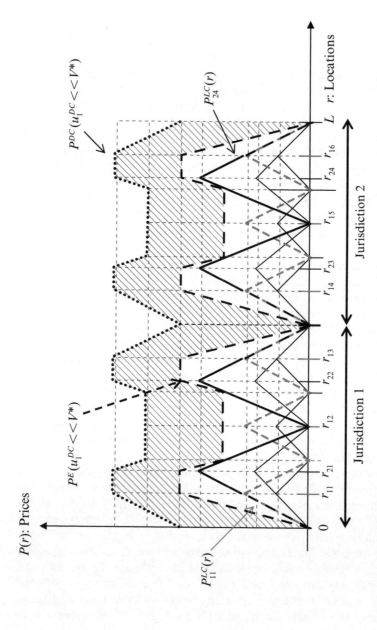

Figure 2.11 Price equilibrium in the case of two classical all-purpose jurisdictions (dotted line) and in the case of the introduction of de-localized membership and uni-functionality of jurisdictions, our interpretation of FOCJ (black dashed line)

Concluding Remarks

In this section, we analysed examples in which overlapping of FOCJ occurs, and we discussed the possible advantages and problems that this overlapping may imply. We specifically analysed the price equilibrium patterns of a system of overlapping FOCJ and compared it with the price equilibrium patterns of a system of classical all-purpose jurisdictions, in order to evaluate the gains that this additional competitive force introduced by FOCJ may or may not imply for the individuals in the region in terms of utility.

We have seen that if mobility of individuals is costless, and there is free entry and exit in jurisdiction formation ($u^{DC} = V^*$), FOCJ and the classical all-purpose jurisdictions lead to the same result, which is the highest possible aggregate utility for individuals. In this case, FOCJ will imply no additional gain in comparison with classical all-purpose jurisdictions.

However, if mobility is costly for individuals, and there are barriers to entry or exit in jurisdiction formation ($u^{DC} < u^*$), FOCJ may increase competition as well as aggregate utility for the individuals in a region. Nevertheless, this will be possible only if there is competition in all types of local public goods. If there is a monopoly service provider, even in only one type, all the gains from the increased competition in all other local public-good types will be redistributed to the monopoly local service provider, and individuals will obtain the same utility as if there were no competition of any type at all, and thus the result in terms of utility for individuals will be equivalent to that observed in the case of classical all-purpose jurisdictions.

Within our model, we can expect that FOCJ increase the utility of the individuals with respect to all-purpose jurisdictions. This is because the assumption of competition in all local public goods types is not necessarily so unrealistic. We could expect to have some degree of competition always, if the market areas are not too big (de-localized membership allows that) and because local public goods will probably have some degree of substitution between types.

It is also important to note that in real local jurisdictions there are alternative sources of competition which we have not formally discussed in the previous analysis, such as political competition, which may limit the monopoly power of the monopoly local government.[95]

Nevertheless, the absence of such alternative forces of competition may be a serious concern, especially if there are local public goods with large market areas (or economies of scale) and little substitution with other local public goods. Market power of a single unit becomes more of a concern in such a world.

Perhaps these kinds of local public goods should be more regulated in order that decentralization in their provision guarantees an increase in the utility level for individuals. On the other hand, local public goods with small market areas and a high substitution with other local public goods will not have this problem of monopolization and they could be provided by a system of FOCJ improving utility for individuals.

2.5 SUMMARY AND EXPLANATION OF THE MAIN RESULTS

In this chapter, we developed a framework designed to understand what can and cannot be achieved by the *unbundling of functions* and *de-localized membership* in jurisdictions for the provision of local public goods. Within this framework, we derived several interesting results related to these issues. In the following section we provide a summary and give some explanations of the main results of the chapter.

Optimal Allocation

We find that an important factor in determining the optimal allocation of local public goods in such a setting is *the existing trade-off between transportation costs and fixed costs*, a classical aspect of location models. On the one hand, if a large number of facilities exist to provide the local public goods, transportation costs for individuals will be reduced, and thus welfare increases. On the other, the existence of a large number of facilities implies higher infrastructure costs, thus reducing welfare. Moreover, the optimal number and size (in terms of individuals) of jurisdictions will be crucially affected by the relationship between transportation and infrastructure costs.

Pricing Policy

Regarding the pricing policy that will be chosen at equilibrium by competing local service providers offering homogeneous local public goods, we find that in general they will choose to charge *discriminatory prices with respect to location, in favour of the more distant locations*. The fact that the use of the local public goods is associated with some transportation costs, gives the local service providers a degree of local monopoly power over the individuals living near them. If local public goods are homogeneous – such as identical schools – they can serve as substitutes for one another, in the sense that individuals must choose only one of the possible facilities offering the local public good in order to enjoy the benefits of education. Nevertheless, their degree of substitution will vary with the individuals' locations, depending on the relative proximity of each facility to each location. A smaller (larger) difference in the distance from an individual's specific location to the different facilities will imply a higher (lower) degree of substitution among them. Only in the special case where the distances to the facilities providing the local public goods are equal, will these facilities be perfect substitutes for the individual located at that specific location. This implies that space and the presence of transportation costs decrease the degree of substitution between local public goods that are identical in all aspects except their location in space, giving local service providers some level of monopoly power in the setting of prices. This monopoly power is reduced as the distance to the local public-good increases, and thus the equilibrium price decreases. Competition at the borders of the region covered by a local service provider will be very intense, because of de-localized membership and the opportunity to charge discriminatory prices.[96]

Location Decisions

With respect to the location decisions made by local service providers offering homogeneous local public goods, the assumption about the flexibility of the local service providers' chosen locations and corresponding market areas is crucial. This flexibility depends on the types of fixed costs involved in the provision of each local public good. There is a wide possible range of degrees of flexibility, depending on the specific local public good, but we can distinguish two extreme cases of fixed cost technologies: *no location sunk cost technology*, in which no location-specific fixed costs are present, and *location sunk cost technology*, in which only location-specific fixed costs are present. With no location sunk cost technology, a local service provider can relocate its local public good without incurring any additional costs; that is, there are no sunk costs in its chosen location and corresponding market segment.[97] In contrast, with location sunk cost technology it is impossible for the local service provider to change its chosen location and corresponding market segment once it has been selected. Local public goods that are located in space are typical examples of sunk cost technologies. Their fixed costs are location specific.[98]

In the case of no location sunk cost technology, the equilibrium locations for competing local service providers will be unique and efficient, in the sense that they will minimize total transport costs for individuals, if local service providers can charge discriminatory prices. The equilibrium locations are efficient in this case because, given the locations of the other local public goods, a local service provider will choose the location for its facility that maximizes its profits. This location is the one that minimizes total transport costs for individuals, since this allows individuals to pay the highest possible price for access to the local public good, and thus the local service provider's profits will be maximized. At any other locations (inefficient locations), total transportation costs will be higher, and thus the prices people are able to pay for the use of local public goods, and the corresponding profits for the local service provider, will be lower. In the case of location sunk cost technology, the efficient locations are also an equilibrium, but there are additional possible location equilibria. Hence, in this case we have a multiplicity of equilibria, and we can also have location equilibria that are not efficient.

Entry Decisions

Regarding the entry decisions of local service providers offering homogeneous local public goods, the assumption about the technology of local public goods is also crucial. In the case of no location sunk cost technology, the equilibrium allocation under free entry of local service providers in the region is unique and is characterized by excessive entry, when the competition represented by other regions is very weak. This means that without the disciplinary force of competition from alternative regions, local competition alone is not enough to ensure optimality. The presence of the opportunity to move to another region reduces the equilibrium profits of local service providers and thus the incentive for entry, leading to a reduction in the inefficiency (excessive entry) in a situation characterized by local competition and no sunk cost technology. Only when we have perfect competition from other regions is the allocation achieved by competing local service providers the optimal one in the case of no sunk cost technology. This (that is, perfect competition from other regions) is Tiebout's implicit assumption in order to obtain optimality in a system of competing local jurisdictions.

In the case of location sunk cost technology, the optimal allocation is a free-entry equilibrium, but we can also have free-entry equilibria with excessive and insufficient entry. In this case we have a *multiplicity of equilibria*. This implies that the precise nature of the free-entry location price equilibrium among competing local service providers offering local public goods with location sunk cost technology in a particular region will depend on the history of that region. The existence of competition from other regions will decrease the profits of the local service providers present in a region and will prevent the entry of new providers, because of the lower profits that an entrant can earn, given a certain number of local service providers. This suggests that very intense competition from other regions can eliminate the potential excessive entry equilibria, as in the no location sunk cost technology case, but it also increases the range of possible insufficient entry equilibria. Insufficient entry cannot be corrected through an increase in competition from other regions. In fact, this inefficiency increases when competition from other regions becomes more intense.

Redistribution and Welfare

If we compare the various free-entry price-location equilibria characterized above in terms of winners and losers among the local service providers and individual customers, we can see that equilibria with higher entry levels are better in terms of utility for individuals and worse for local service providers in terms of profits than equilibria with lower levels of entry. In aggregate terms, individuals benefit from an increase in the number of local service providers, because the increased competition reduces equilibrium prices in aggregate terms, and transportation costs are also reduced due to the presence of additional facilities. For local service providers, an increase in the number of providers reduces their profits in aggregate terms, because the additional competition reduces equilibrium prices, and there are additional fixed costs due to the new facilities.

If we evaluate the various free-entry price-location equilibria characterized above in terms of welfare, we can identify the well-known trade-off between transportation costs and fixed costs as seen in location models. On the one hand, a high number of facilities will decrease total transportation costs and thus increase welfare (because individuals' utility increases), while on the other, a higher number of facilities results in higher fixed costs and thus lower welfare (because local service providers' profits decrease). The losses to local service providers caused by lower prices when the number of local public goods increases, represent gains for the individuals, and hence this does not affect overall welfare.

We have shown that the inefficiencies identified above (excessive and insufficient entry) are bounded. Welfare at both extremes of this range of possible free-entry price-location equilibria is at the lowest possible level, and it is the same at both extremes. Note that deviations from the optimal allocation are more costly in terms of welfare when they represent a reduction in the number of local public goods than when they represent an increase.

The presence of competition from other regions may increase welfare in the analysed region, but it may also decrease welfare. The result will depend on the type of technology of the local public goods provided. If competition from other regions increases, welfare at the free-entry price-location equilibria with no location sunk cost technology increases, but at the free-entry price-location equilibria with location sunk cost technology, it may decrease. In this case, the equilibria with excessive entry are reduced, but those with insufficient entry are expanded. If we have perfect competition from other regions, the free-entry price-location equilibrium with no location sunk cost technology is the optimal one in terms of welfare. The free-entry price-location equilibria with location sunk cost technology characterized by excessive entry are also eliminated in this case, but those with insufficient entry are expanded, and the new potential equilibria are less favourable in terms of welfare than the previous ones. This implies, therefore, that the presence of distant competition is not always welfare increasing. The result will depend on the type of technology of the local public good provided.

Note that in the case of local public goods with location sunk cost technology, the optimal allocation can be sustained as a free-entry price-location equilibrium, but distributions with insufficient and excessive entry can also be sustained as free-entry price-location equilibria by independent local service providers. Thus, with this type of technology, a monopoly local government (metropolitan local government) could solve the inefficiency arising from the coordination problem of the independent local service providers (the possibility of excessive or insufficient entry) and maximize welfare by providing all the local public goods in the optimal number and locations in the region. In this case, there would be no incentives for independent local service providers to enter the region and it will be maximizing its profits.

Elastic Demand

All the previous results hold under the assumption that the demand for local public goods is not responsive to price. In our setting, this implies that individuals travel only once to a facility in order to enjoy the local public goods offered there (or alternatively, the service provided by the local public goods is delivered only once to a residential location). However, we can imagine situations in which individuals may choose to visit the facility more frequently (or to request the service more frequently at their residential locations), depending on the price charged for the service.

If the individual demand for local public goods is responsive to price, and given a number of local service providers and their local public-good locations, the price equilibrium will be identical to that identified in the inelastic demand case. However, the profit function for local service providers will not depend on transportation costs in this case. This is because if transportation costs increase, for example, the equilibrium prices will increase (because the monopoly power increases), but the quantity demanded will decrease (because demand is now sensitive to price), and thus profits will not vary.

If the local public-good technology is characterized by no location sunk costs and there is free entry in the region, the free-entry price-location equilibrium will be characterized by excessive entry, as in the inelastic demand case. Thus, this result does not depend on demand elasticity and is in this sense robust. Nevertheless, if the local public-good technology is characterized by location sunk costs and there is free entry in the region, the free-entry price-location equilibrium may be characterized by insufficient or excessive entry, as in the inelastic demand case, but it can also be characterized only by excessive entry. This is because in this case, no matter how high or low the transportation costs are, they will not affect profits and thus not affect entry. However, different transportation costs will imply a different optimal number of local public goods (with a high transportation cost implying a higher number of local public goods at the optimal allocation). Thus, if transportation costs are very high in relation to the other parameters of the model, resulting in a higher number of local public goods at the optimal allocation, and this does not affect entry, then we would have equilibria with insufficient and with excessive entry. However, if the transportation costs are very low in relation to the other parameters of the model, resulting in a lower number of local public goods at the optimal allocation, and this, as we explained, does not affect entry in the case of price-responsive demand, then we would only have equilibria with excessive entry, even in the case of location sunk cost technology.

Moreover, if the demand for local public goods is price responsive, the optimal allocation will no longer be sustained as a free-entry price-location equilibrium under location sunk cost technology, if the frictions (transportation costs and fixed costs), are relatively small. In this case, a monopoly local government (metropolitan local government) could only partially solve the inefficiency generated by independent local service providers (which in this case would only be that of excessive entry), because when the optimal allocation is no longer sustainable and there are incentives for independent local service providers to enter the region, a monopoly local government will have to choose the smallest number of facilities consistent with no entry, and this will lead to some excessive capacity in the region.

Mill Pricing

All the previous results hold under the assumption that local service providers are free to charge their preferred prices. We have seen that at equilibrium, they will charge discriminatory prices based on location. However, a discriminatory price policy is usually difficult to implement in practice. There may be technical problems in implementation or institutional constraints that prevent price discrimination. Hence, in many cases local service providers will have to charge *mill prices* (that is, the price is the same for all individuals at the point of service, regardless of where they live).

As is well known in location economic theory, no price-location equilibrium would exist in our setting if local service providers charged mill prices. Nevertheless, as shown by D'Aspremont et al. (1979), under quadratic transportation costs, this lack of equilibrium can be solved. Using a slightly modified version of our model, in which transportation costs are now quadratic rather than linear, we analyse what happens to the equilibrium patterns identified earlier under discriminatory pricing if local service providers are no longer free to set prices and are forced to charge constant fees, independent of location. For this analysis, we assume that the local public-good technology is characterized by no location sunk costs, and that the option to move to another region is not present.

With respect to the equilibrium locations under quadratic transportation costs, in the case of discriminatory pricing, the efficient locations are equilibrium locations, as in the case with linear transport costs. This implies that the fact that the efficient locations are an equilibrium under discriminatory pricing is a relatively robust result with regard to the form of the transport cost function. In the case of mill pricing, the efficient locations may not be an equilibrium in a system of competing local service providers. This is because under mill pricing, local service providers have to charge the same price for all locations, and thus, in order to reduce price competition, they will seek to locate as far away as possible from their competitors, that is, at inefficient locations. In the case of discriminatory pricing, price competition is present at every point in space, and thus providers have no opportunity to reduce price competition by changing their locations. Therefore, as explained earlier, providers will maximize their profits by choosing the locations that minimize total transportation costs, which are the efficient locations. This implies that in this setting, discriminatory pricing with respect to location is more favourable in terms of welfare than mill pricing, because the equilibrium locations in the case of discriminatory pricing are equivalent to the optimal ones.

The equilibrium allocation under mill pricing and quadratic transportation costs is characterized by excessive entry of local service providers offering local public goods in the region, as in the case of discriminatory pricing. Nevertheless, in the case of mill pricing, the inefficiency is increased in comparison with discriminatory pricing: more excessive entry is observed. This is because in the case of mill pricing, competition is less intense than in the case of discriminatory pricing, where local service providers compete in price for each location in space, and at the borders of the service areas, competition is so intense that equilibrium prices fall to zero. This implies that the profits for a given number of providers are higher under mill pricing than under discriminatory pricing, serving as an incentive for additional entry in the mill pricing case.

The results above clearly show that the inefficiencies identified under discriminatory pricing are increased under mill pricing, and that in general the opportunity to charge discriminatory prices based on location increases competition and improves welfare in a spatial context.

Heterogeneous Local Public Goods

As noted in the general introduction, an important aspect of the idea of FOCJ is the possibility that these units may overlap, in the sense that many different service providers may extend over the same geographical area, potentially increasing competition and utility for individuals.[99] However, we have shown that in our setting for the case of local service providers providing homogeneous local public goods, optimality requires no overlapping, and at equilibrium they will never overlap.

The possibility of overlapping service areas, along with the idea of unbundling the services provided by local service providers are linked to the existence of different types of local public goods which are not perfect substitutes for each other.

Thus, in order to analyse the question of *overlapping* service areas and the idea of *unbundling* the services provided by local service providers, it is necessary to consider a setting containing different types of local public goods. In the final part of this chapter, we analysed some examples in which overlapping and unbundling of functions occur, and we discussed the possible advantages and problems resulting from this. We specifically analysed the price equilibrium patterns of a system of overlapping uni-functional competing local service providers, in which the local public goods are perfect complements between types (such as schools and universities) and perfect substitutes within a type (as with identical schools). We compared this with the price equilibrium patterns of a system of classical all-purpose jurisdictions, in order to determine the potential utility gains or losses that the additional force of competition resulting from the unbundling of services may imply for the individuals in the region.

We showed that if competition from other regions is very fierce, a system of overlapping uni-functional competing local service providers (our interpretation of FOCJ) and the classical all-purpose jurisdictions will lead to the same result, which is the highest possible aggregate utility for individuals. In this case, the possibility of unbundling will bring no additional gain in comparison with classical all-purpose jurisdictions. However, if competition from other regions is very weak, the possibility of unbundling activities may increase competition and aggregate utility for the individuals in a region. Nevertheless, this will be possible only if there is competition in all types of local public goods. If there is a monopoly local service provider in the region, even for only one type of service, all the gains from the increased competition in all other types of local public goods will be redistributed to the monopoly local service provider, and individuals will obtain the same utility as if there were no competition in any type at all. The result in terms of utility for individuals will be equivalent to the case of the classical all-purpose jurisdictions. Crucial to this result is the assumption of perfect complementarity among the local public goods of different types. If there is some degree of substitution possible between types of local public goods, a monopoly local service provider in one type could not obtain all the gains from increased competition in the other types.

Finally, we discussed an argument that is commonly put forward in favour of FOCJ, which is that the various government services differ with respect to the economies of scale in production and thus the optimal geographical area. Frey and Eichenberger (1999: 5) state:

> The various public services (for example parks, schools, waste treatment plants, national defense and so on) extend very differently over physical space and have different degrees of scale economies (or diseconomies). Moreover demand varies strongly over space because it depends on several factors which can differ strongly according to location. As a consequence it is efficient when not all services are provided by the same governmental unit but instead supplied by specialized functional jurisdictions adjusted to the corresponding tasks.

With respect to this point, the fact that an APJ (all-purpose jurisdiction) provides all the local public goods in an area does not necessarily imply that it will not take advantage of the economies of scale associated with their provision. Actually, in our setting, it would provide the optimal number of each type of local public good in order to increase its profits, which implies taking advantage of the economies of scale. This is because by providing the optimal number and locations for the local public goods, the total transport costs plus fixed costs are minimized and so it can charge the highest possible prices to the population, maximizing its profits.[100]

The problem may be related to the possibility that the APJ is too small for the provision of some local public goods with large economies of scale and which need a larger population in order to take advantage of them. The other related problem is the integer problem mentioned in the general introduction. As explained there, uni-functionality of FOCJ would reduce the severity of the integer problem, at least for the provision of some local public goods, namely those whose optimal consumption group is small in comparison with the region's total population. In this sense it is true that the fact that 'various government services differ with respect to the

economies of scale in production and thus the optimal geographical area'
is an argument in favour of FOCJ, but not for the reason of exploiting the
economies of scale. As we explained, because an APJ provides all the local
public goods in an area, this does not necessarily imply that it will not take
advantage of the economies of scale associated with their provision.

APPENDIX 2A1   THE OPTIMAL ALLOCATION FOR HOMOGENEOUS LOCAL PUBLIC GOODS

In this appendix we characterize the optimal allocation in more detail for
the case of one type of local public good, $K = 1$. The planner's problem in
this case is:

$$\text{Max}_{\underline{r}(m),\phi(r)} \int_{r=0}^{N} V(\cdot)dr \qquad (2A1.1)$$

$$\text{s.t.} \int_{r=0}^{N} \phi(r)dr \geq mG, \qquad (2A1.2)$$

where

$$\int_{r=0}^{N} V(\cdot)dr$$

correspond to the aggregate constraint indirect utility function.

Optimal Locations for a Given Number of Facilities, *m*

To solve this, let us begin by assuming that the number of facilities, m, is
given, and let us then ask what their optimal location, $\underline{r}^*(m)$, would be,
which is the location that maximizes (2A1.1) s.t. (2A1.2). First, assume that
there is only one facility, $m = 1$. Which location would be the optimal one
from the planner's viewpoint? It is straightforward to show that this is the
centre location. Formally, the planner's problem in this case is:

$$\text{Max}_{r_1,\phi(r)} \int_{r=0}^{N} V(\cdot)\, dr \qquad (2A1.3)$$

$$\text{s.t.} \int_{r=0}^{N} \phi(r)dr \geq G. \qquad (2A1.4)$$

We assume that individuals have quasilinear preferences, represented by the following quasilinear utility function, $u(z, G) = z + g(G)$.[101]

Using this explicit form of utility function, the planner's problem is then:[102]

$$\text{Max}_{r_1} \int_{r=0}^{N} [Y - a(|r - r_1|) - \phi(r) + g(G)]dr \qquad (2A1.5)$$

$$\text{s.t.} \int_{r=0}^{N} \phi(r)dr \geq G. \qquad (2A1.6)$$

Solving this, we obtain $r_1{}^* = \frac{1}{2}L$.[103]

Assume now that there are two facilities, $m = 2$. What would be the optimal location for both facilities in this case? The planner's problem would be:

$$\text{Max}_{r_1, r_2, \phi(r)} \int_{r=0}^{N} [Y - a(|r - r_{j_1(r)}|) - \phi(r) + g(G)]dr \qquad (2A1.7)$$

$$\text{s.t.} \int_{r=0}^{N} \phi(r)dr \geq 2G, \qquad (2A1.8)$$

where $j_1(r)$ corresponds to the specific facility j of the local public good chosen by the individual located at r, where $j \in \{1, 2\}$.

Because both facilities are identical, except for their location, each individual will patronize the nearest facility of each type. Thus, the indirect utility function will depend only on the location of the nearest facility for each person located at r, and the planner's problem can be expressed as follows:

$$\text{Max}_{r_1, r_2} \int_{r=0}^{N} Y dr - \int_{r=0}^{r_1} a(r_1 - r)dr - \int_{r=r_1}^{(r_1+r_2)/2} a(r - r_1)dr$$

$$- \int_{r=(r_1+r_2)/2}^{r_2} a(r_2 - r)dr - \int_{r=r_2}^{N} a(r - r_2)dr - \int_{r=0}^{N} \phi(r)dr + \int_{r=0}^{N} g(G)dr$$

$$(2A1.9)$$

$$\text{s.t.} \int_{r=0}^{N} \phi(r)dr \geq 2G. \qquad (2A1.10)$$

Solving this, we obtain $r_1^* = 1/4L$ and $r_2^* = 3/4L$.[104] We can generalize this for any given number of facilities, m. In this case, the optimal location for each facility, $j \in \{1, 2, \ldots, m\}$ of the m facilities will be:

$$\underline{r}^* = (r_1^*, r_2^*, \ldots, r_m^*), \qquad (2A1.11)$$

where

$$r_j^* = \left[\frac{(2j-1)}{2m}\right]L. \qquad (2A1.12)$$

From this we can see that for any given number of facilities m, their optimal locations are those that minimize total transport costs.

Optimal Number of Facilities Given their Optimal Locations

Now we can return to the original planner's problem, as described by equations (2A1.1) and (2A1.2). We now need to determine the optimal number of facilities, m^*, using the fact that for any m, their optimal locations are described by equations (2A1.11) and (2A1.12). Using the explicit form of our utility function, the planner's problem is then:

$$\text{Max}_{\underline{r}^*(m)} \int_{r=0}^{N} [Y - a(|r - r_{j(r)}|) - \phi(r) + g(G)]d \qquad (2A1.13)$$

$$\text{s.t.} \int_{r=0}^{N} \phi(r)dr \geq mG, \qquad (2A1.14)$$

where $j(r)$ corresponds to the specific facility j of the local public good chosen by the individual located at r, where $j \in \{1, 2, \ldots, m\}$. The maximization problem presented in equations (2A1.13) and (2A1.14) can be rewritten as follows:

$$\text{Max}_{\underline{r}^*(m)} \int_{r=0}^{N} Ydr - TTC(m) - mG + \int_{r=0}^{N} g(G)dr, \qquad (2A1.15)$$

where

$$TTC(m) = \int_{r=0}^{N} a(|r - r_{j(r)}|)dr$$

correspond to the total transportation costs incurred by the individuals in aggregate, when there are m facilities located at the optimal locations.

Formally, that is:

$$TTC(m) = \int_0^N a(|r - r_{j(r)}|)dr = \int_0^{r_1} a(r_1 - r)dr + \int_{r_1}^{(r_1+r_2)/2} a(r - r_1)dr$$

$$+ \int_{(r_1+r_2)/2}^{r_2} a(r_2 - r)dr + \ldots \int_{r_m}^N a(r - r_m)dr. \qquad (2A1.16)$$

We can solve this in order to determine exactly how the total transportation costs depend on m. Given that at the optimum the facilities are symmetrically distributed in space, as described by equations (2A1.11) and (2A1.12), we can calculate the average distance travelled by individuals, which we denote by $r^a(m)$, and thus we can more easily calculate the total transportation costs.

$$r^a(m) = \tfrac{1}{4}\left(\frac{N}{m}\right) \quad m < N$$
$$= 0 \qquad m = N \qquad (2A1.17)$$

Thus, the total transportation costs will be given by the following expression:

$$TTC(m) = r^a(m)aN = \tfrac{1}{4}\left(\frac{N}{m}\right)aN \quad m < N$$
$$= 0 \qquad m = N. \qquad (2A1.18)$$

Substituting equation (2A1.18) into (2A1.15) and solving the integrals, the planner's problem presented in equation (2A1.15) can now be written as follows:

$$\text{Max}_m \, YN - \tfrac{1}{4}\left(\frac{N}{m}\right)aN - mG + g(G)N. \qquad (2A1.19)$$

From the FOC[105] we obtain the optimal number of facilities:

$$m^* = \frac{1}{2}\left(\frac{a}{G}\right)^{\frac{1}{2}}N. \qquad (2A1.20)$$

From equation (2A1.20) we can see that the optimal number of facilities in the region crucially depends on the trade-off between transportation costs and the costs of supplying the local public goods.

Note that it is probable that m^* is not an integer, and therefore, because it is not possible to provide fractions of a local public good, the optimal number of facilities at the second-best allocation (given this additional restriction that m must be an integer) will be contained in $(m^* - 1, m^* + 1)$ and will be the integer that maximizes equation (2A1.19). The integer problem is discussed in detail in Scotchmer (1985), so it will be ignored in the following analysis and we shall assume that m^* is an integer.

APPENDIX 2A2   MONOPOLY PRICE EQUILIBRIUM FOR DIFFERENT LEVELS OF DISTANT COMPETITION

In order to show the nature of the monopoly price equilibrium, we will define it for different ranges of value of u^{DC}.

1 $u^{DC} \leq u^A$

In this case (as with u_3^{DC} in Figure 2.1), the utility achieved in a situation of autarky exceeds that achieved in an alternative region, and thus the equilibrium price function and the corresponding constraint indirect utility achieved at equilibrium will be:

$$P^E(r) = P^A(r, u^A) \tag{2A2.1}$$

$$V^E(r) = u^A. \tag{2A2.2}$$

In this case, $\Pi[P^E(r)] > 0$ and the aggregate constraint indirect utility is lower than the maximum that it is possible to achieve, which is given by equation (2.14). This can be seen in Figure 2.1, where the utility achieved at each location at equilibrium, u^A, is smaller than V^*.

2 $u^A < u^{DC} < V^*$

In this case (for example, u_2^{DC} in Figure 2.1), the utility achieved in the other regions exceeds that obtained in a situation of autarky, and thus the equilibrium price function and the corresponding constraint indirect utility achieved at equilibrium will be:

$$P^E(r) = P^{DC}(r, u^{DC}) \tag{2A2.3}$$

$$V^E(r) = u^{DC}. \tag{2A2.4}$$

In this case, $\Pi[P^E(r)] > 0$, but it is smaller than in the other case, and the aggregate constraint indirect utility is lower than the potential maximum, but still higher than it was before. This is because competition from the other regions is now more intense.

3 $u_1^{DC} = V^*$

In this case ($u_1^{DC} = V^*$ in a *continuous black* line in Figure 2.1), the equilibrium price function and the corresponding constraint indirect utility achieved at equilibrium will be:

$$P^E(r) = P^{DC}(r, u^{DC} = V^*) = P^*(r) \tag{2A2.5}$$

$$V^E(r) = u^{DC} = V^*. \tag{2A2.6}$$

Only in this case will the monopolist charge prices equal to $P^*(r)$ at equilibrium, thus making the aggregate constraint indirect utility the maximum that is possible to achieve, given the resources constraint. Consequently, $\Pi[P^E(r)] = 0$.

4 $V^* < u^{DC}$

If $V^* < u^{DC}$ (for example u_1^{DC} in Figure 2.1), the price structure that will guarantee a minimum utility level of u_1^{DC} will be that in which $\Pi[P^E(r)] < 0$ (because for V^*, $\Pi[P^*(r, V^*)] = 0$). Thus, the local service provider will prefer not to provide the local public good in this case.

Accordingly, for a given level of distant competition ($u^{DC} = \gamma V^*$)[106] and autarky restriction ($u^A = Y$), we can then characterize the price equilibrium as follows:[107]

$$P^E(r) = \begin{cases} g(G) - ar & \text{for} & u^{DC} \leq u^A \\ g(G) - ar - (u^{DC} - Y) & \text{for} & u^A \leq u^{DC} \leq V^* \\ G^{\frac{1}{2}} a^{\frac{1}{2}} - ar & \text{for} & u^{DC} = V^* \end{cases} \tag{2A2.7}$$

$$X_1 = [-r^b, r^b] \tag{2A2.8}$$

$$r^b = \begin{cases} \frac{1}{a}[g(G)] & \text{for} & u^{DC} \leq u^A \\ \frac{1}{a}[g(G) - (u^{DC} - Y)] & \text{for} & u^A \leq u^{DC} \leq V^* \\ G^{\frac{1}{2}} a^{\frac{1}{2}} & \text{for} & u^{DC} = V^* \end{cases} \tag{2A2.9}$$

$$\Pi[P^E(r)] = \begin{cases} \frac{1}{a}[g(G)]^2 - G & \text{for} & u^{DC} \leq u^A \\ \frac{1}{a}[g(G) - (u^{DC} - Y)]^2 - G & \text{for} & u^A \leq u^{DC} \leq V^* \\ 0 & \text{for} & u^{DC} = V^* \end{cases} \tag{2A2.10}$$

APPENDIX 2A3 PRICE EQUILIBRIUM FOR TWO COMPETING LOCAL SERVICE PROVIDERS FOR DIFFERENT LEVELS OF DISTANT COMPETITION

In order to show the nature of the price equilibrium in our setting, we define it, as before, for different ranges of the value of u^{DC}. For simplicity, we assume that we have a region whose size[108] is such that, given the provision cost of the local public good (G) and the transportation costs per unit of distance (a), the optimal number of facilities corresponds to $m^* = 2$. Given equation (2.10) this implies that the size of the region in terms of G and a is given by $L = 4G^{\frac{1}{2}}a^{-\frac{1}{2}}$. We also assume that the two facilities are located at the optimal locations in the region, which correspond in this case to $r_1^* = 1/4L = G^{\frac{1}{2}}a^{-\frac{1}{2}}$ and $r_2^* = 3/4L = 3G^{\frac{1}{2}}a^{-\frac{1}{2}}$, respectively. Furthermore, we assume that the local public good is so preferred that $[g(G) - G^{\frac{1}{2}}a^{\frac{1}{2}}] > 2G^{\frac{1}{2}}a^{\frac{1}{2}}$, and thus $P_1{}^A(r, u^A)$ is as we can see in Figure 2A3.1 in a *thin dashed* line. We specify that $\bar{u} = Y - 3G^{\frac{1}{2}}a^{\frac{1}{2}} + g(G)$.

1 $u^{DC} \leq \bar{u}$

In this case (for example, u_1^{DC}, u_2^{DC} or $u_3^{DC} = \bar{u}$ in the figure), $P_1^{LC}(r)$ is lower than $P_1^{DC}(r, u^{DC})$ and $P_1^A(r, u^A)$ for all r, and thus the equilibrium price vector, $\underline{P^E} = [P_1^E(r), P_2^E(r)]$, and the corresponding constraint indirect utility achieved at equilibrium will be given by:

$$P_1^E(r) = \begin{cases} P_1^{LC}(r) = t_2(r) - t_1(r) & \text{if} \quad 0 \leq r \leq 2G^{\frac{1}{2}}a^{-\frac{1}{2}} \\ 0 & \text{if} \quad 2G^{\frac{1}{2}}a^{-\frac{1}{2}} \leq r \leq 4G^{\frac{1}{2}}a^{-\frac{1}{2}} \end{cases} \quad (2A3.1)$$

$$P_2^E(r) = \begin{cases} P_2^{LC}(r) = t_1(r) - t_2(r) & \text{if} \quad 2G^{\frac{1}{2}}a^{-\frac{1}{2}} \leq r \leq 4G^{\frac{1}{2}}a^{-\frac{1}{2}} \\ 0 & \text{if} \quad 0 \leq r \leq 2G^{\frac{1}{2}}a^{-\frac{1}{2}} \end{cases} \quad (2A3.2)$$

$$V^E(r) = \begin{cases} u_2[r, P_2^E(r)] = Y - t_2(r) + g(G) & \text{for} \quad 0 \leq r \leq 2G^{\frac{1}{2}}a^{-\frac{1}{2}} \\ u_1[r, P_1^E(r)] = Y - t_1(r) + g(G) & \text{for} \quad 2G^{\frac{1}{2}}a^{-\frac{1}{2}} \leq r \leq 4G^{\frac{1}{2}}a^{-\frac{1}{2}} \end{cases}$$

$$(2A3.3)$$

This can be seen in Figure 2A3.1, where a *continuous black* line shows the pricing scheme $P_i^*(r, V^*)$ for $i \in \{1, 2\}$, with which all individuals obtain the same and maximum utility V^*.[109] The figure shows only the function for the local service provider of facility 1, because the case of the local service provider offering facility 2 is symmetric. In *dotted* lines we show

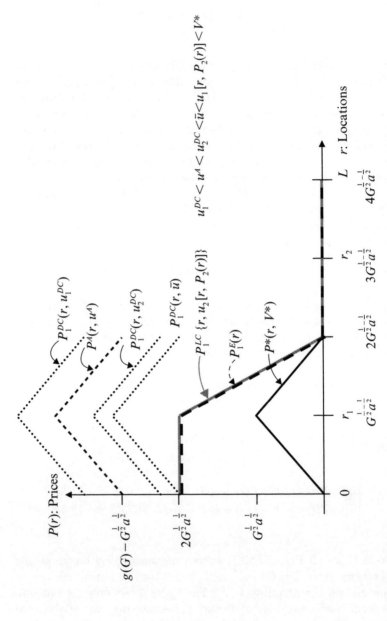

Figure 2A3.1 *Equilibrium price function for competing local service provider 1 ($P_1^E(r)$ in a thick dashed line) when distant competition is very weak* ($u^{DC} \leq \bar{u}$)

$P_1^{DC}(r, u^{DC})$ for some values of $u^{DC} \leq \bar{u}$, along with $P^A(r, u^A)$ in a *thin dashed* line, as noted above, $P_1^{LC}(r)$ in a *continuous grey* line and $P_1^E(r)$ in a *thick dashed* line. Note that for every value of u^{DC}, we obtain one different price function $P_1^{DC}(r, u^{DC})$, and we have a unique price function $P_1^{LC}(r)$. In the figure we can see that for those cases where the exit option is very unattractive, represented by a u^{DC} beneath some level given by u, the equilibrium price function will be unique and determined only by the local competition, $P_1^{LC}(r)$, independent of the exact value of u^{DC}. This is because the effect of nearby competition dominates the effect of distant competitors for $u^{DC} \leq \bar{u}$ (given the assumption made about u^A).

Note that at location $r = |r_j - r_i|/2$ (which corresponds to location $r = 2G^{1/2}a^{-1/2}$ in the figure), neither competing local service provider has a location advantage relative to the other, $t_j(r) - t_i(r) = 0$, so they will compete until prices fall to zero. Beyond this, one of them will have an advantage over the other, so it will be able to charge positive prices, but the maximum that the other one will be able to charge at equilibrium in this region is zero.

In this case, the aggregate constraint indirect utility achieved by individuals will be different for each r in region $0 \leq r \leq 2G^{\frac{1}{2}}a^{-\frac{1}{2}}$, and symmetrical for region $2G^{\frac{1}{2}}a^{\frac{1}{2}} \leq r \leq 4G^{\frac{1}{2}}a^{-\frac{1}{2}}$. We can see that the utility achieved at equilibrium at each r will decrease with distance from the centre of the region. The minimum utility achieved by each individual in the region will be $V(r) = Y - 3G^{\frac{1}{2}}a^{\frac{1}{2}} + g(G)$, which will be reached at the extreme points of the region ($r = 0$ and $r = L$, where each local service provider has the greatest monopoly power). Then, as one approaches the centre of the region, utility increases until it reaches its highest value, V^*, for the individual living at the centre ($r = |r_j - r_i|/2$). We can see that competition between local service providers guarantees that only the individual located at the centre location obtains the highest possible utility, V^*. This is because that is the only point where both providers compete without one having an advantage over the other, and so they have to make their best offer.

We can see in equations (2A3.1) and (2A3.2) that each local service provider's opportunity to charge positive prices for identical local public goods exists only because of its location advantage relative to the other for each r, and thus for each provider, equilibrium prices are determined by the differential transportation costs of patronizing the other provider.

2 $\bar{u} < u^{DC} \leq V^*$

If u^{DC} increases, $u^{DC} > \bar{u}$, and at values such as, for example, u_4^{DC}, u_5^{DC} and u_6^{DC} in Figure 2A3.2, $P_1^{DC}(r, u^{DC})$ and $P_1^{LC}(r)$ will intersect, and thus the equilibrium prices will be $P_1^E(r, u_4^{DC})$, $P_1^E(r, u_5^{DC})$ and $P_1^E(r, u_6^{DC})$ respectively, as shown in *thick dashed* lines in Figure 2A3.2. In general, the equilibrium

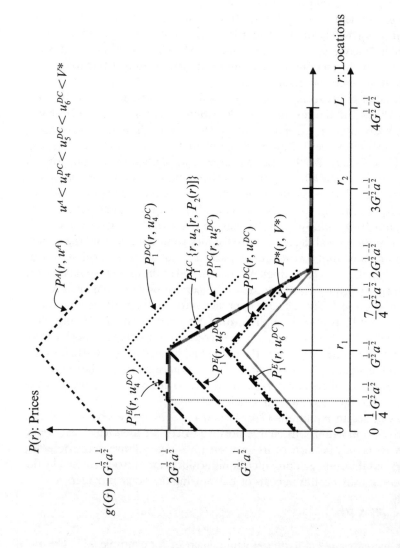

Figure 2A3.2 Equilibrium price function for competing local service provider 1 ($P_1^E(r)$) in thick dashed lines) when distant competition is binding ($u^{DC} > \bar{u}$).

price vector, $\underline{P^E} = [P_1^E(r), P_2^E(r)]$, and the corresponding constraint indirect utility achieved at equilibrium will be given in this case by:

$$P_1^E(r) = \begin{cases} \min[P_1^{DC}(r, u^{DC}); \ P_1^{LC}(r) = t_2(r) - t_1(r)] & \text{if} \quad 0 \le r \le 2G^{\frac{1}{2}}a^{-\frac{1}{2}} \\ 0 & \text{if } 2G^{\frac{1}{2}}a^{-\frac{1}{2}} \le r \le 4G^{\frac{1}{2}}a^{-\frac{1}{2}} \end{cases}$$

(2A3.4)

$$P_2^E(r) = \begin{cases} \min[P_2^{DC}(r, u^{DC}); \ P_2^{LC}(r) = t_1(r) - t_2(r)] & \text{if } 2G^{\frac{1}{2}}a^{-\frac{1}{2}} \le r \le 4G^{\frac{1}{2}}a^{-\frac{1}{2}} \\ 0 & \text{if} \quad 0 \le r \le 2G^{\frac{1}{2}}a^{-\frac{1}{2}} \end{cases}$$

(2A3.5)

$$V^E(r) = \begin{cases} \max[u_1^{DC}; \ u_2(\cdot) = Y - t_2(r) + g(G) & \text{for} \quad 0 \le r \le 2G^{\frac{1}{2}}a^{-\frac{1}{2}} \\ \max[u_2^{DC}; \ u_1(\cdot) = Y - t_1(r) + g(G) & \text{for} \quad 2G^{\frac{1}{2}}a^{-\frac{1}{2}} \le r \le 4G^{\frac{1}{2}}a^{-\frac{1}{2}} \end{cases}$$

(2A3.6)

The equilibrium price function will be unique for each value of u^{DC}. We can also see that at each equilibrium, if $u^{DC} < V^*$, $\Pi_i[P_i^E(r)] > 0$ and the constraint indirect utility function achieved by each individual will be less than V^* for all of them, except the one located at the centre of the region (as before). Only when $u^{DC} = V^*$, $\underline{P^E} = P^*$, $\Pi_i[P_i^E(r)] = 0$ and all the individuals will obtain V^*, implying that the aggregate constraint indirect utility is maximum.

We can see that when distant competition becomes intense, as reflected in $u^{DC} > \bar{u}$, the local monopoly power exercised by each of the local service providers in the region will now be constrained by this distant competition. This can be seen in Figure 2A3.2, for example in the case where $u^{DC} = u_4^{DC}$, where the local monopoly power of the local service provider operating facility 1 is now restricted in the area $r \in [0, 1/4G^{1/2}a^{-1/2}]$. This is because that was where it could most effectively exploit its local monopoly power (recall that it could offer the lowest utility at $r = 0$, because that was the most distant location). When competition from other regions becomes even more intense, as in the case where $u^{DC} = u_6^{DC}$, the local monopoly power of the local service provider operating facility 1 is now restricted in a larger area, $r \in [0, 7/4G^{1/2}a^{-1/2}]$. Only in the case where $u^{DC} = V^*$ ($\gamma = 1$) is the local monopoly power of the local service providers completely restricted, $\underline{P^E} = P^*$, and all the individuals obtain V^* at all locations.

Note that the equilibrium price functions set by the competing local service providers involve mill and discriminatory pricing[110] for some regions in their market area, depending on the level of the distant competition. If the distant competition is relatively weak ($u^{DC} \le \bar{u}$), then the equilibrium price function for local service provider 1 (symmetrical for local service provider 2) will be characterized by mill pricing for $r \in [0, r_1]$ and discriminatory pricing in favour of the more distant locations for $r \in [r_1, (r_2 - r_1)/2]$. For $\bar{u} < u^{DC} < u_5^{DC}$, the mill-pricing region is reduced and the equilibrium price function for local service provider 1 will be characterized by discriminatory pricing at both extremes of its market area. If $u_5^{DC} \leq u^{DC} \leq V^*$, the equilibrium price function set by the competing local service providers will involve only discriminatory pricing.

APPENDIX 2A4 PRICE-LOCATION EQUILIBRIUM AMONG COMPETING LOCAL SERVICE PROVIDERS UNDER FLEXIBLE TECHNOLOGY[111]

The Case of Two Competing Local Service Providers

Absence of distant competition
For the moment we assume that the distant competition restriction is very weak and is therefore not binding, which means that $P_i^{LC}(r, u_j^{LC}) < P_i^{DC}(r, u^{DC})$ for all the relevant range. Thus, $\underline{P^E}$ is described by equation (2.35) and (2.36).

The values of $(r_1^E, r_2^E, \underline{P^E})$ that satisfy equation (2.50) are called a 'location-price equilibrium'. It can be shown that such an equilibrium exists, and that $(r_1^E, r_2^E, \underline{P^E})$ is a location-price equilibrium with locations (r_1^E, r_2^E) if and only if:

$$TTC(r_1^E, r_2^E, \underline{P^E}) \leq TTC(r_1, r_2^E, \underline{P^E}) \quad \forall r_1 \in X$$
$$TTC(r_2^E, r_1^E, \underline{P^E}) \leq TTC(r_2, r_1^E, \underline{P^E}) \quad \forall r_2 \in X, \tag{2A4.1}$$

where $TTC(r_1, r_2)$ represents the total transportation costs incurred in aggregate terms by individuals when the local public goods are located at (r_1, r_2).

In order to understand this result, consider the location decision made by local service provider 1 for its local public good$_1$, r_1, given the location of local public good$_2$, r_2, and the equilibrium price functions given by $\underline{P^E}$. The profit function of local service provider 1 and the $TTC(r_1, r_2)$ are given, respectively, by:

$$\Pi_1 = \int_{X_1(\underline{P^E})} [t_2(r) - t_1(r)]dr - G \tag{2A4.2}$$

$$TTC(r_1, r_2) = \int_{X_1(\underline{P^E})} t_1(r)dr + \int_{X_2(\underline{P^E})} t_2(r)dr. \tag{2A4.3}$$

Recall that X_i is the market area for local service provider $i \in \{1,2\}$, and $X = \sum_{i=1}^{2} X_i$ (assuming that the market is completely covered). Thus the profit function for local service provider 1 can be written as follows:

$$\Pi_i = \int_{X_1(\underline{P^E})} t_2(r)dr - TTC(r_1, r_2) + \int_{X_2(\underline{P^E})} t_2(r)dr - G$$

$$= \int_{X(\underline{P^E})} t_2(r)dr - TTC(r_1, r_2) - G. \qquad (2A4.4)$$

We can see from equation (2A4.4) that, given the location of local public good$_2$, r_2, local service provider 1 will choose the location r_1 that minimizes $TTC(r_1, r_2)$ in order to maximize its profits. In Figure 2A4.1, we show $t_1(r)$ in a *thick black dotted* line, $t_2(r)$ in a *thick grey dashed* line.[112]

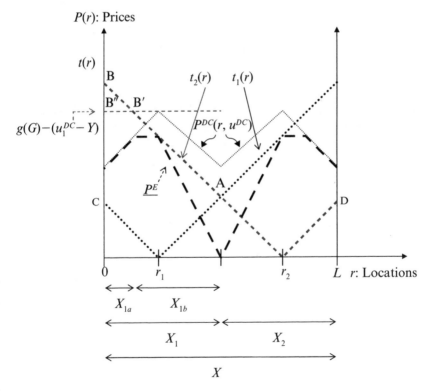

Figure 2A4.1   *Price-location equilibrium among competing local service providers under flexible technology and under the presence of distant competition*

The relationship between the profits of local service provider 1, the transportation costs involved in patronizing facility 2, $t_2(r)$ and $TTC(r_1, r_2)$ can be seen in this figure. The first term of equation (2A4.4) corresponds to the area $0LD$ r_2B in the figure and the second term $(TTC(r_1, r_2))$ corresponds to the area $0r_1C + r_1r_2A + r_2LD$. So, the profits of local service provider 1 are given by the area r_1ABC, minus fixed costs (G). Thus, any location for r_1, that implies higher total transport costs will reduce the profits of local service provider 1. Hence, local service provider 1 will choose the location r_1 that minimizes $TTC(r_1, r_2)$.

Presence of distant competition
Let us now consider the restriction imposed by distant competition on the equilibrium prices, in order to see whether this affects the equilibrium locations of the location-price equilibria identified above. Assume that $P_i^{DC}(r, u_i^{DC}) < P_i^{LC}(r)$ for some region, which means that $\underline{P^E} = [P_1^E(r), P_2^E(r)]$ will be given by:

$$P_i^E(r) = \min[P_i^{DC}(r, u^{DC}); \; P_i^{LC}(r)] \tag{2A4.5}$$

$$\text{s.t. } \Pi_i[P_i^E(r)] \geq 0. \tag{2A4.6}$$

The profit function of local service provider 1 and the $TTC(r_1, r_2)$ are now given, respectively, by:

$$\Pi_1 = \int_{X_{1a}(\underline{P^E})} [P_1^{DC}(r, u^{DC})]dr + \int_{X_{1b}(\underline{P^E})} [P_1^{LC}(r)]dr - G \tag{2A4.7}$$

$$TTC(r_1, r_2) = \int_{X_1(\underline{P^E})} t_1(r)dr + \int_{X_2(\underline{P^E})} t_2(r)dr, \tag{2A4.8}$$

where X_{ia} is the area in which $P_1^{DC}(r, u_1^{DC}) < P_1^{LC}(r)$, and X_{ib} is the area in which $P_1^{DC}(r, u_1^{DC}) > P_1^{LC}(r)$ and $X_{1a} + X_{1b} = X_1$.

We can see that the profit function of local service provider 1 can be written as follows:

$$\begin{aligned}
\Pi_1 &= \int_{X_{1a}(\underline{P^E})} [g(G) - (u^{DC} - Y) - t_1(r)]dr + \int_{X_{1b}(\underline{P^E})} [t_2(r) - t_1(r)]dr - G \\
&= \int_{X_{1a}(\underline{P^E})} [g(G) - (u^{DC} - Y)]dr + \int_{X_{1b}(\underline{P^E})} [t_2(r)]dr - \int_{X_1(\underline{P^E})} [t_1(r)]dr - G
\end{aligned}$$

$$= \int\limits_{X_{1a}(\underline{P^E})} [g(G) - (u^{DC} - Y)]dr + \int\limits_{X_{1b}(\underline{P^E})} [t_2(r)]dr +$$

$$\int\limits_{X_2(\underline{P^E})} [t_2(r)]dr - TTC(r_1, r_2) - G. \tag{2A4.9}$$

From equation (2A4.9) we can see that, given the location of local public good$_2$, r_2, the only factor which local service provider 1 can influence in order to maximize its profits is the total transport costs for (r_1, r_2), by choosing a location r_1. Accordingly, in order to maximize its profits, it will choose the location r_1 that minimizes total transport costs for (r_1, r_2). In Figure 2A4.1 we have drawn $g(G) - (u_1^{DC} - Y)$ in a *thin grey dashed* line. Thus, we can clearly see that profits of local service provider 1 will now be given by the area $r_1AB'B''C$ minus fixed costs, and total transport costs (r_1, r_2) by the area $0r_1C + r_1r_2A + r_2LD$, as before. The area $B''B'B$ gives the reduction in profits for local service provider 1 due to the existence of distant competition. As we can see from the figure, given r_2, the prices that local service provider 1 can charge at each location are independent of its location decision (determined by $t_2(r)$, the *thick grey dashed* line, and by $g(G) - (u_1^{DC} - Y)$, the *thin grey dashed* line). Thus, the best it can do in order to maximize its profits is to choose r_1 in order to minimize total transport costs at (r_1, r_2).

Hence, the restriction imposed by distant competition on equilibrium prices has no effect on the equilibrium location pairs identified above.

The Case of m Competing Local Service Providers

We can generalize the previous result for any given number of local service providers, m. For this purpose, we again assume that space in the region is described by a circle of perimeter L rather than an interval $[0, L]$, and we denote by X the set of locations on this circle.

We assume that the distant competition is very weak and hence $P_i^{LC}(r, u_j^{LC}) < P_i^{DC}(r, u^{DC})$ for all the relevant range, because we have shown for the case of $m = 2$ that the existence of distant competition has no effect on the equilibrium location pairs. Thus, in this case, given the locations $\underline{r} = (r_1, r_2, \ldots, r_m)$, the price equilibrium $\underline{P^E}$ will be given by equations (2.42) and (2.43). Let us define $\underline{r^E}_{-i} = \{r_1^E, \ldots, r_{i-1}^E, r_{i+1}^E, \ldots, r_m^E\}$ and $\underline{r^E} = \{r_1^E, \ldots, r_m^E\}$. We identify a location-price equilibrium as $(\underline{r^E}, \underline{P^E})$, such that the following condition is satisfied:

$$\Pi_i(r_i^E, \underline{r^E}_{-i}, \underline{P^E}) \geq \Pi_i(r_i, \underline{r^E}_{-i}, \underline{P^E}) \quad \forall r_i \in X, \tag{2A4.10}$$

where $i \in \{1, 2, \ldots, m\}$. As in the case of two local service providers, it can be shown that such location-price equilibria exist, and that $(\underline{r}^E, \underline{P^E})$ is a location-price equilibrium with locations $\underline{r}^E$ if and only if:

$$TTC(r_i^E, \underline{r}_{-i}^E, \underline{P^E}) \leq TTC(r_i, \underline{r}_{-i}^E, \underline{P^E}) \quad \forall r_i \in X. \qquad (2A4.11)$$

As before, this implies that the existence of a location-price equilibrium depends on the existence of locations such that each minimizes total transport costs with regard to the locations of the other local public goods. In this case, there is only one equilibrium vector: that which minimizes total transport costs, which represents the optimal locations $\underline{r}^* = (r_1^*, r_2^*, \ldots, r_m^*)$ (the symmetrical locations), as described in Appendix 2A1.

In fact, we have a whole range of vectors that minimize TTC. They differ from one another only in the exact location of the facilities, but at all equilibria the facilities will all be separated from one another by the same distance. Hence, we consider all these equilibria to be equivalent, and we refer to a unique equilibrium in this case.

APPENDIX 2A5   PRICE-LOCATION EQUILIBRIA AMONG COMPETING LOCAL SERVICE PROVIDERS UNDER FIXED TECHNOLOGY[113]

In this appendix we show that the range of possible location-price equilibria identified in the case of flexible technology is enlarged in the case of fixed technology.

For this, we analyse the case of two competing local service providers following the Hotelling line, $X = [0, L]$. Suppose that local service providers 1 and 2 have located their facilities at $r_1 = r_1^* = L/4$ and $r_2 = r_2^* = 3L/4$, respectively, as we can see in Figure 2A5.1. This is the price-location equilibrium when technology is flexible, as explained in Appendix 2A4. We can see that the profits obtained by local service provider 2 are given by the area $r_2'EFLC$, with the area $r_2'CL$ representing its fixed costs.

Suppose now that local service provider 2 is located at $r_2' = L/2$, while local service provider 1 is still at r_1^*, as we can see in the figure. Is this a location-price equilibrium? We can see that it is not a location-price equilibrium for the case of flexible technology, because local service provider 2 will prefer to move to r_2^* in order to reduce total transport costs and thus maximize profits as we discussed in Appendix 2A4.

But does it represent a location-price equilibrium for the fixed technology case? In that case, local service provider 2 faces the problem that if it

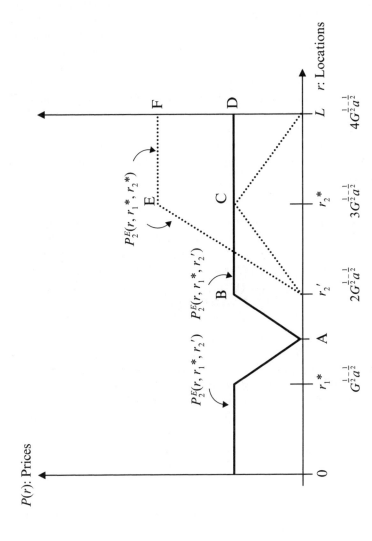

Figure 2A5.1 Additional location equilibria among competing local service providers under fixed technology

wants to change its current location, it must once again incur fixed costs (or some portion of them). In order to decide whether to stay at r_2' or to move to the most profitable location (in terms of higher revenues), r_2*, it must compare the profits it obtains at its current location, given by the area $ABDL$ in the figure,[114] with those it could obtain by relocating to r_2*, given by the area $r_2'EFLC$.[115] We can see that for this specific case, the profits gained from staying at r_2' are greater (in the area ABr_2') than those obtained from moving to r_2*. Thus, the provider will stay at r_2'.

If local service provider 2 stays at r_2', the best location that local service provider 1 can choose in this case (the one that minimizes total transport costs, given r_2') is r_1*, where it already is. Thus, it will also stay there. This implies that in this case, $r_1* = L/4$, $r_2' = L/2$ is a location-price equilibrium for the fixed technology case.

We have thus shown that, with fixed technology, the range of possible location-price equilibria is enlarged and we also have equilibria that are inefficient.

APPENDIX 2A6   INFLUENCE OF DISTANT AND
                LOCAL COMPETITION ON THE
                PRICE-LOCATION EQUILIBRIUM
                AMONG m COMPETING LOCAL
                SERVICE PROVIDERS UNDER
                FLEXIBLE TECHNOLOGY

In this appendix we show the nature of the location-price equilibrium in the case where technology is completely flexible as to location and how it will depend upon the disciplinary influence imposed on the local service providers by the two forces of competition (distant and local competition, reflected by u^{DC} and m, respectively). We analyse the effect of an increase in the intensity of the distant competition and of the local competition on the location-price equilibrium.

We assume that a circle of perimeter L describes space in the region and we examine the case of local service provider i and normalize its location as $r_i = 0$.

The Effect of an Increase in the Intensity of Distant Competition on the Price-location Equilibrium

For this analysis we assume that there is a given number of local service providers in the region, m_1, and we examine the effect of an increase in the intensity of the distant competition, represented by an increase in the level of utility offered at the alternative region (u^{DC}), on the location-price equilibrium.

In Figure 2A6.1, $P_i^{DC}(r, u^{DC})$ is shown in a *dotted* line for two different levels of distant competition (u_1^{DC} and u_2^{DC}, where $u_1^{DC} > u_2^{DC}$); $P_i^{LC}(r, m_1)$ in a *continuous grey* line for the given number of local service providers (m_1) and $P_i^E(r, m_1, u^{DC})$ in a *black dashed* line, which correspond to the equilibrium price set by local service provider i in this case for the two different levels of u^{DC}(u_1^{DC} and u_2^{DC}). Here we can see that a very unfavourable exit option, reflected by a low u^{DC} such as u_2^{DC}, means that the local service providers' monopoly power is restricted only by local competition, and distant competition thus does not influence their equilibrium prices. Therefore, $P_i^E(r) = P_i^{LC}(r, m_1)$ for all $r \in [-r^b, r^b]$.

On the other hand, an increase in the intensity of the distant competition, represented by a higher level of utility offered at the alternative region, u_1^{DC}, means that the local monopoly power enjoyed by each of the local service providers within its region is now constrained by distant competition. Here we can see that local service provider i is now forced to charge lower prices in the entire centre region $r \in [-r^0, r^0]$ than it would if the exit option utility were smaller, as with u_2^{DC}. This is because this is the area where it could most effectively exploit its local monopoly power (recall that it could offer the lowest utility at $r_i = 0$, because this was the location most distant from the other local service providers in the region). The utility gains for individuals located in that area (arising from reductions in the prices they must pay to consume the local public good) due to the existence of this distant competition are given by the shaded area in Figure 2A6.1.

The Effect of an Increase in the Intensity of Local Competition on the Price-location Equilibrium

For this analysis we assume that there is a given level of distant competition, u_1^{DC}, and we examine the effect of an increase in the intensity of local competition, represented by a higher number of local service providers in the region (m), on the location-price equilibrium.

In Figure 2A6.2, $P_i^{DC}(r, u_1^{DC})$ for u_1^{DC} is shown in a *dotted* line, $P_i^{LC}(r, m)$ for two different numbers of local service providers in the region (m_1 and m_2, where $m_2 > m_1$) in a *continuous grey* line, and in a *black dashed* line $P_i^E(r, m, u_1^{DC})$, which correspond to the equilibrium price set by local service provider i in this case for the two different numbers of local service providers (m_1 and m_2). A given level of local competition represented by m_1 implies a market area for local service provider i, $X_i(m_1) = [-r^b(m_1), r^b(m_1)]$ and a price equilibrium $P_i^E(r, m_1, u_1^{DC})$, as shown in a *black dashed* line in the figure. We can see that if local competition becomes more intense, as represented by a

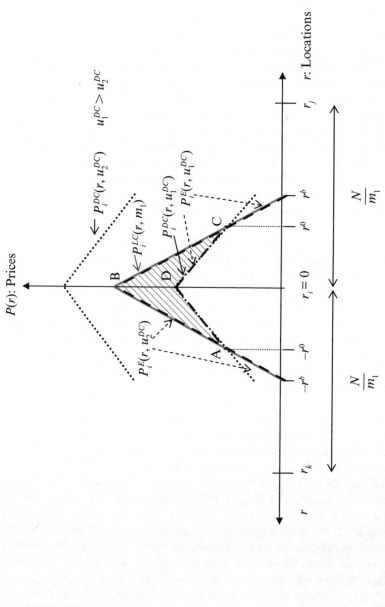

Figure 2 A6.1   The effect of an increase in the intensity of distant competition on the location-price equilibrium

164

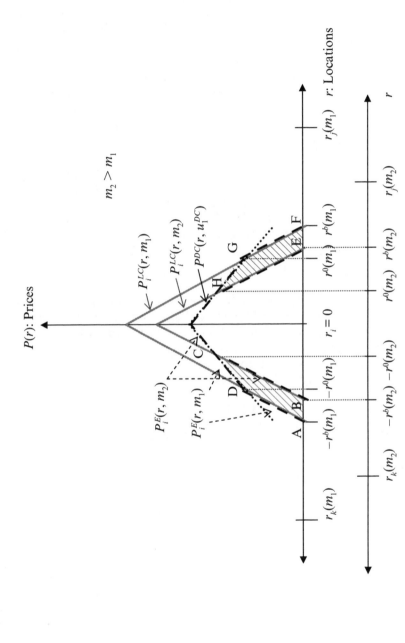

Figure 2A6.2   The effect of an increase in the intensity of local competition on the location-price equilibrium

higher number of local service providers, such as m_2, the local monopoly power enjoyed by each of the local service providers in the region will be constrained by this local competition, and thus their market areas will be reduced to $X_i(m_2) = [-r^b(m_2), r^b(m_2)]$, while the prices that local service provider i can charge for all $r \in [-r^b(m_2), -r^0(m_2)]$ and $r \in [r^0(m_2), r^b(m_2)]$ will be lower than before. This is because a higher number of local service providers will reduce the distance between them, thus making them better substitutes. The utility gains for the individuals located in this area of increased local competition (in terms of the reductions in the prices they must pay to consume the local public goods) are represented by the shaded area in Figure 2A6.2.

APPENDIX 2A7   DETERMINATION OF THE EQUILIBRIUM NUMBER OF LOCAL SERVICE PROVIDERS UNDER THE PRESENCE OF DISTANT COMPETITION WHEN TECHNOLOGY IS FLEXIBLE

In this appendix we determine the equilibrium number of local service providers with flexible technology $m_{flex}^E(u^{DC})$, for a given level of distant competition u^{DC}, if there is free entry in the establishment of local service providers. This implies that entry ceases when the existing local service providers make zero profits, $\Pi_i(m, u^{DC}) = 0$.

In order to simplify the calculations, we specify that:

$$x = [g(G) - u^{DC} + Y]. \qquad (2A7.1)$$

Hence, in order to determine $m_{flex}^E(u^{DC})$, we must solve:

$$\Pi_i(m, u^{DC}) = \frac{N^2 a}{2m^2} - G - \left[\left(\frac{N}{m} - \frac{x}{a} \right) \left(\frac{Na}{m} - x \right) \right] = 0. \qquad (2A7.2)$$

Solving (2A7.2), we obtain the equilibrium number of local service providers with flexible technology depending on u^{DC}, which is given by:

$$m_{flex}^E(u^{DC}) = \left[\frac{x + \left(\dfrac{x^2 - aG}{2} \right)^{\frac{1}{2}}}{G + \dfrac{x^2}{a}} \right] N. \qquad (2A7.3)$$

In order to understand the meaning of this result, we analyse two extreme cases of distant competition: extremely intense and insignificant.

First, we analyse the case of extremely intense distant competition, represented by $u^{DC} = V^* = Y - G^{\frac{1}{2}}a^{\frac{1}{2}} + g(G)$.[116]

Replacing $u^{DC} = V^*$ in equations (2A7.1) and (2A7.3), we obtain:

$$m^E_{flex}(u^{DC} = V^*) = \frac{1}{2}a^{\frac{1}{2}}G^{-\frac{1}{2}}N = m^* \qquad (2A7.4)$$

$$x^E_{flex}(u^{DC} = V^*) = a^{\frac{1}{2}}G^{\frac{1}{2}}. \qquad (2A7.5)$$

This result means that when the distant competition is so intense that $u^{DC} = V^*$, then the number of local service providers at equilibrium will be the optimal one (m^*). This is the implicit assumption made by Tiebout in order to obtain optimality in a system of competing local service providers.

Now we analyse the case of insignificant distant competition, represented by $u^{DC} \leq \underline{u}$, where:[117]

$$\underline{u} = Y - \frac{Na}{m} + g(G). \qquad (2A7.6)$$

Replacing equation (2A7.6) in equations (2A7.1) and (2A7.3), we can see that in this case, the equilibrium number of local service providers with flexible technology will be given by:

$$m^E_{flex}(u^{DC} \leq \underline{u}) = \frac{1}{\sqrt{2}}a^{\frac{1}{2}}G^{-\frac{1}{2}}N > m^* \qquad (2A7.7)$$

$$x^E_{flex}(u^{DC} \leq \underline{u}) = \sqrt{2}a^{\frac{1}{2}}G^{\frac{1}{2}}. \qquad (2A7.8)$$

We observe *excessive entry* (or *excessive capacity in the region*) in the sense that the equilibrium number of competing local service providers is larger than the optimal one.

We can see that the equilibrium number of local service providers decreases steadily as u^{DC} increases for $u^{DC} \in [\underline{u}, V^*]$, because it increases steadily with $x \in [x^*, \underline{x}]$. This is the relevant range of u^{DC} and the corresponding x, because, given $m^E_{flex}(u^{DC} \leq \underline{u})$ from equation (2A7.7), $\underline{u} = Y - 2^{\frac{1}{2}}a^{\frac{1}{2}}G^{\frac{1}{2}} + g(G)$ is the minimum utility that will be achieved by individuals in a system of competing local service providers, and V^* is the maximum utility that can be achieved by the individuals in such a system. The equilibrium number of local service providers will then be closer to the optimal number when distant competition becomes intense (higher u^{DC} near to V^*, implying a lower x near to x^*). But only when $u^{DC} = V^*$ do we get the optimal number of competing local service providers. If $u^{DC} < V^*$,

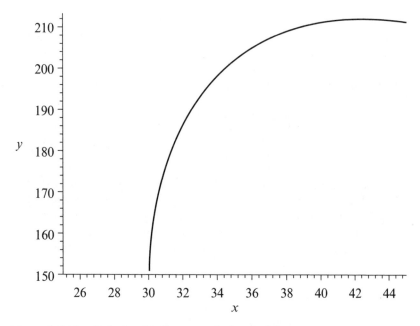

Figure 2A7.1   *Relationship between the level of distant competition (implicitly reflected in the x-axis, where* $x = g(G) - u^{DC} + Y$ *) and the equilibrium number of local service providers in the region (represented by the y-axis), for* $G = 100$, $N = 1000$ *and* $a = 9$

implying an $x > x^*$, then the equilibrium number of competing local service providers will always be higher than the optimal one, and we then have excessive entry.

This steadily decreasing relationship between distant competition (u^{DC}) and the number of competing local service providers in the region (m) can be seen in Figure 2A7.1, where we have drawn equation (2A7.3) for given values of $G = 100$, $N = 1000$ and $a = 9$. Hence, in this case, $x^E_{flex}(u^{DC} = V^*) = 30$, $m^E_{flex}(u^{DC} = V^*) = m^* = 150$, $x^E_{flex}(u^{DC} \leq \underline{u}) = 42.43$ and $m^E_{flex}(u^{DC} \leq \underline{u} = 212.13$. We can see that, in the absence of distant competition, the equilibrium number of competing local service providers is larger than the optimal ($212.13 > 150$) and we then have excessive entry. As distant competition increases, reflected in a reduction of x in the figure, the equilibrium number is reduced and only when we have perfect distant competition ($u^{DC} = V^*$), is the equilibrium number equivalent to the optimal one.

APPENDIX 2A8   DETERMINATION OF THE
MINIMUM EQUILIBRIUM
NUMBER OF SYMMETRICALLY
LOCATED LOCAL SERVICE
PROVIDERS UNDER THE
PRESENCE OF DISTANT
COMPETITION WHEN
TECHNOLOGY IS FIXED

In this appendix we determine the equilibrium number of local service provides with fixed technology $m_{fix}^{min}(u^{DC})$. In the presence of an active distant
competition, the profit function of the entrant is given by:[118]

$$\Pi_e(u^{DC}) = \frac{ad^2}{8} - G - \left[\left(\frac{ad}{2} - x\right)\left(\frac{d}{2} - \frac{x}{a}\right)\right], \tag{2A8.1}$$

where x is specified in equation (2A7.1), in order to simplify the calculations. Hence, the maximum distance between the local service providers
consistent with no entry, and the corresponding minimum equilibrium
number of competing local service providers when an exit option exists, will
be given by:[119]

$$d_{fix}^{max}(u^{DC}) = \frac{2(2x - \sqrt{2x^2 - 2aG})}{a} \tag{2A8.2}$$

$$m_{fix}^{min}(u^{DC}) = \frac{aN}{2(2x - \sqrt{2x^2 - 2aG})}. \tag{2A8.3}$$

In order to understand the meaning of this result, we analyse two
extreme cases for the levels of distant competition.

First, we analyse the case of insignificant distant competition, $u^{DC} \le \underline{u} =
Y - (ad/2) + g(G)$.[120] Replacing $u^{DC} = \underline{u}$ in equations (2A7.1), (2A8.2) and
(2A8.3), we can see that in this case the maximum distance between local
service providers consistent with no entry and the corresponding minimum
equilibrium number of competing local service providers will be given by:

$$m_{fix}^{min}(u^{DC} = \underline{u}) = \frac{1}{2\sqrt{2}}a^{\frac{1}{2}}G^{-\frac{1}{2}}N, \tag{2A8.4}$$

$$d_{fix}^{max}(u^{DC} = \underline{u}) = 2\sqrt{2}a^{-\frac{1}{2}}G^{\frac{1}{2}}. \tag{2A8.5}$$

Note that equations (2A8.4) and (2A8.5) are equivalent to m_{fix}^{min} in equation
(2.69) and $d_{fix}^{max}(m_{fix}^{min})$ in equation (2.70), respectively.

Let us now see what happens if there is extremely intense distant competition, $u^{DC} = V^*$.[121] Replacing $u^{DC} = V^*$ in equations (2A7.1), (2A8.2) and (2A8.3), we get:

$$m_{fix}^{min}(u^{DC} = V^*) = \frac{1}{4}a^{\frac{1}{2}}G^{-\frac{1}{2}}N.$$ (2A8.6)

$$d_{fix}^{max}(u^{DC} = V^*) = 4a^{\frac{1}{2}}G^{-\frac{1}{2}}.$$ (2A8.7)

We can see that:[122]

$$m_{fix}^{min}(u^{DC} = V^*) < m_{fix}^{min}(u^{DC} \leq \underline{u}) < m^*.$$ (2A8.8)

This result means that when the distant competition is so intense that $u^{DC} = V^*$, then the minimum number of local service providers at equilibrium will be even lower than it would have been without any distant competition. Thus, the presence of distant competition in the case of fixed

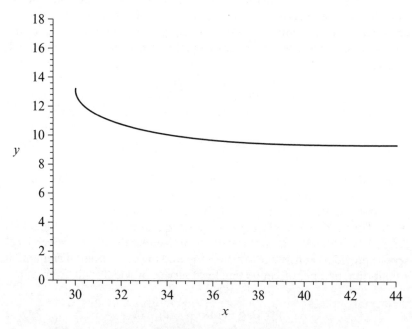

Figure 2A8.1   *Relationship between the level of distant competition (implicitly reflected in the x-axis, where $x = g(G) - u^{DC} + Y$) and the equilibrium distance between the local service providers in the region (represented by the y-axis), for $G = 100$, $N = 1000$ and $a = 9$*

technology causes the number of competing local service providers to deviate even further from its optimal level.

We have seen that the existence of distant competition will decrease the profits of a given number of local service providers, and it will more strongly discourage the entry of new providers, because of the decrease in potential profits for an entrant, given a particular number of providers.

We can see that $d_{fix}^{max}(u^{DC})$ increases steadily with u^{DC} and that $m_{fix}^{min}(u^{DC})$ decreases steadily with u^{DC} for $u^{DC} \in [\underline{u}, V^*]$, because $d_{fix}^{max}(u^{DC})$ decreases and $m_{fix}^{min}(u^{DC})$ increases steadily with $x \in [x(u^{DC} = V^*), x(u^{DC} = \underline{u})]$. This is the relevant range of u^{DC} and the corresponding x. The minimum equilibrium number of local service providers will decrease as distant competition increases, and thus the problem of insufficient entry will become more severe.

This steadily increasing relationship between $d_{fix}^{max}(u^{DC})$ and u^{DC} and the steadily decreasing relationship between $m_{fix}^{min}(u^{DC})$ and u^{DC} can be seen in Figures 2A8.1 and 2A8.2, where we have drawn equations (2A8.2) and

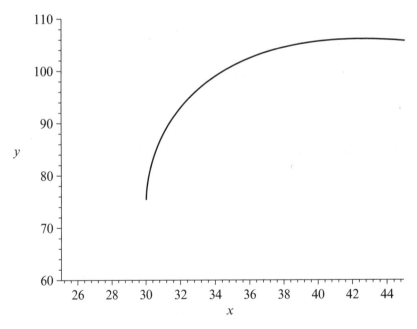

Figure 2A8.2　*Relationship between the level of distant competition (implicitly reflected in the x-axis, where $x = g(G) - u^{DC} + Y$) and the equilibrium number of local service providers in the region (represented by the y-axis), for $G = 100$, $N = 1000$ and $a = 9$*

(2A8.3), respectively, for the given values of $G = 100$, $N = 1000$ and $a = 9$. There, $x(u^{DC} = V^*) = 30$, $d_{fix}^{max}(u^{DC} = V^*) \approx 13.3$, $m_{fix}^{min}(u^{DC} = V^*) = 75$, $x(u^{DC} = \underline{u}) \approx 42.43$, $d_{fix}^{max}(u^{DC} = \underline{u}) \approx 9.4$ and $m_{fix}^{min}(u^{DC} = \underline{u}) \approx 106.6$.[123]

APPENDIX 2A9   THE OPTIMAL NUMBER OF FACILITIES IN THE CASE OF AN ELASTIC DEMAND

In this appendix we determine the optimal number of facilities, m^{ED*}, in the case of an elastic demand. The corresponding section explained that this is equivalent in this case to the number of evenly spaced facilities that a monopolist will choose in order to maximize its profits.

First, we analyse the price $P_i^*(r)$ that the monopolist will want to charge at each r for local public good i. The revenue function for local public good i, if the monopolist charges the price $P_i^*(r)$, is given by:[124]

$$R_i(r) = 1 - \frac{t_i(r)}{P_i(r) + t_i(r)}. \tag{2A9.1}$$

We can see that, in order to maximize its revenues for local public good i, the monopolist will charge the highest possible price at each location, which is, as explained earlier (equation (2.31)):

$$P_i(r) = P_i^A(r) = g(G) - t_i(r). \tag{2A9.2}$$

Given this price, the quantity demanded by an individual located at r from facility i will be given by:

$$q_i(r) = \frac{1}{g(G)}. \tag{2A9.3}$$

Thus, the revenue function will be given by:

$$R_i(r) = P_i(r)q_i(r) = [g(G) - t_i(r)]\frac{1}{g(G)} = 1 - \frac{t_i(r)}{g(G)}. \tag{2A9.4}$$

If we normalize the location of local public good i as $r_i = 0$, then the profit function of the monopolist can be written as:[125]

$$\Pi(m) = m\left[2\int_0^{\frac{N}{2m}} R_i(r)dr - G\right] = N - \frac{aN^2}{4mg(G)} - mG. \tag{2A9.5}$$

If we maximize equation (2A9.5) with respect to m, we obtain m^{ED*}, which is then given by the following expression:

$$m^{ED*} = \frac{1}{2}\left[\frac{a}{Gg(G)}\right]^{\frac{1}{2}} N. \qquad (2A9.6)$$

Note that, contrary as what happens in the case of an inelastic demand, $g(G)$ influences the optimal number of facilities (m^{ED*}) in this case. In order to understand this relationship, let us analyse what happens with m^{ED*} if $g(G)$ increases. In this case individuals will be willing to pay a higher price for the use of the local public good, as we can see in equation (2A9.2). Nevertheless and because demand is sensitive to price changes, this higher price will imply a reduction in the quantity demanded (equation (2A9.3)), which consequently individuals will travel less. As a result, the impact of transportation cost on revenues will be reduced, as we can see in equation (2A9.4).[126] Accordingly, as $g(G)$ increases, the total revenues of the monopolist will be less sensitive to transportation cost, and so the optimal number of facilities will be smaller, in order to reduce the fixed costs that additional facilities imply.

We should also note here that the monopolist will only provide the m^{ED*} local public goods if its profits are positive, and thus the following condition is satisfied:[127]

$$\frac{aG}{g(G)} \leq 1. \qquad (2A9.7)$$

APPENDIX 2A10   OPTIMAL ALLOCATION AND EQUILIBRIUM ALLOCATION OF COMPETING LOCAL SERVICE PROVIDERS UNDER THE POSSIBILITY OF DISCRIMINATORY PRICING USING QUADRATIC TRANSPORT COSTS

In this appendix we analyse the optimal allocation and equilibrium allocation of competing local service providers under the possibility of price discrimination, as in previous sections, but now we consider a slightly modified version of the model presented before, in which transportation costs are quadratic rather than linear and are given by $t_j(r) = a(|r_j - r|)^2$.[128]

Optimal Allocation Using Quadratic Transport Costs

The determination of the optimal allocation under quadratic transport costs is analogous to that observed in the case of linear transport costs, which was analysed in detail in previous sections. Thus, we shall characterize it directly, without explaining the details of the analysis.

The optimal allocation under quadratic transport costs consists of the placement of local public goods at locations that minimize total transport costs, as in the case of linear transport costs. In the case of an asymmetrical space structure, such as the Hotelling (1929) setting,[129] the optimal locations for two facilities would be at $1/4L$ and $3/4L$, respectively.

In the case of a symmetrical space structure, such as the circle of the Salop (1979) setting,[130] the optimal number of local service providers under quadratic transport costs, m^{*Q} and the corresponding optimal distance between the local public goods they provide, d^{*Q}, are given by:[131]

$$m^{*Q} = \left(\frac{1}{6}\right)^{\frac{1}{3}} \left(\frac{a}{G}\right)^{\frac{1}{3}} L \qquad (2A10.1)$$

$$d^{*Q} = 6^{\frac{1}{3}} \left(\frac{G}{a}\right)^{\frac{1}{3}} L. \qquad (2A10.2)$$

Equilibrium Allocation under Discriminatory Pricing, Using Quadratic Transport Costs

Price-location equilibrium with two competing local service providers[132]
As stated in Result 2.5 and explained in Appendix 2A4, the equilibrium locations of two competing local service providers offering local public goods with flexible technology are independent of the specific form of the transport-cost function.

Accordingly, and as explained for the case of linear transport costs (Appendix 2A4), there is a unique equilibrium pair in our two-dimensional setting, independent of the specific form of the transport-cost function: that which minimizes total transportation costs, which is the optimal location pair (r_1^*, r_2^*), where $r_1^* = L/4$ and $r_2^* = 3L/4$. This means that, independent of the specific form of the transport-cost function, the unique price-location equilibrium is efficient when price discrimination is possible.

Free-entry price-location equilibrium[133]
The unique free-entry price-location equilibrium under quadratic transport costs and discriminatory pricing will be characterized by a number of m^{EDQ} local service providers, with their corresponding local public goods located at the symmetrical locations, as in the case of linear transport costs.[134]

However, the free-entry equilibrium number of local service providers will be higher in this case than the one under linear transport costs. This is because under quadratic transport costs, the transport costs for the individual increase more with the distance to the local public goods. Accordingly, the local monopoly power of the local service providers increases when transport costs are quadratic, and therefore the equilibrium prices (P_i^{EDQ}) will now be higher than in the linear transport costs case (P_i^{EDL}), as we can see in Figure 2A10.1. Consequently, equilibrium profits increase, which provides a greater incentive for entry than in the linear transport-cost case.

In this case with quadratic transport costs, the equilibrium prices for local service provider i, depending on the distance between local public goods (d), if we normalize the location of local public good i to $r_i = 0$, will be given by:[135]

$$P_i^{EDQ}(r) = ad^2 - 2adr. \tag{2A10.3}$$

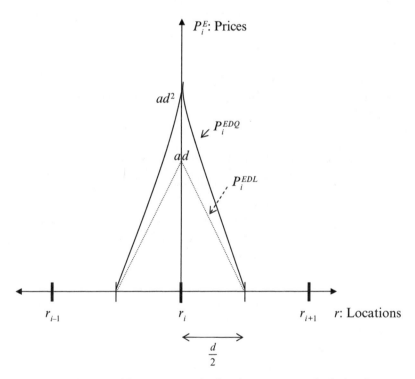

Figure 2A10.1   *Equilibrium prices for local service provider* i, *for the case of linear transport costs (*P_i^{EDL}*) and for the case of quadratic transport costs (*P_i^{EDQ}*)*

The equilibrium profits for local service provider i, depending on the distance between local public goods, will in this case be given by:[136]

$$\Pi_i^{EDQ}(d) = \frac{ad^3}{2} - G. \qquad (2A10.4)$$

Accordingly, the unique free-entry price-location equilibrium under quadratic transport costs and discriminatory pricing is characterized by:[137]

$$m^{EDQ} = \left(\frac{1}{2}\right)^{\frac{1}{3}} \left(\frac{a}{G}\right)^{\frac{1}{3}} L \qquad (2A10.5)$$

$$d^{EDQ} = 2^{\frac{1}{3}} \left(\frac{G}{a}\right)^{\frac{1}{3}}. \qquad (2A10.6)$$

We can then see that:

$$m^{EDQ} > m^{*Q}. \qquad (2A10.7)$$

This implies that the free-entry price-location equilibrium under discriminatory pricing and quadratic transport costs is characterized by the excessive entry of local service providers offering local public goods with flexible technology in the region, as in the case of linear transport costs (Appendix 2A7).

APPENDIX 2A11   PRICE EQUILIBRIA IN A SYSTEM OF ONE-PURPOSE COMPETING JURISDICTIONS UNDER HETEROGENEOUS LOCAL PUBLIC GOODS FOR DIFFERENT LEVELS OF DISTANT COMPETITION

In order to show the nature of the price equilibrium P^E in a system of one-purpose competing jurisdictions under heterogeneous local public goods, we define it, as in the case of homogeneous local public goods, for different ranges of the value of distant competition, represented by u^{DC}. For simplicity, we assume that the local public good is so preferred that $[g(G_1, G_2) - 3G_1^{\frac{1}{2}} a_1^{\frac{1}{2}}] > 2G_2^{\frac{1}{2}} a_2^{\frac{1}{2}}$, and thus $P_T^A(r, u^A)$ results as we can see in a *black continuous* line in Figure 2A11.1. We have also drawn $P_T^{DC}(r, u^{DC})$ there in *dotted* lines, as well as $P_{11}^{LC}(r)$ and $P_{12}^{LC}(r)$ in *grey continuous* lines. Let us specify that $\bar{u} = Y - 5G_1^{\frac{1}{2}} a_1^{\frac{1}{2}} + g(G_1, G_2)$.

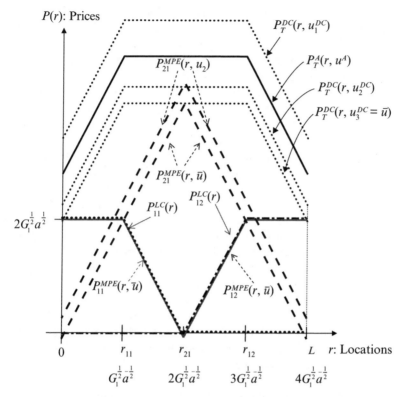

Figure 2A11.1 *Maximum price equilibrium (MPE) for the local service providers facing local competition when $u^{DC} \leq \bar{u}$*

1 $u^{DC} \leq \bar{u}$

We see that in the case of a very weak distant competition, such as $u^{DC} \leq u^A$ (as with u_1^{DC} in Figure 2A11.1), the autarky option dominates the alternative of moving to another region, and $P_T^A(r, u^A)$ is then the maximum price function that can be charged for the consumption of all types of local public goods, while still persuading individuals to stay in the region and participate in the consumption of the local public goods. For a stronger distant competition, such as $u^A \leq u^{DC} \leq \bar{u}$ (as with u_2^{DC} and u_3^{DC} in Figure 2A11.1), the alternative of moving to another region dominates the autarky option, and $P_T^{DC}(r, u^{DC})$ then represents the maximum price function that can be charged for the consumption of all types of local public goods, in order to ensure that individuals remain in the region and participate in the consumption of the local public goods.

Note that, as in the case of one type of local public good, we have a different price function $P_T^{DC}(r, u^{DC})$ for every value of u^{DC}, and the price functions $P_{11}^{LC}(r)$ and $P_{12}^{LC}(r)$ will be unique. This means that, regardless of how low the utility obtained by moving to another region or staying in autarky may fall, local competition imposes an upper limit for the prices that can be set by competing local service providers offering the same local public good.

As explained in the main body of the chapter, in this case of two types of local public goods, the two types are in a sense complements; both must be consumed in order to obtain utility from their consumption. Thus, the maximum price that each local service provider can set will depend negatively on the price set by the providers of the other type. This means that in this case, for each value of u^{DC}, we will have a whole range of possible price equilibrium functions for each local service provider, which will depend on the prices set by the local service provider offering the other type. This is different from the results in the case of one local public-good type, where we observed a unique price equilibrium function for each local service provider at each value of u^{DC}.

In order to determine the nature of these multiple price equilibria in price functions for each value of u^{DC}, we take, for example, $u_3^{DC} = \bar{u}$. In Figure 2A11.1 we can see the alternative of moving to another region dominates the autarky option, and thus $P_T^{DC}(r, u_3^{DC} = \bar{u})$ is the maximum price function that can be charged for the consumption of all types of local public goods, in order to persuade individuals to stay in the region and to participate in the consumption of the local public goods.

One possible equilibrium is the 'maximum price equilibrium' (MPE) for the local service providers facing local competition (in this case, the providers of local public-good type 1). In this equilibrium, local service provider 11 and local service provider 12 will charge the highest prices they can, $P_{11}^{LC}(r)$ and $P_{12}^{LC}(r)$, respectively (in a *continuous grey* line in Figure 2A11.1), and thus the maximum price that local service provider 21 can charge is derived from equation (2.127). Thus, the equilibrium price vector $\underline{P^{MPE}} = [P_{11}^{MPE}(r), P_{12}^{MPE}(r), P_{21}^{MPE}(r)]$, and the corresponding constraint indirect utility achieved at equilibrium at each location will be given by:

$$P_{11}^{MPE}(r, u^{DC}) = P_{11}^{LC}(r) \tag{2A11.1}$$

$$P_{12}^{MPE}(r, u^{DC}) = P_{12}^{LC}(r) \tag{2A11.2}$$

$$P_{21}^{MPE}(r, u^{DC}) = \{\min[P_T^A(r), P_T^{DC}(r)]\} - P_{1j}^{LC}(r) \tag{2A11.3}$$

$$V^{MPE}(r) = \max[u^A, u^{DC}], \tag{2A11.4}$$

where j is the specific type 1 facility chosen by the individual located at r.

This equilibrium can be seen in Figure 2A11.1 where we have drawn $P_{11}^{MPE}(r)$ in a *thick black dotted* line, $P_{12}^{MPE}(r)$ in a *dotted and dashed black* line and $P_{21}^{MPE}(r)$ in a *dashed black* line. At any other equilibrium, for $u_3^{DC} = \bar{u}$, the prices that local service provider 11 and local service provider 12 can charge will be lower. This equilibrium is also characterized by the fact that the price function charged by the monopolist local service provider (in this case the provider of local public-good type 2) is the lowest of all the possible equilibria, and $\Pi_{21}[P_{21}^{MPE}(r, u^{DC})] > 0$. This means that at all of the possible equilibria, the monopoly local service provider will always obtain positive profits, for these values of u^{DC}.

We can see that if the exit option becomes less favourable, as in the case of u_2^{DC} in Figure 2A11.1, the equilibrium price functions at MPE for local service provider 11 and local service provider 12, will still be $P_{11}^{MPE}(r)$, $P_{12}^{MPE}(r)$, respectively, because their local competition prevents them from charging higher prices, in spite of the fact that their distant competition is now less intense. Therefore, local service provider 21 can use all of its monopoly power and increase its equilibrium prices until each individual obtains the lower utility u_2^{DC}. $P_{21}^{MPE}(r, u_2^{DC}) > P_{21}^{MPE}(r, \bar{u})$ for all r, as we can see in the figure.

Another possible equilibrium is the 'minimum price equilibrium' (*mpe*) for the local service providers facing local competition (in this case, the providers of local public-good type 1). In this equilibrium, local service provider 11 and local service provider 12 charge the minimum prices they can (in the sense that they just cover their costs), and thus the maximum price that local service provider 21 can charge is the figure derived from equation (2.127). We can see that there are multiple possible price levels for the local service providers which satisfy the condition that local service provider 11 and local service provider 12 cover their costs, which means that $\Pi_{11} = \Pi_{12} = 0$. One possible equilibrium is drawn in Figure 2A11.2 (for $u^{DC} = \bar{u}$), where $P_{11}^{mpe}(r)$, $P_{12}^{mpe}(r)$ and $P_{21}^{mpe}(r)$ are shown in a *grey dashed line*, in a *dotted and dashed black* line and in a *black dashed* line, respectively. Thus, there is a whole range of equilibrium price vectors $\underline{P^{mpe}} = P_{11}^{mpe}(r), P_{12}^{mpe}(r), P_{21}^{mpe}(r)$, which can be characterized as follows:

$$\Pi[P_{11}^{mpe}(r, u^{DC})] = 0 \tag{2A11.5}$$

$$\Pi[P_{12}^{mpe}(r, u^{DC})] = 0 \tag{2A11.6}$$

$$P_{21}^{mpe}(r, u^{DC}) = \{\min[P_T^A(r), P_T^{DC}(r)]\} - P_{1j}^{mpe}(r, u^{DC}) \tag{2A11.7}$$

$$V^{mpe}(r) = \max[u^A, u^{DC}], \tag{2A11.8}$$

where j is the specific type 1 facility chosen by the individual located at r.

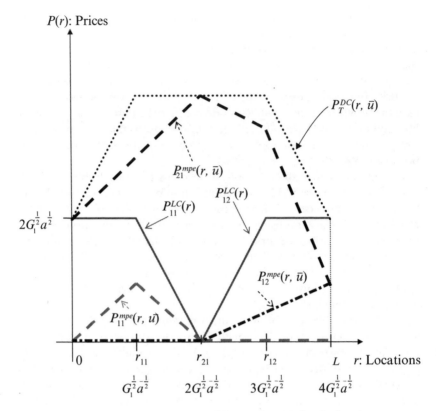

Figure 2A11.2   Minimum price equilibrium (mpe) for the local service providers facing local competition when $u^{DC} \leq \bar{u}$.

However, these are only some of the whole range of possible equilibria in price functions that exist for each u^{DC}. The case in which local service provider 21 charges a higher price than $P_{21}^{MPE}(r, u^{DC})$, and thus local service provider 11 and local service provider 12 must charge lower prices than $P_{11}^{MPE}(r)$, $P_{12}^{MPE}(r)$, respectively, in order to guarantee that the individuals obtain u^{DC} and consume the local public goods, will also be an equilibrium. It is also possible to have asymmetrical equilibria (an example of one possible asymmetrical equilibrium can be seen in Figure 2A11.2) and the equilibrium price functions may also be discontinuous. The only element that is common to all possible equilibria is that the utility obtained by the individuals at each location will be the same for all of them and will be at its maximum between u^{DC} and u^A.

2 $\bar{u} < u^{DC} \leq \underline{u}$

Let us now examine the nature of the price equilibria when the distant competition utility increases from $\bar{u}$, for example, to u_4^{DC} as can be seen in a *thin dotted* line in Figure 2A11.3. In this case, the MPE can be seen in Figure 2A11.3, where we have drawn $P_{11}^{MPE}(r)$ in a *thick black dotted* line, $P_{12}^{MPE}(r)$ in a *dotted and dashed black* line and $P_{21}^{MPE}(r)$ in a *dashed black* line. Here we see that when distant competition becomes intense, so that $u^{DC} > \bar{u}$, the local monopolistic power enjoyed by each of the local service providers in the region is now constrained by this distant competition, as seen in the case with only one type of local public good. The local monopoly power of local service provider 11 (and equivalently for local service provider 12) is now restricted in the area $r \in [0, 1/2G_1^{1/2}a^{-1/2}]$. This is because this was where it could exploit its local monopoly power most effectively (recall that it could offer the lowest utility at $r = 0$, because this was the most distant location).

The maximum equilibrium price for local service provider 11, $P_{11}^{MPE}(r, u_4^{DC})$ (and equivalently for local service provider 12) will be equal to $P_{11}^{LC}(r)$, except in the region $r \in [0, 1/2G_1^{1/2}a^{-1/2}]$, where it will be lower, because distant competition becomes relevant in this region. The minimum equilibrium price for local service provider 21 that characterizes this equilibrium, $P_{21}^{MPE}(r, u_4^{DC})$, will be smaller than $P_{21}^{MPE}(r, \bar{u})$ at all locations in this region. Thus, the equilibrium price vector $\underline{PMPE} = [P_{11}^{MPE}(r), P_{12}^{MPE}(r), P_{21}^{MPE}(r)]$ and the corresponding constraint indirect utility achieved at equilibrium at each location will be given by:

$$P_{11}^{MPE}(r, u^{DC}) = \min[P_{11}^{LC}(r), P_T^{DC}(r, u^{DC})] \qquad (2A11.9)$$

$$P_{12}^{MPE}(r, u^{DC}) = \min[P_{12}^{LC}(r), P_T^{DC}(r, u^{DC})] \qquad (2A11.10)$$

$$P_{21}^{MPE}(r, u^{DC}) = [P_T^{DC}(r) - P_{1j}^{MPE}(r, u^{DC})] \qquad (2A11.11)$$

$$V^{MPE}(r) = u^{DC}. \qquad (2A11.12)$$

As before, there are a whole range of price equilibria for u_4^{DC} (and thus for each value of u^{DC}) with lower values of $P_{11}(r, u_4^{DC})$ and $P_{12}(r, u_4^{DC})$ (not necessarily symmetrical or continuous, as shown earlier) and higher values of $P_{21}(r, u_4^{DC})$. We do not know which particular price equilibrium will result. What we do know with certainty, however, is that the maximum prices we observe for local service provider 11 and local service provider 12 at equilibrium, given u_4^{DC}, will be $P_{11}^{MPE}(r, u_4^{DC})$ and $P_{12}^{MPE}(r, u_4^{DC})$, respectively, and that the minimum price that local service provider 21 will be able to charge at equilibrium will be $P_{21}^{MPE}(r, u_4^{DC})$. Thus, as u^{DC} increases, the

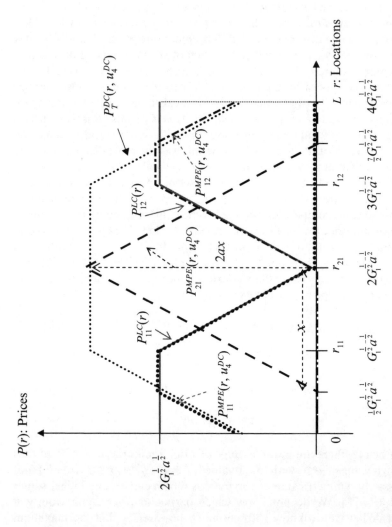

Figure 2A11.3 Maximum price equilibrium (MPE) for the local service providers facing local competition when $\bar{\bar{u}} < u^{DC} \le \underline{u}.$

maximum equilibrium prices for local service provider 11 and local service provider 12 will fall for some locations, and the minimum equilibrium price for local service provider 21 will be reduced throughout the entire region. At equilibrium, the utility for individuals will always be equal to u^{DC}.

Note that the minimum equilibrium price for local service provider 21 has a limit, because it must guarantee that $\Pi_{21}[P_{21}^{MPE}(r, u_4^{DC})] \geq 0$. This implies that there is some value u for which the minimum equilibrium price exactly covers the provision costs G_2, $\Pi_{21}[P_{21}^{MPE}(r, \underline{u})] = 0.$[138]

3 $\underline{u} < u^{DC} \leq V^*$

Let us now see what happens when the distant competition becomes more intense, where $u^{DC} > \underline{u}$, for example u_5^{DC}, as shown in *thin dotted* lines in Figure 2A11.4. We see here that there is a whole range of MPE for a given u^{DC}, not just one as before. One possible MPE is given by $P_{11}^{MPE}(r, u_5^{DC})$, $P_{12}^{MPE}(r, u_5^{DC})$ and $P_{21}^{MPE}(r, u_5^{DC})$, as shown in the figure in a *thick black dotted* line, in a *dotted and dashed black* line and in a *dashed black* line respectively. We can verify that for these prices, $\Pi_{21} = 0$. However, this is only one of the possibilities. As stated earlier, there is a whole range of equilibrium price vectors in this case, $\underline{P^{MPE}} = [P_{11}^{MPE}(r), \ P_{12}^{MPE}(r), \ P_{21}^{MPE}(r)]$, which can be characterized as follows:

$$\Pi_{21}[P_{21}^{MPE}(r, u^{DC})] = 0 \tag{2A11.13}$$

$$P_{11}^{MPE}(r, u^{DC}) = \{\min[P_{11}^{LC}(r), P_T^{DC}(r)]\} - P_{21}^{MPE}(r, u^{DC}) \tag{2A11.14}$$

$$P_{12}^{MPE}(r, u^{DC}) = \{\min[P_{12}^{LC}(r), P_T^{DC}(r)]\} - P_{21}^{MPE}(r, u^{DC}) \tag{2A11.15}$$

$$V^{MPE}(r) = u^{DC}. \tag{2A11.16}$$

Accordingly, as distant competition increases beyond some level, the number of possible equilibria is enlarged.

Note that the MPE in Figure 2A11.4 is the only MPE with continuous price functions: 'continuous MPE' (CMPE). All other MPEs, for a given u^{DC}, will have discontinuous equilibrium price functions. We can also find asymmetrical MPEs. As before, the only element common to all of the equilibria is the fact that the utility achieved by individuals at each location is determined by the possible exit option, u^{DC}, and not by the competition in the region, because of the existence of one monopoly local service provider.

We can see that as u^{DC} increases (for example, from $\underline{u}$ to u_5^{DC} in Figure 2A11.4), the slope of $P_{21}^{CMPE}(r, u^{DC})$ becomes smaller at the CMPE. As before, a whole range of possible price equilibria exist between these

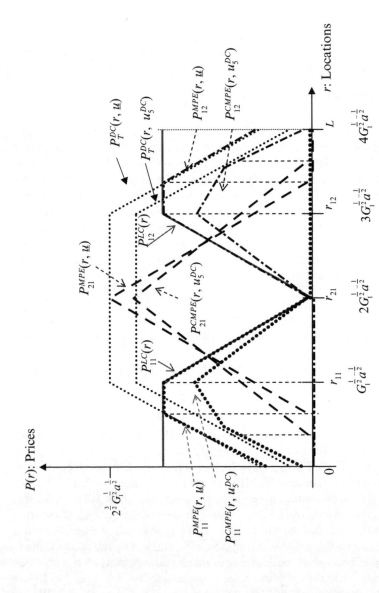

Figure 2A11.4 Continuous maximum price equilibrium (CMPE) for the local service providers facing local competition when $\underline{u} < u^{DC} < V^*$

extreme equilibrium prices, and we do not know which price equilibrium will result. But what we do know with certainty is that the maximum prices we observe for local service provider 11 and local service provider 12 in equilibria with continuous price functions will be $P_{11}^{CMPE}(r, u^{DC})$, $P_{12}^{CMPE}(r, u^{DC})$ respectively, and that the minimum continuous price functions that local service provider 21 will be able to charge at equilibrium will be $P_{21}^{CMPE}(r, u_5^{DC})$.

When the utility offered by the exit option reaches its highest possible value, $u^{DC} = V^*$ (perfect distant competition), then the CMPE will appear as shown in Figure 2A11.5, where $P_{11}^{CMPE}(r, V^*)$, $P_{12}^{CMPE}(r, V^*)$ and $P_{21}^{CMPE}(r, V^*)$, are drawn in a *thick black dotted* line, in a *dotted and dashed black* line and in a *dashed black* line respectively.

This is the only continuous equilibrium that exists for $u^{DC} = V^*$. All the other equilibria will have discontinuous equilibrium price functions, and they may be asymmetrical. They can be characterized as follows:

$$\Pi_{11}[P_{11}^{MPE}(r, V^*)] = 0 \qquad (2A11.17)$$

$$\Pi_{12}[P_{12}^{MPE}(r, V^*)] = 0 \qquad (2A11.18)$$

$$\Pi_{21}[P_{21}^{MPE}(r, V^*)] = 0 \qquad (2A11.19)$$

$$P_{11}^{MPE}(r, V^*) = \{\min[P_{11}^{LC}(r), P_T^{DC}(r, V^*)]\} - P_{21}^{MPE}(r, V^*) \qquad (2A11.20)$$

$$P_{12}^{MPE}(r, V^*) = \{\min[P_{12}^{LC}(r), P_T^{DC}(r, V^*)]\} - P_{21}^{MPE}(r, V^*) \qquad (2A11.21)$$

$$P_{21}^{MPE}(r, V^*) = P_T^{DC}(r, V^*) - P_{1j}^{MPE}(r, V^*) \qquad (2A11.22)$$

$$V^{MPE}(r) = V^*, \qquad (2A11.23)$$

where j is the specific type 1 facility chosen by the individual located at r.

As before, the only element common to all equilibria is that the utility achieved by individuals at each location is determined by the possible exit option, u^{DC}, and not by the competition in the region, because of the existence of one monopoly local service provider. Therefore, only when $u^{DC} = V^*$ will the equilibrium utility for each individual at each location be V^*, and thus the aggregate constraint indirect utility will be the maximum possible for this economy. Only in this case will the price equilibrium among independent competing local service providers achieve the maximum possible utility for the individuals in the region. For any $u^{DC} < V^*$, any price equilibrium among competing local service providers will result in a lower utility for individuals, which will be equal to u^{DC}.

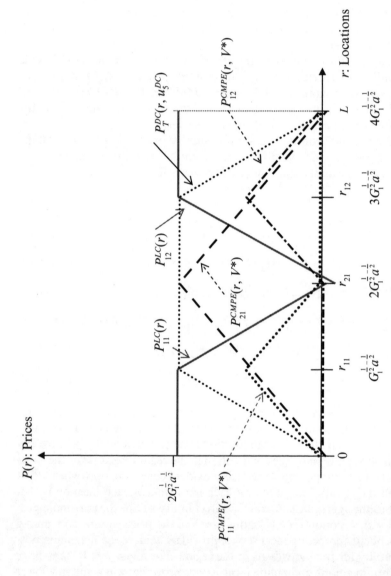

Figure 2A11.5   Continuous maximum price equilibrium (CMPE) for the local service providers facing local competition when $u^{DC} = V^*$

186

NOTES

1. 'Uni-functionality of jurisdictions' means that different local service providers provide each facility of the various types of local public goods.
2. 'De-localized membership' means that individuals have the opportunity to choose the local service provider they want independently of where they live.
3. For example, local public goods for which it pays for groups to consume collectively (those with high fixed costs), but for which it is possible to exclude others from consuming the groups' own units of the goods (such as school systems, domestic refuse collection, collective transportation services and so on).
4. As explained in the general introduction, we refer to 'local service providers' rather than 'local governments' as providers of the local public goods, in order to clarify that there is no political process involved in our analysis and that the only objective of the local service providers in our setting is to maximize profits. This is the main difference compared with the FOCJ concept, where voting is involved and there may be several objectives. However, our analysis is valid even for political competition to the extent that running public services is a source of tax income for any politician.
5. This situation is equivalent to those in which a delivery fee is charged for local public goods supplied to residential locations (as with refuse collection), or in which the level of service decreases with increasing distance (as with police protection).
6. Accordingly, local service providers can also be viewed as private firms that supply the service.
7. When there are high costs involved in changing one's place of residence, or the number of competing regions is low and there are entry and exit barriers to the formation of new jurisdictions, competition among regions will be very weak, and this will be reflected in a very low utility level achievable in alternative regions. On the other hand, where there is costless mobility of people among regions, and a large number of regions exist, or there is free entry and exit in the formation of regions, competition among regions will be very fierce, and we assume that the achievable utility in alternative regions will be the highest possible within the economy in question (that is, the utility obtained when the local public goods are provided efficiently, at the optimal allocation).
8. By 'homogeneous local public goods', we mean local public goods that are identical in all aspects except for their location in space. In a spaceless framework, these local public goods would be perfect substitutes.
9. In this setting, an allocation is identified principally by a number of facilities for each type of local public good, in which each facility is described by its location, its number of customers and the residential location of its customers (size of the jurisdiction or market area). Moreover, an optimal allocation (or an efficient allocation) will be an allocation for which welfare is maximized.
10. By 'heterogeneous local public goods', we mean local public goods offering different services, which are to some degree complementary. We consider the extreme case of local public goods that are perfect complements, such as schools and universities.
11. The use of a quasilinear utility function is explained in note 105 (Appendix 2A1), where it is shown that our results do not change dramatically if other forms of utility functions are used.
12. This situation is equivalent to those in which there is a delivery cost for local public goods supplied to residential locations (as with refuse collection) or deterioration in the level of service with increasing distance (as with police protection).
13. We call it a 'constraint indirect utility function' because it exhibits the additional constraint that the amount of each type of local public good is given.
14. Note that there is no political process like voting involved in the analysis and that the only objective of the local service providers in our setting is to maximize profits.
15. Note that it is probable that m^* is not an integer. Nevertheless and as we explain in Appendix 2A1, we set this problem aside in the following analysis and assume that m^* is an integer.

16.   The determination of equation (2.14) is as follows: from Appendix 2A1 we can see that

$$\int_{r=0}^{N} V[r, \underline{r}^*(m^*)]dr = YN - \frac{1}{4}\left(\frac{N}{m^*}\right)aN - m^*G + g(G)N$$

Thus, substituting equation (2.10) into this expression, we obtain equation (2.14).

17.   Equation (2.17) was obtained as follows. The aggregate constraint indirect utility of providing the local public good in a collective manner will be higher than that obtained under auto-provision if the cost of collective provision is lower than by auto-provision. The minimum cost of providing the local public good in a collective manner is $a^{\frac{1}{2}}G^{\frac{1}{2}}$ (this is the cost per individual on average, as we can see in equation (2.16)), and the cost of auto-provision of the local public good is G. For the first cost to be lower than the second, the following must hold: $a^{\frac{1}{2}}G^{\frac{1}{2}} < G \Rightarrow a < G$.

18.   Formally, this means:

$$\int_{t=0}^{N} V[r, r^*(m^*), G]dr > \int_{r=0}^{A} Ydr.$$

Using equation (2.14), we can obtain equation (2.18).

19.   As we explained in the introduction, we assume that the objective of local service providers is to maximize profits, because these entities are completely independent from the central government and behave as private firms in this model.

20.   Recall first, that the individuals in this model assume the transport costs. Alternatively we could have supposed that the transport costs are internalized by the service providers (as with refuse collection) or that the transport costs are represented as a decreasing level of service with distance between the public facility and the beneficiaries' residential location (as with police protection). In both cases, the results that we obtained would not be changed.

Second, we assume that the local service providers are allowed to choose the price structure they prefer (which means that they can also charge different prices for individuals coming from different locations, that is, they can charge discriminatory prices) and that they can verify the location of origin of each individual.

21.   The determination of equation (2.23) is as follows: $V[r, P(r), G] = Y - t(r) - P(r) + g(G) \geq u^{DC} \Rightarrow (P^{DC}(r, u^{DC}) = Y - t(r) + g(G) - u^{DC}$. The determination of equation (2.24) is as follows: $V[r, P(r), G] = Y - t(r) - P(r) + g(G) \geq u^{A} = Y \Rightarrow (P^{A}(r, u^{A}) = g(G) - t(r)$. Note that, as we explain in Appendix 2A1, we assume that individuals have quasilinear preferences, represented by the following quasilinear utility function, $u(z, G) = z + g(G)$. This implies that the constraint indirect utility function for an individual located at r, will be given by $V[r, P(r), G] = z[r, P(r)] + g(G) = Y - t(r) - P(r) + g(G)$.

22. V^* is given by equation (2.16) and corresponds to the highest constraint indirect utility level that each individual can possibly achieve with the current resources, when staying at the region and using the local public good.

23.   We assume that $g(G) - G^{\frac{1}{2}}_2 a^{\frac{1}{2}}_2 > 0$, which implies that $u^A < V^*$. Otherwise, it would be preferable not to produce the local public good and remain in a situation of autarky. If $g(G) - G^{\frac{1}{2}}_2 a^{\frac{1}{2}}_2 = 0$, then the maximum price this monopoly local service provider can charge is $P^*(r)$ (in Figure 2.1), which implies that the aggregate constraint indirect utility achieved by the individuals under this system will be the maximum one. However, in this case, individuals will obtain the same utility whether the local public-good is provided or not. So, in order to guarantee that it is better to provide the local public good, we consider local public goods for which $g(G) - G^{\frac{1}{2}}_2 a^{\frac{1}{2}}_2 > 0$ rather than $g(G) - G^{\frac{1}{2}}_2 a^{\frac{1}{2}}_2 \leq 0$, as demonstrated in equation (2.18).

24.   'Discriminatory pricing with respect to locations' means that the local service provider charges individuals different prices for using the facility, depending on where they come from. Thus, individuals coming from nearer locations with respect to the facility must

pay higher prices than those coming from more distant locations. Recall that in our setting, the individuals face the transport costs and the prices correspond to those charged by the local service provider at the facility location.

25. We assume that $u^A < V^*$, as explained above.

26. We assume that the cost of providing the local public good, G, has already been incurred and so it is irrelevant for the decision of setting prices.

27. The determination of (2.30) is as follows: $V[r, P_i(r)] = Y - t_i(r) - P_i(r) + g(G) \geq u^{DC} \Rightarrow P_i^{DC}(r, u^{DC}) = Y - t_i(r) + g(G) - u^{DC}$. The determination of (2.31) is as follows: $V[r, P_i(r)] = Y - t_i(r) - P_i(r) + g(G) \geq u^A = Y \Rightarrow P_i^A(r, u^{DC}) = g(G) - t_i(r)$. The determination of (2.32) is as follows: $V[r, P_i(r)] = Y - t_i(r) - P_i(r) + g(G) \geq Y - t_j(r) - P_j(r) + g(G) = V_j[r, P_j(r)] \Rightarrow P_i^{LC}\{r, u_j[r, P_j(r)]\} = t_j(r) - t_i(r) + P_j(r)$. In the market area of i, $P_j(r) = 0$, because it has no advantage with respect to i that allows it to charge positive profits, so $P_i^{LC}\{r, u_j[r, P_j(r)]\} = t_j(r) - t_i(r)$.

28. Alternatively, if we do not have de-localized membership and the two jurisdictions each have a predefined territory occupied by individuals who are forced to patronize the local public good of the jurisdiction where they live (as is normally the case in classical jurisdictions), then each jurisdiction would face only distant competition, as in the case where $m = 1$, and the price equilibria would be like those shown in *dotted* lines in Figures 2A3.1 and 2A3.2 (symmetrical for both facilities), where local service providers would be restricted only by the distant competition and by customers' possible choice of remaining in autarky, as reflected by $P^A(r, u^A)$ in a *dashed* line. Thus, de-localized membership is crucial for guaranteeing a minimum utility level for individuals which is higher than that of classical jurisdictions.

29. In Appendix 2A6 we show the nature of this price equilibrium and how it will depend upon the disciplinary influence imposed on the local service providers by the two forces of competition (distant and local competition, reflected by u^{DC} and m, respectively).

30. As we can see in Appendix 2A3, $\bar{u}$ correspond to the maximum utility level represented by the distant competition for which this restriction is not binding for the determination of the equilibrium prices.

31. We assume that $u^A < V^*$, as explained above.

32. This corresponds to the central location for the example in Appendix 2A3.

33. Equation (2.44) is given by the first line of equation (2A2.9), where we can see that the borders of the region that the monopolist seeks to cover are determined by the locations where the prices it can charge in order to encourage people to participate in the consumption of the local public good are zero. For farther away locations it would be obliged to charge negative prices or in other words to pay people to participate. This would obviously reduce profits.

34. Equation (2.47) is given by the second line of equation (2A2.9).

35. The fact that the distant competition restriction is not binding means that $P_i^{LC}(r, u_j^{LC}) < P_i^{DC}(r, u^{DC})$ for all of the relevant range. Thus, $\underline{P}^E$ is described by equations (2.35) and (2.36).

36. Lederer and Hurter (1986) derived a similar result.

37. In a three-dimensional space, we can find locations (r_1, r_2) for which if $\underline{r}_2$ is held fixed, r_1 minimizes total transport costs $(r_1, \underline{r}_2)$, and if $\underline{r}_1$ is held fixed, $\underline{r}_2$ minimizes total transport costs $(\underline{r}_1, r_2)$, but (r_1, r_2) may be different from (r_1^*, r_2^*), which are the locations that minimize total transport costs globally. An example of a pair of locations with these characteristics can be found in Lederer and Hurter (1986).

38. Of course, another school could be built at a different location and the one at the original location could be sold, but this undertaking would involve high costs. For example, finding a buyer for the old school would be difficult, because the facility is specially designed for educational services, and thus changing its current use would be very costly.

39. As we explained above, this change in the model is made only to avoid the special cases that appear at the extremes of the interval, and thus to make every point in the region equivalent. This allows us to concentrate on the general results.

40. Note that when technology is flexible, the equilibrium locations are the symmetrical locations, as we explained above.

41. The determination of (2.53) is as follows: from the analysis above, we know that $P_i^{LC}(r) = t_j(r) - t_i(r)$, where j (with $j \neq i$ and $i, j \in \{1, 2, \ldots, m\}$) is the jurisdiction, different from i, with the smallest transport cost from r. Because locations are are symmetrical at equilibrium and r_i is normalized to 0, $P_i^{LC}(r) = t_j(r) - t_i(r) = a|r_j - r| - a|r| = a|r_j| - 2a|r| = aN/m - 2a|r|$ (since $r_j = N/m$ when locations are symmetrical).

42. This corresponds to the area $(-r^bBr^b) - G$ in Figure 2A6.1.

43. Note that we defined $P^{DC}(r, u^{DC})$ as the price function that describes the maximum prices that the local service provider can charge at each location in order to guarantee to its customers the same level of utility that they could achieve at the distant region (u^{DC}) and so persuade them to remain in the region, and that we defined $P_i^{LC}(r, m)$ as the price function that describes the maximum prices that provider i can charge at each location, in order to prevent its customers from switching to other providers, when there are m local service providers in the region.

44. As we can see in Figure 2A6.1, the determination of (2.62) is as follows: $P^{LC}(r^0) = P^{DC}(r^0)$. Because the local service providers are identical and are symmetrically distributed within the region, all their market areas will be identical at equilibrium and will depend on m.

45. Equation (2.63) was obtained as follows. We can write equation (2.61) as the equilibrium profits of local service provider i in the absence of distant competition ($\Pi_i(m)$) minus the price decreases due to the existence of distant competition, represented by u^{DC} (area ABCD in Figure 2A6.1) and so: $\Pi_i(m, u^{DC}) = \Pi_i(m) - r_i^0[P_i^{LC}(r = 0, m) - P_i^{DC}(r = 0, u^{DC})]$, where $[P_i^{LC}(r = 0, m) - P_i^{DC}(r = 0, u^{DC})] = Na/m - [g(G) - u^{DC} + Y]$. Therefore, using equations (2.57) and (2.62) we obtain equation (2.63).

46. Note that, in order to simplify the calculations, we specify x in equation (2A7.1).

47. For the following analysis we assume that the costs of changing a location are so high, that once a location is chosen, it is impossible to change it.

48. Equation (2.68) was obtained as follows:

$$\Pi_e = 2\left[\int_0^{r_e^b} P_e^{LC}(r)dr \right] - G,$$

where $P_e^{LC}(r) = (Na/2m) - 2ar$ and $r_e^b = N/4m$.

49. Note that m_{fix}^{max} is equivalent to the free-entry equilibrium number of local service providers under flexible technology, m_{flex}^E, as we can see in equation (2A7.7).

50. In a symmetrical equilibrium, the equilibrium distance between the facilities will be given by $d(m_{fix}) = N/m_{fix}$ and given equation (2.69) we can obtain equation (2.70).

51. Note that this monopoly local service provider will appropriate all the benefits of the optimal allocation, but welfare will be maximized (it is only a redistribution problem).

52. In Appendix 2A7 we can see the impact of the level of distant competition on $m_{flex}^E(u^{DC})$ and accordingly on $m_{fix}^{max}(u^{DC})$.

53. The $m_{fix}^{min(u^{DC}=V^*)}$ was obtained as follows: $\Pi_e(u^{DC} = V^*) = N^2a/8m^2 - G - r^0[P_e^{LC}(r = r_e) - P_e^{DC}(r = r_e, u^{DC} = V^*)]$, where $r^0 = N/2m - a^{-\frac{1}{2}}G^{\frac{1}{2}}$ and $[P_e^{LC}(r = r_e) - P_e^{DC}(r = r_e, u^{DC} = V^*)] = aN/2m - a^{\frac{1}{2}}G^{\frac{1}{2}}$. Specifying $\Pi_e(u^{DC} = V^*) = 0$, we obtain the minimum equilibrium $m_{fix}^{min}(u^{DC} = V^*) = \frac{1}{4}a^{\frac{1}{2}}G^{-\frac{1}{2}}N$.

54. As proposed by Prescott and Visscher (1977), it can be argued that firms enter in sequence because some entrants become aware of a profitable market before others, or they require longer periods of time in which to 'tool up'.

55. If N/d_{fix}^{max} were not an integer, we would observe uniform spacing between local public

goods, given by d_{fix}^{max}, except for that of the last provider, which would choose the location at the centre of the remaining interval consistent with non-negative profits. In this case, the equilibrium number of local service providers would be the integer in the interval

$$\left[\frac{N}{d_{fix}^{max}}, \frac{N}{d_{fix}^{max}} + 1 \right].$$

That is, for example if $N = 14$, $d_{fix}^{max} = 4$ and thus $N/d_{fix}^{max} = 3.5$, and then the equilibrium number of local service providers would be 4, and we would have $|r_2 - r_1| = |r_1 - r_3| = 4$ and $|r_3 - r_4| = |r_4 - r_2| = 3$, if local service provider 3 had chosen to locate near local service provider 1. It may also be that $|r_2 - r_1| = |r_3 - r_2| = 4$ and $|r_3 - r_4| = |r_4 - r_1| = 3$, if local service provider 3 had chosen to locate near local service provider 2, rather than 1.

56. In this case the maximum distance between two local service providers without inviting entry is given by $d_{fix}^{max}[m_{fix}^{min}(u^{DC})]$ in equation (2.71).

57. Even though the following analysis corresponds to the symmetrical free-entry location price equilibria, the implications for the asymmetrical equilibria can be derived from it.

58. As we explained above, this change in the model is made only to avoid the special cases that appear at the extremes of the interval, and thus to make every point in the region equivalent. This allows us to concentrate on the general results.

59. Equation (2.81) was obtained as follows:

$$V^T[r^E(m), P^E] = \int_X V[r, r^E(m), P^E] =$$

$$m \int_{X_i} V[r, r^E(m), P^E] = m \left\{ [Y + g(G)] \frac{N}{m} - \left(\frac{1}{2} \frac{aN}{m} + \frac{1}{4} \frac{aN}{m} \right) \frac{N}{m} \right\} = N[Y + g(G)] - \frac{3}{4} \frac{aN^2}{m}.$$

60. As noted above, this monopoly local service provider will appropriate all the benefits of the optimal allocation, but welfare will be maximized (it is only a redistribution problem).

61. The inefficiency generated by independent local service providers in this case will be only excessive entry.

62. This price structure ($P_i(r)$) defines the prices charged by service provider i, at the point where it locates its facility (r_i). The specific price charged by it to each individual who comes to its facility to consume the local public good provided there, can be different, depending on the location of origin of each individual (r). This is why the price structure of each local service provider depends on r. Recall that the transport costs are assumed by the individuals in this model. Alternatively we could have assumed that the transport costs are internalized by the service providers or that the transport costs are represented as a decreasing level of service with distance between the public facility and the beneficiaries' residential location. In both cases the results that we obtained would not change.

63. In order to have positive demand, the maximum price that local service provider i can charge at each location for one unit of the local public good is $P_i(r) = g(G) - t_i(r)$. This is because the participation constraint must be satisfied, and thus $V[r, P_i(r)] = Y - t_i(r) - P_i(r) + g(G) \geq u^A = Y \Rightarrow P_i(r) \leq g(G) - t_i(r) \Rightarrow P_i^T(r) \leq g(G)$.

64. As we explained above, this change in the model is made only to avoid the special cases that appear at the extremes of the interval, and thus to make every point in the region equivalent. This allows us to concentrate on the general results.

65. The number and locations of the local public goods chosen by this profit-maximizing monopolist will be the same as those chosen by a region-wide planner whose objective is to maximize the aggregate utility achieved by the N individuals living in the region, subject to the resources constraint.

66. Despite the fact that the transport costs are borne by the individuals, the configuration that minimizes total transport costs is the one that will provide maximum profits for the monopolist, because individuals will then be willing to pay more for the local public good, since they have to spend less for transportation.

67. In the case of an inelastic demand in our present setting, $q_i(r) = 1$, the optimal number of facilities will be given by equation (2.10), as before.

68. This is because its revenue function increases with price, as we can see in equation (2A9.1).

69. Equation (2.90) was obtained as follows: if we normalize the location of the local public good supplied by local service provider i to $r_i = 0$, then its profit function can be written as:

$$\Pi_i(m) = 2\left[\int_0^{\frac{N}{2m}} P_i^E(r)q_i(r)dr\right] - G,$$

where $P_i^E(r) = (aN/m) - 2ar$ and $q_i(r) = 1/[(aN/m) - ar]$. Solving the integral, we obtain: $\Pi_i(m) = 2N/m[1 - \ln(2)] - G$. Under free entry and no location-specific fixed costs, the equilibrium number of evenly spaced local service providers will be: $\Pi_i(m) = 0 \Rightarrow m_{flexED} = 2N[1 - \ln(2)]/G$.

70. This is because m_{flexED} can never be smaller than m^{ED*}, but it can be larger. To show this, suppose that m_{flexED} is less than m^*, and thus we have insufficient entry. The following must then be true:

$$m_{flexED} < m^* \Rightarrow \frac{2N[1 - \ln(2)]}{G} < \frac{1}{2}\left[\frac{a}{Gg(G)}\right]^{\frac{1}{2}} N \Rightarrow \frac{aG}{g(G)} > \{4[1 - \ln(2)]\}^2 > 1.$$

But this would contradict the condition on the parameters given by equation (2A9). Therefore, we always have excessive entry in this case, as in the inelastic demand case.

71. Equation (2.94) was obtained as follows: in the case of price-responsive demand, the profits that a new entrant can make, given m evenly spaced local service providers, will be given by:

$$\Pi_e(m) = 2\left[\int_0^{\frac{N}{4m}} P_i^E(r)q_i(r)dr\right] - G,$$

where $P_i^E(r) = aN/2m - 2ar$ and $q_i(r) = 1/[(aN/2m) - ar]$. Solving the integral, we obtain: $\Pi_e(m) = \frac{N}{m}[1 - \ln(2)] - G$. Therefore, the minimum equilibrium number of evenly spaced local service providers consistent with no entry will be given by: $\Pi_e(m) = 0 \Rightarrow m_{fixED}^{min} = N[1 - \ln(2)]/G$.

72. This condition was obtained as follows:

$$m_{fixED}^{min} \leq m^{ED*} < m_{fixED}^{max} \Rightarrow \frac{N[1 - \ln(2)]}{G} \leq \frac{1}{2}\left[\frac{a}{Gg(G)}\right]^{\frac{1}{2}} N \Rightarrow 1 > \frac{aG}{g(G)} \geq \{2[1 - \ln(2)]\}^2.$$

73. This condition was obtained as follows:

$$m^{ED*} < m_{fixED}^{min} < m_{fixED}^{max} \Rightarrow \frac{1}{2}\left[\frac{a}{Gg(G)}\right]^{\frac{1}{2}} N < \frac{N[1 - \ln(2)]}{G} \Rightarrow 1 > \{2[1 - \ln(2)]\}^2 > \frac{aG}{g(G)}.$$

74. Recall that in the inelastic demand case, the optimal number of local service providers (m^*) and the symmetrical equilibrium number of evenly spaced local public goods

under fixed technology (m_{fix}^E) were given by equations (2.10) and (2.69), respectively. On the other hand, in the price-responsive demand case, the optimal number of local service providers (m^{ED*}) and the symmetrical equilibrium number of evenly spaced local public goods under fixed technology (m_{fixED}^E) were given by equations (2.86) and (2.95), respectively.

75. Here we are assuming that the value of the local public good to individuals, $g(G)$, as well as the individuals' income, Y, are sufficiently high.

76. As explained above, in equilibrium they charge higher prices to individuals coming from nearer locations to use the local public good, than to individuals located farther away relative to it. This is because as the distance to the local public good increases, the monopoly power of the local service provider decreases (local public goods become better substitutes), and the equilibrium prices it can charge to the individuals located there are reduced.

77. As before, we assume that space in the region is described by an interval $[0, L]$.

78. Equations (2.98) and (2.99) were obtained as follows. For simplicity we assumed that $0 \le r_1 \le r_2 \le L$. In the present case, given the prices and locations of each facility, the consumer who is indifferent between these two local public goods will be located at w, which is determined by solving:

$$v - P_1 - a(w - r_1)^2 = v - P_2 - a[(r_2 - r_1) - (w - r_1)]^2 \Rightarrow w = \frac{(r_2 - r_1)}{2} + \frac{(P_2 - P_1)}{2a(r_2 - r_1)} + r_1.$$

Thus, the profits of local service provider 1, depending on locations and prices, will be given by:

$$\Pi_1 = P_1 \left[\frac{(r_2 - r_1)}{2} + \frac{(P_2 - P_1)}{2a(r_2 - r_1)} + r_1 \right].$$

Local service provider$_1$ will choose a price that maximizes its profits, given the locations and the price set by the other local service provider, and thus:

$$\frac{\partial \Pi_1}{\partial P_1} = 0 \Rightarrow P_1 = \frac{a}{2}(r_2 + r_1)(r_2 - r_1) + \frac{P_2}{2}.$$

This is equivalent for local service provider$_2$:

$$P_2 = a \left[L - \frac{(r_2 + r_1)}{2} \right](r_2 - r_1) + \frac{P_1}{2}.$$

Solving this system of equations, we obtain the equilibrium prices P_1^{LC}, P_2^{LC} and the corresponding market areas and profits for the given locations.

79. This is equivalent to the result derived by D'Aspremont et al. (1979) in the case of competing firms.

80. Equations (2.100) and (2.101) were obtained as follows: in the case of local service provider i, for w_{i+1}, the utility of going to r_i and r_{i+1} must be the same, and thus:

$$Y - P_i - a(w_{i+1} - r_i)^2 + g(G) = Y - P_{i+1} - a[(r_{i+1} - r_i) - (w_{i+1} - r_i)]^2 - g(G).$$

We can see that:

$$(w_{i+1} - r_i) = \frac{(r_{i+1} - r_i)}{2} + \frac{(P_{i+1} - P_i)}{2a(r_{i+1} - r_i)}.$$

Similarly, for w_{i-1} we can see that:

$$(r_i - w_{i-1}) = \frac{(r_i - r_{i-1})}{2} + \frac{(P_{i-1} - P_i)}{2a(r_i - r_{i-1})}.$$

Thus,

$$X_i = [w_{i-1}, w_{i+1}] \Rightarrow D_i^{LC} = (w_{i+1} - r_i) + (r_i - w_{i-1}) =$$

$$\frac{1}{2}\left[\frac{P_{i+1} - P_i}{a(r_{i+1} - r_i)} + \frac{P_{i-1} - P_i}{a(r_i - r_{i-1})} + r_{i+1} - r_{i-1}\right].$$

This implies that:

$$\Pi_i^{LC} = P_i D_i^{LC} - G = P_i \frac{1}{2}\left[\frac{P_{i+1} - P_i}{a(r_{i+1} - r_i)} + \frac{P_{i-1} - P_i}{a(r_i - r_{i-1})} + r_{i+1} - r_{i-1}\right] - G.$$

81. Equation (2.102) was obtained by maximizing profits, given by equation (2.101), with respect to price.
82. The proof of this can be found in Economides (1989).
83. As explained in the general introduction, 'FOCJ' refers to our interpretation of the concept relative to the aspects of it that we considered.
84. Note that the assumption of perfect complementarities between types may be considered an extreme assumption and even unrealistic. Nevertheless, we use it as an instrument that allows us to identify where the problems with a decentralized provision of local public goods like FOCJ could be in order to take measures to solve them and so improve such a system.
85. Note that we are focusing here on the possible consequences of a decentralized provision of local public goods on the utility levels of the individuals, but in terms of welfare all the situations are equivalent, because the number of facilities and their locations are given.
86. Equations (2.111) and (2.112) were obtained as follows. We earlier defined $TTC(m_i)$ for $i \in \{1, 2, \ldots, K\}$ as the total transport costs incurred in aggregate terms by individuals, when there are m_i facilities of local public-good type i located at the optimal locations, as explained in Appendix 2A1. $TTC(m_i)$ was described by equation (2A1.18). Accordingly, if $K = 2$, the planner's problem presented in equations (2.109) and (2.110) can be written as follows:

$$\text{Max}_{m_1, m_2} YN - \frac{1}{4}\left(\frac{N}{m_1}\right)aN - \frac{1}{4}\left(\frac{N}{m_2}\right)aN - m_1 G_1 - m_2 G_2 + g(G_1, G_2)N.$$

From the FOC we obtain the optimal number of facilities of each type, given by equations (2.111) and (2.112), respectively.
87. The determination of equation (2.114) is as follows: we know that

$$\int_{r=0}^{N} V[r, \underline{r}^*(m^*)]dr = YN - TTC(m_1^*) - TTC(m_1^*) - m_1^* G_1 - m_1^* G_1 + Ng(G_1, G_2).$$

Hence, by substituting equations (2A1.18), (2.111) and (2.112) into this expression, we obtain equation (2.114).
88. The determination of (2.125) is as follows: $V[r, P_T(r)] = Y - t_{21}(r) - t_{1j}(r) - P_T(r) + g(G_1, G_2) \geq u^{DC} \Rightarrow P_T^{DC}(r, u^{DC}) = Y - t_{21}(r) - t_{1j}(r) + g(G_1, G_2) - u^{DC}$. The determination of (2.126) is as follows: $V[r, P_T(r)] = Y - t_{21}(r) - t_{1j}(r) - P_T(r) + g(G_1, G_2) \geq u^A = Y \Rightarrow P_T^A(r, u^A) = g(G_1, G_2) - t_{21}(r) - t_{1j}(r) - P_{1j}(r)$.
89. We assume that $g(G_1, G_2) - 3G_1^{1/2}a^{1/2} > 0$, which implies that $u^A < V^*$. Otherwise, it would be better not to produce the local public goods and remain in autarky.
90. The determination of (2.127) is as follows: $V[r, P_{21}(r)] = Y - t_{21}(r) - t_{1j}(r) - P_{21}(r) -$

$P_{1j}(r) + g(G_1, G_2) \geq u^{DC} \Rightarrow P^{DC}(r, u^{DC}) = Y - t_{21}(r) - t_{1j}(r) - P_{1j}(r) + g(G_1, G_2) - u^{DC}.$
The determination of (2.128) is as follows: $V[r, P_{21}(r)] = Y - t_{21}(r) - t_{1j}(r) - P_{21}(r) - P_{1j}(r) + g(G_1, G_2) \geq u^A = Y \Rightarrow P^A(r, u^A) = g(G_1, G_2) - t_{21}(r) - t_{1j}(r) - P_{1j}(r).$

91. This can be seen in the fact that an increase in the price charged by local service provider$_{21}$ reduces the price that local service provider$_{11}$ can charge.
92. This can be seen in the fact that an increase in the price charged by local service provider$_{12}$ increases the price that local service provider$_{11}$ can charge.
93. In Appendix 2A11 we determine $\underline{u}$.
94. Note that 'classical all-purpose jurisdictions' refer to the Tiebout concept of jurisdiction, which was explained in the general introduction. The municipalities of Santiago are similar to this concept of jurisdiction, as stated above.
95. These other dimensions of competition are beyond the remit of the analysis presented here.
96. Note that in the case of educational systems, we can observe some price discrimination among different locations. For example, many universities charge differentiated fees to local and foreign students, with higher rates for foreign students. In this case, price discrimination operates in the opposite direction from that seen in our model of competing local service providers. This implies that for these universities, price discrimination is not a response to spatial competition but is a result of other forces, such as cooperation (collusion), the opportunity for price discrimination in segregated markets and so on.
97. This is the case, for example, with the technology used for collective transportation services such as buses and taxis. In this case, there may be high fixed costs involved in acquiring the buses and taxis that serve a specific area, but these vehicles can easily be reallocated to other areas if necessary, at almost no cost. Thus, if competition in one region is too intense, the local service provider offering the transportation services can easily (in terms of cost) reallocate its buses to another region where it can achieve higher profits. Another example of a local public good with no location sunk cost technology is a refuse collection service.
98. This is the case, for example, with schools. Once they are located at a point in space, it would be very costly to change their location. Of course, a new school could be built at another location and the one at the original location could be sold, but high costs would be involved in this undertaking. For example, finding a buyer for the old school would be difficult, because the facility is specially designed for educational services, and thus changing its current use would be very costly.
99. Recall that in the classical all-purpose jurisdictions (or Tiebout's jurisdictions), which provide all types of local public goods (as do Santiago's municipalities), the overlapping of jurisdictions is not possible, because each one has a territorial monopoly over its region, so all the people living there are forced to pay taxes to it and use the services it provides.
100. Of course the individuals will get a low level of utility, because of the high prices charged by this monopolist, but the level of welfare will be maximized, because the number and locations for the local public goods are optimal.
101. Quasilinear utility functions are commonly used, particularly in problems related to the provision of public goods, because they are very easy to work with. At any rate, the results that follow do not change dramatically if other forms of utility functions are used. If, for example, we use a Cobb–Douglas utility function, $u(z, G) = z^\beta G^\alpha$, the optimal location for one facility from the planner's viewpoint would also be the centre location, as we see below. In this case, the planner's problem would be:

$$\text{Max}_{r_1} \int_{r=0}^{N} [Y - a(|r - r_1|) - \phi(r)]^\beta G^\alpha \, dr$$

$$\text{s.t.} \int_{r=0}^{N} \phi(r) dr \geq G.$$

Replacing the restriction in the function and solving the integrals, we can express the maximization problem as follows: $\text{Max}_{r_1} G^\alpha[YN - ar_1N + ar_1^2 + (a/2)N^2 - G]^\beta$. The FOC will be given by: $\partial(\cdot)/\partial r_1 = G^\alpha(-aN + 2ar_1)^\beta$. From here, we can see that $r_1^* = N/2 = L/2$.

102. Recall that $z = Y - a(|r - r_1|) - \phi(r)$, which describes the amount of income that is left free for an individual located at r for consumption of the composite good, after travelling to the chosen facilities providing the local public good and paying the tax or fee charged by the planner at r in order to finance it. This implies that the aggregate constraint indirect utility function will be given in this case by:

$$\int_{r=0}^{N} V(\cdot)dr = \int_{r=0}^{N} [Y - a(|r - r_1|) - \phi(r) + g(G)]\, dr.$$

103. This was obtained as follows. Replacing equation (2A1.6) in (2A1.5) and solving the integrals, we can express the maximization problem as: $\text{Max}_{r_1}[YN - ar_1N + ar_1^2 + (a/2)N^2 - G + Ng(G)]$. The FOC will be given by: $\partial(\cdot)/\partial r_1 = (-aN + 2ar_1) = 0$. We can then see that $r_1^* = N/2 = L/2$.

104. This was obtained as follows. Substituting equation (2A1.10) into (2A1.9) and solving the integrals, we can express the maximization problem as:

$$\text{Max}_{r_1,r_2}\left[YN - \frac{3}{4}ar_1^2 - \frac{3}{4}ar_2^2 + \frac{a}{2}r_1r_2 - \frac{a}{2}N^2 + ar_2N - 2G - Ng(G) \right].$$

From the FOC, we obtain the following:

$$\frac{\partial(\cdot)}{\partial r_1} = \left(-\frac{3}{2}ar_1 + \frac{1}{2}ar_2 \right) = 0 \Rightarrow r_2 = 3r_1$$

and

$$\frac{\partial(\cdot)}{\partial r_2} = \left(-\frac{3}{2}ar_2 + \frac{1}{2}ar_1 \right) = 0 \Rightarrow r_2 + 2N = 3r_2.$$

From this system of equations we obtain $r_1^* = (1/4)N = (1/4)L$ and $r_2^* = (3/4)N = (3/4)L$.

105. The FOC in this case is:

$$\frac{\partial(\cdot)}{\partial m_1} = \left(\frac{1}{4}\frac{N^2}{m_1^2}a - G \right) = 0$$

From here we obtain $m^* = (1/2)[(a/G)]^{1/2}N$.

106. Recall that the parameter $\gamma \in [0, 1]$ reflects the level of competition presented by other regions for the analysed region. A higher value of γ reflects more intense competition from other regions. Hence, $\gamma = 0$ reflects no competition from other regions, which would imply extremely high mobility costs, and $\gamma = 1$ reflects perfect competition from other regions.

107. We assume that individuals have quasilinear preferences, represented by $u(z, G) = z + g(G)$, where $z = Y - t(r) - P(r)$ and that the transportation cost for an individual located at r and patronizing a facility located at r_1 is given by $t(r) = a\,(|r - r_1|)$, where we normalized $r_1 = 0$.

We assume that there is an adequate potential market on both sides of the facility, so that the market borders are symmetrical to the facility, $-r^{bl} = r^{br}$, and r^b is then determined as follows: $P^E(r^b) = 0$. Equation (2A2.10) was determined as follows:

$$\Pi[P^E(r)] = 2\left[\int_0^{r^b} P^E(r)dr\right] - G.$$

108. By the 'size of the region' we mean both physical extent and number of individuals living there. This is because, as we explained above, each point in space is identified with one individual, and so $L = N$.

109. For these prices, the local service provider will get zero profits, because its revenues just cover its costs, G. This is verified in the figure, where the area under $P_i^*(r, V^*)$ corresponds to G.

110. The fact that the competing local service providers charge mill prices at equilibrium for some regions is explained by the asymmetrical structure of space in models *à la* Hotelling (1929), with the presence of endpoints. In a symmetrical space, such as the Salop circle (1979), the equilibrium prices will involve discrimination for the whole region.

111. In order to simplify the following analysis, we assume that the exit option dominates the autarky option ($u^{DC} > u^A = Y$). 'Flexible technology' refers to the local service provider's opportunity to relocate its local public good without incurring any additional costs.

112. Although this figure shows the situation under the presence of distant competition, it also serves to show the relationship between the profits of local service provider 1, the transportation costs involved in patronizing facility 2, $t_2(r)$ and $TTC(r_1, r_2)$ in the absence of distant competition.

113. Fixed technology refers here to the situation in which it is very costly for a local service provider to change its local public goods' location and corresponding market segment once it has been chosen.

114. We did not include the fixed costs here, because these have already been incurred.

115. Here we assumed that all the fixed costs are sunk costs and must then be incurred again if the local public goods' location is changed.

116. $V^* = Y - G^{1/2}a^{1/2} + g(G)$ is the constraint indirect utility achieved by each individual at the optimum in this economy, as shown in equation (2.16).

117. The distant competition utility $\underline{u}$ is the maximum utility that can be achieved in another region that does not affect the monopoly power of a given number of local service providers in the analysed region. If u^{DC} is equal to or less than this, the distant competition restriction will be irrelevant for the determination of equilibrium prices and the corresponding equilibrium number of local service providers in the analysed region. This utility corresponds to that obtained at $r_i = 0$, in the absence of distant competition. In this case, $P_i^E = P_i^{LC}(r = 0, m) = (Na/m)$, and so the indirect utility will be given in this case by equation (2A7.6).

118. Equation (2A8.1) was obtained as follows. As explained in the chapter, if locations are fixed and symmetrical, the most profitable location for an entrant (r_e) will be the midpoint between two existing facilities in the region. Thus, if we normalize location $r_e = 0$,

$$\Pi_e(u^{DC}) = 2\left[\int_0^{r^0} P_i^{DC}(r, u^{DC})dr + \int_r^{r^b} P_i^{LC}(r)dr\right] - G,$$

where

$$P_e^{DC}(r) = x - ar, \quad P_e^{LC}(r) = \frac{ad}{2} - 2ar, \quad r_e^0 \Rightarrow P_e^{DC} = P_e^{LC} \Rightarrow r_e^0 = \frac{d}{2} - \frac{x}{a} \text{ and } r_e^b = \frac{d}{4}.$$

119. Equation (2A8.2) was obtained as follows: $\Pi_e(u^{DC}) = 0$.

120. The distant competition utility $\underline{u}$ is the maximum utility that can be achieved in another region, which does not affect the equilibrium prices for an entering local service provider. Note that this utility is different from the one in equation (2A7.6).

121. Recall that V^* is the constraint indirect utility achieved by each individual at the optimum in this economy, which is given by equation (2.16). So, $x^*(u^{DC} = V^*) = a^{\frac{1}{2}}G^{\frac{1}{2}}$.

122. Recall that m^* was given by equation (2.10).
123. Recall that for $G = 100$, $N = 1000$ and $a = 9$, the optimal number of local public goods, $m^* = 150$.
124. Equation (2A9.1) was obtained as follows:

$$R_i(r) = P_i(r)q_i(r) = P_i(r)\frac{1}{P_i(r) + t_i(r)} = 1 - \frac{t_i(r)}{P_i(r) + t_i(r)}.$$

125. Equation (2A9.5) was obtained as follows:

$$\Pi(m) = m\left[2\int_0^{\frac{N}{2m}} R_i(r)dr - G\right] = m\left\{2\int_0^{\frac{N}{2m}}\left[1 - \frac{ar_i}{g(G)}\right]dr - G\right\} = N - \frac{aN^2}{4mg(G)} - mG.$$

126. The impact of transportation costs on revenues is given by $\partial R_i(r)/\partial t_i(r) = -1/g(G)$. So, as $g(G)$ increases, the impact of transportation costs on revenues is reduced.
127. Equation (2A9.7) was obtained as follows: replacing m^* in the profit function of the monopolist, we get $\Pi(m) = N - \{aG/[g(G)]\}^{\frac{1}{2}}N$. In order for it to be worthwhile for the monopolist to provide the local public goods, these profits must be positive.
128. We assumed that the technology of the local public goods is flexible and that the exit option (distant competition) is not present, in order to simplify the analysis and concentrate on the general results.
129. Recall that in this case, space in the region is described by the interval $X = (0, L)$.
130. Recall that in this case, space in the region is described by a circle of perimeter L.
131. To provide an idea of the main points of the proof, we sketch out its central arguments here. As shown in previous sections, the optimal allocation is characterized by a number of local public goods (m) and their corresponding locations in the region that minimize social total cost (STC), which is given by $STC = TTC + mG$. We show that for a given m, the symmetrical locations of local public goods minimize total transport costs and are in this sense the optimal ones. The same is valid for the case of quadratic transport costs. Hence, in the case of quadratic transport costs, total transport costs for m local public goods at the symmetrical locations are given by:

$$TTC = m^2\int_0^{\frac{L}{2m}} ar^2 dr = \frac{aL^3}{12m^2}$$

The STC of the provision of m facilities is then given by: $STC = TTC + mG = (aL^3/12m^2) + mG$. Accordingly,

$$\frac{\partial STC}{\partial m} = 0 \Rightarrow m^*\varrho = \left(\frac{1}{6}\right)^{\frac{1}{3}}\left(\frac{a}{G}\right)^{\frac{1}{3}}L.$$

132. As before, we assume that space in the region is described by an interval $[0, L]$.
133. As before, we assume that space in the region is described by a circle of perimeter L rather than an interval $[0, L]$. This change in the model is made only to avoid the special cases that appear at the extremes of the interval and thus to make every point in the region equivalent, which allows us to concentrate on the general results.
134. This is because, as explained for the case of two competing local service providers, the equilibrium locations of competing local service providers offering local public goods with flexible technology and under the possibility of discriminatory pricing are inde-

pendent of the specific form of the transport-cost function. So, in the case of quadratic transport costs, the equilibrium locations will be the symmetrical locations, as in the case of linear transport costs (Appendix 2A4).

135. Equation (2A10.3) was obtained as follows: as in the linear transport-cost case, the maximum prices that local service provider i can charge at each r within its market area are those that make individuals indifferent to the choice of patronizing the second-nearest provider of the local public goods. This implies: $Y - P_i - ar^2 + g(G) = Y - a(d - r)^2 + g(G) \Rightarrow P_i(r) = ad^2 - 2adr$.

136. Equation (2A10.4) was obtained as follows:

$$\Pi_i^{EDQ}(d) = 2 \int_0^{\frac{d}{2}} P^{EDQ}(r)dr - G = \frac{ad^3}{2} - G.$$

137. It can be seen that, the free-entry equilibrium number of local service providers under quadratic transport costs (given by equation (2A10.5)) is higher than the one under linear transport costs (given by equation (2A7.7)), as explained above.

138. In order to calculate $\underline{u}$, we must find some x (as shown in Figure 2A11.3), for which: $x(2ax) = 4G_1$, which implies $x = 2^{\frac{1}{2}} G_1^{\frac{1}{2}} a^{-\frac{1}{2}}$. So u^{DC} will be equal to the utility achieved at $r = 2G_1^{\frac{1}{2}} a^{-\frac{1}{2}}$, where $P_{21}(r = 2G_1^{\frac{1}{2}} a^{-\frac{1}{2}}) = 2^{\frac{3}{2}} G_1^{\frac{1}{2}} a^{\frac{1}{2}}$. Therefore, we can see that $\underline{u^{DC}} = Y - (1 + 2^{\frac{3}{2}})G_1^{\frac{1}{2}} a^{\frac{1}{2}} + g(G_1, G_2)$.

3. Cooperation between competing jurisdictions

3.1 INTRODUCTION

One alleged problem of a system of uni-functional competing jurisdictions involves coordination among the large number of jurisdictions. Many critics of FOCJ[1] argue that there should be some coordination among these entities. As we explained in Chapter 2, pure competition among FOCJ[2] may fail to achieve an optimal allocation of local public goods under some circumstances.

For example, when for one reason or another, local service providers have to charge mill prices (that is, the price at the point of service is the same for all individuals, regardless of where they live), the efficient locations may not be an equilibrium under a system of competing local service providers. This is because under mill pricing, local service providers must charge the same price for all locations, and thus, in order to relax price competition, they will seek to locate as far away as possible from their competitors, at inefficient locations.[3] Another example of a failure of competition in this setting is the possible excessive or insufficient entry of local service providers, resulting in the corresponding excessive or insufficient capacity of local public goods in the region.[4]

Accordingly, the absence of coordination among FOCJ may lead to inefficiencies such as *inefficient location choices for the local public goods* or *excessive or insufficient entry of local service providers*, with a correspondingly reduced level of welfare.

The proponents of this type of competition among local service providers argue that coordination among FOCJ often makes sense, and it is also possible if required; r_f however, it is not always desirable. They maintain that coordination among local service providers (or governments) is not good in itself, but often leads to the formation of a cartel among the members of the classe politique, which they can use to evade, or even exploit, the population's wishes (Frey and Eichenberger, 1995; Frey, 1997).

In this chapter, we address the question of cooperation among FOCJ in order to shed some light on the possible benefits and problems arising from cooperation among these entities, and analyse the equilibrium allocation of a system of FOCJ characterized by cooperation, in order to compare this equilibrium allocation with that achieved under competition and with the optimal allocation.

Structure of the Chapter

This chapter is structured as follows. In Section 3.2, the model is presented. For our analysis we use the framework presented in the previous chapter for the case of homogeneous local public goods. There, once local service providers decide to enter the local public goods market, they must make decisions about two variables: the *location* of their facility and the *prices* they will charge their customers. Here, we focus exclusively on the price and location choices of two local service providers already in the region. By cooperation among local service providers, we mean that local service providers reach agreements together as to their locations and/or prices. Two possible forms of cooperation between local service providers are analysed: *partial cooperation* and *full cooperation*.

By, 'partial cooperation' we mean that local service providers choose some of their decision variables (here, their locations or prices), in a cooperative manner and the other variables in a non-cooperative manner. We analyse the case in which local service providers choose their locations non-cooperatively, but they are aware that after choosing their locations, they will cooperate in the area of prices. We make this assumption in order to examine whether cooperation in pricing, by reducing price competition, may solve the problem of inefficient location choices (maximum differentiation) that emerges under full competition and mill pricing, as explained in the previous chapter.

By, 'full cooperation' we mean that local service providers choose all their decision variables in a cooperative manner. In our setting, this means that providers agree about both their locations and prices. Nevertheless, we should distinguish between full cooperation among uni-functional local service providers and the case of a monopoly provider (or monopoly local government) operating several facilities in the region. A monopoly provider will choose its locations and prices so as to maximize the aggregate profits of all facilities, because it owns all of them. However, even under full cooperation, providers are still independent units, and they can break their agreements at any time, if this would maximize their individual profits.

In Section 3.3, the case of partial cooperation is analysed. In order to analyse the equilibrium allocation under partial cooperation, we investigate the case of two existing local service providers, which simultaneously select their locations at the beginning of the timeframe in a non-cooperative manner. Once chosen, these locations are permanently fixed, but local service providers will then choose prices at each of an infinite succession of time periods. We are interested in the equilibrium behaviour when providers cooperatively arrange a trigger strategy equilibrium in prices, and they select their locations knowing that a particular such trigger strategy equilibrium will ensue.

In the first part of Section 3.3, the equilibrium locations are analysed under the assumption of an asymmetrical geographical structure, such as the Hotelling setting. We also analyse the case of mill pricing.

We shall see that there are two opposing forces in this framework when a local service provider chooses its location under partial cooperation, taking the location of the other as given. On the one hand, moving closer to the competitor will bring a higher proportion of profits in the single-shot equilibrium and thus a higher share of the cooperative profits, giving an incentive to move closer. On the other, moving too close to the competitor may mean moving away from the efficient locations (those which minimize total transport costs and thus maximize total cooperative profits), and therefore this will reduce the total amount of the cooperative profits. We can expect that, in a Hotelling setting, these two opposing forces may lead to a location equilibrium between that of minimum differentiation (both facilities located at the centre of the region at $L/2$) and the efficient one (at $L/4$ and $3L/4$, which are those that minimize total transport costs), and in this sense improve welfare in comparison to pure competition (where we get maximum differentiation, at 0 and L, as explained above), since total transport costs will be reduced. Nevertheless, we shall see that minimum differentiation is the only equilibrium under partial cooperation. Thus, in both cases, namely under competition and under partial cooperation, the equilibrium locations will be inefficient when the providers charge mill prices in this setting, and they will be equivalent in terms of welfare (total transport costs will be identical in both cases).

However, as we saw in Chapter 2, under competition, discriminatory pricing leads to an equilibrium with efficient locations. Thus, we might hypothesize that discriminatory pricing could also change the minimum differentiation equilibrium result under partial cooperation and could also lead to efficient equilibrium locations for the local public goods. The inefficiency problem would originate from the charging of mill prices, and not from the presence of partial cooperation. Nevertheless, and as we shall show, the opportunity to charge discriminatory prices does not change the equilibrium locations existing under partial cooperation with mill pricing, and therefore the equilibrium locations will also be those of minimum differentiation in this case. This implies that partial cooperation will always be inefficient in this framework, and that discriminatory pricing will lead to the efficient locations only if partial cooperation is ruled out.

Minimum differentiation seems to be a robust equilibrium outcome under partial cooperation, which implies that partial cooperation is always inefficient in this setting. Nevertheless, we should note that this strong argument is based on the very specific geographical structure of the Hotelling model, featuring the presence of endpoints, which gives each provider the incentive to fight to obtain a larger captive market than the other, in order to enjoy higher bargaining power and thus a higher proportion of the cooperative profits.

It is true that the Hotelling setting may be an appropriate one for the description of differentiated product markets. If we take the classical example of two producers of a lemon-flavoured soft drink, such as Sprite and Seven-Up, which differ from each other in the sweetness of the product (with location 0 being a product without sugar and location 1 the sweetest product), and we assume that consumers are uniformly distributed in the unit interval with respect to their preferences for sweetness, it is clear that these endpoints will never meet, and thus, given the location of the competitor, a firm will increase its captive market if it moves nearer to it.

However, in other contexts, the initial asymmetry of space in models such as Hotelling's may not be the best way to represent the real forces of competition. In a geographical context, for example, if we consider competition in global markets, we may find that space is continuous rather than having endpoints, and thus when a multinational firm decides where to install a plant, it must consider, aside from other variables, that if it moves nearer to the competitor's location and its corresponding local market, it will gain additional customers from its competitor at that end of the market, because they are now relatively nearer to it, but on the other hand it will lose some customers at the other end of the market, because they will now be relatively farther away from it and closer to the competitor.

Thus, in the second part of Section 3.3, we consider partial cooperation in a model where space is symmetrical, in the sense that it does not have endpoints, in order to examine whether the outcome of minimum differentiation is also robust to changes in the geographical structure of the model. We will see there that with a symmetrical geographical structure, competition and partial cooperation will lead to the same location choices at equilibrium under both mill and discriminatory pricing, which are the optimal locations.

In general, we shall see that under the assumption of a symmetrical geographical structure such as the Salop setting, we always obtain efficient equilibrium location choices for the local public goods by the local service providers. The problem of inefficient equilibrium location choices arises when there is some hinterland to be captured. As mentioned above, within such an asymmetrical geography, discriminatory pricing with respect to location can help solve this problem and achieve the optimal location choices at equilibrium, if competition is guaranteed and partial cooperation is ruled out. However, a discriminatory price policy is usually difficult to implement in practice.[5] Thus, in many cases local service providers must charge mill prices. Hence, under an asymmetrical geographical structure, competition and partial cooperation will both lead to inefficient location choices.

Could full cooperation lead to the optimal allocation of local public goods in this case? We address this question in Section 3.4. Normally, we would expect that full cooperation would be equivalent to a monopoly situation, and it can be seen that within both symmetrical and asymmetrical geographical structures and under both price regimes, a monopoly local service provider would choose the optimal locations for its local public goods in order to maximize its profits, and would therefore be efficient in this sense. Friedman and Thisse (1993) argue that, in a Hotelling-type model with quadratic transportation costs, the equilibrium locations under mill pricing and full cooperation with equal profits are the efficient locations.

Accordingly, in our setting, this would imply that full cooperation among local service providers in an asymmetrical geography with mill pricing should lead to the efficient location choices for their local public goods at equilibrium, and in this sense it would imply an increase in efficiency in comparison with competition (where we obtain the inefficient location choices of maximum differentiation) or with partial cooperation (where we get minimum differentiation) under mill pricing. Nevertheless, and as we show in this chapter, full cooperation is not completely equivalent to the case of a monopoly local service provider, as explained above. Under mill pricing, full cooperation can lead to inefficient location choices within an asymmetrical space, as competition and partial cooperation would also do under mill pricing in such a setting.

Under full cooperation, local service providers will still be independent units, and thus once the locations of their local public goods are chosen in a cooperative manner, assuming that they are difficult to modify once chosen,[6] the providers may still deviate from the agreement in the area of pricing, because prices can easily be changed. If the penalty for deviating from the cooperative price agreement is very high, there will be no incentive to deviate from the cooperative optimal prices (that is, the prices that maximize cooperative profits at a given location pair) once locations have been chosen, and thus local service providers will cooperatively choose the locations that will maximize the optimal cooperation prices, as a monopolist would do, and these will be the efficient locations. What happens, however, if the penalty for deviating from the cooperation price agreement is very low? It is probable that in these cases the cooperative optimal prices will no longer be sustainable at any location pair, and thus local service providers will have to consider this when cooperatively choosing locations and prices.

If the penalty for deviating from the cooperative price agreement is very high, as reflected in a relatively high value of the discount parameter, full cooperation with optimal prices will be sustainable at any location pair chosen cooperatively by the local service providers. Thus, they will choose the locations that maximize their cooperative profits, which are the efficient locations, as Friedman and Thisse argue. But if the penalty for deviating from the cooperative price agreement is very low, as reflected in a relatively low value of the discount parameter, full cooperation with optimal prices will not be sustainable at all locations, and it may not be sustainable at the efficient locations. Therefore, in order to choose the location pair that maximizes their cooperative profits, local service providers will have to look for a location pair that will bring the highest possible *sustainable cooperative profits*, given such a low discount parameter. In the case of relatively low discount parameters, sustainable cooperative profits will be maximized at locations farther from the efficient ones, and for low enough values of the discount parameter, at equilibrium we obtain maximum differentiation under full cooperation, as we did under competition. Thus, for a low discount parameter, competition, partial cooperation and full cooperation all lead to inefficient location choices for local public goods under mill pricing and an asymmetrical space, which are equivalent in terms of welfare (total transport costs are identical in all three cases).

Finally, in Section 3.5, we offer some concluding remarks.

3.2 THE MODEL

In this chapter we use almost the same model as that described in Chapter 2, featuring two local service providers which have to choose the locations and prices for their local public goods in a region. We consider only the case of homogeneous local public goods. Thus, both local public goods are identical. However, in order to simplify the analysis and make it more general, in this chapter we shall make some minor modifications.

As before, space in the region is described by the interval $X = (0, L)$ in the case of an asymmetrical space as in the Hotelling model, and by a circle of perimeter L, in the case of a symmetrical space as in the Salop model, where at each point $r \in X$ the amount of land is $L(r) = 1$. Space is considered to be homogeneous except for the presence of the facilities offered by each local service provider, which are each located at one specific location r_j

where $j \in \{1, 2\}$. Without loss of generality, we take $r_1 \leq r_2$ throughout the chapter. We assume that N identical individuals are uniformly distributed throughout the region, that they are fixed to their locations, and that $L = N$. There is a reservation price denoted by v. In order to enjoy the local public goods, an individual located at r must travel to a single selected facility. The full price to an individual located at r who chooses facility j is:

$$P^F = P_j + t_j(r), \tag{3.1}$$

where P_j is the price charged by local service provider$_j$ at each r,[7] and $t_j(r)$ is the travel cost for an individual located at r and patronizing facility j. In the case of mill pricing, we assume quadratic transportation costs, $t_j(r) = a(r_j - r)^2$, in order to guarantee the existence of a price equilibrium with positive prices for any location pair.[8] In the case of discriminatory pricing, this existence problem does not exist, and thus we assume linear transportation costs in that case, so that $t_j(r) = a(r_j - r)$. Each individual will choose the facility with the lowest full price, if that full price does not exceed the reservation price v.

As in the previous chapter, we assume that each local service provider selects its prices and locations so as to maximize its profits, but unlike the previous case, we assume that it has zero production costs. For the given locations and prices of the local public goods offered by both local service providers, the profits of local service provider$_j$ in competition will be given by:

$$\Pi_j^{LC} = \int_{X_j(P)} P_j dr, \tag{3.2}$$

where P_j is the price structure chosen by the local service provider$_j$, $j \in \{1, 2\}$, $P = (P_1, P_2)$ is the vector describing the price structure chosen by each local service provider, and $X_j(P) \in X$ corresponds to the interval describing the location of the individuals choosing to patronize facility j (the market area), given P. In the case of mill pricing, the prices will not depend on distance, and thus $\Pi_j^{LC} = P_j D_j$, where $D_j = \int_{x_j(p)}^{1dr}$ is the total demand experienced by local service provider$_j$.

3.3   PARTIAL COOPERATION

In this section, we analyse the equilibrium allocation of a system of FOCJ under *partial cooperation* (that is, the non-cooperative choice of locations followed by cooperative pricing), in order to compare these equilibrium allocations with those achieved under competition and with the optimal allocation.

For this purpose, we investigate the case of two existing local service providers which simultaneously select their locations at the beginning of the timeframe in a non-cooperative manner. Once chosen, these locations are permanently fixed, but the local service providers will then choose prices at each of an infinite succession of time periods. We are interested in the equilibrium behaviour when local service providers cooperatively arrange a trigger strategy equilibrium. They will select their locations knowing that a particular such trigger strategy equilibrium will ensue.

The trigger strategy equilibrium that we use is as follows. The cooperative prices chosen will be those that maximize common cooperative profits (these would be the same prices chosen by a monopoly local service provider with two facilities at the given locations) and they will split these profits in the same proportion as at the single-shot non-cooperative equilibrium (for their given locations). This sharing rule appropriately reflects the relative power of the local service providers in our model.[9]

Given the trigger strategy described above, if $r_1 \neq r_2$, the profits of local service provider 1 and local service provider 2 under partial cooperation will be given by:

$$\Pi_1^K = \frac{\Delta}{1 + \Delta} \Pi^K,$$
$$\Pi_2^K = \frac{1}{1 + \Delta} \Pi^K \qquad (3.3)$$

where Π^k represents the total cooperative profits (these are equal to the maximum profits a monopoly local service provider with two facilities at the given locations can achieve), and Δ is given by:

$$\Delta = \frac{\Pi_1^{LC}}{\Pi_2^{LC}}, \qquad (3.4)$$

where Π_j^{LC} are the equilibrium profits for local service provider j at the single-shot non-cooperative equilibrium (for their given locations). If $r_1 = r_2$, they will split the total cooperative profits in equal parts.

In all of the following sections, 'cooperation', refers to partial cooperation.

Asymmetrical Geographical Structure: The Hotelling Setting

Mill pricing
In this section, we analyse the case of partial cooperation in a Hotelling-style model under mill pricing.[10] We shall see that in this case, the equilibrium

locations will be inefficient and will be characterized by minimum differentiation (that is, both facilities at the centre of the region).

Characterization of the single-shot non-cooperative equilibrium As explained in Chapter 2, the equilibrium prices, market areas, demands and profits at the single-shot non-cooperative equilibrium as a function of locations are given by equations (2.98) and (2.99). We can see that both Π_1^{LC} and Π_2^{LC} fall as r_1 rises, and both fall as r_2 falls. Thus, in the single-shot equilibrium, local service providers increase their profits as they move farther apart, and so the equilibrium locations in this case are those of maximum differentiation, 0 and L, respectively.

We assume that v/a is large enough so that local service providers compete for all points in space, implying that for each provider alone, it will always be profitable to cover the entire market. Therefore, throughout our analysis, we assume that:[11]

$$\frac{v}{a} \geq 3L^2. \tag{3.5}$$

Cooperative profits Let us now investigate the nature of the cooperative profits for each local service provider, Π_1^K and Π_2^K (equation (3.3)). Given the trigger strategy equilibrium described above, providers will be interested in the total amount of the cooperative profits, Π^K, as well as in the proportion of profits they would gain in the single-shot equilibrium, because this will determine the share of the total cooperative profits they will obtain. In this case, if $r_1 \neq r_2$, Δ and the corresponding share of the cooperative profits for local service provider 1 and local service provider 2, respectively, will be given by:

$$\Delta = \frac{\Pi_1^{LC}}{\Pi_2^{LC}} = \frac{(2L + r_1 + r_2)^2}{(4L - r_1 - r_2)^2} \tag{3.6}$$

$$\frac{\Delta}{1 + \Delta} = \frac{(2L + r_1 + r_2)^2}{(4L - r_1 - r_2)^2 + (2L + r_1 + r_2)^2}$$

$$\frac{1}{1 + \Delta} = \frac{(4L - r_1 - r_2)^2}{(4L - r_1 - r_2)^2 + (2L + r_1 + r_2)^2}. \tag{3.7}$$

As mentioned earlier, if $r_1 = r_2$, they will split the total cooperative profits in equal shares.

We can see that if $r_1 \neq r_2$, Δ increases with r_1, which implies that if local service provider 1 moves nearer to its competitor, the share of the cooperative profits it obtains will increase.[12] We can also see that Δ increases with r_2, and thus if local service provider 2 moves closer to its competitor, the share of the cooperative profits it obtains will also increase. Thus, if total cooperative profits were independent of location, both local service providers would have incentives to move closer to each other.

However, as we explain in Appendix 3A1, total cooperative profits depend on the locations of the local service providers, and therefore this effect must also be considered by providers when choosing a location.

The results of Appendix 3A1 can be summarized as follows:

Result 3.1 Under mill pricing, total cooperative profits (Π^K) are maximized when local service providers place their facilities at the efficient locations, $r_1 = L/4$ and $r_2 = 3L/4$, respectively.

We can then see that if $r_1 \neq r_2$, the cooperative profits obtained by each local service provider for given locations will be given by:[13]

$$\Pi_1^K = \frac{\Delta}{1 + \Delta} \Pi^K$$

$$= \begin{cases} \left[\dfrac{(2L + r_1 + r_2)^2}{(4L - r_1 - r_2)^2 + (2L + r_1 + r_2)^2} \right] L \left[v - a \left(\dfrac{r_2 - r_1}{2} \right)^2 \right] & \text{if } r_1 < \dfrac{r_2}{3} \quad \wedge \quad r_2 > \dfrac{2L}{3} + \dfrac{r_1}{3} \\[4mm] \left[\dfrac{(2L + r_1 + r_2)^2}{(4L - r_1 - r_2)^2 + (2L + r_1 + r_2)^2} \right] L(v - ar_1^2) & \text{if } r_1 > \dfrac{r_2}{3} \quad \wedge \quad r_1 > L - r_2 \; . \\[4mm] \left[\dfrac{(2L + r_1 + r_2)^2}{(4L - r_1 - r_2)^2 + (2L + r_1 + r_2)^2} \right] L[v - a(L - r_2)^2] & \text{if } r_2 < \dfrac{2L}{3} + \dfrac{r_1}{3} \wedge r_1 < L - r_2 \end{cases}$$

$$\Pi_2^K = \frac{1}{1 + \Delta} \Pi^K$$

$$= \begin{cases} \left[\dfrac{(4L - r_1 - r_2)^2}{(4L - r_1 - r_2)^2 + (2L + r_1 + r_2)^2} \right] L \left[v - a \left(\dfrac{r_2 - r_1}{2} \right)^2 \right] & \text{if } r_1 < \dfrac{r_2}{3} \quad \wedge \quad r_2 > \dfrac{2L}{3} + \dfrac{r_1}{3} \\[4mm] \left[\dfrac{(4L - r_1 - r_2)^2}{(4L - r_1 - r_2)^2 + (2L + r_1 + r_2)^2} \right] L(v - ar_1^2) & \text{if } r_1 > \dfrac{r_2}{3} \quad \wedge \quad r_1 > L - r_2 \\[4mm] \left[\dfrac{(4L - r_1 - r_2)^2}{(4L - r_1 - r_2)^2 + (2L + r_1 + r_2)^2} \right] L[v - a(L - r_2)^2] & \text{if } r_2 < \dfrac{2L}{3} + \dfrac{r_1}{3} \wedge r_1 < L - r_2 \end{cases}$$

$$(3.8)$$

If $r_1 = r_2$, the cooperative profits obtained by each provider at given locations will be given by:

$$\Pi_1^K = \Pi_2^K = \frac{1}{2}\Pi^K = \begin{cases} \frac{1}{2}L[v - a(L - r_j)^2] & \text{if} \quad r_1 = r_2 < \dfrac{L}{2} \\ \frac{1}{2}L(v - \frac{1}{4}aL^2) & \text{if} \quad r_1 = r_2 = \dfrac{L}{2} \\ \frac{1}{2}L[v - a(r_j)^2] & \text{if} \quad r_1 = r_2 > \dfrac{L}{2} \end{cases} \tag{3.9}$$

We now examine how the cooperative profits for each provider will depend upon the facilities' locations.

COOPERATIVE PROFITS WHEN $r_1 \neq r_2$ Two forces determine the cooperative profits of local service provider 1 depending on its location, given r_2 (and equivalently for local service provider 2), if $r_1 \neq r_2$. On the one hand, as we explained earlier, $\partial[\Delta/(1+\Delta)]/\partial r_1 > 0$ for all location pairs, which means that $\partial\Pi_1^K/\partial r_1 > 0$, implying an advantage for local service provider 1 if it moves closer to local service provider 2. We call this the 'bargaining power force.'

On the other hand, we can see that $\partial\Pi^K/\partial r_1 > 0$ or $\partial\Pi^K/\partial r_1 = 0$ or $\partial\Pi^K/\partial r_1 < 0$, depending on locations, which means that $\partial\Pi_1^K/\partial r_1 > 0$, $\partial\Pi_1^K/\partial r_1 = 0$ and $\partial\Pi_1^K/\partial r_1 < 0$, respectively. Given r_2, $\partial\Pi^K/\partial r_1 > 0$ ($\partial\Pi^K/\partial r_1 < 0$) if moving closer implies a decrease (increase) in total transport costs. Generally, if the locations of local public goods are very far from each other, moving nearer will imply a reduction in total transport costs, and thus $\partial\Pi^K/\partial r_1 > 0$. However, if the locations of the local public goods are already close to each other, moving even closer will increase total transport costs, and thus $\partial\Pi^K/\partial r_1 < 0$.[14] This will give the local service providers an incentive to move closer to the efficient locations. We call this the 'efficiency force.'

In order to determine the net effect of these two forces in equation (3.8), we start by analysing the case in which $r_2 = L$ and $r_1 = 0$, and examine the incentives for local service provider 1 to move closer to local service provider 2, which means discovering the conditions required so that $\partial\Pi_1^K/\partial r_1 > 0$.

We can see that if $r_1 \in [0, L/3]$, then $\Pi^K = L\{v - a[(L - r_1)/2]^2\}$, and thus $\partial\Pi^K/\partial r_1 > 0$. On the other hand, we know that $\partial\{(\Delta/(1+\Delta)\}/\partial r_1 > 0$ for all locations. Thus, in this case both effects operate in the same direction, and so $\partial\Pi_1^K/\partial r_1 > 0$ for all of this interval. If $r_1 \in [L/3, L[$, we can see that $\Pi^K = L(v - ar_1^2)$, and so $\partial\Pi^K/\partial r_1 < 0$. Thus, for this interval the effects work in opposite directions. On the one hand, moving towards local service provider 2 increases the share of cooperative profits gained by local service provider 1, but on the other, moving towards local service provider 1 decreases total cooperative profits. We can see that in this case, the bargaining power effect will always offset the efficiency effect, if v/a is large enough so that:

$$\frac{v}{a} \geq 7.\overline{6}L^2. \tag{3.10}$$

Thus, if v/a satisfies condition (3.10), $\partial \Pi_1^K / \partial r_1 > 0$, and therefore local service provider 1 will increase its cooperative profits if it moves closer to local service provider 2.

If we now analyse the case in which $r_2 < L$, we find that the condition on v/a, so that the bargaining power effect always offsets the efficiency effect and thus $\partial \Pi_1^K / \partial r_1 > 0$, is relaxed. This implies the following result:

Result 3.2 Under mill pricing, if the facilities are located at different locations ($r_1 \neq r_2$) and the reservation price is relatively high with respect to transport costs so that $v/a \geq 7.\overline{6}L^2$, local service provider 1 (local service provider 2) will increase its partial cooperative profits if it moves closer to local service provider 2 (local service provider 1).[15]

COOPERATIVE PROFITS WHEN $r_1 = r_2$ We now examine how the cooperative profits for both local service providers depend upon location, if they are at the same location. It is clear that when $r_1 = r_2$, the profits for both local service providers in the one-shot equilibrium will be identical and equal to zero, and thus, given our trigger strategy equilibrium, under cooperation they will split the total cooperative profits into two equal halves. Let us see what happens to the cooperative profits of local service provider 1 (and equivalently for local service provider 2) if it deviates from this location. Three cases will arise, depending on the initial locations $r_1 = r_2$.

The first case is when $r_1 = r_2 > L/2$. Here we can see that Π_1^K increases if local service provider 1 moves away, choosing a location $r_1 = r_2 - \varepsilon$, where ε is positive and very small. This is because at $r_1 = r_2 - \varepsilon$ the total cooperative profits are nearly unchanged, but the proportion that local service provider 1 now obtains from them is greater than 1/2, because it now has a bigger captive market to its left, and thus higher bargaining power. If it moved in the other direction and chose the location $r_1 = r_2 + \varepsilon$, its cooperative profits would be smaller than at $r_1 = r_2$, because the total cooperative profits are nearly unchanged, but the proportion of them that it now obtains is lower than 1/2. In this case, it would have a smaller captive market and thus less bargaining power than at $r_1 = r_2$.

The second case is when $r_1 = r_2 < L/2$. Here, as in the previous analysis, Π_1^K increases if local service provider 1 moves away, choosing the location $r_1 = r_2 + \varepsilon$.

The final case is when $r_1 = r_2 = L/2$. In this case, Π_1^K decreases if local service provider 1 moves away from local service provider 2 in either direction. Accordingly, we can summarize the findings in the following result:

Result 3.3   Under mill pricing, and if the reservation price is relatively high with respect to transport costs so that $v/a \geq 7.\overline{6}L^2$, if $r_1 = r_2 \neq L/2$ the partial cooperative profits for local service provider 1 (and equivalently for local service provider 2) will increase if it moves away and chooses a location $r_1 = r_2 - \varepsilon$, if $r_2 > L/2$, and $r_1 = r_2 + \varepsilon$ if $r_2 < L/2$, where ε is very small and positive. If $r_1 = r_2 = L/2$, then partial cooperative profits for local service provider 1 (and equivalently for local service provider 2) will decrease if it moves away from local service provider 2.

Existence of a unique, inefficient equilibrium   Given Results 3.2 and 3.3, we can show that only one possible location equilibrium exists under cooperation, and that is the one of minimum differentiation, $r_1{}^* = r_2{}^* = L/2$. On the one hand, locations for which $r_1 \neq r_2$ will not be equilibrium locations, because local service provider 1 and local service provider 2 will always have incentives to move nearer to each other, as shown in Result 3.2. On the other hand, all locations at which $r_1 = r_2 \neq L/2$ are not equilibrium locations, because both local service providers will have an incentive to move a small distance away from their competitor, in the direction of the larger captive market, as shown in Result 3.3. The only location pair at which no provider has an incentive to choose another location under cooperation is that of minimum differentiation, at the centre of the market. Thus:

Result 3.4   Under mill pricing, given that the reservation price is relatively high with respect to transport costs so that $v/a \geq 7.\overline{6}L^2$, if a partial cooperative equilibrium exists, it is unique and occurs at the centre of the region at $r_1{}^* = r_2{}^* = L/2$.

In Appendix 3A2 we describe this locational duopoly as a repeated game, in which the local service providers share a common discount parameter, $\delta \in \,]0, 1]$. As explained in detail there, the following result can be derived:

Result 3.5   Under mill pricing and given that the reservation price is relatively high with respect to transport costs so that $v/a \geq 7.\overline{6}L^2$ and that the discount parameter is relatively high so that $\delta \geq \frac{1}{2}$, a partial cooperative equilibrium exists, which is unique and occurs at the centre of the region at $r_1^* = r_2^* = L/2$.

Discriminatory pricing

In the previous section, we saw that under mill pricing and partial cooperation, the equilibrium locations are those of minimum differentiation (both local public goods placed at the centre of the region). We already know that the equilibrium locations under mill pricing and competition are those of maximum differentiation (both local public goods placed at the borders of the region). Thus, under both competition and partial cooperation, the equilibrium locations will be inefficient[16] as well as equivalent in terms of welfare (total transport costs will be the same in both cases) when mill prices are charged in this setting.

However, as we saw in Chapter 2, discriminatory pricing under competition leads to an equilibrium with efficient locations (at 1/4 and 3/4, which are those that minimize total transport costs). Thus, we may postulate that discriminatory pricing might also change the minimum differentiation equilibrium result under partial cooperation and in this case also lead to efficient equilibrium locations for the local public goods. The inefficiency problem would originate from the charging of mill prices and not from the existence of partial cooperation.

Nevertheless, as we show in the following section, the opportunity to charge discriminatory prices does not change the equilibrium locations existing under partial cooperation with mill pricing, and thus the equilibrium locations will also be those of minimum differentiation in this case. This implies that discriminatory pricing will lead to the efficient locations only if partial cooperation is not possible.

Characterization of the single-shot non-cooperative equilibrium The equilibrium prices, market areas and profits at the single-shot non-cooperative equilibrium as a function of locations are given by:[17]

$$
P_1^{LC}(r) = \begin{cases} t_2(r) - t_1(r) & \text{if} \quad 0 \le r \le r_1 + \dfrac{r_2 - r_1}{2} \\ 0 & \text{if} \quad r_1 + \dfrac{r_2 - r_1}{2} \le r \le L \end{cases}
$$

$$
X_1 = \left[0, r_1 + \frac{r_2 - r_1}{2} \right]
$$

$$
\Pi_1^{LC} = r_1(r_2 - r_1)a + \left(\frac{r_2 - r_1}{2} \right)^2 a \tag{3.11}
$$

$$P_2^{LC}(r) = \begin{cases} t_1(r) - t_2(r) & \text{if} \quad r_1 + \dfrac{r_2 - r_1}{2} \leq r \leq L \\[2mm] 0 & \text{if} \quad 0 \leq r \leq r_1 + \dfrac{r_2 - r_1}{2} \end{cases}$$

$$X_2 = \left[r_1 + \frac{r_2 - r_1}{2}, L \right]$$

$$\Pi_2^{LC} = (L - r_2)(r_2 - r_1)a + \left(\frac{r_2 - r_1}{2} \right)^2 a \tag{3.12}$$

We assume that v/a is large enough so that local service providers compete for all points in space, implying that for each provider alone, it will always be profitable to cover the entire market. Thus, throughout this analysis we assume that:[18]

$$\frac{v}{a} \geq L. \tag{3.13}$$

We can see in equations (3.11) and (3.12) that if both local service providers were located in the same place, they would have no relative advantage compared to the other, and thus equilibrium prices and profits would be zero under competition. Only the distance between them gives each some relative advantage with respect to the other, allowing them to charge positive prices in some areas.

As we have shown in Chapter 2, local service provider $_j$, in order to maximize its profits, will choose a location that minimizes total transport costs, given the location of the other local service provider. Thus, the efficient locations ($L/4$, $3L/4$), which are those that minimize total transport costs, represent an equilibrium in this case. This is different from the result in the case of mill pricing under competition, where the only equilibrium locations were those of maximum differentiation (at 0 and L).

This can be seen in Figure 3.1. Given $r_2 = 3L/4$, if local service provider 1 chooses to locate at $r_1 = 2L/4$, its profits will be given by the area 0ABC. If it moves away from local service provider 2 and chooses a location such as $r_1' = L/4$, its profits will be given by the area 0DEF, which is larger than the area 0ABC. But if it moves even farther away from local service provider 2, choosing a location such as $r_1'' = 0$, its profits will be given by the area 0GH, which is smaller than the area 0DEF. In the case of mill pricing, local service providers can always increase their profits if they move away from their competitors.

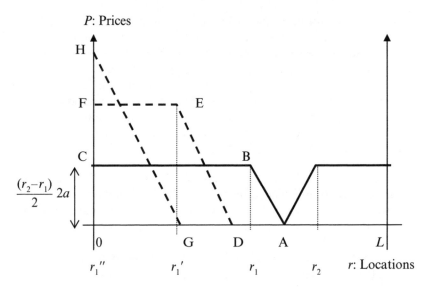

Figure 3.1 *Profits for local service provider 1 for different locations*
(r_1, r'_1 and r''_1), given that local service provider 2 is located at
$r_2 = 3L/4$.

Thus, discriminatory pricing will solve the problem of inefficient locations chosen by competing local service providers under mill pricing, by inducing them to choose the efficient locations.

Would discriminatory pricing, then, also lead to efficient location choices under partial cooperation?

Given the trigger strategy equilibrium described earlier, local service providers will be interested in the proportion of profits they would gain in the single-shot equilibrium, because this will determine the share they will obtain of the total cooperative profits. In this case:

$$\Delta = \frac{\Pi_1^{LC}}{\Pi_2^{LC}} = \frac{\frac{3}{4}r_1 + \frac{1}{4}r_2}{L - \frac{3}{4}r_2 - \frac{1}{4}r_1}. \tag{3.14}$$

We can see here that in terms of its share of cooperative profits, given r_2, local service provider 1 will always benefit from moving closer to local service provider 2 (increasing r_1), as in the case of mill pricing, because the proportion of its profits at the single-shot equilibrium increases, thus increasing the share it will obtain from the cooperative profits. The same argument is valid for provider 2. Therefore, if the total amount of cooperative profits were independent of location, both providers would have incentives to move towards each other. However, as we shall see next, total cooperative profits do depend on the locations chosen by providers, and thus, a move to the right by local service provider 1 (nearer to local service provider 2) may result in its gaining a higher share of total cooperative profits, but it may also lead to a reduction in total cooperative profits if it means moving away from the efficient locations, and this may leave the provider with smaller profits than at a more distant location. Thus, we can expect that these two opposing forces will form an equilibrium at some location pair between the optimal locations (L/4 and 3L/4) and the minimum differentiation locations (with both facilities at the centre of the market, at L/2).

Cooperative profits In order to investigate the nature of the cooperative profits for each local service provider, given the trigger strategy equilibrium that we used as described above, let us first examine the total cooperative profits, Π^K. In Figure 3.2, we can see the prices a monopoly provider with two local public goods at r_1 and r_2 would charge in order to maximize its profits, which we denote by $P^K(r)$. Thus, in order to maximize total cooperative profits, these would be the prices that each provider (local service provider 1 and local service provider 2) will set under cooperation, given r_1 and r_2, and thus the total cooperative profits will be given by the total area under $P^K(r)$:[19]

$$\Pi^K = \int_0^L P^K(r)dr = vL - \frac{a}{2}r_1^2 - \frac{a}{2}(L - r_2)^2 - \frac{a}{4}(r_2 - r_1)^2. \qquad (3.15)$$

In cooperation, each of the local service providers will obtain a portion of these total cooperative profits, which we denote by Π_1^K and Π_2^K, respectively, with $\Pi^K = \Pi_1^K + \Pi_2^K$. These shares will be in the same proportion as the profits in the single-shot game. Thus, the profits each provider will obtain under cooperation as a function of their locations are given by the following expressions:

$$\Pi_1^K$$

$$= \begin{cases} \left(\dfrac{\Delta}{1+\Delta}\right)\Pi^K = \left(\dfrac{3r_1 + r_2}{4L - 2r_2 + 2r_1}\right)\left[vL - \dfrac{a}{2}r_1^2 - \dfrac{a}{2}(L - r_2)^2 - \dfrac{a}{4}(r_2 - r_1)^2\right] & \text{if } r_1 \neq r_2 \\[2ex] \dfrac{1}{2}\Pi^K = \dfrac{1}{2}\left[vL - \dfrac{a}{2}r_1^2 - \dfrac{a}{2}(L - r_2)^2 - \dfrac{a}{4}(r_2 - r_1)^2\right] & \text{if } r_1 = r_2 \end{cases}$$

$$\Pi_2^K$$

$$= \begin{cases} \left(\dfrac{1}{1+\Delta}\right)\Pi^K = \left(\dfrac{4L - 3r_2 - r_1}{4L - 2r_2 + 2r_1}\right)\left[vL - \dfrac{a}{2}r_1^2 - \dfrac{a}{2}(L - r_2)^2 - \dfrac{a}{4}(r_2 - r_1)^2\right] & \text{if } r_1 \neq r_2 \\[2ex] \dfrac{1}{2}\Pi^K = \dfrac{1}{2}\left[vL - \dfrac{a}{2}r_1^2 - \dfrac{a}{2}(L - r_2)^2 - \dfrac{a}{4}(r_2 - r_1)^2\right] & \text{if } r_1 = r_2 \end{cases}$$

$$(3.16)$$

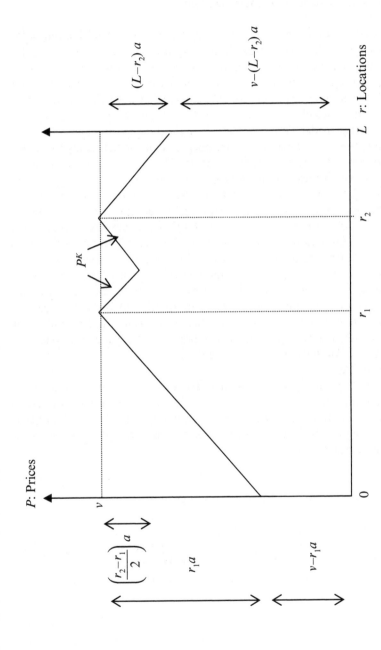

Figure 3.2   Prices set by each local service provider under partial cooperation, given that their facilities are located at r_1 and r_2, respectively

We now want to see how the cooperative profits for both local service providers will depend upon their locations.

COOPERATIVE PROFITS WHEN $r_1 \neq r_2$ If $r_1 \neq r_2$, we can see in equation (3.16) the two forces that determine the cooperative profits for local service provider 1, depending on its location, given r_2 (and equivalently for local service provider 2). On the one hand, as in the case of mill pricing, we observe the bargaining power force. We can see that $\partial(\Delta/1 + \Delta)/\partial r_1 > 0$ for all location pairs, which means that $\partial\Pi_1^K/\partial r_1 > 0$, implying an advantage for local service provider 1 if it moves closer to local service provider 2.[20] On the other hand, we can also note the presence here of the 'efficiency force.' We can see that $\partial\Pi^K/\partial r_1 > 0$, $\partial\Pi^K/\partial r_1 = 0$ or $\partial\Pi^K/\partial r_1 < 0$, depending on the locations, which means that $\partial\Pi_1^K/\partial r_1 > 0$, $\partial\Pi_1^K/\partial r_1 = 0$ and $\partial\Pi_1^K/\partial r_1 < 0$, respectively. Given r_2, $\partial\Pi^K/\partial r_1 > 0$ ($\partial\Pi^K/\partial r_1 < 0$) if moving closer implies a decrease (increase) in total transport costs. Generally, if the locations of local public goods are very far from each other, moving closer will cause a reduction in total transport costs, and thus $\partial\Pi^K/\partial r_1 > 0$. But if the locations of the local public goods are already very close together, moving even closer will increase total transport costs, and so $\partial\Pi^K/\partial r_1 < 0$.[21] This will give the local service providers an incentive to move closer to the efficient locations.

In order to understand the meaning of equation (3.16) and to see how these two forces interact with each other in determining the cooperative profits of local service provider 1 in relation to the given locations (and equivalently for local service provider 2), we analyse this situation in Appendix 3A3.

We can see in the appendix that the bargaining power force always dominates the efficiency force, and thus a local service provider will always have an incentive to move nearer to another provider, if the reservation price is relatively high with respect to the transport costs and so the following condition is satisfied:

$$\frac{v}{a} > 4.5L. \tag{3.17}$$

Accordingly, we can summarize the findings in the following result:

Result 3.6 Under discriminatory pricing, if $r_1 \neq r_2$ and the reservation price is relatively high with respect to the transport costs so that $v/a > 4.5L$, local service provider 1 (local service provider 2) will increase its partial cooperative profits if it moves closer to local service provider 2 (local service provider 1).

COOPERATIVE PROFITS WHEN $r_1 = r_2$ We now examine how the cooperative profits for both local service providers depend upon location, if they are at the same location. This analysis is identical to the one in the case of mill pricing, which was explained in detail above. Thus, we go directly to the result.

Result 3.7 Under discriminatory pricing and if the reservation price is relatively high with respect to transport costs so that $v/a > 4.5L$, if $r_1 = r_2 \neq L/2$ the partial cooperative profits for local service provider 1 (and equivalently for local service provider 2) will increase if it moves away, choosing the location $r_1 = r_2 - \varepsilon$, if $r_2 > L/2$, and $r_1 = r_2 + \varepsilon$, if $r_2 < L/2$, where ε is positive and very small. If $r_1 = r_2 = L/2$, then the partial cooperative profits for local service provider 1 (and equivalently for local service provider 2) under discriminatory pricing will decrease if it moves away from local service provider 2.

Existence of a unique inefficient equilibrium Given Results 3.6 and 3.7, we can show that only one possible location equilibrium exists under cooperation, and that is the one with minimum differentiation, $r_1^* = r_2^* = L/2$, as in the case of mill pricing. On the one hand, locations where $r_1 \neq r_2$ will not be equilibrium locations, because local service provider 1 and local service provider 2 will always have an incentive to move closer to each other, as shown in Result 3.6. On the other, all locations at which $r_1 = r_2 \neq L/2$ are not equilibrium locations, because each local service provider will have an incentive to move slightly away from its competitor, in the direction of the larger captive market, as shown in Result 3.7. The only location pair at which no local service provider has an incentive to choose another location, under partial cooperation, is that of minimum differentiation, at the centre of the market. Thus:

Result 3.8 Under discriminatory pricing and given that the reservation price is relatively high with respect to transport costs so that $v/a > 4.5L$, if a partial cooperative equilibrium exists, it is unique and occurs at $r_1^* = r_2^* = L/2$.

Equivalent to the case of mill pricing, in Appendix 3A2 we describe this locational duopoly as a repeated game, in which the local service providers share a common discount parameter, $\delta \in]0, 1[$. As explained in detail there, the following result can be derived:

Result 3.9 Under discriminatory pricing and given that the reservation price is relatively high with respect to transport costs so that $v/a > 4.5L$ and that the discount parameter is relatively high so that $\delta \geq 1/2$, a partial cooperative equilibrium exists, which is unique and occurs at $r_1^* = r_2^* = L/2$.

Accordingly, the strategic aspect with respect to cooperation dominates, contributing to the result of minimum differentiation. Thus, in spite of the opportunity for price discrimination, the equilibrium locations under partial cooperation are inefficient, as in the case of mill pricing. The advantages of minimum differentiation at the centre under partial cooperation are the access to hinterlands of equal size, as well as the potential to impose substantial penalties for deviation from the cooperative outcomes. In order to distinguish between the role of the hinterland and the disciplinary role of potential penalties, we now analyse a setting without a hinterland, in which space is symmetrical, that is, the Salop setting.

Symmetrical Geographical Structure: The Salop Setting

As discussed in the previous sections, minimum differentiation seems to be a robust equilibrium outcome under partial cooperation. Nevertheless, and as we noted earlier, this strong argument is based on the very specific geographical structure of the Hotelling model, featuring the presence of endpoints, which gives local service providers the incentive to fight to obtain a larger captive market than the other, in order to enjoy higher bargaining power and thus a higher proportion of the cooperative profits.

Thus, we should consider partial cooperation in a model where space is symmetrical, in the sense that it does not have endpoints. To that end, we consider a model similar to that of Salop (1979) and Economides (1988), the significant difference being that here we allow for partial cooperation among local service providers. As expected, and as we show in the following section, we can see that in such a symmetrical space, the outcome of minimum differentiation from partial cooperation under mill pricing no longer holds, and that the equilibrium location choices will be those of maximum differentiation (at the symmetrical locations), which are also the efficient ones. This holds even in competition, which similarly contradicts the result of inefficient equilibrium locations under mill pricing in a Hotelling context. As we shall see, this is also true for price discrimination. Thus, in this context, competition and cooperation under both price regimes will lead to the same result, which is the choice of the optimal locations at equilibrium.

In this case, with the absence of a hinterland, the share of the cooperative profits obtained by each local service provider at equilibrium will always be 1/2, independent of their location, because at any location pair, no local service provider will have an advantage over the other (since there is no captive market or hinterland). When a local service provider moves nearer to its competitor, its gains on one side of the market are the same as its losses on the other side. Thus, assuming that cooperation is sustainable, if total cooperative profits did not depend upon location, providers would be indifferent to their locations. However, total cooperative profits do, of course, depend upon location, and thus, given the location of the other, a local service provider will choose the location that minimizes total transport costs, in order to maximize total cooperative profits and therefore its own cooperative profits. This implies that the efficient locations will be the equilibrium locations in this context.

Mill pricing
In this section we analyse the case of partial cooperation with mill pricing in a Salop-style model. We shall see that the equilibrium locations are those of maximum differentiation (at the symmetrical locations), which are also the efficient ones.

Characterization of the single-shot non-cooperative equilibrium Given prices and locations, under competition, the market areas and corresponding demands and profits of local service provider 1 and local service provider 2, respectively, are given by:[22]

$$X_1^{LC}(\underline{P}, d) = [w_1, w_2] \Rightarrow D_1^{LC} = \frac{L}{2} + \frac{(P_2 - P_1)L}{2ad(L - d)}$$

$$X_2^{LC}(\underline{P}, d) = [w_2, w_1] \Rightarrow D_2^{LC} = \frac{L}{2} + \frac{(P_1 - P_2)L}{2ad(L - d)} \tag{3.18}$$

$$\Pi_1^{LC}(\underline{P}, d) = \frac{P_1 L}{2} + \frac{P_1(P_2 - P_1)L}{2ad(L - d)},$$

$$\Pi_2^{LC}(\underline{P}, d) = \frac{P_2 L}{2} + \frac{P_2(P_1 - P_2)L}{2ad(L - d)} \tag{3.19}$$

where d is the distance between r_1 and r_2, to the right of local service provider 1; $(L - d)$ is the distance to the left of local service provider 1; w_1 is the location of the individual indifferent to the choice between local service provider 1 and local service provider 2, to the left of local service provider 1; and w_2 is the location of the individual indifferent to the choice between local service provider 1 and local service provider 2, to the right of local service provider 1, as we can see in Figure 3.3.

We assume that v/a is large enough to ensure that the providers compete for all points in space, implying that for each provider alone, it will always be profitable to cover the entire market. Therefore, throughout the analysis we assume that:[23]

$$\frac{v}{a} \geq \frac{3}{4} L^2. \tag{3.20}$$

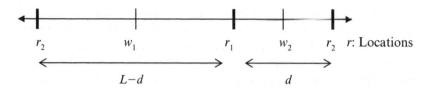

Figure 3.3   *Location of a consumer indifferent to the choice of patronizing*
                local public good₁ at r₁ or local public good₂ at r₂, which is
                represented by w₁ and w₂, in the Salop setting

The equilibrium prices, market areas, demands and profits at the single-shot non-cooperative equilibrium as a function of location will be given by:[24]

$$P_1^{LC}(d) = P_2^{LC}(d) = ad(L - d) \tag{3.21}$$

$$X_1^{LC}(d) = X_2^{LC}(d) \Rightarrow D_1^{LC}(d) = D_2^{LC}(d) = \frac{L}{2} \tag{3.22}$$

$$\Pi_1^{LC}(d) = \Pi_2^{LC}(d) = \frac{L}{2}ad(L - d). \tag{3.33}$$

We can see that in a state of competition, the profits of each local service provider will be maximized when $d = L/2$.[25] Thus, the symmetrical locations are a single-shot non-cooperative equilibrium. As we saw in Chapter 2, the symmetrical locations are those that minimize total transport costs, and thus for two existing local service providers, the symmetrical locations are the efficient ones.

Here we can see that the profits in the single-shot non-cooperative equilibrium will always be equal, independent of location. This implies that, in this case:

$$\Delta = \frac{\Pi_1^{LC}}{\Pi_2^{LC}} = 1 \tag{3.24}$$

$$\frac{\Delta}{1 + \Delta} = \frac{1}{1 + \Delta} = \frac{1}{2}. \tag{3.25}$$

Therefore, given the trigger strategy equilibrium described earlier, both local service providers will obtain half of the total cooperative profits at equilibrium, independent of their locations.

Cooperative profits   Let us now investigate the nature of the cooperative profits for each local service provider, Π_1^K and Π_2^K. From equations (3.24) and (3.25), we know that they will be given by:

$$\Pi_1^K = \Pi_2^K = \frac{1}{2}\Pi^K. \tag{3.26}$$

Given the trigger strategy equilibrium used above, the cooperative prices that will be set by each provider (local service provider 1 and local service provider 2) in cooperation, given r_1 and r_2, will be identical to the prices that would be chosen by a monopoly provider with local public goods at r_1 and r_2 in order to maximize its total profits.

Accordingly, and as we explain in detail in Appendix 3A4, the cooperative profits of each local service provider will be given by:

$$\Pi_1^K = \Pi_2^K = \left[v - \frac{a(L-d)^2}{4} \right]\frac{L}{2} \quad \text{if} \quad d < \frac{L}{2}$$

$$\Pi_1^K = \Pi_2^K = \left(v - \frac{ad^2}{4} \right)\frac{L}{2} \quad \text{if} \quad d > \frac{L}{2}. \quad (3.27)$$

$$\Pi_1^K = \Pi_2^K = \left(v - \frac{aL^2}{16} \right)\frac{L}{2} \quad \text{if} \quad d = \frac{L}{2}$$

Existence of an efficient equilibrium   From equation (3.27) it can be seen that the cooperative profits of each local service provider are maximized when $d = L/2$, and therefore each provider, given the location of the other, will seek to locate its facility at the opposite side of the market area in order to maximize its cooperative profits. Thus, we can summarize the findings as follows:

Result 3.10   In the absence of a hinterland, under mill pricing and assuming that the reservation price is relatively high with respect to transport costs so that $v/a \geq 3/4\ L^2$, if a partial cooperative equilibrium exists, it is unique and occurs at the efficient locations, $d^* = L/2$.

Result 3.10 implies that, in a symmetrical space such as this one, the outcome of minimum differentiation under partial cooperation and mill pricing no longer holds, and that the equilibrium location choices will be those of maximum differentiation (at the symmetrical locations), which are also the efficient ones. We have seen that this holds in competition as well, which contradicts the result of inefficient equilibrium locations under mill pricing in a Hotelling context.

As explained earlier, in this case with its absence of a hinterland, the share of the cooperative profits obtained by each local service provider at equilibrium will always be $\frac{1}{2}$, independent of location. This is because at any location pair, neither local service provider will have an advantage over the other (there is no captive market or hinterland). When a local service provider moves nearer to its competitor, its gains on one side of the market are the same as its losses on the other. Thus, if total cooperative profits did not depend upon location, providers would be indifferent to their location. However, total cooperative profits do in fact depend upon location, and thus, given the location of the other, a provider will choose the location that minimizes total transport costs, in order to maximize total cooperative profits and therefore its own cooperative profits. This implies that the efficient locations, those of maximum differentiation (at the symmetrical locations), will be the equilibrium locations in this setting.

In Appendix 3A5 we describe this locational duopoly as a repeated game, in which the local service providers share a common discount parameter: $\delta \in \,]0, 1[$. As explained in detail there, following result can be derived:

Result 3.11 In the absence of a hinterland, under mill pricing and assuming that the reservation price is relatively high with respect to transport costs so that $v/a \geq 3/4 \, L^2$ and that the discount parameter is relatively high so that

$$\delta \geq \frac{1}{2} \left(\frac{16\dfrac{v}{a} - 9L^2}{16\dfrac{v}{a} - 7L^2} \right),$$

a cooperative equilibrium exists, which is unique and occurs at the efficient locations, $d^* = L/2$.

We have seen that by changing our assumption from a Hotelling definition of space to a symmetrical space, the result of minimum differentiation under partial cooperation changes dramatically, and we obtain maximum differentiation under partial cooperation. As stated above, in this case of a symmetrical space, the equilibrium locations under cooperation and under competition are the same, and they are also the efficient locations. Thus, the presence of a hinterland is crucial to the result of inefficient location choices under competition and partial cooperation with mill pricing.

Discriminatory pricing

In this section, we analyse the case of partial cooperation in a Salop-style model with discriminatory pricing. We shall see that the equilibrium locations are also those of maximum differentiation (the symmetrical locations) in this case.

Characterization of the single-shot non-cooperative equilibrium The equilibrium prices, market areas and profits at the single-shot non-cooperative equilibrium as a function of location are given by:[26]

$$P_j^{LC}(r) = \begin{array}{ll} t_i(r) - t_j(r) & \text{if } r \in X_j \\ 0 & \text{if } r \in X_i \end{array}$$

$$X_i = X_2 = [w_1, w_2] \Rightarrow D_1^{LC} = D_2^{LC} = \frac{L}{2} \qquad (3.28)$$

$$\Pi_1^{LC} = \Pi_2^{LC} = \frac{ad}{2}(L - d),$$

where $t_j(r)$ is always the shortest distance to local public good$_j$; d is the distance between r_1 and r_2, to the right of local service provider 1; $(L - d)$ is the distance to the left of local service provider 1; w_1 is the location of the individual indifferent to the choice between local service provider 1 and local service provider 2, to the left of local service provider 1; and w_2 is the location of the individual indifferent to the choice between local service provider 1 and local service provider 2, to the right of local service provider 1, as we can see in Figure 3.4.

We assume that v/a is large enough so that the local service providers will compete for all points in space, implying that for each provider alone, it will

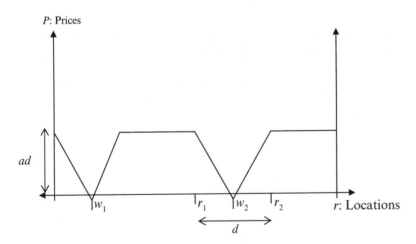

Figure 3.4 Equilibrium prices at the single-shot non-cooperative equilibrium as a function of location under price discrimination in the Salop setting

always be profitable to cover the entire market. Thus, throughout the analysis we assume that:[27]

$$\frac{v}{a} \geq \frac{L}{2}.$$ (3.29)

We can see that if both providers are located at the same place ($d=0$), they will have no relative advantage over each other, and thus equilibrium prices and profits will be zero.

As in the case of mill pricing, we can see that under competition, the profits of each provider are maximized when $d=L/2$.[28] Thus, the symmetrical locations are a single-shot non-cooperative equilibrium, as in the case of discriminatory pricing. In Chapter 2, we showed that the symmetrical locations are those that minimize total transport costs, and thus, for two existing providers, the symmetrical locations are the efficient ones.

As in the mill-pricing case, we can see that the profits in the single-shot non-cooperative equilibrium will always be equal, independent of location. This also implies in this case that:

$$\Delta = \frac{\Pi_1^{LC}}{\Pi_2^{LC}} = 1$$ (3.30)

$$\frac{\Delta}{1+\Delta} = \frac{1}{1+\Delta} = \frac{1}{2}.$$ (3.31)

Therefore, given the trigger strategy equilibrium described above, both local service providers will obtain half of the total cooperative profits at equilibrium, independent of their location.

Cooperative profits   Let us now investigate the nature of the cooperative profits for each local service provider, Π_1^K and Π_2^K. From equations (3.30) and (3.31), we know that they are given by:

$$\Pi_1^K = \Pi_2^K = \frac{1}{2}\Pi^K.$$ (3.32)

Given the trigger strategy equilibrium used above, the cooperative prices that each local service provider (local service provider 1 and local service provider 2) will set in cooperation, given r_1 and r_2, will be identical to the prices chosen by a monopoly local service provider with local public goods at r_1 and r_2 in order to maximize its total profits.

In Figure 3.5 we can see the prices that would be chosen by a monopoly local service provider with two local public goods at r_1 and r_2 in order to

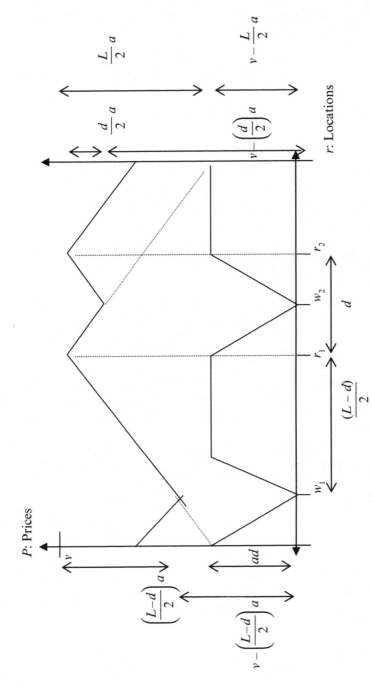

Figure 3.5   Prices set by each local service provider under partial-cooperation, given that their facilities are located at r_1 *and* r_2, *respectively*

maximize its profits, which we denote by $P^K(r)$. Thus, the total area under $P^K(r)$ will give total cooperative profits:[29]

$$\Pi^K = \int_0^L P^K(r)dr = vL - \frac{ad^2}{4} - \frac{a(L-d)^2}{4}. \tag{3.33}$$

Accordingly, the cooperative profits of each provider will be given by:

$$\Pi_1^K = \Pi_2^K = \frac{1}{2}\Pi^K = \frac{vL}{2} - \frac{ad^2}{8} - \frac{a(L-d)^2}{8}. \tag{3.34}$$

Existence of a unique and efficient equilibrium From equation (3.34) we can see that, as in the case of mill pricing, the cooperative profits of each local service provider are maximized when $d = L/2$, and thus each provider, given the location of the other, will seek to place its facility at the opposite side of the market in order to maximize its cooperative profits. Therefore, we can summarize the findings as follows:

Result 3.12 In the absence of a hinterland, assuming discriminatory pricing and that the reservation price is relatively high with respect to transport costs so that $v/a \geq L/2$, if a partial cooperative equilibrium exists, it is unique and occurs at the efficient locations, $d^* = L/2$.

Thus, by changing our assumption from a Hotelling definition of space to a symmetrical space without the presence of a hinterland, independent of the price regime, we obtain maximum differentiation under partial cooperation.

Note that in this case of a symmetrical space, as in the case of mill pricing, the equilibrium locations are the same under partial cooperation and under competition, and they are the efficient ones.

In Appendix 3A6 we describe this locational duopoly as a repeated game, in which the local service providers share a common discount parameter: $\delta \in]0, 1[$. As explained in detail there, the following result can be derived:

Result 3.13 In the absence of a hinterland, assuming discriminatory pricing and that the reservation price is relatively high with respect to transport costs so that $v/a \geq L/2$ and that the discount parameter is relatively high so that $\delta \geq 1/2$, a cooperative equilibrium exists which is unique and occurs at the efficient locations, $d^* = L/2$.

We have seen here, as in the case of mill pricing, that the equilibrium locations under partial cooperation within a symmetrical geography will be those of maximum differentiation (the symmetrical locations), which are also the efficient ones. Therefore, when there is no hinterland, competition and partial cooperation will lead to the same result under both price regimes, which is the optimal location choice at equilibrium.

3.4   FULL COOPERATION

As discussed in the previous section, within a symmetrical geography, the equilibrium location choices of the local service providers for their local public goods will be efficient. This holds both under competition and under partial cooperation, as well as under both price regimes, mill and discriminatory pricing. The problem of inefficient equilibrium location choices arises in the presence of some hinterland to be captured.

We have seen that within such an asymmetrical geography, discriminatory pricing with respect to location can help to solve this problem and achieve the optimal location choices at equilibrium, if competition is guaranteed and thus partial cooperation is impossible. However, a discriminatory price policy is usually difficult to implement in practice. On the one hand, there can be technical problems in implementing it. For example, it can be difficult to verify customers' addresses, and people will have incentives to claim that they live farther away in order to obtain lower prices. On the other hand, there may also be political problems in implementing this policy, because price discrimination is generally seen as 'unfair.' Thus, it is likely that local service providers will have to charge mill prices.

As argued by Friedman and Thisse (1993), in a Hotelling-style model, the equilibrium locations of two firms under mill pricing and full cooperation with equal profits will correspond to the efficient locations, 1/4 and 3/4, respectively. Thus, in our setting, full cooperation of local service providers within an asymmetrical geography and mill pricing should lead to the efficient location choices for their local public goods at equilibrium, and in this sense, full cooperation will lead to an increase in efficiency in comparison with competition (where we obtain the inefficient location choices of maximum differentiation) or with partial cooperation (where we get minimum differentiation) under mill pricing. This seems to be a plausible result, because full cooperation appears to be equivalent to a monopoly situation, and we can show that a monopolist will always choose the optimal locations for its local public goods in order to maximize its profits in this setting.

Nevertheless, we should bear in mind that in spite of their full cooperation, the local service providers will still be independent entities, and thus, once the locations of their local public goods are chosen in a cooperative manner, assuming that these are difficult to change once selected,[30] they may still deviate in the area of prices, because prices can easily be changed. If the penalty for deviating from the cooperative price agreement is very high, there will be no incentive to deviate from the optimal cooperation prices (that is, the prices that maximize cooperative profits at a given location pair) once the locations are chosen, and thus local service providers will cooperatively choose those locations which maximize optimal cooperation prices, as a monopolist would do, and these are the efficient locations. However, what happens if the penalty for deviating from the cooperative agreement is very low? It is probable that in those cases, the optimal cooperative prices will no longer be sustainable at any location pair, and thus local service providers must take this into account when cooperatively choosing their locations and prices. Could this imply that the equilibrium location choices under full cooperation in this case would be different from the efficient locations?

In order to analyse this question, we examine the equilibrium allocation of a system of FOCJ characterized by *full cooperation* and *mill pricing*, in order to compare these equilibrium allocations with those achieved under competition and partial cooperation as well as with the optimal allocation. We investigate the case of two existing local service providers, which cooperatively select the locations of their local public goods at the beginning of the timeframe. Once chosen, these locations are permanently fixed, but the providers will cooperatively choose mill prices at each of a infinite succession of time periods. We also examine the equilibrium behaviour of the providers in this setting.

We shall see that if the penalty for deviating from the cooperative price agreement is very high, as reflected in a relatively high value of the discount parameter, full cooperation with optimal pricing will be sustainable at any location pair chosen cooperatively by the local service providers. Thus, they will choose the location pair that maximizes their cooperative profits, which represents the efficient locations, as argued by Friedman and Thisse. However, if the penalty for deviating from the cooperative price agreement is very low, as reflected in a relatively low value of the discount parameter, full cooperation with optimal pricing will not be sustainable at all locations, and it may not be sustainable at the efficient locations. Thus, in order to choose the location pair that maximizes their cooperative profits, local service providers will have to find a location pair that results in the highest possible *sustainable cooperative profits*, given this low discount parameter. We see that when the discount parameters are relatively low, sustainable cooperative profits will be maximized at locations farther away from each other than the efficient ones, and when the values of the discount parameter are low enough, at equilibrium maximum differentiation under full cooperation, as under competition, will be obtained.

We show that for low values of the discount parameter, the incentives to deviate in pricing, for a given discount parameter, decrease as the distance between the two local public goods increases, implying that the maximum sustainable cooperation prices that local service providers can agree to charge will increase with the distance between them. The explanation for this is as follows. As providers cooperatively choose to locate farther away from each other, two effects can be noted on their incentives to deviate in pricing. The first is that profits under competition increase, which implies an increase in the incentive to deviate in pricing, because the penalty for deviating is less severe. But there is also a second effect, which is that the profits from deviating are reduced when the providers cooperatively choose to locate at more distant locations, and thus deviation in price becomes less attractive. This is because when the local public goods are located far from each other, the mill price that must be charged by one local service provider in order to underbid the other and obtain all of the market is very low, because transportation costs are very high. This effect will lead to a reduction in the incentive to deviate in price. We show that with a low discount parameter, this second effect outweighs the first, and thus the maximum sustainable cooperative prices that providers can agree to charge increase with the distance between them.

As stated earlier, if the discount parameter is very low, local service providers will cooperatively choose locations farther away from each other than the efficient locations, in order to maximize sustainable cooperative profits. If the discount parameter, δ, is higher than some threshold level, $\bar{\delta}$, then the equilibrium locations under full cooperation will be the efficient ones. However, if $\delta < \bar{\delta}$, then the equilibrium locations under full cooperation will be inefficient, and the local will cooperatively choose locations that are farther away from each other than the efficient locations. As δ decreases, the distance between the two local public goods at equilibrium will increase, and if $\delta \leq \underline{\delta}$, then the equilibrium locations will be those of maximum differentiation under full cooperation. Therefore, for lower values of the discount parameter, the equilibrium locations under mill pricing and full cooperation will generally be inefficient.

Characterization of the Single-shot Non-cooperative Equilibrium

Chapter 2 showed that the equilibrium prices, market areas, demands and profits at the single-shot non-cooperative equilibrium as a function of locations are given by equations (2.98) and (2.99). As explained there, in the single-shot equilibrium, local service providers increase their profits as they move farther apart, and so the equilibrium locations in this case are those of maximum differentiation, 0 and L respectively.[31]

Cooperative Profits under Optimal Pricing

Given the fact that both local service providers are identical in all aspects at the beginning of the negotiation, and that they cooperatively arrange prices and locations, it is likely that they will divide their cooperative profits into equal shares, and thus we assume that:

$$\Pi_1^K = \Pi_2^K = \frac{1}{2}\Pi^K. \tag{3.35}$$

Accordingly, local service providers will then be interested in the total amount of the cooperative profits, in order to determine the location pair and prices that they will cooperatively choose. Let us disregard for the moment the option of deviating in price after the locations are set in a cooperative manner, and investigate the nature of the total cooperative profits under optimal pricing (that is, the prices that maximize total cooperative profits at a given location pair).

First, we investigate the optimal prices, P^{Kop}, in order to determine the level of the maximum total cooperative profits and to examine how they will depend upon the chosen locations. As stated earlier, these prices will be equal to those chosen by a monopoly local service provider with two facilities at r_1 and r_2 in order to maximize its profits.

Thus, in Appendix 3A1 we analyse the prices that a monopolist would choose. There we can see that P^M, which is equal to the optimal price set by local service providers under cooperation, will be given by equation (3A1.6). Thus, given the locations of the local public goods, the profits that would be obtained by a monopoly provider, which are equivalent to the total cooperative profits under optimal pricing, will be given by equation (3A1.7). As explained in the appendix, for a monopoly local service provider, the locations that will maximize its profits are the efficient ones, $r_1 = L/4$ and $r_2 = 3L/4$, because these are the locations that minimize total transport costs, and thus total profits are maximized. Therefore, as shown in Result 3.1, total cooperative profits will be maximized in this case when the local service providers place their facilities at the efficient locations.

Inefficient Equilibrium Locations for Low Values of the Discount Parameter

From the previous result, we know that a monopolist with two facilities would install them at the efficient locations $r_1 = L/4$ and $r_2 = 3L/4$, respectively, in order to maximize its profits, and that it would charge the following price:[32]

$$P^M = v - \frac{1}{16}aL^2. \qquad (3.36)$$

Nevertheless, full cooperation is not equivalent to a monopoly, because both local service providers are still independent units, and thus, once they choose their locations, they still have the opportunity to deviate from the agreed-upon cooperative prices. Of course, if deviating from the optimal prices once the locations are chosen were not profitable, the threat of deviation would not be relevant, and full cooperation with optimal pricing would be sustainable at any location pair chosen cooperatively by the providers. In this case, they will choose the location pair that maximizes their cooperative profits, as a monopolist would do, which represents the efficient locations, as argued by Friedman and Thisse. However, what happens when the threat of price deviation becomes relevant? Would this alter the location choices cooperatively arranged by the providers?

To answer these questions, in Appendix 3A7 we describe this locational duopoly as a repeated game, in which the local service providers share a common discount parameter, $\delta \in \,]0, 1[$. As explained in detail there, in order for cooperation with the providers located at the efficient locations (which are those which maximize total cooperative profits through optimal pricing) to be stable, the discount parameter must be sufficiently high so that:

$$\delta \geq \bar{\delta} = \frac{1}{2} \left(\frac{16\frac{v}{a} - 17L^2}{16\frac{v}{a} - 13L^2} \right). \qquad (3.37)$$

Accordingly, the following result can be derived:

Result 3.14   Under mill pricing and full cooperation, if the discount parameter is sufficiently high so that $\delta \geq \bar{\delta}$, local service providers will cooperatively choose to locate at the efficient locations $r_1 = L/4$ and $r_2 = 3L/4$, respectively.

We can see that $\bar{\delta}$ increases with v/a, and as $v/a \to \infty \Rightarrow \bar{\delta} \to \frac{1}{2}$. Therefore, for any constellation of parameters, if $\delta \geq 1/2$, cooperation will always be stable at the efficient locations, and thus the local service providers will cooperatively choose these locations.

Accordingly, it is clear that for high values of the discount parameter, where $\delta \geq \bar{\delta}$, full cooperation will always lead to the efficient location choices for the local public goods. Nevertheless, if the discount parameter is relatively low, so that $\delta < \bar{\delta}$, cooperation with optimal pricing may no longer be sustainable at the efficient locations. Thus, in this case, local service providers will have to choose the locations and prices that maximize *sustainable cooperative profits*. $P^{Ksop}(r_1, \delta)$ denotes the optimal cooperative prices that are sustainable, given a low δ.

Then if $\delta < \bar{\delta}$, we need to know what these sustainable optimal cooperative prices, $P^{Ksop}(r_1, \delta)$, and the corresponding sustainable cooperative profits look like, in order to determine which locations would maximize them. These would be the locations that local service providers will cooperatively choose if $\delta < \bar{\delta}$. We consider only symmetrical locations, because only symmetrical location pairs will maximize sustainable cooperative profits, given a low value of the discount parameter.

Let us start by determining the maximum cooperative prices, for a given location pair, that are sustainable under a low discount parameter δ, which we define as $P^{K\max}(r_1, \delta)$. This is given by:[33]

$$P^{K\max}(r_1,\delta) = aL(L - 2r_1)\left(\frac{3\delta - 2}{2\delta - 1}\right).$$
(3.38)

We can see that:

$$\frac{\partial P^{K\max}(r_1,\delta)}{\partial \delta} > 0$$
(3.39)

$$\frac{\partial P^{K\max}(r_1,\delta)}{\partial r_1} < 0.$$
(3.40)

This means that as δ increases, it decreases the restriction on the prices the providers can charge in cooperation for a given location pair so that price deviation is not profitable, and thus they can charge higher prices under cooperation. This is because a higher δ makes the penalty for deviation more severe, and therefore price cooperation can be sustained at higher prices. It can be shown that if δ is sufficiently high, $\delta \geq 1/2$, then the restriction on the prices charged in cooperation for a given location pair so that deviation is not profitable is no longer binding, and cooperation with optimal prices will be sustainable at any location pair.

On the other hand, if local service providers decide to locate their local public goods farther away from each other (lower r_1), the restriction on the prices they can charge in cooperation for a given, relatively low δ, $\delta < 1/2$, so that deviation is not profitable, is relaxed, and thus they can charge higher prices under cooperation. This is because the incentives for price deviation at a given location pair decrease as the distance between the two local public goods increases, implying that the maximum sustainable cooperation prices that providers can agree to charge increases with the distance between them. The explanation for this is as follows. As local service providers cooperatively choose to locate farther away from each other, there are two effects on their incentives to deviate in prices. The first is that profits under competition increase, which implies an increase in the incentive for price deviation, because the penalty for deviating is less severe. However, there is also a second effect, which is that the profits from deviation are reduced when the providers cooperatively choose to place their facilities at more distant locations, and thus price deviation becomes less attractive. This is because when the local public goods are located far from each other, the mill price that must be charged by one local service provider in order to underbid the other is very low, since transportation costs are very high. This effect reduces the incentive to deviate in prices. Under a low discount parameter, this second effect outweighs the first, and therefore the maximum sustainable cooperative prices that providers can agree to charge increases with the distance between them.

Let us now examine what the sustainable optimal cooperation prices, $P^{Ksop}(r_1, \delta)$, along with the corresponding sustainable optimal cooperative profits, will look like if $\delta < 1/2$, in order to determine which locations will maximize them and thus to discover the locations that local service providers will cooperatively choose in this case.

We can see that if $\delta < 1/2$, $P^{Ksop}(r_1, \delta)$ is given by the following expression:

$$P^{Ksop}(r_1, \delta) = \min[P^{Kop}(r_1), P^{Kmax}(r_1, \delta)], \tag{3.41}$$

where $P^{Kop}(r_1)$ and $P^{Kmax}(r_1, \delta)$ are given by equations (3A1.6) and (3.38), respectively.

Thus, the equilibrium location choices of local service providers under full cooperation, if $\delta < 1/2$, will be given by:

$$r_1^E = \arg \max[P^{Ksop}(r_1, \delta)] \tag{3.42}$$

$$r_2^E = L - r_1^E. \tag{3.43}$$

In order to make this clear, we have drawn $P^{Kop}(r_1)$ and $P^{Kmax}(r_1, \delta)$ to represent local service provider 1 (and symmetrically for local service provider 2) in Figure 3.6, for given values of v, a and L, and for different location pairs and δ. We can see that for high values of δ, where $\delta \geq \bar{\delta}$, for example at δ_1 in the figure, $r_1^E = L/4 = r_1^*$, because $P^{Ksop}(r_1, \delta)$ is given in this case by the semi-circle between point A and C and by the segment

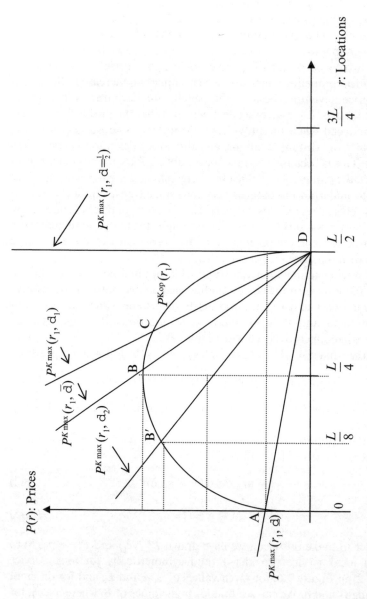

Figure 3.6 $P^{Kop}(r_1)$ *(in the semi-circle line) and* $P^{K\,max}(r_1, \delta)$ *(in the segments starting at point* D*) (in the segments starting at point* D*) for local service provider 1, for given values of* v, a *and* L, *and for different locations for its facility;* r_1, *and for different levels of the discount parameter,* δ

236

between point C and D. However, if $\delta < \bar{\delta}$, for example at δ_2 in the figure, $P^{Ksop}(r_1, \delta)$ will be given in this case by the semi-circle between point A and B' and by the segment between point B' and D, and thus $r_1^E = L/8 < r_1^*$. As δ decreases, r_1^E also decreases, and if $\delta \leq \underline{\delta}$, where:[34]

$$\underline{\delta} = \frac{1}{2}\left(\frac{4\dfrac{v}{a} - 9L^2}{4\dfrac{v}{a} - 7L^2}\right), \tag{3.44}$$

then $r_1^E = 0$, and thus we get maximum differentiation under full cooperation.

This implies that if the discount parameter is relatively low, local service providers will cooperatively choose locations farther away from each other than the efficient ones, in order to maximize their sustainable cooperative profits.

As stated earlier, we can see that both $\underline{\delta}$ and $\bar{\delta}$ increase with v/a, and as $v/a \to \infty \Rightarrow \underline{\delta} \wedge \bar{\delta} \to 1/2$. Therefore, as $v/a \to \infty$, $\delta < 1/2$, will imply that the equilibrium location under full cooperation will be that of maximum differentiation. We can summarize the findings in the following result:

Result 3.15 If the discount parameter is relatively low so that $\delta < \bar{\delta}[v/a, L]$, the equilibrium locations under full cooperation will be inefficient and will be characterized by a greater distance between local public goods than the optimal one. If the discount parameter is so low that $\delta < \underline{\delta}(v/a, L)$, the equilibrium locations under full cooperation will be those of maximum differentiation.

This implies that within an asymmetrical geographical structure, if the threat of price deviation is sufficiently low (that is, the discount parameter is sufficiently high), full cooperation between local service providers will lead to the efficient location choices for local public goods at equilibrium, and in this sense it will solve the efficiency problem obtained with mill pricing under competition (where we obtain the inefficient location choices of maximum differentiation) as well as under partial cooperation (where we obtain minimum differentiation). Nevertheless, if the threat of price deviation is relatively high (the discount parameter is low), full cooperation between providers will lead to inefficient location choices for their local public goods at equilibrium, and if it is sufficiently high, it will also lead to maximum differentiation, as in the case of competition. In this last case, competition, partial cooperation and full cooperation will be equivalent in terms of welfare.

3.5   CONCLUDING REMARKS

In this chapter, we have analysed whether cooperation among local service providers such as FOCJ might solve some of the allocation problems that emerge in competition, particularly the inefficient equilibrium location choices by providers for their local public goods that may emerge in competition under some circumstances.

We have seen that the geographical structure of the analysed setting is crucial for the determination of local service providers' equilibrium location choices for their local public goods, and that in general, when the geography is symmetrical, as in the Salop setting, the local service providers' equilibrium location choices for their local public goods will be efficient. This holds under competition as well as under cooperation, and under both analysed price regimes, mill and discriminatory pricing. The problem of inefficient equilibrium location choices arises when the geographical structure of the setting is asymmetrical, so that endpoints are present, as in the Hotelling setting.

We have shown that under this kind of asymmetrical geography, and assuming quadratic transportation costs, the equilibrium locations chosen by two competing local service providers for their local public goods under mill pricing will be those of maximum differentiation (that is, the providers place their local public goods at 0 and L, respectively). This is because in competition, providers will seek to locate their facilities as far as possible from their competitors, in order to reduce price competition. In this setting, the optimal locations for the local public goods would be at $L/4$ and $3L/4$, which are the locations that minimize total transport costs, as shown above. Thus, competition will fail in this case, leading to inefficient locations for the local public goods.

We also show that discriminatory pricing with respect to location can help solve this problem and achieve the optimal location choices at equilibrium, if competition is guaranteed. However, discriminatory price policies are usually difficult to implement in practice, for both technical and political reasons. It is therefore probable that local service providers will have to charge mill prices, implying that within an asymmetrical geographical structure, competition will fail in this case, leading to inefficient locations for the local public goods (those of maximum differentiation), as explained earlier.

As we have argued in this chapter, we might imagine that in this context, where the geography is asymmetrical and local service providers are obliged to charge mill prices, cooperation (whether partial or full) between local service providers may partially or completely solve the problem of inefficient location choices for local public goods that emerges under competition, because some degree of cooperation will reduce price competition and thus may lead to more efficient locations (those that reduce total transport costs).

The analysis in this chapter has shown that, the equilibrium locations in the case of cooperation will crucially depend on the stability of this cooperation, as reflected in the value of the discount parameter, δ. We have shown that if δ is sufficiently high (implying high stability of cooperation), so that $\delta > \frac{1}{2}$, then partial cooperation will be stable, but it will lead to inefficient location choices (minimum differentiation, with both facilities at $L/2$), which are equivalent in terms of welfare to the equilibrium location choices under competition. This is because under partial cooperation, in contrast to what happens in competition, local service providers will always have an incentive to move closer to their competitors in order to increase their bargaining power and thus their cooperative profits. This implies that the only possible equilibrium under partial cooperation is that of minimum differentiation, because it ensures hinterland areas of equal size. In contrast, full cooperation in this case will lead to the efficient locations for local public goods.

Given smaller values of the discount parameter, so that $\overline{\delta} < \delta < \frac{1}{2}$, partial cooperation will never be stable, and thus we obtain the result we observed under competition (maximum differentiation) in the case of partial cooperation as well. Full cooperation will also lead in this case to the efficient locations for local public goods. Thus, for relatively high values of the discount parameter, full cooperation will lead to the efficient locations for local public goods, improving the situation with respect to competition. This is because if the stability of cooperative prices is guaranteed by a sufficiently high value of δ, local service providers will cooperatively choose the locations that maximize their cooperative profits, and these are, as in the case of a monopoly provider, the efficient locations. However, if $\delta < \overline{\delta}$, then full cooperation will also lead to inefficient location choices (farther apart than the efficient locations). This is because at low values of the discount parameter, local service providers will have incentives to choose locations farther from the efficient ones in a cooperative manner, in order to reduce the incentives for price deviation after the locations are chosen, and thus to maximize sustainable cooperative profits. Nevertheless, if $\underline{\delta} < \delta < \overline{\delta}$, in spite of the fact that the equilibrium locations under full cooperation will be inefficient, these location choices will be better in terms of welfare than under competition, because total transport costs will be lower. Only in the case where δ is so low that $\delta \leq \underline{\delta}$ will full cooperation also lead to maximum differentiation, and thus it will be as unfavourable as competition in terms of welfare. These results are summarized in Figure 3.7.

PRICE REGIME

<table>
<tr><th rowspan="2">LEVEL OF COOPERATION</th><th colspan="3">MILL PRICING</th><th colspan="2">DISCRIMINATORY PRICING</th></tr>
<tr><th colspan="3"></th><th colspan="2"></th></tr>
<tr>
<td>NO COOPERATION: FULL COMPETITION</td>
<td colspan="3">Maximum differentiation: $r_1 = 0 \wedge r_2 = L$</td>
<td colspan="2">Optimal locations: $r_1 = \frac{1}{4}L \wedge r_2 = \frac{3}{4}L$</td>
</tr>
<tr>
<td>PARTIAL COOPERATION</td>
<td colspan="3"><table><tr><td>$\delta < \frac{1}{2}$
No equilibrium</td><td>$\delta \geq \frac{1}{2}$
Maximum differentiation: $r_1 = r_2 = \frac{1}{2}L$</td></tr></table></td>
<td colspan="2"></td>
</tr>
<tr>
<td>FULL COOPERATION</td>
<td>$\delta \leq \underline{\delta}$
Maximum differentiation: $r_1 = 0 \wedge r_2 = L$</td>
<td>$\underline{\delta} < \delta < \bar{\delta}$
$0 < r_1^E < \frac{1}{4}L \wedge \frac{3}{4}L < r_2^E < L^{**}$</td>
<td>$\delta \geq \bar{\delta}^*$
Optimal locations: $r_1 = \frac{1}{4}L \wedge r_2 = \frac{3}{4}L$</td>
<td>$\delta < \frac{1}{2}$
No equilibrium</td>
<td>$\delta \geq \frac{1}{2}$
Maximum differentiation: $r_1 = r_2 = \frac{1}{2}L$</td>
</tr>
</table>

Notes:

*Remember that, as explained in the chapter, we can easily see that δ increases with v/a, and as $v/a \to \infty \Rightarrow \delta \to 1/2$. Therefore, for any constellation of parameters, if $\delta \geq 1/2$, cooperation will always be stable at the efficient locations, and thus the local service providers will cooperatively choose these locations.

**Remember that we considered only symmetrical locations, because only symmetrical location pairs will maximize sustainable cooperative profits, given a low value of the discount parameter. Accordingly, $r_2^E = L - r_1^E$.

Figure 3.7   Equilibrium locations chosen by two local service providers for their local public goods in the Hotelling setting

Therefore, in general, partial cooperation will never improve the situation in comparison with competition in terms of welfare, but full cooperation may improve it, if the discount parameter is sufficiently high. Nevertheless, if the discount parameter is relatively low, competition, partial cooperation and full cooperation will be equivalent in terms of welfare, and in this case cooperation will not help solve, in welfare terms, the problem of inefficient locations for local public goods that arises under competition.

A number of questions emerge from the previous analysis that remain for future research. First, we should analyse what happens to the equilibrium locations under full cooperation if the technology of the local public goods is characterized by no location sunk costs, rather than location sunk costs, as we assumed in the analysis above. This would clearly change the results obtained here, because now local service providers would be able to deviate in both price and location after the cooperative prices and locations have been agreed upon. Thus, local service providers will have to take this situation into account when cooperatively choosing their locations and prices. Second, we should determine whether this result still holds for more than two local service providers. Clearly, the equilibrium configuration for local public goods would be affected by cooperative pricing in this case, but it is not so clear that the results would be identical to those in our case involving two local service providers. Third, we should examine what happens to the equilibrium locations for local public goods if we consider the case of cooperation in a situation where there are various different types of local public goods, with different degrees of substitutability between them. The locations of these local public goods would now depend not only on the locations of the local public goods of the same type, but also on the locations of the other types of local public goods, as well as their strategy of competition or cooperation.

Finally, in the analysis above, we examined whether cooperation between local service providers such as FOCJ might solve some of the allocation problems that emerge in competition, and we focused only on the possible inefficient location choices for local public goods in competition. We should also analyse the potential effects of cooperation on some of the other inefficiencies generated under competition, such as excessive and insufficient entry. For example, in the case of a monopoly local service provider, the equilibrium number of facilities and their locations will be equivalent to the optimal ones, because these minimize total transport costs plus fixed costs, thus maximizing aggregate profits without giving incentives for entry. Nevertheless, this optimal allocation may not be an equilibrium in a setting of full cooperation, because in this case, local service providers are still independent units which aim to maximize their individual profits.

APPENDIX 3A1   DETERMINATION OF THE TOTAL COOPERATIVE PROFITS, Π^K, IN THE HOTELLING SETTING UNDER MILL PRICING AND PARTIAL COOPERATION

Chapter 3 showed that total cooperative profits are equivalent to the profits that a profit-maximizing monopoly local service provider with two facilities would make. Accordingly, this appendix examines the prices set by a profit-maximizing monopoly provider with two facilities in the Hotelling setting in order to determine the monopoly profits and thus the total cooperative profits, π^K.

First we analyse the prices that a monopoly provider with two facilities at r_1 and r_2 would choose in order to maximize its profits.

It can be shown that if v/a is large enough so that $v/a \geq 3L^2$, a monopolist with local public goods at r_1 and r_2, in order to maximize total profits, will set prices at each facility that will allow it to cover the entire market and to minimize total transport costs, so people will pay the maximum they can afford. Thus, the prices that a monopolist will charge for local public good$_1$ and local public good$_2$, P_1^M and P_2^M respectively, must satisfy the following conditions:

$$P_1^M = P_2^M = P^M \tag{3A1.1}$$

$$P^M = \min\left\{ P^{max}(rpc = 0),\ P^{max}\left[rpc = r_1 + \left(\frac{r_2 - r_1}{2}\right) \right],\ P^{max}(rpc = L) \right\}, \tag{3A1.2}$$

where rpc is the location of the, 'reservation price consumer', which is the consumer paying the full price of v; P^{max} $(rpc = 0)$ is the maximum price that the monopoly provider can charge so that the reservation price consumer is located at 0; P^{max} $\{rpc = r_1 + [(r_2 - r_1)/2]\}$ is the maximum price that the monopoly provider can charge so that the reservation price consumer is located at $r_1 + (r_2 - r_1)/2$; and P^{max} $(rpc = L)$ is the maximum price that the monopoly provider can charge so that the reservation price consumer is located at L.

Condition (3A1.1) guarantees that total transport costs are minimized in the sense that, given the locations of the local public goods, each consumer will patronize the nearest facility. Condition (3A1.2) guarantees that the market is completely covered, which will allow the monopolist to maximize its profits, if $v/a \geq 3L^2$.

We can see that $P^{max}(rpc = 0)$, $P^{max}\{rpc = r_1 + [(r_2 - r_1)/2]\}$ and $P^{max}(rpc = L)$ are given by the following expressions:

$$P^{\max}(rpc = 0) = v - ar_1^2 \tag{3A1.3}$$

$$P^{\max}\left[rpc = r_1 + \left(\frac{r_2 - r_1}{2}\right)\right] = v - a\left(\frac{r_2 - r_1}{2}\right)^2 \tag{3A1.4}$$

$$P^{\max}(rpc = L) = v - a(L - r_2)^2. \tag{3A1.5}$$

This implies that P^M, which is equal to the price that local service providers will charge under cooperation, P^K, will be given by:

$$P^M = P^K = \begin{cases} \left[v - a\left(\dfrac{r_2 - r_1}{2}\right)^2\right] & \text{if} \quad r_1 < \dfrac{r_2}{3} \quad \wedge \quad r_2 > \dfrac{2L}{3} + \dfrac{r_1}{3} \\[2ex] (v - ar_1^2) & \text{if} \quad r_1 > \dfrac{r_2}{3} \quad \wedge \quad r_1 > L - r_2 \,. \\[2ex] [v - a(L - r_2)^2] & \text{if} \quad r_2 < \dfrac{2L}{3} + \dfrac{r_1}{3} \quad \wedge \quad r_1 < L - r_2 \end{cases} \tag{3A1.6}$$

Thus, the profits that would be obtained by a monopoly local service provider, given the locations of the local public goods, which are equivalent to the total cooperative profits in this case, will be given by:

$$\Pi^M = \Pi^K = \begin{cases} L\left[v - a\left(\dfrac{r_2 - r_1}{2}\right)^2\right] & \text{if} \quad r_1 < \dfrac{r_2}{3} \quad \wedge \quad r_2 > \dfrac{2L}{3} + \dfrac{r_1}{3} \\[2ex] L(v - ar_1^2) & \text{if} \quad r_1 > \dfrac{r_2}{3} \quad \wedge \quad r_1 > L - r_2 \\[2ex] L[v - a(L - r_2)^2] & \text{if} \quad r_2 < \dfrac{2L}{3} + \dfrac{r_1}{3} \quad \wedge \quad r_1 < L - r_2 \end{cases} \tag{3A1.7}$$

From equation (3A1.7) we can see that for a monopoly provider, the locations that will maximize its profits are the efficient ones,[35] $r_1 = L/4$ and $r_2 = 3L/4$, because these are the locations that minimize total transport costs, and thus total profits are maximized. Therefore, total cooperative profits are maximized when local service providers are located at the efficient locations.

APPENDIX 3A2   LOCATIONAL DUOPOLY AS A REPEATED GAME IN THE HOTELLING SETTING UNDER MILL PRICING AND PARTIAL COOPERATION

This appendix describes this locational duopoly as a repeated game, in which the local service providers share a common discount parameter, $\delta \in]0, 1[$. The incentive for local service provider $_j$ to deviate in one period, when $r_1^* = r_2^* = L/2$, will be given by:[36]

$$U_j(r_1^*, r_2^*) = \Pi_j^D(r_1^*, r_2^*) - \Pi_j^K(r_1^*, r_2^*)$$

$$- \left\{ \frac{\delta}{1-\delta} [\Pi_j^K(r_1^*, r_2^*) - \Pi_j^{LC}(r_1^*, r_2^*)] \right\}, \quad (3A2.1)$$

where $\Pi_j^D(r_1^*, r_2^*)$ is the profit that local service provider $_j$ (for $j \in \{1, 2\}$) would obtain if it deviated from the cooperative price strategy for $r_1^* = r_2^* = L/2$ and charged a price that would maximize its profits in one period, given that the other provider is charging the agreed-upon cooperative prices. Thus:

$$\Pi_1^D(r_1^*, r_2^*) = \Pi_2^D(r_1^*, r_2^*) = \Pi^K(r_1^*, r_2^*) = vL - \frac{aL^2}{4}. \quad (3A2.2)$$

This is because local service provider $_j$ will charge a price that is a little bit lower than $P^K(r_1^*, r_2^*)$ in order to capture the entire market, and thus its profits in this case can be approximated by $\Pi^K(r_1^*, r_2^*)$. Thus, if we substitute equations (2.98) and (3A2.2) into equation (3A2.1), we obtain:

$$U_j(r_1^*, r_2^*) = \frac{vL}{2} - \frac{aL^2}{8} - \left[\frac{\delta}{1-\delta} \left(\frac{vL}{2} - \frac{aL^2}{8} \right) \right]. \quad (3A2.3)$$

For $r_1^* = r_2^* = L/2$ to be a cooperative equilibrium, local service provider $_j$ must have no incentives to move, and therefore:

$$U_j(r_1^*, r_2^*) \le 0. \quad (3A2.4)$$

Only if $\delta \ge 1/2$ will equation (3A2.4) hold.

APPENDIX 3A3   COOPERATIVE PROFITS OF LOCAL SERVICE PROVIDER 1 FOR DIFFERENT r_1 AND r_2 IN THE HOTELLING SETTING UNDER DISCRIMINATORY PRICING AND PARTIAL COOPERATION[37]

In Figure 3A3.1 we have drawn equation (3.16) for $L = 1, a = 1$ and $v = 5$.[38] We can see there that, given r_2, moving nearer to local service provider 2 will always increase the cooperative profits of local service provider 1.

For example, if $r_2 = 1$ (local service provider 2 is located at one extreme of the market), the profits that local service provider 1 will obtain under cooperation, depending on its location, are represented in Figure 3A3.2 (which is a section of Figure 3A3.1 for $r_2 = 1$). It is clear that Π_1^K increases with r_1.

In Figure 3A3.3–3A3.5 (which are sections of Figure 3A3.1 for $r_2 = 3/4$, $r_2 = 1/2$ and $r_2 = 1/4$) we can see what happens to the profits that local service provider 1 will obtain under cooperation, depending on its location, if $r_2 = 3/4, 1/2$ or $1/4$, respectively. It is also clear that they increase with r_1 in the relevant interval for $r_1 < r_2$, [0, 3/4], [0, 1/2] and [0, 1/4], respectively.

From these figures we can also see that the cooperative profits of local service provider 1 decrease as the given location of local service provider 2 decreases. This makes sense, because if local service provider 2 is located nearer to local service provider 1, it has more hinterland or captive market to its right in the one-shot equilibrium, and thus higher bargaining power, implying lower equilibrium profits for local service provider 1 under cooperation.

Therefore, we have seen that for these given values of L, a and v, and given that $r_1 < r_2$, the bargaining power force always dominates the efficiency force, and thus:

$$\frac{\partial \Pi_1^K(\overline{r_2})}{\partial r_1} > 0 \qquad\qquad (3A3.1)$$

$$\frac{\partial \Pi_2^K(\overline{r_1})}{\partial r_2} < 0. \qquad\qquad (3A3.2)$$

This means that for both local service providers, moving nearer to the competitor's given location will always increase their own cooperative profits, and thus they will always have an incentive to move nearer to each other.

Note that this result will only be sustained under specific relationships among L, a and v. We now investigate the assumptions under which this result holds with respect to these variables.

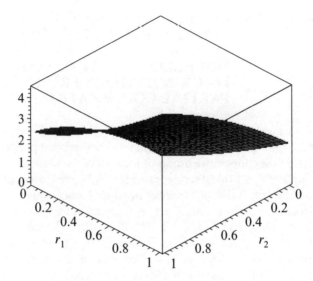

*Figure 3A3.1   Cooperative profits of local service provider₁, for different r_1
and r_2, valid for $r_1 < r_2$*

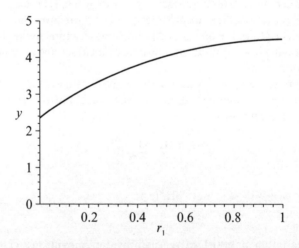

*Figure 3A3.2   Cooperative profits for local service provider₁ (on the
y-axis) at each r_1, given $r_2 = 1$*

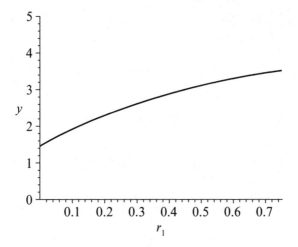

Figure 3A3.3 *Cooperative profits for local service provider$_1$ (on the y-axis) at each r_1, given $r_2 = 3/4$*

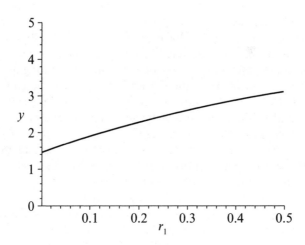

Figure 3A3.4 *Cooperative profits for local service provider$_1$ (on the y-axis) at each r_1, given $r_2 = 1/2$*

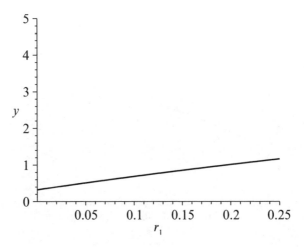

*Figure 3A3.5   Cooperative profits for local service provider₁ (on the
                 y-axis) at each r_1, given $r_2 = 1/4$*

For this purpose, assume first that $r_2 = L$. In this case, if local service provider 1 is located at the other end of the market, at $r_1 = 0$, we can see that $\partial \Pi_1^K / \partial r_1 = v$, implying that local service provider 1 will always have an incentive to move nearer to local service provider 2, regardless of the level of transport costs a or the size of the region L, as long as the individuals have a positive reservation price.[39] If $r_1 = L/8$, we can see that $(\partial \pi_1^K / \partial r_1) = (64/81)v + (29/864)aL$. Therefore, here again, regardless of the values of a and L, there will always be an incentive to move even closer to local service provider 2. If $r_1 = 2L/8$, we can see that $(\partial \pi_1^K / \partial r_1) = (16/25)v - (9/400)aL$. In this case, so that $(\partial \pi_1^K / \partial r_1) > 0$, and thus local service provider 1 has an incentive to move towards local service provider 2, the following condition must be satisfied: $v/a > 0.035\ L$, and thus, for some values of a and L, v must be large enough so that local service provider 1 has an incentive to move towards local service provider 2. If local service provider 1 is located even closer to local service provider 2, at $r_1 = 4L/8$, we can see that $(\partial \pi_1^K / \partial r_1) = (4/9)v - (7/24)aL$. So that $(\partial \pi_1^K / \partial r_1) > 0$, the following condition must be satisfied in this case: $v/a > 0.65\ L$. If $r_1 = 6L/8$, we can see that $(\partial \pi_1^K / \partial r_1) = (16/49)v - (531/784)aL$, and therefore $v/a > 2.07L$, so that $(\partial \pi_1^K / \partial r_1) > 0$. We can continue with this reasoning and find that, as r_1 converges to $r_2 = L$ (but does not reach it, because $r_1 \neq r_2$), the condition that must be satisfied so that local service provider 1 always has an incentive to move nearer to local service provider 2 converges to:

$$\frac{v}{a} > 4.5 \, L. \tag{3A3.3}$$

If we now analyse the requirements for a, L and v that are needed for $(\partial \pi_1^K / \partial r_1) > 0$ to hold, if local service provider 2 has some captive market to its right and is located at, for example, $r_2 = 6L/8$, we find that, as r_1 converges to $r_2 = 6L/8$ (but does not reach it, because $r_1 < r_2$), the condition that must be satisfied so that local service provider 1 always has an incentive to move nearer to local service provider 2 converges to $v/a > 1.8 \, L$. Thus, we can see that the condition is relaxed with respect to equation (3A3.3), and as the captive market of local service provider 2 increases (r_2 decreases), the condition becomes even more relaxed.

APPENDIX 3A4 DETERMINATION OF THE COOPERATIVE PROFITS, Π_1^K AND Π_2^K, IN THE SALOP SETTING UNDER MILL PRICING AND PARTIAL COOPERATION

The chapter, showed that total cooperative profits are equivalent to the profits that a profit-maximizing monopoly local service provider with two facilities would make. Accordingly, this appendix examines the prices set by a profit-maximizing monopoly provider with two facilities in the Salop setting in order to determine the monopoly profits and thus the total cooperative profits, Π_1^K and Π_2^K, in this case.

First we analyse the prices that a monopoly provider with two facilities at r_1 and r_2 would choose in order to maximize its profits.

It can be seen that if v/a is large enough so that $v/a \geq 3/4 \, L^2$, a monopolist with local public goods at r_1 and r_2, in order to maximize total profits, will set prices for each facility that allow it to cover the entire market while minimizing total transport costs, so that customers pay the most they can afford. Therefore, the prices that a monopolist will charge for local public good$_1$ and local public good$_2$ (P_1^M and P_2^M respectively), must satisfy the following conditions:

$$P_1^M = P_2^M = P^M \tag{3A4.1}$$

$$P^M = \min[P^{\max}(rpc = w_2), P^{\max}(rpc = w_1)], \tag{3A4.2}$$

where rpc is the location of the 'reservation price consumer', which is the one who pays the full price of v; $P^{\max}$ ($rpc = w_2$) is the maximum

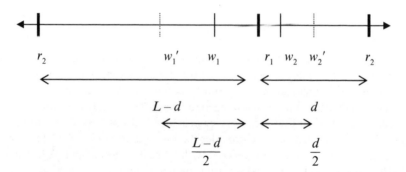

Figure 3A4.1   Location of a consumer indifferent to the choice of patronizing local public good₁ at r_1 *or local public good₂ at* r_2, *which is represented by* w_1 *and* w_2, *in the Salop setting*

price the local service provider can charge so that the reservation price consumer is located at w_2; and $P^{\max}$ $(rpc = w_1)$ is the maximum price that the provider can charge so that the reservation price consumer is located at w_1.

Condition (3A4.1) guarantees that total transport costs will be minimized in the sense that, given the locations of the local public goods, each consumer will patronize the nearest facility. If $P_1^M = P_2^M$, the consumers who are indifferent between facilities, w_1' and w_2' in Figure 3A4.1, will be located at the same distance from both facilities. But if $P_1^M \neq P_2^M$, for example $P_1^M > P_2^M$, then, as we can see in the figure, w_1 and w_2 will be closer to the more expensive facility and thus there will be consumers (those located at $r \in [w_1', w_1]$ and $r \in [w_2', w_2]$) who incur higher transport costs than they would have if $P_1^M = P_2^M$, and thus in this case, total transport costs will be higher and the monopolist's total profits lower. Condition (3A4.2) guarantees that the market will be completely covered, which will allow the monopolist to maximize its profits, if $v/a \geq 3/4L^2$.

We can see that, for given locations (and corresponding d), $P^{\max}(rpc = w_2)$ and $P^{\max}(rpc = w_1)$ will be given by:[40]

$$P^{\max}(rpc = w_2) = v - \frac{ad^2}{4}$$

$$P^{\max}(rpc = w_1) = v - \frac{a(L - d)^2}{4}. \tag{3A4.3}$$

Thus the equilibrium prices and corresponding profits for a monopolist with local public goods located at r_1 and r_2 will be given by:

$$PM = \min\left[v - \frac{a(L-d)^2}{4}, v - \frac{ad^2}{4} \right] \tag{3A4.4}$$

$$\Pi^M = \min\left\{ \left[v - \frac{a(L-d)^2}{4} \right]L, \left(v - \frac{ad^2}{4} \right)L \right\}. \tag{3A4.5}$$

As explained above, the cooperative prices that will be set by each provider (local service provider 1 and local service provider 2) under cooperation, given r_1 and r_2, will be identical to the prices chosen by a monopoly provider with local public goods at r_1 and r_2 in order to maximize its total profits.

Therefore, the cooperative profits of each local service provider will be given by:

$$\Pi_1^K = \Pi_2^K = \frac{1}{2}\Pi^K = \frac{1}{2}\Pi^M = \min\left\{ \left[v - \frac{a(L-d)^2}{4} \right]\frac{L}{2}, \left(v - \frac{ad^2}{4} \right)\frac{L}{2} \right\}. \tag{3A4.6}$$

Thus, if $d < L/2$, then $P^{\max}$ $(rpc = w_1) < P^{\max}$ $(rpc = w_2)$; if $d > L/2$, then $P^{\max}$ $(rpc = w_1) > P^{\max}$ $(rpc = w_2)$; and if $d = L/2$, then $P^{\max}$ $(rpc = w_1) = P^{\max}$ $(rpc = w_2)$. Thus, the cooperative profits of each provider, given d, can alternatively be expressed as follows:

$$\Pi_1^K = \Pi_2^K = \left[v - \frac{a(L-d)^2}{4} \right]\frac{L}{2} \quad \text{if} \quad d < \frac{L}{2}$$

$$\Pi_1^K = \Pi_2^K = \left(v - \frac{ad^2}{4} \right)\frac{L}{2} \quad \text{if} \quad d > \frac{L}{2} \tag{3A4.7}$$

$$\Pi_1^K = \Pi_2^K = \left(v - \frac{aL^2}{16} \right)\frac{L}{2} \quad \text{if} \quad d = \frac{L}{2}.$$

APPENDIX 3A5   LOCATIONAL DUOPOLY AS A REPEATED GAME IN THE SALOP SETTING UNDER MILL PRICING AND PARTIAL COOPERATION

This appendix describes this locational duopoly as a repeated game, in which the local service providers share a common discount parameter, $\delta \in]0, 1[$. The incentives for local service provider$_j$ to deviate in one period, when $d^* = L/2$, will be given by:[41]

$$U_j(d^*) = \Pi_j^D(d^*) - \Pi_j^K(d^*) - \left\{ \frac{\delta}{1-\delta}[\Pi_j^K(d^*) - \Pi_j^{LC}(d^*)] \right\}, \qquad (3A5.1)$$

where $\Pi_j^D(d^*)$ is the profit that local service provider$_j$ (for $j \in \{1, 2\}$) will obtain if it deviates from the cooperative price strategy for $d^* = L/2$, charging a price that maximizes its profits in one period, while the other provider continues to charge the agreed-upon cooperation prices. Thus:[42]

$$\Pi_1^D(d^*) = \Pi_2^D(d^*) = vL - \frac{5}{16}aL^3 \qquad (3A5.2)$$

$$\Pi_1^K(d^*) = \Pi_2^K(d^*) = \frac{vL}{2} - \frac{aL^3}{32} \qquad (3A5.3)$$

$$\Pi_1^{LC}(d^*) = \Pi_2^{LC}(d^*) = \frac{aL^3}{8}. \qquad (3A5.4)$$

Thus, if we substitute equations (3A5.2), (3A5.3) and (3A5.4) into equation (3A5.1), we obtain:[43]

$$U_j(d^*) = \frac{vL}{2} - \frac{9aL^3}{32} - \left[\frac{\delta}{1-\delta} \left(\frac{vL}{2} - \frac{5aL^3}{32} \right) \right]. \qquad (3A5.5)$$

In order for $d^* = L/2$ to be a cooperative equilibrium, local service provider$_j$ must have no incentive to deviate, and thus:

$$U_j(d^*) \leq 0. \qquad (3A5.6)$$

We can see that for equation (3A5.6) to hold, and thus for partial cooperation to be an equilibrium, δ must satisfy the following condition:

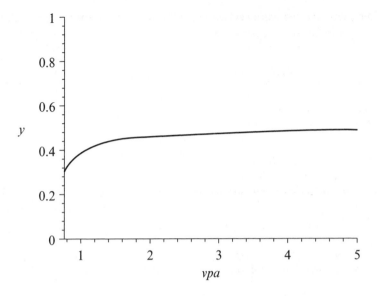

Figure 3A5.1 *Minimum δ so that* d* *will be an equilibrium,* y = δ,
vpa = v/a *and* L = 1

$$\delta \geq \frac{1}{2}\left(\frac{16\frac{v}{a} - 9L^2}{16\frac{v}{a} - 7L^2}\right). \tag{3A5.7}$$

In Figure 3A5.1, we have drawn equation (3A5.7) for L = 1. We can
see that for the relevant values of *v/a*, which are *v/a* ∈ [$\frac{3}{4}L^2$, ∞], δ ∈ [$\frac{3}{10}$, $\frac{1}{2}$], and
δ increases with *v/a* and converges to δ = 1/2.

APPENDIX 3A6   LOCATIONAL DUOPOLY AS A REPEATED GAME IN THE SALOP SETTING UNDER DISCRIMINATORY PRICING AND PARTIAL COOPERATION

This appendix describes this locational duopoly as a repeated game, in
which the local service providers share a common discount parameter,
δ ∈]0, 1[. First we analyse the incentives of a provider to deviate from the
cooperative agreement, as a function of *d*.

The incentive for local service provider$_j$ to deviate from cooperation is given by the following expression:[44]

$$U_j(d) = \Pi_j^P(d) - \Pi_j^K(d) - \left\{ \frac{\delta}{1-\delta}[\Pi_j^K(d) - \Pi_j^{LC}(d)] \right\}, \quad (3A6.1)$$

where

$$\Pi_j^P(d) = vL - \frac{aL^2}{4} \quad (3A6.2)$$

for any d, and $\Pi_j^{LC}(d)$ and $\Pi_j^K(d)$ are given by equations (3.28) and (3.34), respectively. Thus, the incentive for local service provider$_j$ to deviate from cooperation, depending on d, can be written as follows:

$$U_j(d) = vL - \frac{aL^2}{4} - \left[\frac{vL}{2} - \frac{ad^2}{8} - \frac{a(L-d)^2}{8} \right] - \left(\frac{\delta}{1-\delta} \left\{ \left[\frac{vL}{2} - \frac{ad^2}{8} \right. \right. \right.$$
$$\left. \left. \left. - \frac{a(L-d)^2}{8} \right] - \left[\frac{ad}{2}(L-d) \right] \right\} \right) \quad (3A6.3)$$

For cooperation to be stable, local service provider$_j$ must have no incentive to deviate, and thus:

$$U_j(d) \leq 0. \quad (3.A6.4)$$

We can see that $\Pi_j^P(d) - \Pi_j^K(d) = \Pi_j^K(d) - \Pi_j^{LC}(d)$ for all d, and therefore, independent of d, cooperation will be stable only if:

$$\delta \geq \frac{1}{2}. \quad (3A6.5)$$

APPENDIX 3A7   LOCATIONAL DUOPOLY AS A REPEATED GAME IN THE HOTELLING SETTING UNDER MILL PRICING AND FULL COOPERATION

This appendix describes this locational duopoly as a repeated game, in which the local service providers share a common discount parameter,

$\delta \in \,]0, 1[$. The incentives for local service provider $_j$ to deviate in one period, for given r_1 and r_2, are given by:[45]

$$U_j(r_1, r_2) = \Pi_j^D(r_1, r_2) - \Pi_j^K(r_1, r_2) - \left\{ \frac{\delta}{1-\delta} \left[\Pi_j^K(r_1, r_2) - \Pi_j^{LC}(r_1, r_2) \right] \right\},$$

(3A7.1)

where $\Pi_j^K(r_1, r_2)$ is the cooperative profit that local service provider $_j$ (for $j \in \{1, 2\}$) would obtain if charging the arranged cooperative price P^K (r_1, r_2) for given r_1 and r_2; $\Pi_j^D(r_1, r_2)$ is the profit that local service provider $_j$ would obtain if it deviated from the cooperative price strategy for given r_1 and r_2, charging a price $P^D(r_1, r_2)$ that maximizes its profits in one period, given that the other local service provider continues to charge the agreed-upon cooperation prices; and $\Pi_j^{LC}(r_1, r_2)$ are the profits under competition.

We can see that the best price for local service provider 1 (and equivalently for local service provider 2) if it deviates from cooperation, along with its corresponding profits, will be given by the following expressions:[46]

$$P_1^D = P^K - a(r_2^2 - r_1^2) \qquad (3A7.2)$$

$$\Pi_1^D = P_1^D L = [P^K - a(r_2^2 - r_1^2)]L. \qquad (3A7.3)$$

We know that the cooperative profits will be given by:

$$\Pi_1^K = P_1^K \frac{L}{2}. \qquad (3A7.4)$$

From the analysis in the chapter we know that if no threat of price deviation existed, local service providers would cooperatively choose to place their facilities at the locations that maximize total cooperative profits, which are $r_1 = L/4$ and $r_2 = 3L/4$, and they will charge the optimal cooperative prices given by equation (3.36), as explained in the chapter.

Let us now investigate the conditions under which there will be no threat of price deviation, and thus the equilibrium locations will be the efficient ones.

If the local service providers are located at the efficient locations (which are those that maximize total cooperative profits through optimal pricing) the optimal cooperation prices and the corresponding best response price for local service provider 1, if it deviates from cooperation at the location pair, will be given by:

$$P^{Kop}\left(r_1 = \frac{L}{4}, r_2 = \frac{3L}{4}\right) = v - \frac{1}{16}aL^2 \tag{3A7.5}$$

$$P^D\left(r_1 = \frac{L}{4}, r_2 = \frac{3L}{4}, P^{Kop}\right) = v - \frac{9}{16}aL^2. \tag{3A7.6}$$

Thus, the profit functions in this case will be given by:

$$\Pi_1^D\left(r_1 = \frac{L}{4}, r_2 = \frac{3L}{4}, P^{Kop}\right) = vL - \frac{9aL^3}{16} \tag{3A7.7}$$

$$\Pi_1^{Kop}\left(r_1 = \frac{L}{4}, r_2 = \frac{3L}{4}, P^{Kop}\right) = \frac{vL}{2} - \frac{aL^3}{32} \tag{3A7.8}$$

$$\Pi_1^{LC}\left(r_1 = \frac{L}{4}, r_2 = \frac{3L}{4}\right) = \frac{8aL^3}{32}. \tag{3A7.9}$$

This will imply that the incentives to deviate in price will be given in this case by:

$$U_j\left(r_1 = \frac{L}{4}, r_2 = \frac{3L}{4}, P^{Kop}\right) = \frac{vL}{2} - \frac{17aL^3}{32} - \left[\frac{\delta}{1-\delta}\left(\frac{vL}{2} - \frac{9aL^3}{32}\right)\right]. \tag{3A7.10}$$

In order for cooperation to be stable, the following must be true:

$$U_j\left(r_1 = \frac{L}{4}, r_2 = \frac{3L}{4}, P^{Kop}\right) \leq 0. \tag{3A7.11}$$

This implies that:

$$\delta \geq \bar{\delta} = \frac{1}{2}\left(\frac{16\frac{v}{a} - 17L^2}{16\frac{v}{a} - 13L^2}\right). \tag{3A7.12}$$

NOTES

1. The concept of FOCJ was developed by Frey and Eichenberger (1995, 1996a, 1997, 1999) and is explained in the general introduction.
2. As explained in the general introduction, 'FOCJ' refers to our interpretation of the concept relative to the aspects of it that we considered.

3. Using the framework of the previous chapter, it can be shown that in a one-shot location Hotelling-type model with quadratic transportation costs, the equilibrium locations chosen by two competing local service providers for their local public goods under mill pricing will be those of maximum differentiation (that is, the local service providers will place their local public goods at 0 and L, respectively. Recall that in a Hotelling setting, space in the region is described by the interval $X = [0, L]$, as explained in detail in Chapter 2). Thus, in this setting, the optimal locations for the local public goods would be at $L/4$ and $3L/4$, respectively, which are those that minimize total transport costs, as shown in Chapter 2. Thus, competition will fail in this case, leading to inefficient locations for the local public goods.

4. In the case of local public goods characterized by *no location sunk cost technology* (that is, there are no sunk costs in its chosen location and corresponding market segment), the equilibrium allocation under free entry of local service providers in the region is characterized by *excessive entry*, when the competition represented by alternative regions is very weak. This is because, given this very weak competition from other regions, the profits of local service providers will be relatively high, giving high incentives for entry. In the case of *location sunk cost technology*, the optimal allocation is a free-entry equilibrium, but we can also have free-entry equilibria with excessive and insufficient entry. This implies that the precise nature of the free-entry location-price equilibrium among competing local service providers offering local public goods with location sunk cost technology in a particular region will depend upon the history of that region. This is because, in this case, once the locations of the local public goods are chosen, they cannot be changed. Hence, the threat of an entrant cannot lead to the reallocation of the local public goods in the region, and thus we can also observe equilibria with insufficient entry in this case.

5. As explained in Chapter 2, on the one hand, there may be technical problems in implementing it. For example, it can be difficult to verify customers' addresses, and people will have incentives to claim that they live farther away in order to obtain lower prices. On the other hand, there can also be political problems in implementing this policy, because price discrimination is generally seen as 'unfair'.

6. We assume here that the local public goods are characterized by fixed technology.

7. In the case of mill pricing, this price is constant for all locations, but in the case of discriminatory pricing, it will depend on location.

8. D'Aspremont et al. (1979) show for the Hotelling geographical structure that if transportation costs are linear, no price equilibrium with positive mill prices exists when the firms are located relatively close to each other. They also show that if quadratic, instead of linear, transportation costs are considered, a price equilibrium solution will exist for any pair of locations. It can be seen that this is also true for the case of a symmetrical geographical structure, such as that of the Salop model.

9. We assume here that monetary transfers between local service providers are possible. This means that if the revenues collected by each provider at the cooperative prices are not in the same proportion as in the single-shot non-cooperative equilibrium, transfers between providers allow these revenues to be reallocated, in order to guarantee that in the end they are in the same proportion as in the single-shot non-cooperative equilibrium.

10. This model is similar to that used by Friedman and Thisse (1993), but with some variations.

11. Equation (3.5) was obtained as follows. For a monopoly local service provider, located at one extreme of the market and charging a price P, the indifferent consumer will be located at w, which will be given by: $v - a(w)^2 - P = 0 \Rightarrow w = [(v - p)/a]^{1/2}$. Therefore, its profits will be given by: $\Pi = wP = [(v - p)/a]^{\frac{1}{2}}P$. Thus, the price that it will choose in order to maximize its profits will be given by: $\partial\Pi/\partial P = [((v - p)/a)^{\frac{1}{2}} - (P/2a)^{-\frac{1}{2}}] = 0 \Rightarrow P = (2/3)v$, and w will be given by: $w = (1v/3a)^{\frac{1}{2}}$. Thus, to ensure that the monopolist local service provider is willing to cover the entire market, $w \geq L \Rightarrow v/a \geq 3L^2$.

12. Therefore $\partial\Delta/\partial r_1 > 0$ implies $\partial[\Delta/(1 + \Delta)]/\partial r_1 > 0$.

13. For equations (3.8) and (3.9), Π^K is given by equation (3A1.7).

14. For example, if $r_2 = 3L/4$, then if $r_1 \in [0, L/4]$, then $\Pi^K = L\{v - a[(r_2 - r_1)/2]^2\}$ and $\partial\Pi^K/\partial r_1 > 0$. But if $r_1 \in [L/4, 3L/4]$, then $\Pi^K = L(v - ar_1^2)$, and thus $\partial\Pi^K/\partial r_1 < 0$. So in this case, $r_1 = L/4$ is the location of local service provider 1 which maximizes Π^K.

15. In the previous analysis we assumed that $r_1 < r_2$. The analysis is symmetrical for $r_1 > r_2$.

16. The efficient (or optimal) locations of two local public goods in this setting are derived in Appendix 2A1 and are given by $r_1 = L/4$ and $r_2 = 3L/4$.

17. This can be derived from Chapter 2.

18. Equation (3.13) was obtained as follows. For a monopoly local service provider to be willing to cover the entire market, the most distant consumer must be willing to pay a positive price. This means that $v - aL \geq 0 \Rightarrow v/a \geq L$.

19. As explained in Appendix 3A1, total cooperative profits are equivalent to the profits that a profit-maximizing monopoly local service provider with two facilities would make.

20. From the analysis above we saw that $\partial\Delta/\partial r_1 > 0$. This implies that $\partial[\Delta/(1 + \Delta)]/\partial r_1 > 0$.

21. For example, if $r_2 = 3L/4$, then $r_1 = L/4$ is the location for local service provider 1 that maximizes Π^K. Thus, if local service provider 1 moves closer to local service provider 2, choosing $r_1 > L/4$, Π^K and thus Π_1^K, will be reduced.

22. Equations (3.18) and (3.19) were obtained as follows: For the case of local service provider 1, for w_2, $P_1 + a(w_2 - r_1)^2 = P_2 + a[(r_2 - r_1) - (w_2 - r_1)]^2$. From here we can see that

$$(w_2 - r_1) = \frac{(r_2 - r_1)}{2} + \frac{(P_2 - P_1)}{2a(r_2 - r_1)} = \frac{d}{2} + \frac{(P_2 - P_1)}{2ad}$$

Equivalently for w_1, we can see that

$$(r_1 - w_1) = \frac{(r_1 - r_2)}{2} + \frac{(P_2 - P_1)}{2a(r_1 - r_2)} = \frac{(L - d)}{2} + \frac{(P_2 - P_1)}{2a(L - d)}$$

Thus,

$$X_1(P, d) = [w_1, w_2] \Rightarrow D_1^{LC} = \int_{w_1}^{w_2} 1 dr = (w_2 - w_1) + (r_1 - w_1) = \frac{L}{2} + \frac{(P_2 - P_1)L}{2ad(L - d)}.$$

This implies that

$$\Pi_1^{LC} = P_1 D_1^{LC}(P, d) = \frac{P_1 L}{2} + \frac{P_1(P_2 - P_1)L}{2ad(L - d)}.$$

The equivalent is true for local service provider 2.

23. Equation (3.20) was obtained as follows: for a monopoly local service provider charging a price P, the indifferent consumers on either side of its facility will be located at: $v - a(w)^2 - P = 0 \Rightarrow w = (v - P/a)^{\frac{1}{2}}$. Thus, its profits will be given by: $\Pi = 2wP = 2[(v - P)/a]^{\frac{1}{2}} P$. Accordingly, the price it will choose in order to maximize its profits will be given by:

$$\frac{\partial\Pi}{\partial P} = 2\left[\left(\frac{v - p}{a}\right)^{\frac{1}{2}} - \frac{P}{2a}\left(\frac{v - P}{a}\right)^{\frac{1}{2}}\right] = 0 \Rightarrow P = \frac{2}{3}v,$$

and w will be given by: $w = (1v/3a)^{\frac{1}{2}}$. Thus, in order for the monopolist local service provider to be willing to cover the entire market, $2w \geq L \Rightarrow v/a \geq 3/4 L^2$.

24. Equation (3.21) was obtained as follows: Given the location and price chosen by local service provider 2, local service provider 1 will choose the price that maximizes its profits. This price will be given by the following expression:

$$\frac{\partial\Pi_1(P_2, d)}{\partial P_1} = \frac{L}{2ad(L - d)}(P_2 - 2P_1) + \frac{L}{2} = 0 \Rightarrow P_1 = \frac{ad(L - d) + P_2}{2}.$$

Similarly, we can determine the price that local service provider$_2$ will charge, given the location and price of local service provider $1 \Rightarrow P_2[ad(L-d) + P_1]/2$. Solving this equation system, we obtain equation (3.21).

25. $(\partial \Pi_1/\partial d\ aL^2/2) - adL = 0 \Rightarrow d^* = L/2.$
26. This can be derived from Chapter 2.
27. Equation (3.29) was obtained as follows. For a monopoly local service provider to be willing to cover the entire market, the most distant consumer must be willing to pay a positive price. This means that: $v - a\ (L/2) \geq 0 \Rightarrow v/a \geq L/2.$
28. $\partial \Pi_j/\partial d = aL/2 - ad = 0 \Rightarrow d^* = L/2.$
29. As explained in Appendix 3A1, total cooperative profits are equivalent to the profits that a profit-maximizing monopoly local service provider with two facilities would make.
30. We are assuming here that the local public goods are characterized by fixed technology.
31. As explained in the case of partial cooperation, we assume that v/a is large enough so that local service providers will compete for all points in space, implying that for each provider alone, it always be profitable to cover the entire market. Therefore, throughout the analysis we will assume that $v/a \geq 3L^2.$
32. Equation (3.36) was obtained by replacing $r_1 = L/4$ and $r_2 = 3L/4$ in equation (3A1.6).
33. Equation (3.38) was obtained as follows. If we substitute equations (3A7.3), (3A7.4) and (3.98) into equation (3A7.1), we get:

$$U_1(r_1, \delta, P^K) = \{P^K - a[(L - r_1)^2 - r_1^2]\}L - P^K\frac{L}{2}$$
$$- \left\{\frac{\delta}{1-\delta}\left[(\{P^K - a[(L-r_1)^2 - r_1^2]\}L) - \left[\frac{aL^2}{2}(L - 2r_1)\right]\right]\right\}.$$

In order for cooperation to be stable, the following must be true: $U_1(r_1, \delta, P^K) \leq 0$. This implies that, given the locations and δ, $P^K(r_1, \delta)$ must satisfy the following condition, so that the cooperative prices will be sustainable: $P^K(r_1, \delta) \leq aL(L - 2r_1)[(3\delta - 2)/2\delta - 1)]$. This will imply that: $P^{K\max}(r_1, \delta) = aL(L - 2r_1)[(3\delta - 2)/2\delta - 1)]$.

34. Equation (3.44) was obtained as follows: If $r_1 = 0 \ ^\wedge r_2 = L - r_1 = L$, then

$$\Pi_1^D(r_1 = 0, r_2 = L) = L\left(v - \frac{5}{4}aL^2\right), \ \Pi_1^{Kop}(r_1 = 0, r_2 = L) = \frac{L}{2}\left(v - \frac{aL^2}{4}\right),$$

and $\Pi_1^{LC}(r_1 = 0, r_2 = L) = \frac{aL^3}{2}$. In order for cooperation to be stable, the following must be true: $U_i(r_1 = 0, r_2 = L, P^{Kop}) \leq 0$. This implies that:

$$\delta \geq \delta = \frac{1}{2}\left[\frac{4\frac{v}{a} - 9L^2}{4\frac{v}{a} - 7L^2}\right]$$

35. The efficient (or optimal) locations of two local public goods in this setting are derived in Appendix 2A1.
36. It can be shown that:

$$U_j(r_1^*, r_2^*) = \Pi_j^D(r_1^*, r_2^*) - \Pi_j^K(r_1^*, r_2^*) - \left\{\sum_{t=1}^{\infty}\delta^t[\Pi_j^K(r_1^*, r_2^*) - \Pi_j^{LC}(r_1^*, r_2^*)]\right\}$$
$$= \Pi_j^D(r_1^*, r_2^*) - \Pi_j^K(r_1^*, r_2^*) - \left\{\frac{\delta}{1-\delta}[\Pi_j^K(r_1^*, r_2^*) - \Pi_j^{LC}(r_1^*, r_2^*)]\right\}.$$

37. In the following analysis we assume that $r_1 < r_2$. This analysis is symmetrical for $r_1 > r_2$.
38. Figure 3A3.1 is only valid for values of r_1 and r_2 for which $r_1 < r_2$. Thus, only the left-hand portion of the figure is valid.
39. If $r_2 = L$, then

$$\frac{\partial \Pi_1^K(r_2 = L)}{\partial r_1} = -\frac{1}{4} \frac{(-4vL^2 + 9ar_1^3 + 12ar_1^2 - 3aL^2r_1)}{(r_1 + L)^2}.$$

40. Equation (3A4.3) was obtained as follows:

For w_2, $v - a\left(\dfrac{d}{2}\right)^2 - P^{\max}(rpc = w_2) = 0 \Rightarrow P^{\max}(rpc = w_2) = v - \dfrac{ad^2}{4}.$

For w_1, $v - a\left[\dfrac{(L-d)}{2}\right]^2 - P^{\max}(rpc = w_1) = 0 \Rightarrow P^{\max}(rpc = w_2) = v - a\dfrac{(L-d)^2}{4}.$

41. It can be shown that:

$$U_j(r_1{}^*, r_2{}^*) = \Pi_j^D(r_1{}^*, r_2{}^*) - \Pi_j^K(r_1{}^*, r_2{}^*) - \left\{\sum_{t=1}^{\infty} \delta^t [\Pi_j^K(r_1{}^*, r_2{}^*) - \Pi_j^{LC}(r_1{}^*, r_2{}^*)]\right\}.$$

$$= \Pi_j^D(r_1{}^*, r_2{}^*) - \Pi_j^K(r_1{}^*, r_2{}^*) - \left\{\frac{\delta}{1-\delta}[\Pi_j^K(r_1{}^*, r_2{}^*) - \Pi_j^{LC}(r_1{}^*, r_2{}^*)]\right\}$$

42. Equation (3A5.2) was obtained as follows: the maximum price that a local service provider can charge in order to capture the entire market, given d^* and the agreed-upon cooperative price P^K, is given by: $v - a(d)^2 - P^D = v - P^K \Rightarrow P^D = P^K - a(d)^2 = v - (5/16)aL^2$. Thus, the profits it will obtain in this manner will be given by: $\Pi_j^D(d^*) = L(P^D) = vL - (5/16)aL^3$ Equations (3A5.3) and (3A5.4) can be directly derived from equations (3.27) and (3.23), respectively.

43. Note that for $\Pi_j^D > \Pi_j^K$, and for positive incentives to deviate to exist, $v/a \geq (7/16)L^2$. We can see that this is satisfied by our condition that $v/a \geq 3/4L^2$. Thus, given our original assumption, it is always true that $\Pi_j^D > \Pi_j^K$.

44. It can be shown that :

$$U_j(d) = \Pi_j^D(d) - \Pi_j^K(d) - \left\{\sum_{t=1}^{\infty} \delta^t [\Pi_j^K(d) - \Pi_j^{LC}(d)]\right\}$$

$$= \Pi_j^D(d) - \Pi_j^K(d) - \left\{\frac{\delta}{1-\delta}[\Pi_j^K(d) - \Pi_j^{LC}(d)]\right\}.$$

45. It can be shown that :

$$U_j(r_1{}^*, r_2{}^*) = \Pi_j^D(r_1{}^*, r_2{}^*) - \Pi_j^K(r_1{}^*, r_2{}^*) - \left\{\sum_{t=1}^{\infty} \delta^t [\Pi_j^K(r_1{}^*, r_2{}^*) - \Pi_j^{LC}(r_1{}^*, r_2{}^*)]\right\}$$

$$= \Pi_j^D(r_1{}^*, r_2{}^*) - \Pi_j^K(r_1{}^*, r_2{}^*) - \left\{\frac{\delta}{1-\delta}[\Pi_j^K(r_1{}^*, r_2{}^*) - \Pi_j^{LC}(r_1{}^*, r_2{}^*)]\right\}.$$

46. Equation (3A7.2) was obtained as follows: Given a high enough value of v/a, a local service provider will always maximize its profits if it chooses the highest possible price that covers the entire market. Thus, given the locations and P^K (r_1, r_2), the best response price for local service provider 1, if it deviates from cooperation, will be the highest possible that covers the entire market, and so it must satisfy the following condition: $v - r_2^2 a - P^D = v - r_1^2 a - P^K \Rightarrow P^D = P^K - a(r_2^2 - r_1^2).$

General conclusion

The growth of megacities is an obvious trend within today's urban land-scape, especially in developing countries.[1] Many problems are associated with these large urban regions, with perhaps one of the most evident and dramatic being the lack of an adequate level of urban infrastructure. The inhabitants of many of these cities are troubled by inadequate refuse collection, the spread of diseases, rising crime rates, inefficient transportation services, and ineffective sewer and drainage systems which often cause massive flooding, among many other problems. In general, these cities offer inadequate levels of collective goods such as refuse collection services, health-care systems, police and fire departments, educational systems, transportation services and water and sewer systems, among others, in order to solve problems arising from the agglomeration of people. These inadequacies are responsible for the dominant feeling today across the various disciplines related to urbanization that most of these cities are simply too big. Most current urban policies implicitly include this assumption. In the view of many, megacities appear as gigantic, dangerous autonomous organisms whose expansion should be curbed.[2]

Nevertheless, in spite of these alleged problems of large urban regions, there are many good reasons why people and economic agents decide to settle there. Some of these reasons are those given by Marshall ([1890] 1920), which are discussed in the general introduction. Others can be found in Fujita and Thisse (2002). There are certainly many other good reasons that motivate people to become or remain residents of these urban giants, some of which we may not even be able to imagine. However, the problems of these megacities are generally so evident and dramatic that their benefits are sometimes overlooked by those who design and implement today's urban policies, many of which are geared towards trying to halt the growth of such cities.

It is true that the lack of adequate urban infrastructure constitutes a severe problem in large urban regions. However, rather than trying to stop these cities from increasing in size, it would be preferable for urban policy-makers to help the cities solve their problems directly. Economists can play an important role by identifying flexible mechanisms that can provide individuals and local governments with incentives to achieve the adequate provision of local public goods in these large and dynamic urban regions.

Discovering such flexible mechanisms for the provision of local public goods is an especially urgent task when we consider the ongoing dissolution of borders, the relatively free mobility of individuals among countries, and the diminishing power of national governments, which until now have served as the providers of many local public goods within their territories, within regional trade zones such as the European Union.

Tiebout (1956) was the first to make advances in this direction, envisaging an original decentralized mechanism to achieve the optimal provision of local public goods. He suggested that in an economy with local public goods, the optimal allocation can be decentralized by means of a system of competing jurisdictions. His idea was that consumers can reveal their preferences by migrating to the jurisdiction that respects their tastes in public goods and tax schemes. Tiebout argued that competition among jurisdictions and 'voting with the feet' may lead to the efficient provision of local public goods. His concept of jurisdiction was one in which local governments offer a bundle of services (*multi-functionality of jurisdictions*) to those living in a predefined region. All residents must pay taxes to the jurisdiction and consume the services it provides (*localized membership*). Currently, jurisdictions in many countries, including the municipalities of Santiago, exhibit similar characteristics to those envisaged by Tiebout.

However, some crucial assumptions that are required for Tiebout's hypothesis to hold are unlikely to be satisfied in reality, especially in countries with large metropolitan regions. This makes it less likely that the optimal provision of local public goods can actually be achieved by competing jurisdictions *à la* Tiebout. One of these potential barriers to the achievement of an adequate level of local public goods in these large urban regions appears to be a lack of competition among local governments that provide local public goods. This is the case in the metropolitan region of Santiago. Competition among Santiago's municipalities is restricted by mobility costs for individuals, the limited number of jurisdictions, and the barriers to entry and exit in municipality formation. At the same time, the metropolitan local government of Santiago[3] is in practice a monopolist with respect to the provision of local public goods or the solution of urban problems involving many municipalities. This lack of competition may be a key factor in preventing the adequate provision of local public goods in the case of large urban agglomerations such as Santiago. Generally, due to the rigidity of current urban policy mechanisms, competition is often absent from the provision of local public goods as well as from the solution of urban problems.

The idea of FOCJ, introduced by Frey and Eichenberger (1995, 1996a, 1997, 1999), constitutes an additional contribution to the search for flexible mechanisms to provide individuals and local governments with effective incentives to achieve the adequate provision of local public goods. This new approach proposes *unbundling the activities of a jurisdiction* and opening up each individual activity to competition. In order to generate competition among these new uni-functional jurisdictions effectively, the proponents of this approach argue in favour of the *de-localization of membership*. These two aspects seem to be crucial for increasing competition among local governments in large metropolitan regions.

Nevertheless, this increased competition among local governments (or local service providers) may also give rise to problems and generate inefficiencies that should be considered in the design of urban policies. In this book, we have developed a framework that can be used to analyse the effects of de-localized membership in jurisdictions and the uni-functionality of jurisdictions on competition among local service providers in large urban agglomerations, as well as the potential impact of the expected increase in competition on the achievement of the optimal provision of local public goods.

MAIN RESULTS OF THE BOOK

Within this framework, the most relevant results for urban policy are as follows. It is true that the de-localized membership in jurisdictions and uni-functionality of jurisdictions proposed by the FOCJ concept offers the potential to greatly improve welfare by increasing competition among local service providers. Nevertheless, some important aspects of this situation should be noted, and we should also be aware of some problems that may arise.

First, if FOCJ[4] are to increase competition and guarantee a high utility level for the individuals in a region, there must be *competition in all types of local public goods*. If there is a monopoly local service provider even in only one type, and we assume that local public goods are perfect complements between types, all the gains from increased competition in the other types of local public goods will be redistributed to this monopoly local service provider, and individuals would obtain the same utility as if there were no competition in any type at all; the result in terms of utility for individuals would be equivalent to that of classical all-purpose jurisdictions.

It is important to note that in real local jurisdictions and in the multi-dimensional concept of FOCJ, there are alternative sources of competition which we have not formally discussed in the previous analysis, such as political competition, which may limit the monopoly power of the monopoly local government. However, these other dimensions of competition are beyond the remit of the analysis presented in this book. Nevertheless, the absence of such alternative forces of competition may be a serious concern, especially if there are local public goods with large market areas (or economies of scale) and little substitution with other local public goods. Market power of a single unit becomes more of an issue in such a world. Perhaps these kinds of local public goods should be more regulated in order that decentralization in the form of FOCJ for their provision will guarantee an increase in the utility level for individuals. On the other hand, local public goods with small market areas and a high substitution with other local public goods will not have this problem of monopolization and they could be provided by a system of FOCJ improving utility for the individuals.

Second, if there is competition in the region (that is, there is more than one local service provider in the region for each type of local public good), FOCJ should be allowed to charge *discriminatory prices* (which is the price policy they will choose at equilibrium). If they were obliged to charge uniform prices regardless of location, the resulting local competition would be less intense. Prices at the extreme boundaries of the local service areas would be higher than under discriminatory pricing, and thus in aggregate, the customers would be worse off than under price discrimination. We have shown that the efficient allocation of local public goods necessarily requires spatial price discrimination. This is also true in Tiebout's setting. In fact, charging taxes (or prices) according to land rent values in order to achieve optimality, as in Tiebout's setting, is a form of spatial price discrimination. Mill pricing will typically increase the inefficiencies identified under discriminatory pricing (at least in the case of no location sunk cost technology), and in general, the opportunity to charge discriminatory prices with respect to location increases competition and is welfare improving in a spatial context.

Third, if there is competition in the region and FOCJ are allowed to charge discriminatory prices, there will be a *maximum price* that local service providers can charge, which will be determined by the differential transport costs of patronizing the provider with the second-lowest transport cost. This will guarantee a minimum aggregate utility level for individuals, which will depend on the intensity of the local competition, independent of the individuals' mobility (their ability or willingness to move from one place of residence to another). This will improve the situation for individuals in comparison with Tiebout's jurisdiction concept.

Fourth, if the technology of the local public good is characterized by no location sunk costs (so that the facilities can be reallocated at no additional cost), and there is very weak competition from other regions (because, for example, individuals have a low propensity to change their place of residence), there will be *excessive entry* of FOCJ providing the local public good, leading to excess capacity in the analysed region. This will result in lower overall welfare in comparison to the optimal allocation; however, for individuals, this will be the most favourable situation in terms of utility, because they will profit from the intense competition among local service providers. On the other hand, if the technology of the local public good is characterized by location sunk costs, very weak competition from other regions may lead to either excessive or insufficient entry. The precise nature of the equilibrium pattern of competing local service providers in this case, and the possible resulting inefficiency, will depend upon the history of that region. In this case, the sunk costs may act as a kind of entry barrier that impedes the entry of additional FOCJ, despite the fact that the FOCJ currently operating in the region are earning profits. In terms of welfare, the equilibria characterized by extremely insufficient entry are equivalent to those with extremely excessive entry, but in the case of insufficient entry, the individuals suffer the greatest losses, while the local service providers active in the region profit from the existence of this entry barrier. In both cases, local competition alone is not sufficient to guarantee optimality.

Finally, coordination among FOCJ, aimed at solving some of the allocation problems that emerge from competition, may also cause inefficiencies. In fact, *partial cooperation* (that is, the non-cooperative choice of locations followed by cooperative pricing) will always be inefficient within our framework, and discriminatory pricing will lead to the efficient locations only if partial cooperation is ruled out. On the other hand, we saw that *full cooperation* (that is, the cooperative choice of locations and prices) is not completely equivalent to the case of a monopoly local government, and it can also lead to inefficient location choices. Therefore, in general, *collusion among FOCJ should be avoided*.

OPEN QUESTIONS FOR FUTURE RESEARCH

We have provided answers to some of the relevant questions regarding the effects of introducing the phenomena of de-localized membership in jurisdictions and the uni-functionality of jurisdictions on competition among local service providers in large urban agglomerations. Nevertheless, many open questions still remain to be answered.

Two factors that are crucial and should be included in a future extension of the model are *income heterogeneity* and *quality differentiation*. In a setting characterized by geographical segregation according to income, excess entry of FOCJ would be expected at the upper end of the income distribution, while insufficient entry and inadequate quality would most likely result at the lower end. The spatial characteristics of the city will crucially affect the location and quality decisions of the competing and independent jurisdictions. For example, complete exclusion may occur under such a system. On the other hand, well-targeted welfare programmes may be able to exploit the competition among FOCJ for the low-cost provision of local public goods.

In our setting, we assumed that individuals in the analysed region had the opportunity to move to an alternative region, and the level of competition represented by the latter for the former was reflected in a parameter, γ. Nevertheless, this parameter was exogenously given in our model and we should extend our setting by endogenizing γ. This would mean explicitly modelling the interaction of local service providers with the characteristics of FOCJ not only within a region, but also between regions.

In order to analyse overlapping jurisdictions and the idea of unbundling the services provided by local service providers, we considered a setting that included different types of local public goods. We saw that the option of unbundling activities can increase competition and aggregate utility for individuals in a region only if there is competition in all types of local public goods. Crucial to this result was the assumption of perfect complementarity among local public goods of different types. If some degree of substitution is possible between types of local public goods, a monopoly local service provider in one type could not obtain all of the gains from increased competition in the other types. Thus, we should incorporate some degree of substitution between types, in order to see how this would affect the results obtained here.

We should also integrate a labour market into the model, in order to explicitly analyse the interdependencies between the availability of jobs and the provision of local public goods. This is because individuals' location decisions seem to be more strongly influenced by job alternatives than by the provision of local public goods, provided that some acceptable level of the latter is present.

A further extension of the work presented here would be an empirical one. Given the privatization measures implemented in Chile since 1973 (intensified with the structural reforms around 1980), using Santiago as a case study would provide ample opportunities to test and contrast the FOCJ concept with the privatization policies actually implemented in Chile. The country's experience with respect to the level of decentralization and the degree of unbundling of various functions, as well as delocalized membership in some of them, would be especially useful in this regard.

As explained in the general introduction, this book analyses the optimal allocation of local public goods in a spatial context[5] and the allocation consequences of increasing competition in their decentralized provision. For this we took two innovative aspects present in the concept of FOCJ: de-localized membership and uni-functionality of jurisdictions. However, and as explained, the concept of FOCJ has many other interesting dimensions, which have been analysed until now using exclusively verbal economic reasoning (particularly in Frey and Eichenberger, 1999). In this sense we should make a formal analysis of other relevant aspects of this concept, for example, by incorporating political competition and democratic control. The incentives of politicians may be different in FOCJ from all-purpose jurisdictions for reasons other than competition and this could have impacts on the provision of local public goods.

Finally, the framework developed in this book and the results derived can be applied to many other general problems of spatial competition, such as location decisions for competing firms, as well as problems of industrial organization, such as the selection of products in a differentiated product market, among others.

NOTES

1. To the best of my knowledge, there is still no analysis of the economic role of megacities in developing countries in the literature.
2. For example, in the case of Chile, more than 40 per cent of the country's population (6 million people) live in the capital city or metropolitan region of Santiago, where more than 47 per cent of the entire country's GDP is produced (INE, 2001). Numerous policies have been implemented in an attempt to reverse this trend towards the concentration of people and economic activity in this large city. One crucial argument offered by policy-makers to justify these kinds of policies is that numerous problems experienced by the city, especially those related to the lack of adequate urban infrastructure, are due simply to its enormous size.
3. As explained in the General introduction, there is no metropolitan government of Santiago, but the 'MINVU' (Ministry of Housing and Urban Planning) in some sense plays the role of a metropolitan local government in the provision of local public goods or solutions to urban problems involving many municipalities (such as metropolitan parks, link roads and so on).
4. As explained in the general introduction, 'FOCJ' refers to our interpretation of the concept relative to the aspects of it that we considered in this book.
5. By 'spatial context' we mean basically considering transport costs.

Bibliography

Aguirre, I., Espinoza, M.P. and Macho-Stadler, I. (1998), 'Strategic entry deterrence through spatial price discrimination', *Regional Science and Urban Economics* **28**: 297–314.

Alesina, A. and Spolaore, E. (1997), 'On the number and size of nations', *Quarterly Journal of Economics* **112**: 1027–55.

Alonso, W. (1964), *Location and Land Use*, Cambridge, MA: Harvard University Press.

Anderson, S.P. and de Palma, A. (1988), 'Spatial price discrimination with heterogeneous products', *Review of Economic Studies* **55**: 573–92.

Arnott, R. and Stiglitz, J. (1979), 'Aggregate land rents, expenditure on public goods, and optimal city size', *Quarterly Journal of Economics* **93**: 471–500.

Arrow, K. and Debreu, G. (1954), 'Existence of an equilibrium for a competitive economy', *Econometrica* **22**: 265–90.

Austin, A. (1998), 'A positive model of spatial district formation', *Regional Science and Urban Economics* **28**: 103–22.

Bairoch, P. (1985), *De Jérico à Mexico. Villes et économie dans l'histoire*, Paris: Gallimard. English translation: *Cities and Economic Development. From the Dawn of History to the Present*, Chicago: University of Chicago Press (1988).

Barros, P.P. (1999), 'Multimarket competition in banking, with an example for the Portuguese market', *International Journal of Industrial Organization* **17**: 335–52.

Baumol, W. (1982), 'Contestable markets: an uprising in the theory of industrial structure', *American Economic Review* **72**: 1–15.

Berglas, E. (1976a), 'Distribution of tastes and skills and the provision of local public goods', *Journal of Public Economics* **6**: 409–23.

Berglas, E. (1976b), 'On the theory of clubs', *American Economic Review* **66**: 116–21.

Berglas, E. (1984), 'Quantities, qualities and multiple public services in the Tiebout Model', *Journal of Public Economics* **25**: 299–321.

Berglas, E. and Pines, D. (1981), 'Clubs, local public goods and transportation models: a synthesis', *Journal of Public Economics* **15**: 141–62.

Bertrand, J. (1883), 'Book review of *Théorie Mathématique de la Richesse Sociale* and of *Recherches sur les principes Mathematiques de la Théorie des Richesses*', *Journal des Savants* **67**: 499–508.

Bester, H., de Palma, A., Leininger, W. Thomas, J. and von Thadden, E.-L. (1996), 'A noncooperative analysis of Hotelling's location game', *Games and Economic Behavior* **12**: 165–86.

Bewley, T.F. (1981), 'A critique of Tiebout's theory of local public expenditures', *Econometrica* **49**: 713–40.

Bird, R. (1993), 'Threading the fiscal labyrinth: some issues in fiscal decentralization', *National Tax Journal* **46**: 207–27.

Braid, R.M. (1991), 'The locations of congestible facilities in adjacent jurisdictions', *Regional Science and Urban Economics* **21**: 617–26.

Brueckner, J. and Lee, K. (1991), 'Economies of scope and multiproduct clubs', *Public Finance Quarterly* **19** (2): 193–208.

Buchanan, J.M. (1965), 'An economic theory of clubs', *Economica* **33**: 1–14.

Buchanan, J. and Goetz, C. (1972), 'Efficiency limits of fiscal mobility: an assessment of the Tiebout model', *Journal of Public Economics* **1**: 25–43.

Carlton, D.W. and Perloff, J.M. (1990), *Modern Industrial Organization*, Glenview, IL and London: Scott, Foresman/Little, Brown Higher Education.

Casella, A. (1992), 'Federalism and clubs: toward an economy theory of overlapping political jurisdictions', *European Economic Review* **36**: 639–46.

Cheshire, P. and Edwin, M. (1999) (eds), *Handbook of Regional and Urban Economics*, Vols I, II, III. Handbooks in Economics, vol. 7. Amsterdam, New York and Oxford: Elsevier Science, North-Holland.

Chiang, A.C. (1984), *Fundamental Methods of Mathematical Economics*, Singapore: McGraw-Hill International Editions.

Core, L.P. (1988), 'Price discrimination: a survey of the theory', *Journal of Economic Surveys* **2**: 135–67.

Cremer, H., de Kerchove, A.-M. and Thisse, J.F. (1985), 'An economic theory of public facilities in space', *Mathematical Social Sciences* **9**: 249–62.

D'Aspremont, C., Gabszewicz, J. and Thisse, J.-F. (1979), 'On Hotelling's "stability in competition" ', *Econometrica* **47**: 1145–50.

de Palma, A., Ginsburgh, V. and Thisse, J.-F. (1987), 'On existence of location equilibria in the 3-firm Hotelling problem', *Journal of Industrial Economics* **36**: 245–52.

de Palma, A. and Liu, Q. (1993), 'The welfare aspects of spatial pricing policies reconsidered for a monopoly case', *Journal of Regional Science* **33**: 1–12.

DiLorenzo, T. (1981), 'Special districts and local public services', *Public Finance Quarterly* **9**: 353–67.

Eaton, B.C. (1976), 'Free entry in one-dimensional models: pure profits and multiple equilibria', *Journal of Regional Science* **16**: 21–33.

Eaton, B.C. and Lipsey, R.G. (1973), 'The principle of minimum differentiation reconsidered: some new developments in the theory of spatial competition', *Review of Economic Studies* **42**: 27–49.

Eaton, B.C. and Lipsey, R.G. (1997), *On the Foundations of Monopolistic Competition and Economic Geography: The Selected Essays of B. Curtis Eaton and Richard G. Lipsey*, Economists of the Twentieth Century series. Cheltenham, UK and Lyme, NH, USA: Edwar Elgar; distributed by American International Distribution Corporation, Williston, VT.

Eaton, B.C. and Schmitt, N. (1994), 'Flexible manufacturing and market structure', *American Economic Review* **84**: 875–88.

Eaton, C. and Wooders, M. (1985), 'Sophisticated entry in a model of spatial competition', *Rand Journal of Economics* **16**: 282–97.

Economides, N. (1987), 'On Nash equilibrium existence an optimality in oligopolistic competition in prices and varieties', *Greek Economic Review* **9**: 198–209.

Economides, N. (1989), 'Symmetric equilibrium existence and optimality in differentiated product market', *Journal of Economic Theory* **47**: 178–94.

Eichenberger, R. (1996), 'Eine "fünfte Freiheit" für Europa: Starkung des politischen Wettbewerbs durch "FOCJ" ' ('A Fifth Freedom for Europe: increase of political competition through "FOCJ" '), *Zeitschrift für Wirtschaftspolitik* **45**: 110–31.

Eppel, D. and Zelenitz, A. (1981a), 'The implications of competition among jurisdictions: does Tiebout need politics?', *Journal of Political Economy* **89**: 1197–217.

Eppel, D. and Zelenitz, A. (1981b), 'The roles of jurisdictional competition and of collective choice institutions in the market for local public goods', *American Economic Review* **71**: 87–92.

Feldstein, M.S. and Inman, R.P. (1977), *The Economics of Public Services. Proceedings of a Conference held by the International Economic Association at Turin, Italy*, London and Basingstoke: Macmillan.

Fershtman, C. and Gandal, N. (1994), 'Disadvantageous semicollusion', *International Journal of Industrial Organization* **12**: 141–54.

Freidman, J.W. (1970), 'A non-cooperative equilibrium for supergames', *Review of Economic Studies* **38**: 1–12.

Frey, B. (1996), 'A directly democratic and federal Europe', *Constitutional Political Economy* **7**: 267–79.

Frey, B. (1997), *Ein neuer Föderalismus für Europa: Die Idee der FOCJ (A New Federalism for Europe: The Idea of the FOCJ)*, version from the lectures given at the Walter Eucken Institute, Freiburg im Breisgan, 4 December 1996.

Frey, B. (2001), 'A utopia? Government without territorial monopoly', *Journal of Institutional and Theoretical Economics* **157**: 162–75.

Frey, B. and Eichenberger, R. (1995), 'Competition among jurisdictions: the idea of FOCJ', in L. Gerken (ed.), *Competition Among Institutions*, New York: St. Martin's Press; London: Macmillan : 209–29.

Frey, B. and Eichenberger, R. (1996a), 'FOCJ: competitive governments for Europe', *International Review of Law and Economics* **16**: 315–27.

Frey, B. and Eichenberger, R. (1996b), 'To harmonize or to compete? That's not the question', *Journal of Public Economics* **60**: 335–49.

Frey, B. and Eichenberger, R. (1997), 'FOCJ: creating a single European market for governments', in D. Schmidtchen and R. Cooter (eds), *Constitutional Law and Economics of the European Union*, Cheltenham, UK and Lyme, NH, USA: Edward Elgar, distributed by American International Distribution Corporation, Williston, VT: 195–215.

Frey, B. and Eichenberger, R. (1999), '*The New Democratic Federalism for Europe: Functional, Overlapping and Competing Jurisdictions*', Studies in Fiscal Federalism and State–Local Finance, Cheltenham, UK and Northampton, MA, USA: Edward Elgar.

Friedman, J. and Thisse, J.-F. (1993), 'Partial collusion fosters minimum product differentiation', *Rand Journal of Economics* **24**: 631–45.

Fujita, M. (1986), 'Optimal location of public facilities: area dominance approach', *Regional Science and Urban Economics* **16**: 241–68.

Fujita, M (1989), *Urban Economic Theory. Land Use and City Size*, Cambridge, New York and Melbourne: Cambridge University Press.

Fujita, M. (2000), 'Thünen and the new economic geography', Kyoto Institute of Economic Research, Discussion Paper No. 521.

Fujita, M. and Thisse, J.-F. (1986), 'Spatial competition with a land market: Hotelling and Von Thünen unified', *Review of Economic Studies* **53**: 819–41.

Fujita, M. and Thisse, J.-F. (2002), *Economics of Agglomeration: Cities, Industrial Location, and Regional Growth*, Cambridge: Cambridge University Press.

Gabszewicz, J.J. and Thisse, J.-F. (1986), 'On the nature of competition with differentiated products', *Economic Journal* **96**: 160–72.

Gabszewicz, J.J., Thisse, J.F., Fujita, M. and Schweizer, U. (1986), *Location Theory*, Chur: Harwood Academic.

Gehrig, T. (1998), 'Competing markets', *European Economic Review* **42**: 277–310.

Gehrig, T. (2000), 'Cities and the geography of financial centers', in J.M. Huriot and J.F. Thisse (eds), *Economics of Cities: Theoretical Perspectives*, Cambridge, New York and Melbourne: Cambridge University Press: 415–45.

Glaeser, E.L., Kolko, J. and Saiz, A. (2001), 'Consumer city', *Journal of Economic Geography* **1**: 27–50.

Greenhut, J.G. and Greenhut, M.L. (1975), 'Spatial price discrimination, competition and locational effects', *Economica* **42**: 401–19.

Greenhut, M.L. and Norman G. (1995), *The Economics of Location. Volume 1: Location Theory. Volume 2: Space and Value. Volume 3: Spatial Microeconomics*, Elgar Reference Collection: International Library of Critical Writings in Economics 42, Aldershot, UK: Edward Elgar; distributed in the US by Ashgate, Brookfield, VT.

Gupta, B. (1992), 'Sequential entry and deterrence with competitive spatial price discrimination', *Economics Letters* **38**: 487–90.

Hamilton, J.H., Thisse, J.-F. and Weskamp, A. (1989), 'Spatial discrimination: Bertrand vs. Cournot in a model of location choice', *Regional Science and Urban Economics* **19**: 87–102.

Helpman, E. (1978), 'On optimal community formation', *Economic Letters* **1**: 289–93.

Hobbs, B.F. (1986), 'Mill pricing versus spatial price discrimination under Bertrand and Cournot spatial competition', *Journal of Industrial Economics* **35**: 173–91.

Hochman, O. (1981), 'Land rents, optimal taxation and local fiscal independence in an economy with local public goods', *Journal of Public Economics* **15**: 59–85.

Hochman, O. (1982a), 'Clubs in an urban setting', *Journal of Urban Economics* **12**: 85–101.

Hochman, O. (1982b), 'Congestable local public goods in an urban setting', *Journal of Urban Economics* **11**: 290–310.

Hochman, O., Pines, D. and Thisse, J.-F. (1995), 'On the optimal structure of local governments', *American Economic Review* **85**: 1224–40.

Holahan, W.L. (1975), 'The welfare effects of spatial price discrimination', *American Economic Review* **65**: 498–503.

Holahan, W.L. and Schuler, R.E. (1981), 'Competitive entry in a spatial economy: market equilibrium and welfare implications', *Journal of Regional Science* **21**: 341–57.

Holler, M.J. and Illing, G. (1991), *Einführung in die Spieltheorie (Introduction in Game Theory)*, Berlin and Heidelberg: Springer-Lehrbuch, Springer-Verlag.

Hoover, E.M. (1937), 'Spatial price discrimination', *Review of Economic Studies* **4**: 182–91.

Hotelling, H. (1929), 'Stability in competition', *Economic Journal* **39**: 41–57.

INE (2001), *Informe 2001*, Instituto Nacional de Estadísticas, Santiago de Chile.

Jehiel, P. (1992), 'Product differentiation and price collusion', *International Journal of Industrial Organization* **10**: 633–41.

Kalai, E. and Stanford, W. (1988), 'Finite rationality and interpersonal complexity in repeated games', *Econometrica* **56**: 397–410.

Kilkenny, M. and Thisse, J.-F. (1999), 'Economics of location: a selective survey', *Computers & Operations Research* **26**: 1369–94.

Krugman, P. (1991), *Geography and Trade*, Cambridge, MA: MIT Press.

Lederer, P. and Hurter, A.P. (1986), 'Competition of firms: discriminatory pricing and location', *Econometrica* **56**: 623–40.

MacLeod, W.B., Norman, G. and Thisse, J.-F. (1987), 'Competition, tacit collusion and free entry', *Economic Journal* **97**: 189–98.

MacLeod, W.B., Norman, G. and Thisse, J.-F. (1988), 'Price discrimination and equilibrium in monopolistic competition', *International Journal of Industrial Organization* **6**: 429–46.

Mankiw, N.G. and Whinston, M.D. (1986), 'Free entrance and social inefficiency', *Rand Journal of Economics* **17**: 48–58.

Marshall, A. (1890), *Principles of Economics*, London: Macmillan, 8th edition published in 1920.

Martinez-Vazquez, J., Rider, M. and Walker, M.B. (1997), 'Race and the structure of school districts in the United States', *Journal of Urban Economics* **41**: 281–300.

Mas-Colell, A., Whinston, M. and Green, J.R. (1995), *Microeconomic Theory*, New York: Oxford University Press.

McGuire, M. (1972), 'Private good clubs and public good clubs: economic model of group formation', *Swedish Journal of Economics* **74**(1): 84–99.

Mills, D. (1991), 'Untimely entry', *Journal of Industrial Economics* **39**: 659–70.

Mills, E.S. (1967), 'An aggregative model of resource allocation in a metropolitan area', *American Economic Review* **57**: 197–210.

Muth, R.F. (1969), *Cities and Housing*, Chicago: University of Chicago Press.

Nash, J.F. (1950), 'The bargaining problem', *Econometrica* **18**: 155–62.

Nelson, M. (1990), 'Decentralization of the subnational public sector: an empirical analysis of the determinants of local government structure in metropolitan areas in the US', *Southern Economic Journal* **57**: 443–57.

Neven, D. (1985), 'Two stage (perfect) equilibrium in Hotelling's model', *Journal of Industrial Economics* **33**: 317–25.

Ng, Y.-K. (1981), 'All "Ng" up in clubs: a "bran-new flawer" of Brennan-flowers', *Public Finance Quarterly* **9**: 75–8.

Norman, G. (1981), 'Spatial competition and spatial price discrimination', *Review of Economic Studies* **48**: 97–111.

Norman, G. (1983), 'Spatial pricing with differentiated products', *Quarterly Journal of Economics* **98**: 291–310.

Norman, G. (1999), *The Economics of Price Discrimination*, Elgar Reference Collection. International Library of Critical Writings in Economics 112. Cheltenham, UK and Northampton, MA, USA: Edward Elgar; distributed by American International Distribution Corporation, Williston, VT.

Novshek, W. (1980), 'Equilibrium on simple spatial (or differentiated product) models', *Journal of Economic Theory* **22**: 313–26.

Novshek, W. and Sonnenschein, H. (1979), 'Marginal consumers and neo-classical demand theory', *Journal of Political Economy* **87**: 1368–76.

Oates, W.E. (1972), *Fiscal Federalism*, Harbrace Series in Business and Economics, New York, Chicago, San Francisco, Atlanta: Harcourt Brace Jovanovich.

Oates, W.E. (1991), *Studies in Fiscal Federalism*, Economists of the Twentieth Century series, Aldershot, UK and Brookfield, US: Edward Elgar.

Olson, M. Jr (1969), 'Strategic theory and its applications: the principle of "fiscal equivalence": the division of responsibilities among different levels of governments', *American Economic Association* **59**: 479–87.

Osborne, M. and Pitchik, C. (1987), 'Cartels, profits and excess capacity', *International Economy Review* **28**: 413–28.

Peitz, M. (1999a), 'A difficulty with the address models of product differentiation', *Economic Theory* **14**: 717–27.

Peitz, M. (1999b). 'The circular road revisited: uniqueness and super-modularity', *Research in Economics* **53**: 405–20.

Petermann, A. (1998), 'Límite Urbano: El caso de su aplicación en Chile' ('Urban boundary: the case of its use in Chile'), thesis for obtaining the degree of Commercial Engineer with mention in Economics, Economic Institute, Pontificia Universidad Católica de Chile, Santiago, Chile.

Petermann, A. (2005), '¿Quién extendió a Santiago? Una breve historia del límite urbano, 1953–1994' ('who extended Santigo? A brief story of the urban boundary, 1953–1994'), in A. Galetovic (ed.), *Santiago: dónde estamos y hacia dónde vamos (Santigo: Where We Are and Where Are We Going To?)*, Santiago de Chile: Centro de Estudios Públicos (CEP), forthcoming.

Pines, D. (1991), 'Tiebout without politics', *Regional Science and Urban Economics* **21**: 469–89.

Pines, D., Sadka, E. and Zilcha, I. (1997), *Topics in Public Economics: Theoretical and Applied Analysis*, Cambridge, New York and Melbourne: Cambridge University Press.

Prescott, E.C. and Visscher, M. (1977), 'Sequential location among firms with foresight', *Bell Journal of Economics* **8**: 378–93.

Salop, S.C. (1979), 'Monopolistic competition with an outside good', *Bell Journal of Economics* **10**: 141–56.

Samuelson, P.A. (1954), 'The pure theory of public expenditures', *Review of Economics and Statistics* **36**: 387–9.

Sandler, T. and Tschirhart, J. (1980), 'The economic theory of clubs: an evaluative survey', *Journal of Economic Literature* **18**: 1481–521.

Schmalensee, R. (1987), 'Competitive advantage and collusive optima', *International Journal of Industrial Organization* **5**: 351–67.

Schmidt-Trenz, H.-J. (1997), 'FOCJ: creating a single European market for governments: comment', in D. Schmidtchen and R. Cooter (eds), *Constitutional Law and Economics of the European Union*, Cheltenham, UK and Lyme, NH, USA: Edwar Elgar, distributed by American International Distribution Corporation, Williston, VT: 216–22.

Scotchmer, S. (1985), 'Profit-maximizing clubs', *Journal of Public Economics* **27**: 25–45.

Scotchmer, S. (1986), 'Local public goods in an equilibrium: how pecuniary externalities matter', *Regional Science and Urban Economics* **16**: 436–81.

Scotchmer, S. and Wooders, M.H. (1987), 'Competitive equilibrium and the core in club economies with anonymous crowding', *Journal of Public Economics* **34**: 159–73.

Sherer, F.M. and Ross, D. (1990), *Industrial Market Structure and Economic Performance*, Boston, MA: Houghton Mifflin.

Sinn, H. (1997), 'The selection principle and market failure in systems competition', *Journal of Public Economics* **66**: 247–74.

Spence, M. (1976), 'Product selection, fixed costs, and monopolistic competition', *Review of Economic Studies* **43**: 217–35.

Stahl, K. (1982), 'Differentiated products, consumer search, and locational oligopoly', *Journal of Industrial Economics* **31**: 97–114.

Stahl, K. (1987), 'Theories of urban business location', in E.S. Mills (ed.), *Handbook of Regional and Urban Economics*, Vol. 2, Amsterdam: North-Holland: 759–820.

Tan, L. (2001), 'Spatial pricing policies reconsidered: monopoly performance and location', *Journal of Regional Science* **41**: 601–16.

Thisse, J.-F. and Vives, X. (1988), 'On the strategic choice of spatial price policy', *American Economic Review* **78**: 122–36.

Tiebout, C.M. (1956), 'A pure theory of local public expenditures', *Journal of Political Economy* **64**: 416–24.

Tirole, J. (1997), *The Theory of Industrial Organization*, Cambridge, MA and London: MIT Press.

United Nations (2002), *World Urbanization Prospects: The 2001 Revision*, New York: United Nations, Population Division.

Varian, H.R. (1992), *Análisis Microeconómico* (Microeconomic análisis), Barcelona: Antonio Bosch Editor, S.A.

Varian, H.R. (1993), *Intermediate Microeconomics. A Modern Approach*, New York and London: Norton.

von Thünen, J.H. (1826), *Der Isolierte Staat in Beziehung auf Landwirtschaft und Nationalökonomie.* Hamburg: Perthes. English translation: *The Isolated State*, Oxford: Pergamon (1966).

Wagner, R. and Weber, W. (1975), 'Competition, monopoly and the organization of government in metropolitan areas', *Journal of Law and Economics* **18**: 661–84.

Young, D.R. (1976), 'Consolidation of diversity: choices in the structure of urban governance', *American Economic Association* **66**: 378–91.

Zodrow, G.Z. (1983) (ed.), *Local Provision of Public Services: The Tiebout Model after Twenty-Five Years*, Studies in Urban Economics, New York: Academic Press.

Index